SCOTTISH ROCK GARDENING
IN THE 20TH CENTURY

SCOTTISH ROCK GARDENING IN THE 20TH CENTURY

Forbes W. Robertson
and
Alastair Mckelvie

Published by The Scottish Rock Garden Club

Copyyright © The Scottish Rock Garden Club 2000

A CIP catalogue record for this book is available from
the British Library
All rights reserved. No reproduction, copy or transmission
of this publication may be made without written permission

Published by The Scottish Rock Garden Club
and available from the Publications Manager
17 Strathview Place, Comrie, Perthshire, UK
PH6 2HG

Softback ISBN 0 9537019 0 5
Hardback ISBN 0 9537019 1 3

Produced by Claymore Graphics,
63 Cotton Street, Aberdeen, UK
AB11 5EG

CONTENTS

		LIST OF FIGURES, SUBJECTS AND SOURCES...	v
		ACKNOWLEDGEMENTS....................................	xi
		INTRODUCTION..	1
CHAPTER			
1		THE BOTANICAL CONTEXT...........................	3
2		PRIVATE COLLECTORS..................................	19
3		THE HISTORY OF THE SCOTTISH ROCK GARDEN CLUB...	30
4		GROWERS OF NOTE...	40
5		ALPINE NURSERIES AND GARDENS..............	60
6		TECHNICAL ADVANCES AND CONSERVATION...	78
		PREAMBLE TO CHAPTERS 7-12......................	92
7		THE SINO-HIMALAYAN REGION....................	95
8		SOUTH WEST ASIA AND THE BALKANS........	133
9		NORTH AND SOUTH AMERICA.......................	163
10		JAPAN..	202
11		NEW ZEALAND AND AUSTRALIA..................	214
12		SOUTH AFRICA..	234
13		THE FUTURE..	237
		BIBLIOGRAPHY...	240
		INDEX OF PEOPLE, PLACES AND TOPICS........	244
		INDEX OF PLANTS...	248

LIST OF FIGURES, SUBJECTS AND SOURCES

1	Sir Isaac Bayley Balfour	RBGE
2	J. McNab's Rock Garden 1880	"
3	George Sherriff	Mrs J.A. Sherriff
4	Map of George Forrest's Travels	OUP
5	George Forrest on horseback	RBGE
6	Sandy Leven with Caithness Glass Trophy	Glassford Sprunt
7	Winning Exhibits at Strathclyde	" "
8	Modern Rock Garden Layout	Ian Young
9	The Great Wall	David Aitken
10	Sales Area in Garden Centre	Alastair McKelvie
11	Display Area in Garden Centre	" "
12	Rock Garden at RBGE	RBGE
13	Rock Garden at Leith Hall	Alastair McKelvie
14	Alpine House at RBGE	RBGE
15	Ron McBeath in RBGE Alpine House	"
16	Four types of stone trough	Ian Young
	Cement Concrete	
	Reconstituted stone Real sandstone	
	Polystyrene fish box	
17	Polystyrene box being roughened by heat gun	" "
18	Painting stages	" "
19	Pile of six completed boxes	" "
20	*Saussurea laniceps*	Ron J. D. McBeath
21	*Draba oreades*	Joel Smith
22	*Incarvillea compacta*	Ron J. D. McBeath
23	*Cremanthodium ellisii*	" "
24	*Cassiope fastigiata*	" "
25	*Cassiope selaginoides*	Peter A. Cox
26	*Cassiope wardii*	Anne Chambers
27	*Rhododendron laudandum*	Peter A. Cox
28	*Rhododendron primuliflorum*	" "
29	*Rhododendron ciliatum*	Anne Chambers
30	*Rhododendron lepidotum*	Margaret &Henry Taylor
31	*Rhododendron racemosum*	Peter A. Cox
32	*Gentiana georgei*	Ron. J. D. McBeath
33	*Gentiana hexaphylla*	" "
34	*Gentiana sino-ornata*	" "
35	*Gentiana veitchiorum*	Ron J. D. McBeath
36	*Corydalis cashmeriana*	Margaret &Henry Taylor
37	*Meconopsis horridula*	Ron J. D. McBeath
38	*Meconopsis grandis*	" "

39	*Meconopsis integrifolia*	Anne Chambers
40	*Meconopsis paniculata*	Ron J. D. McBeath
41	*Meconopsis psedudointegrifolia*	John A. Richards
42	*Meconopsis quintuplinervia*	Ron J. D. McBeath
43	*Meconopsis villosa*	" "
44	*Primula aureata*	Joel Smith
45	*Primula strumosa*	" "
46	*Primula ioessa*	Anne Chambers
47	*Primula calderiana*	Fred Hunt
48	*Primula forrestii*	Peter A. Cox
49	*Primula sikkimensis*	Ron J. D. McBeath
50	*Primula tanneri tsariensis*	Peter A. Cox
51	*Primula whitei*	Anne Chambers
52	*Primula macrophylla*	Margaret &Henry Taylor
53	*Primula chionantha*	John A. Richards
54	*Primula minutissima*	Margaret &Henry Taylor
55	*Primula reidii*	" " "
56	*Primula gracilipes*	Joel Smith
57	*Primula rosea*	Margaret &Henry Taylor
58	*Androsace delavayi*	" " "
59	*Omphalogramma elwesiana*	Ron J. D. McBeath
60	*Anemone rupicola*	Margaret &Henry Taylor
61	*Anemone obtusiloba*	" " "
62	*Paraquilegia anemonoides*	" " "
63	*Trollius pumilus*	Ron J. D. McBeath
64	*Potentilla cuneata*	Joel Smith
65	*Delphinium tatsienense*	Heather Salzen
66	*Potentilla eriocarpa*	Ron J. D. McBeath
67	*Saxifraga hypostoma*	RBGE
68	*Arisaema candidissimum*	Ron J. D. McBeath
69	*Arisaema nepenthoides*	" "
70	*Arisaema flavum* var. *tibeticum*	Anne Chambers
71	*Arisaema triphyllum*	Heather Salzen
72	*Lilium flavidum*	Ron J. D. McBeath
73	*Lilium nanum*	Anne Chambers
74	*Lilium lophophorum*	Ron J. D. McBeath
75	*Lilium sherriffiae*	Fred Hunt
76	*Lilium souliei*	John A. Richards
77	*Nomocharis aperta*	Peter A. Cox
78	*Nomocharis pardanthina*	Ron J. D. McBeath
79	*Daiswa polyphylla*	" "
80	*Achillea ageratifolia*	Michael Almond
81	*Arabis caucasica*	Lynn Almond
82	*Draba polytricha*	" "

83	*Campanula aucheri/tridentata* aff.	Michael Almond
84	*Campanula betulifolia*	" "
85	*Campanula versicolor*	" "
86	*Edraianthus graminifolius*	" "
87	*Dianthus scardicus*	" "
88	*Ramonda serbica*	" "
89	*Corydalis bulbosa*	" "
90	*Corydalis ochroleuca*	" "
91	*Acantholimon* sp.	Lynn Almond
92	*Androsace hedraeantha*	Michael Almond
93	*Androsace villosa*	" "
94	*Cyclamen cilicium*	" "
95	*Cyclamen parviflorum*	" "
96	*Primula amoena*	" "
97	*Trollius ranunculinus*	" "
98	*Saxofraga sempervivum*	" "
99	*Saxifraga marginata*	" "
100	*Daphne oleoides/Helleborus cyclophyllus*	" "
101	*Viola graeca*	" "
102	*Crocus abantensis*	" "
103	*Crocus biflorus* ssp. *mazzaricus*	" "
104	*Crocus chrysanthus*	" "
105	*Crocus cancellatus* ssp. *mazzaricus*	" "
106	*Crocus fleischeri*	" "
107	*Crocus pallasii* ssp. *pallasii*	" "
108	*Crocus sieberi* ssp. *sublimis*	" "
109	*Crocus sieberi* ssp. *atticus*	" "
110	*Iris afghanica*	RBGE
111	*Iris attica*	Lynn Almond
112	*Iris unguicularis*	Heather Salzen
113	*Iris winogradowii*	RBGE
114	*Friitllaria acmopetala*	Michael Almond
115	*Fritillaria bithynica*	Michael Almond
116	*Fritillaria crassifolia* ssp. *kurdica*	Lynn Almond
117	*Fritillaria davisii*	" "
118	*Fritillaria latifolia* var. *nobilis*	Michael Almond
119	*Muscari macrocarpum*	" "
120	*Ornithogalum oligophyllum*	" "
121	*Scilla sibirica* ssp. *armena*	Lynn Almond
122	*Sternbergia candida*	" "
123	*Sternbergia sicula*	Heather Salzen
124	*Strenbergia lutea*	Michael Almond
125	*Tulipa biflora*	" "
126	*Erigeron aureus*	Polly Stone

127	*Erigeron compositus*	" "
128	*Erigeron pinnatisectus*	" "
129	*Hymenoxis acaulis caespitosa*	" "
130	*Townsendia condensata*	" "
131	*Townsendia exscapa*	" "
132	*Townsendia montana*	" "
133	*Cornus canadensis*	Heather Salzen
134	*Kalmia polifolia*	" "
135	*Phyllodoce empetriformis*	Polly Stone
136	*Gentiana algida*	" "
137	*Phlox adsurgens*	Fred Hunt
138	*Phacelia sericea*	Polly Stone
139	*Phlox diffusa*	" "
140	*Phlox hendersonii*	" "
141	*Phlox hirsuta*	Margaret &Henry Taylor
142	*Phlox hoodii*	Polly Stone
143	*Phlox speciosa*	Margaret &Henry Taylor
144	*Polemonium viscosum*	Polly Stone
145	*Eriogonum flavum* var. *piperi*	" "
146	*Lewisia rediviva minor*	Fred Hunt
147	*Androsace laevigata*	Margaret &Henry Taylor
148	*Androsace montana*	Polly Stone
149	*Dodecatheon clevelandii*	Margaret &Henry Taylor
150	*Dodecatheon conjugans*	Polly Stone
151	*Dodecatheon poeticum*	Margaret &Henry Taylor
152	*Primula angustifolia*	Polly Stone
153	*Primula parryi*	" "
154	*Anemone multifida*	Heather Salzen
155	*Aquilegia jonesii*	Polly Stone
156	*Caltha leptosepala* var. *sulphurea*	" "
157	*Ranunculus adoneus*	" "
158	*Pulsatilla patens*	" "
159	*Ranunculus eschscholtzii eximius*	" "
160	*Elmera racemosa*	" "
161	*Penstemon eriantherus*	" "
162	*Penstemon newberryi*	" "
163	*Penstemon procerus* var. *tolmiei*	" "
164	*Iris douglasiana*	Margaret &Henry Taylor
165	*Iris innominata*	" " "
166	*Iris tenax*	" " "
167	*Calochortus venustus*	Fred Hunt
168	*Erythronium grandiflorum*	Margaret &Henry Taylor
169	*Erythronium hendersonii*	Polly Stone
170	*Erythronium montanum*	" "

171	*Fritillaria affinis*	Fred Hunt
172	*Fritillaria glauca*	" "
173	*Fritillaria recurva*	" "
174	*Trillium erectum*	Polly Stone
175	*Trillium chloropetalum*	" "
176	*Trillium luteum*	Fred Hunt
177	*Trillium grandiflorum roseum*	" "
178	*Trillium rivale* 'Purple Heart'	" "
179	*Trillium ovatum*	Margaret & Henry Taylor
180	*Pernettya mucronata*	Heather Salzen
181	*Nassauvia revoluta*	Ian Brooker
182	*Oxalis adenophylla*	" "
183	*Oxalis enneaphylla*	" "
184	*Saxifraga magellanica*	Heather Salzen
185	*Calceolaria uniflora*	Ian Brooker
186	*Ourisia coccinea*	" "
187	*Ourisia fragrans*	" "
188	*Nierembergia patagonica*	" "
189	*Tropaeolum incisum*	" "
190	*Tropaeolum polyphyllum*	" "
191	*Viola atropurpurea*	" "
192	*Viola coronifera*	" "
193	*Viola nivalis*	" "
194	*Viola philippii*	" "
195	*Viola sacculus*	Ian Brooker
196	*Alstroemeria pseudospathulata*	" "
197	*Epimedium grandiflorum*	Polly Stone
198	*Adenophora triphylla* var. *japonica*	RBGE
199	*Campanula chamisonnis superba*	Alf Evans
200	*Diapensis lapponica* var. *obovata*	" "
201	*Shortia soldanelloides* forma *alpina*	Polly Stone
202	*Shortia soldanelloides* 'Askival Icebell'	" "
203	*Shortia soldanelloides*	" "
204	*Andromeda polifolia*	Alf Evans
205	*Cassiope lycopodioides*	Polly Stone
206	*Gaultheria adenothrix*	" "
207	*Phyllodoce aleutica*	Alf Evans
208	*Rhododendron aureum*	" "
209	*Rhododendron camtschaticum*	" "
210	*Rhododendron dauricum*	" "
211	*Rhododendron keiskii*	" "
212	*Gentiana triflora*	" "
213	*Glaucidium palmatum*	" "
214	*Dicentra peregrina*	Polly Stone

215	*Hylomecon japonicum*	Alf Evans
216	*Primula japonica*	" "
217	*Primula sieboldii*	Alastair McKelvie
218	*Primula takedana*	Polly Stone
219	*Adonis amurensis*	Alf Evans
220	*Aquilegia flabellata* var. *pumila*	Polly Stone
221	*Astilbe simplicifolia*	" "
222	*Arisaema japonicum*	" "
223	*Celmisia angustifolia*	Harold McBride
224	*Celmisia hookeri*	" "
225	*Celmisia semicordata*	" "
226	*Celmisia sessiliflora*	Forbes Robertson
227	*Haastia pulvinaris*	Harold McBride
228	*Leucogenes grandiceps*	Heather Salzen
229	*Leucogenes leontopodium*	Harold McBride
230	*Raoulia eximia*	John A. Richards
231	*Aciphylla aurea*	Harold McBride
232	*Notothlaspi australe*	" "
233	*Notothlaspi rosulatum*	" "
234	*Gentiana serotina*	" "
235	*Gentiana saxosa*	Harold Mcbride
236	*Clematis marmoraria*	" "
237	*Ranunculus buchananii*	" "
238	*Ranunculus lyallii*	" "
239	*Bulbinella angustifolia*	Heather Salzen
240	*Gazania krebsiana*	" "
241	*Rhodohypoxis baurii* var. *baurii*	RBGE
242	*Lapeirousia silenoides*	Heather Salzen
243	*Romulea bulbocodium*	RBGE
	Frontispiece: Spring in the Rock Garden	Ian Young

§ ACKNOWLEDGEMENTS §

This book was commissioned to celebrate the Millennium by the Council of the Scottish Rock Garden Club to whom we are grateful for the necessary financial support for the project. We are also indebted to the trustees of the Stanley Smith Horticultural Trust for financial assistance.

We particularly wish to thank those members of the SRGC who devoted time and effort to supply us with information about themselves and their rock gardening activities and who also lent us some of their most valued transparencies for the illustrations. Transparencies were lent by David Aitken, Michael and Lynn Almond, Ian Brooker, Anne Chambers, Peter Cox, Fred Hunt, Ron McBeath, Harold McBride, John Richards, Heather Salzen, Joel Smith, Henry and Margaret Taylor, Polly Stone and Ian Young.

We are indebted to Jane Hutcheon, Librarian of the Royal Botanic Garden Edinburgh for permission to draw upon the Garden's slide collection which includes the photograph of George Forrest which is reproduced with the permission of his relatives. The map of Forrest's area of exploration in China is taken from J.M. Cowan's "The Journeys and Plant Introductions of George Forrest", 1952 OUP. It is reproduced with the permission of the Oxford University Press. We wish to thank Mrs J. A. Sherriff for the excellent photograph of George Sherriff and also Angus Robertson for comments on the New Zealand Flora.

We would like to thank Fred Carrie for assistance with computing problems especially those of compatibility between the various systems used. Especial thanks are due to Mike Reid for assistance with selecting the illustrations used in the book from the many submitted and for carrying out the laborious but essential process of assembling them on to the 80 colour plates.

The assistance of David and Gordon Rait of Claymore Graphics at all stages in the preparation of the book is gratefully acknowledged

Finally grateful thanks are due to our wives who, for almost a two-year period, had to put up with a life dominated by production of the book perhaps at times to the detriment of other more important things.

Although the book was commissioned by the Council of the SRGC the views expressed in the book are those of the authors and are not necessarily those of the Council.

Forbes W. Robertson
Alastair McKelvie

October 1999

§ INTRODUCTION §

To prepare a volume in celebration of a Millennium is to venture upon uncharted territory without the benefit of precedent or convention to act as guide. Different authors will opt for different routes, according to their interests and experience. In the present instance we took the view that, whatever else was included, there must be a major historical component which covered the history of rock gardening in Scotland and which revealed the Royal Botanic Garden, Edinburgh and the Scottish Rock Garden Club as the mainsprings of knowledge and enterprise. Restriction of our account to the Scottish scene derives not from chauvinist inclination but simply because that was our remit.

In preparing this account we have paid tribute to the men and women who, whether as collectors, skilled growers or gardeners have made their distinctive contribution to our favourite branch of horticulture. Such information serves a dual purpose. On the one hand, we would hope that present members will find interest in the early history of the Club, the various ways its activities have developed since its inception and would like to be reminded of those who have particularly contributed to its success. But, on the other hand, we also have an eye on history since this kind of information will be of value to any future historian of this branch of horticulture who may wish to identify the principal players. Evidence of this nature acquires increasing value as time passes not only for its factual content but also because it offers our successors a glimpse into the social mores of a bye-gone age for comparison with their contemporary scene. A Millennium volume would seem a particularly suitable repository for such evidence.

So much for the people, the rest of the book presents an overview of the more important alpine and rock plants which have been introduced during the 20th century. Here the treatment departs from convention since species are grouped in natural families according to the major region of the world from whence they come, with the exception of western Europe. The European alpine flora is so well known and many of the species have been with us so long that it was decided to concentrate on species from further afield. We believe there is value in grouping species according to geographical origin since it immediately focuses attention on the families and genera which have made the greatest contribution to the rock garden flora from different regions. Also, plants from a given region with well defined climatic conditions often share similar physiological requirements which often point to similar cultural needs. Each species has its own distribution, habitats and ecological associations which play an important part in defining its identity. The more we are aware of such attributes the greater our appreciation of the differences between related species. Unfortunately there is neither space nor time to apply this approach in systematic fashion but at least we can take account of where species come from, since their origins often co-incide with the more important floristic regions.

This survey also has some historical significance. Just as we are intrigued to know what our ancestors were growing a century or more ago so our descendants will like to know which species dominated our rock garden flora, which were deemed difficult to grow and to what extent particular species were represented by more than one variety, or cultivar as modern terminology has it. They will have a measure of progress in technique by comparing how far they can easily grow species which we find difficult.

So this is the route we have followed and we can only hope that our readers will find something of interest in the succeeding pages.

§ CHAPTER 1 §

The Botanical Context

THE ROLE OF THE ROYAL BOTANIC GARDEN EDINBURGH

During the 20th century both the exploration of the Himalayan and Chinese flora and the introduction of new species to the garden are closely entwined with the fortunes of the Royal Botanic Garden Edinburgh (RBGE). Successive Regius Keepers have collaborated with and advised famous collectors in the identification and naming of new plants they brought back as herbarium specimens, while the garden staff spared no effort to germinate the imported seed and propagate the new species which poured in so abundantly. Although the localities and style of collecting have changed the tradition has been maintained so that the role of the garden runs like a connecting thread from the beginning of the century to the present day.

ISAAC BAYLEY BALFOUR

At the beginning of the century the Regius Keeper was Isaac Bayley Balfour (1853-1922), later Sir Isaac (Fig.1), who, more than any other single person, advanced the cause of Himalayan exploration in several different ways. A native of Edinburgh, he trained as a doctor, but, like his father, John Hutton Balfour, a former Regius Keeper of the Botanic Garden, the study of plants claimed his entire attention. After experience as a field botanist on an expedition to Mexico he was appointed Professor of Botany at the University of Glasgow in 1874, where he remained for six years before moving to Oxford as the Sherardian Professor of Botany. In 1887 he returned to Edinburgh as Regius Keeper of the Royal Botanic Garden for a period of 34 years. During his long reign he completely reorganised the garden, diversifying the plantings, adding conservatories, a lecture theatre and entirely reconstructing the rock garden to arrive at its present natural lay-out, in place of the collection of pots and containers which had preceded it. He became particularly interested in the plants of the Himalayas and Western China and, with the aid of the collectors like Forrest, who worked these areas, he established Edinburgh's pre-eminence in these floras. It is difficult to exaggerate the importance of Bayley Balfour in establishing the Edinburgh Garden as an internationally recognised centre both for the taxonomy and for the tasteful display of an immense collection of plants from these regions.

THE CLASSIC ERA OF COLLECTING

By one of those unpredictable coincidences, in 1904 Balfour was consulted by A.K. Bulley, a Liverpool cotton broker, owner of a famous garden at Ness, with a commercial section which developed into the seed and plant firm of Bees Ltd. Bulley had a passion for introducing new plants for profitable sale by his firm and he wanted Balfour's advice as to where he should focus his efforts. Both were already familiar with the collections of that remarkably versatile Irishman Augustine Henry in Western China as well as the collections of the French Missionaries like David and Delavay, while E.H. Wilson, sent out to the same area by Messrs Veitch, the premier nursery firm of the time, had brought back a great deal of valuable new material. So Bulley was advised to concentrate on Western China and to employ as collector a young man called George Forrest, who was working as an assistant in the Herbarium. Bulley took the advice and Forrest was soon off on the first of his seven expeditions in the course of which he established his reputation as the most famous Scottish plant collector of the twentieth century. By the time Forrest died prematurely in 1932, while out duck shooting with Chinese friends, he had collected over 30,000 first class herbarium specimens (Fletcher and Brown 1970), had sent back seed measured in pounds and hundredweights and had introduced an immense number of new plants into cultivation which would eventually transform our gardens. All the preserved material came to the Edinburgh Herbarium. Most of the collected seed was cleaned in Edinburgh, from where it was distributed to members of the syndicates who supported the expeditions, to growers and to other scientific institutions, while the propagating staff concentrated on raising the new plants. Balfour realised that he was presented with a botanical and horticultural goldmine. He spent the rest of his life on the taxonomy and floristic relations of Western Chinese plants and in supervising their successful cultivation for use in the garden. In the latter respect his right-hand man was Lewis Baxter Stewart, a native of Kirriemuir, who joined the Botanic Garden in 1901 as Glasshouse Foreman. For his first decade in the Garden he was responsible for supplying teaching material for the University classes in Botany. From 1911 to 1932 he was Plant Propagator, and was appointed Curator in 1932. To Stewart must go the credit for establishing so much of Forrest's introductions in cultivation. He merits special recognition in the annals of rock-gardening.

WILLIAM WRIGHT SMITH

Bayley Balfour's successor was William Wright Smith (1875-1956), also knighted. A native of Lochmaben, Dumfriesshire and graduate of Edinburgh University, he started his career as lecturer in Botany at Edinburgh University. Soon after, he left for India where he was appointed Director of the Government Herbarium of the Royal Botanic Garden, Calcutta, where he stayed until 1911. During that period he became familiar with the Indian and Burmese flora in several expeditions to Sikkim and the borders of Nepal, Tibet and Bhutan, where he collected plants on the Tibetan border, north of Kanchenjunga, at altitudes of over 4300m and visited the alpine regions between the Tibetan valley of Chumbi and Eastern Sikkim. He left India to become Deputy Keeper of the Edinburgh Garden, where he continued his studies of Sino-Himalayan plants, especially of primulas and rhododendrons. He was deeply involved with the material brought back by Forrest and, later, Ludlow and Sherriff and was admirably qualified by first-hand experience and his taxonomic expertise to make the most of it. He and Forrest collaborated in preparing an account of the genus *Primula*. Many of the species of this genus are notoriously difficult to grow, taxing the skills of Stewart and another skilled propagator, Robert L. Harrow, to the utmost. As noted by Fletcher and Brown (1970), between 1912 and 1921 Wright Smith published in Notes from the Royal Botanic Garden, Edinburgh, descriptions of more than 550 new species from the genera *Saxifraga, Androsace, Delphinium, Gentiana, Codonopsis, Senecio, Aster, Corydalis, Salvia, Cremanthodium, Astragalus, Daphne, Potentilla, Vaccinium, Magnolia, Abelia, Berberis, Jasminum, Spiraea, Lonicera* and *Cotoneaster* together with various reintroductions and an account of the lilies of China.

HAROLD ROY FLETCHER

Wright Smith was followed by Harold Roy Fletcher (1897-1978) as Regius Keeper. Fletcher was a member of the Garden staff from 1934 to 1951 when he was appointed Director of the Royal Horticultural Society at Wisley but he was soon back in Edinburgh as Regius Keeper in 1956. Encouraged by Wright Smith he developed an interest in primulas and collaborated with him in a long series of papers on the taxonomy of the genus. Fletcher had previously worked on the flora of Siam, when he was a member of staff of the Dept. of Botany at the University of Aberdeen under Professor Craib, a native of Banff.

By the middle of the century the great era of discovery of Sino-Himalayan plants was entering a new phase in which the emphasis would be on the general flora and floristic relations of Western China, Sikkim and Bhutan. Many short expeditions, devoted to intense general collecting of the flora became the norm. Such expeditions were either sent out from the Royal Botanic Garden Edinburgh or the scientists joined expeditions mounted in part or entirely under other auspices. Often they have been to the same areas as those traversed by Forrest, Cooper, Ludlow and Sherriff, Kingdon Ward or Rock. In many instances the horticultural interests were incidental to the aim of documenting the flora, although this was not always so. Inevitably, however, such expeditions bring back seed of rediscovered plants of horticultural value, species which may have briefly flowered in the past but which are worth trying to re-establish. Also plants from new locations may prove better adapted to our conditions. In addition, as fashions change, genera little noticed or ignored by the earlier collectors add to the diversity of rock-garden plants. So the great Sino-Himalayan tradition continues at Edinburgh in long unbroken continuity from the beginning of the century. We must now consider the several famous collectors associated with the Garden.

GEORGE FORREST

Forrest (1873-1932) was born in Falkirk where he attended Falkirk Southern School. Fourteen years later his family moved to Kilmarnock, where his father set up a draper's business. When Forrest left Kilmarnock Academy he was apprenticed as pharmacist with a local firm, although he never completed his apprenticeship. His life-long interest in natural history was established during his youth, stimulated by a local minister friend who was a keen naturalist. Benefiting by a small inheritance he left for Australia where he tried his luck in the goldfields and worked on a sheep farm. In 1902 he returned to Scotland to stay with his widowed mother, near Edinburgh. His association with the Royal Botanic Garden started when he got a job as assistant in the herbarium. He impressed Bayley Balfour by his competence and reliability. As we have seen this led to employment by Bulley who was glad to have a robust young fellow to collect for him in Yunnan (Fig.5). The upshot was that Forrest found himself sailing for Rangoon as Bulley's collector in 1904.

On arrival he made his way to the mountainous region where four great rivers rise, the Mekong, the Salween, the Yangtsekiang and the Irrawaddy and where the valleys running north and south are separated by steep mountain ranges. On this expedition he operated rather like a general naturalist, since, in addition to plants, he also collected birds, adding some 90 new species to the avifauna of the region, small mammals and butterflies and moths, as well as gathering information and artefacts relating to the native people and their ways. This was the expedition when Forrest nearly lost his life. In July 1905 he was staying at the French mission on the upper Mekong River, when they received news that Tibetan lamas far to the north had rebelled against the Chinese, killing the local garrison, and were heading towards them. Since neither the missionaries nor their converts could expect any mercy they fled, with the Tibetans in pursuit.

Forrest narrowly eluded capture, escaping the fate of the missionaries who were brutally tortured before being killed. All but one of his 17 collectors were killed and he was hunted by the Tibetans, who were determined to get him. One of their poisonous arrows penetrated his hat and for days he was in the utmost danger. To confuse his pursuers tracking his footprints he had to discard his boots. After being pursued for a week, during which, lurking unobserved in the forest he could often see his enemy, starving, his feet in a terrible state, and not caring whether he lived or died, he stumbled on a village which turned out to be friendly and where he found food and shelter. The Austrian botanist and Himalayan explorer Handel-Mazzetti, who had his account at first hand when he was staying in the same town in Yunnan, wrote that no one unfamiliar with the wild and rugged country could appreciate what Forrest had endured. Handel-Mazzetti was, himself, a great botanist in the same areas as Forrest and brought back more than 13,000 specimens to Vienna, well documented in his published diaries (Handel-Mazzetti 1996).

At home, the news was that Forrest had perished although a couple of days later his improbable survival was reported. After such an experience many would have opted to avoid such a hazardous part of the world, but it was not long before he was back. That says a great deal about what manner of man he was.

A few general aspects of his enterprise are worth noting. E.H.M. Cox, later of Glendoick Nursery, author of "Plant Hunting in China", knew Forrest well, subscribed to his expeditions and discussed them with him. He also had first-hand knowledge of the kind of conditions where Forrest collected since he had been with Farrer during part of his last, ill-fated journey in Burma. Cox made the point that Forrest was the first of a new kind of plant collector. Hitherto, scientific or government funded institutions or commercial firms had sent out collectors. The first two of Forrest's expeditions were funded by Bulley, although the collaboration ended acrimoniously on account of Bulley's failure to pay Forrest's salary on time to his wife or to provide sufficient money for the expedition. But the rest were supported by small syndicates of growers who received the collected seed in return for their outlay. Cox rated this arrangement a real benefit since no one institution or garden could cope adequately with the volume of material Forrest sent back.

A great many of the new introductions were difficult to grow or their particular requirements were unknown. The greater the number of growers who handled them, in different climatic and soil conditions, the greater the chance of survival somewhere. In this context, Cox also remarked that in the 20s and 30s the contributions of Forrest, Kingdon Ward and Rock flooded into the UK and USA, exceeding the capacity of the available growers to deal with all of them. Hence the more flamboyant species got most attention, to the neglect of many a good plant which might have survived in cultivation, given a less hurried response.

Among the most faithful of Forrest's subscribers was J.C. Williams of Caerhays and Warrington Park. Like Bayley Balfour, rhododendrons were a special interest. Indeed, he paid Forrest a bonus for each collected rhododendron which was described as a new species by Balfour. Another regular supporter was D.M. McLaren, later Lord Aberconway, for whom Forrest organised a collecting trip which went ahead even after he had died. Cox drew particular attention to Forrest's innovation in training local people to act as efficient collectors. This was no mean achievement. Although unfamiliar with any language other than his own, Forrest learnt Chinese and established excellent rapport with the local people. His collectors mostly came from the single village of Mosso and so were friends or relatives, who established a valuable esprit de corps and became dedicated to their task. His general policy was to set up a base in some strategic area and radiate from there in successive collecting forays. Often his collectors would range far afield in their search and would even continue their work while Forrest was back in the UK. Although his field notes indicate localities it is not possible to reconstruct his routes in detail, nor is it generally possible to distinguish between what he or his collectors found. It was his practice to return repeatedly to profitable areas, to make sure nothing was missed, so he got to know parts of the Lichiang in familiar detail.

On his first trip he had for part of the time, the company of Mr Litton, the British Consul at Teng-Yueh. They went to Lichiang together and travelled to the upper Salween as far north as latitude 27° 0', through country inhabited by the Lissus who had not seen a white man before. After Litton died of blackwater fever in 1905 Forrest had no European assistance or company in the field, apart from a Major Johnston who joined the last expedition but whom Forrest found of little assistance, since he preferred socialising to botany, and had to return home soon since he found the going too rough.

Forrest generally had about 20 collectors to organise, plan their collecting trips and advise them on particular plants to look for. He always carried a supply of medicines and drugs to treat either himself, his collectors or the local villagers. He was an expert and productive photographer, working with old-style 1/4 and 1/2 plate cameras, which needed long exposure times and posed problems in development when the temperature was too high. And of course there was his correspondence. We have it from the eldest of his three sons (1973) that he sent home a letter to his wife every week and these were very full and of great interest. He corresponded prodigiously with Bayley Balfour and Wright Smith about his botanical discoveries; sometimes the letters ran to 30 pages. Since he wrote so well and so directly, it is a pity he never recorded his experiences and the country he travelled through for the benefit of the general public. A few short articles in the Royal Horticultural Journal, the Geographical Journal and the Gardeners' Chronicle and some technical items in the Edinburgh Botanic Garden Notes are all that he left in the public domain. He was pressed to write up his travels but always declined. Perhaps he had this in mind for the retirement he never enjoyed.

Forrest comes across as a very self-reliant person who felt entirely at ease in the domain of wild nature. He had an iron constitution, having survived blackwater fever, typhoid and malaria, which he treated himself, at least in the early stages. He was very jealous of the territory which he considered his own stamping ground and resented Kingdon Ward's and Rock's incursions. Having worked the area so thoroughly and for so long that was probably not surprising. But he got on very well with Handel-Mazzetti and advised the Austrian on the route to follow when he set off to collect in the area of Forrest's first expedition which ended so disastrously.

An account of Forrest's travels and more important discoveries was published in 1952 by Dr McQueen Cowan, then Deputy Keeper of RBGE

Cowan's map (Fig.4) indicates the general area of Forrest's seven explorations in Yunnan. He usually entered by Bhamo to Teng-yueh and the Salween Divide. He collected in the Lichiang Range repeatedly as well as on the Chungtien Plateau, the Mekong-Salween and the surrounding country and beyond to the north of Li-tu-ping.

ROLAND E. COOPER

Roland Cooper (1890-1967) was the other Edinburgh-based European botanist who collected for A.K. Bulley. He was orphaned at an early age and brought up by his aunt and uncle, the Wright Smiths. His uncle was, of course, later to become Regius Keeper of the Royal Botanic Garden Edinburgh and University Professor of Botany. Before that he acted as Director of the Government Herbarium in Calcutta. Naturally Cooper went with him in 1907 and, during the next four years, developed into a competent botanist. He collected plants in Sikkim and attended courses in Botany. He came to Edinburgh when his uncle became Deputy Keeper of the Royal Botanic Garden and continued his studies in horticulture. As a result of another enquiry from Bulley about a suitable man to collect for him Professor Bayley Balfour recommended Cooper. After considering various alternatives it was decided that Cooper should make for Sikkim where he found himself in the field from June to October in 1913. Nothing very remarkable seems to have come out of this trip so it was decided to try a different area. After the protracted diplomatic negotiations required for entry to such a secluded country, Cooper crossed into Bhutan a year later, accompanied by a Bhutanese escort and his Sikkimese collectors, recruited in Darjeeling, with the objective of finding new primulas and rhododendrons.

Bhutan is bounded by Sikkim to the west, Tibet to the east and north and by Assam and Bengal to the south. The country can be divided into three areas: the valley of Paro and Timpu where the flora approximates to that of Sikkim, from which it is separated by the western side of the Chumbi valley; the valley of Punakha, Tongsa and Pumthang in the central area; the valley of Kurmed and Kumted in the east.

Cooper spent almost a full year travelling across from Paro in the west to Townga in the east, a distance of some 320km across steeply precipitous mountain terrain, penetrating to areas which had not been seen by Europeans before and which were only rarely frequented by the Bhutanese. This expedition was curtailed by the First World War when Cooper joined the Indian Army in 1916. But by that time he had made a substantial collection of primulas. Of the 19 new species or varieties he listed, seven are mentioned in the Encyclopedia of Alpines (1994), indicating that they were at some time in cultivation but, sadly, apart from *P. bracteosa*, most of his introductions did not survive. Those which did, for at least a time, include *PP. chaemophila, eburnea, erythrocarpa, strumosa, umbratilis*, the rare and attractive *xanthopa* and the beautiful ivory coloured variety *hopeana* of *sikkimensis*.

In several respects Cooper was very unfortunate in the timing of his expeditions. Although his collecting was successful and well organised his contributions were inevitably eclipsed by those of Forrest. The War not only curtailed his second expedition but had other consequences. One of his consignments of plants was sunk by enemy action, while a great proportion of his collected material had to be stored in Calcutta where they suffered from neglect and insect attack. It was not until 1950 that all his herbarium material in Edinburgh was finally examined. So in spite of his efforts there is little to remember him by in the rock garden. After the War he worked in Burma and later returned to Edinburgh where he became Assistant Curator and, later, Curator of the RBG until he retired in 1950. During this later period he became well known to the alpine garden fraternity in Scotland and was an enthusiastic founder member of the SRGC.

LUDLOW AND SHERRIFF

After Forrest the most important Scottish collector was George Sherriff (Fig.3) whose name is always linked with that of the Englishman Frank Ludlow because they enjoyed such a long friendship, during which they travelled to so many remote places in the Himalayas, that they have to be considered together. Although they documented their plant collections well enough and kept diaries neither wrote up their experiences for the general public, unlike their contemporary Frank Kingdon Ward, who explored the same general region but also had a flair for graphic description which ensured the popularity of his many books. So we have to rely on Harold Fletcher's account of their journeys in his "A Quest of Flowers" (1975) and also on George Taylor's comments, which are particularly valuable since he accompanied them on one of their major expeditions. He knew them as companions in the field and is unstinting in his appreciation of their qualities.

Frank Ludlow (1885-1972), born in London, graduated from Cambridge in 1908 with a BA in the Natural Sciences. As a student he studied Botany under Kingdon Ward's father, Professor Marshal Ward. After University he took a post as Vice-President of Sind College in Karachi where he also taught Biology and English. After the First World War, during which he was commissioned in the Indian Infantry, he joined the Indian Education Service as Inspector of European Schools. During 1922 he received a request to identify candidates for the post of headmaster of a school to be opened at Gyantse in Tibet for the purpose of introducing upper class Tibetans to Western education. Attracted by the chance of obtaining first hand experience of such an alien and little known culture he submitted his own name, although success would hardly advance his career in the Indian Education service. He got the post and spent three years in Tibet, returning to Srinagar in 1927. In 1929 he was invited to spend the winter with the Consul General of Kashgar. There he met George Sheriff and established a friendship which was to last until Sherriff died. Ludlow was an outstanding naturalist with particular interests in ornithology to which he made major contributions in the way of specimens and reports during his travels. Taylor notes that Ludlow was expert with a catapult, a great advantage when collecting specimens in areas where firearms were forbidden.

George Sherriff (1898-1967), was a native of Larbert, near Stirling. After a school career at Sedbergh he entered the Royal Military Academy at Woolwich to become a professional soldier. Commissioned in the Royal Garrison Artillery in the First World war, he was gassed in 1918 and spent the rest of the War in hospital. By 1919 he was in the Mountain Artillery on the North West frontier. In 1928 he entered the Consular Service and was appointed British Vice-Consul in Kashgar, although, later he resigned from the Consular Service. During the Second World War he rejoined the Royal Artillery. In 1943 he succeeded Ludlow as British resident in Lhasa.

Some thirteen years younger than Ludlow, Sherriff was a very different person, being very much the sportsman, a first class shot who could bring down a swift on the wing, and man of action with a very practical bent. But their different talents were complementary and they made a strong team in the field. Unlike Ludlow, Sherriff had private means which he drew upon to help finance their expeditions and pay for the cost of transporting live specimens back to Britain. Their interests and enthusiasm for collecting plants grew over time and both developed into expert field workers. Taylor remarks on what nowadays seems a curious foible. During all their years of friendship and shared hardships and successes they never referred to each other than by their surnames. In 1950 Ludlow and Sherriiff retired to Britain. Ludlow spent the rest of his life working on the plant collections they had sent to the British Museum while Sherriff settled on a farm near Kirriemuir, where he and his wife established a garden at Ascreavie, which became well known for their success in growing so many of the Himalayan plants that Sherriff had collected.

Over a period of 30 years Ludlow and Sherriff carried out seven expeditions, collecting plants in all the areas covered by their predecessors in Bhutan and Tibet as well as previously unexplored areas of both Bhutan and South East Tibet. They can be briefly summarised as follows:

(i) **1933**, a five month journey chiefly to the Trashiyangtse Valley in East Bhutan and thence over the Himalayan Range into Tibet.
(ii) **1934**, an expedition to the basins of the Tawang Chu and Nyam Jang Chu in Tibet, entering and returning by the Trashiyangse valley.
(iii) **1936**. In the company of Dr. K. Lumsden they explored the upper reaches of the Subansiria, which Kingdon Ward had visited in 1935. The plant gatherings totalled some 2000 and they were able to send home by sea two crates of live plants. Fletcher notes that, on this trip, out of 65 species and varieties of primula, 14 were new to science. Out of 69 rhododendron

collections 15 were new while for meconopsis there was a new species, *M. sherriffii* and a new yellow form of *M. horridula*.

(iv) **1937.** On this occasion Ludlow was unable to leave his duties and Sherriff went on his own to the high massif known as the Black Mountain to the Indian Survey.

(v) **1938.** On this trip George Taylor joined Ludlow and Sherriff. Taylor was a professional Botanist, later Director of Kew. Whereas Ludlow and Sherriff concentrated on groups and species of potential garden value, Taylor was more catholic in his collecting since he was interested in the general flora of the region. The genus *Meconopsis* was his speciality which culminated in his definitive account of the genus.

This was a ten months trip within the drainage of the Tsangpo, from the vicinity of Molo to the entrance of the Tsangpo Gorge, resulting in more than 4000 gatherings, a large quantity of seed and a substantial number of living plants sent by air to be widely distributed among British growers. Together, this was the largest and most comprehensive plant collection from Tibet ever made but the outbreak of the Second World War and the consequent neglect of both the living plants and seeds, and even the loss by bombing of some of the herbarium material in the British Museum, meant that its potential contribution to our gardens was not realised or only in part.

(vi) **1946.** Ludlow and Sherriff, accompanied by Mrs Sherriff and Col. Henry Elliott as Medical Officer, explored south east Tibet. They travelled in winter to be at the collecting area by spring. However, Sherriff developed a heart condition and had to return to India, but not before collecting in the lower reaches of the Polyigrong and Po Tsangpo and visiting Showa Dzong and Gompo Ne. This was the most ambitious of all their expeditions and would doubtless have been much more successful had not Sherriff fallen ill. It was also the last of their Tibetan expeditions since neither the Tibetan nor Indian Governments would grant permission for further expeditions in the areas they wished to visit.

(vii) **1949.** This was the last of their Himalayan expeditions since both Ludlow and Sherriff were now retired and preparing to return home. This time they went to Bhutan, accompanied by both Mrs Sherriff and Dr. J. H. Hicks as Medical Officer. This seven months trip, marred by an accident to Mrs Sherriff who was thrown by her mule, resulted in about 5000 gatherings, many bulbs and tubers, nearly 100 lots of live plants, which were flown to UK from Calcutta and a great deal of seed. Highlights of the findings on this expedition included *Lilium sherriffiae* and the rediscovery of *Meconopsis sherriffii* growing in great numbers in the upper Po Chu and Mangde Chu.

When we come to evaluate the contribution of the Ludlow and Sherriff expeditions to the rock garden and alpine house the conclusions are somewhat paradoxical. They collected a large number of species new to science, and made thereby a valuable contribution to the botany of the areas in which they travelled. Many of these species, seen in their natural habitat, appeared desirable garden plants, especially of such genera as *Aconitum*, *Delphinium*, *Gentiana*, *Pedicularis* and *Primula*, but only a small proportion of these became firmly established in cultivation. The same was largely true of the species they rediscovered, species which had first been found by their predecessors such as Hooker, Delavay, Bailey, Cooper and Forrest. The valuable collection gathered during the fifth expedition was neglected because of wartime priorites. But, like many of Forrest's discoveries, many of their introductions proved unable to flourish under British conditions.

Sherriff regularly sent seed to the Royal Botanic Garden Edinburgh as well as many other experienced growers. Often they would germinate, flower and, in several instances, reach the stage of exhibition and award of a RHS Award of Merit, but generally they soon faded away. Fletcher listed nearly 540 species and varieties, other than forest trees, which were collected either as herbarium specimens, often also as seed or, less frequently, living plants. Of the newly found species, other than rhodendrons, only 36% are mentioned in the Encyclopedia of Alpines. These will include species which once were in cultivation but are no longer extant. Furthermore, only about 10% of them appear in the 1997-8 Plant Finder – such is the attrition among introduced species.

GEORGE TAYLOR

George Taylor (1904–1997) was a native of Edinburgh and a graduate of the University. He was a professional botanist who in turn became Deputy Keeper of Botany at the British Museum, followed in 1956 by appointment as Director of Kew and, later, by a knighthood. He earns a place in our list of Scottish collectors chiefly because he accompanied Ludlow and Sherriff on their fifth, ten month expedition within the drainage of the Tsangpo, from the vicinity of Molo to the entrance of the Tsangpo Gorge. As noted earlier Taylor was primarily concerned with the general flora rather than species of potential horticultural value. However, he had a particular interest in the genus *Meconopsis*, culminating in his study of the genus, published in 1934. In the preface of the book, which is a model of critical taxonomy, he expressed his indebtedness to George Forrest, who "by his magnificent collections added so materially to our knowledge of the genus and with whom I had many opportunities of discussing the behaviour of certain species in the field."

POST-WAR HIMALAYAN EXPEDITIONS

After World War II the long standing dedication of RBGE to the study of the Sino-Himalayan flora continued. A number of expeditions have been sent out under the auspices of the Garden, manned by Garden staff some of whom have also taken part in expeditions initiated by other organisations such as the Alpine Garden Society and/or the Royal Horticultural Society. Almost all of them have been mounted in collaboration with the Kunming Institute of Botany, a member of a tri-partite agreement which included the Chinese Academy of Sciences and RBGE, to promote co-operation and exchange of plant material and information to mutual advantage. Although the names of the Chinese botanists who took part in these joint expeditions are not mentioned here, since they would not mean much to most readers, the success of these expeditions depended in no small measure on their enthusiastic co-operation.

The contemporary expeditions are very different from those of Forrest and Ludlow and Sherriff who worked and travelled in the interior for months on end. Modern travel can take one quickly to suitable collecting areas. Roads built to serve logging needs can often be used for lorry transport in place of mule trains. Detailed advance planning is designed to enable several experienced botanists to collect intensively over a 4-5 week period. All the emphasis is on maximum return for effort and money expended – in line with the prime themes of contemporary society. The aim of most of these expeditions was to add to our understanding of the flora of the region by collecting herbarium specimens, seed and often living plant material. In such cases the horticultural spin-off was incidental.

In several instances, however, noted below, introductions to horticulture was the main aim. When this was so the collected seed was widely distributed to botanical gardens and specialist nurseries as well to private growers known for their experience in growing certain species. Thus there has been a steady injection of wild material which often appears in the Plant Finder under the code name of a particular expedition or collector. It has to be acknowledged that the greater part of the material introduced this way to the trade and thence to gardeners consists of re-introductions of species which may have become scarce or vanished, forms of well-established species, perhaps different in some respects and, quite rarely, species entirely new to cultivation unless they happen to belong to genera which have been hitherto rather ignored such as say *Arisaema* or *Polygonatum*.

The most important of these expeditions, together with their destination and European personnel are summarised below. Members of RBGE staff are indicated by an asterisk while Scottish participants, not attached to the RBGE, are identified by a plus sign after their name. The code names which appear in the Plant Finder are in brackets.

YUNNAN
1981 The Cangshan Sino-British Expedition to the Cangshan Range above Dali in north west Yunnan. (SBE)
Personnel: D. F. Chamberlain*, P.A.Cox+, R. Lancaster, R.J.Mitchell + (Leader). This was the first major, western expedition of its kind since 1947.

1985 The Kunming, Edinburgh Yulongshan Expedition to Lijang and the Yulong Shan mountains in north west Yunnan.
Personnel: D.F. Chamberlain*. The aim was to study rhododendrons.

1987 Sino- British Lijang Expedition. (SBL)
Personnel: D.F. Chamberlain*, C. Grey-Wilson (Kew), R.J.D.McBeath*, A.D. Schilling (Kew). Horticultural material was collected as well as herbarium specimens.

1990 The Chungtien–Lijiang-Dali Expedition to the Zhongdian plateau, Lijang-Yulong Shan and Dali-Tsang Shan areas of Yunnan (CLD).
Personnel: C.D.Brickell (RHS), E.J.Cowley (Kew), A.C. Leslie (RHS), D.G. Long*, R.J.D. McBeath,*, D.S. Paterson*.
The main aim of the expedition was to collect seed of garden plants. More than 8,000 packets of seed were distributed.

1992 Sino-Scottish Expedition to North West Yunnan (SSY)
Personnel: D.F. Chamberlain*, P.A. Cox +, Sir P. Hutchison, I.W.J. Sinclair*.
The aim was to study rhododendrons. Sir P. Hutchison was formerly Chairman of RBG Edinburgh Trustees.

1993 The Kunming, Edinburgh, Göteborg Expedition to Yunnan, especially the Mekong Valley, the Zhongdian Plateau, Daxue Shan and Beima Shan. (KEG)
Personnel: J.C.M. Alexander*, B. Alden (Göteborg), D.G. Long*, R.J.D. McBeath*, H.J. Noltie*, M.F. Watson.*

1994 The Kagur Pu Expedition to north west Yunnan.
Personnel: D.F. Chamberlaain*, P.A. Cox+, R.D. Hyam*, E.G. Millais,
The aim was to study rhododendrons.

1994 The Alpine Garden Society Expedition to North West Yunnan, especially the Zhongdian Plateau, Daxue Shan, Haba Shan and Beima Shan .(ACE).
Personnel: C.D. Brickell (Leader,RHS), E.J. Cowley (Kew), P. Cunnington, C. Grey-Wilson, G. Hans, R.J.D.McBeath*, J.M. Mitchell*, R. Potterton, E. Strangman, T. Wiltshire (Wisley).
The expedition was in two parts – a spring reconnaisance and an autumn seed collection. Not all personnel participated in both trips. Nearly 900 accessions, both seed and live plants were collected.

SICHUAN
1986 Sichuan Expedition to central and northern Sichuan. (CHM)

Personnel: P.A. Cox +, Sir P. Hutchison, D. Maxwell-Macdonald +.

1989 Sichuan Expedition. (CCH)
Personnel: D.F. Chamberlain*, P.A. Cox +, Sir P. Hutchison.
Rhododendrons and primulas were the chief interests.

1991 The Chengdu Expedition to west and central Sichuan (CBE).
Personnel: D.F. Chamberlain*, D.G. Knott*
Rhodendrons were the main aim.

TAIWAN
1993 The Taiwan Expedition to the Hsueshan Range and the Yushan Massif. (ETE)
Personnel: S. Clarke*, M.F. Gardner*, J.D. Main*, D.G. Mann*, D.S. Paterson*.
This entirely RBGE expedition was largely horticultural in intent.

NEPAL
1981 Expedition to Makalu and Barun Khola.
Personnel: R.J.D. McBeath. This was chiefly to collect seeds. Finds included *Lilium nanum* 'Ron McBeath', a yellow form of *Rhododendron lepidotum* and many plants of *Rhododendron pumilum*.

1983 Expedition to Marsyandi Valley.
Personnel: G. Kirkpatrick*, R.J.D. McBeath*
Primarily horticultural including seed collections of *Arisaema, Stellera, Primula, Saxifraga*, including *S. cinerea*, many forms of *S. andersonii* and *S. lowndesii* which was new to cultivation.

1989 Kew - Edinburgh Expedition to Kachenjunga. (KEKE)
Personnel: S.Crawford, A.Dunkley, C.Grey-Wilson, D.G.Long*, R.J.D.McBeath*, H. Noltie*, M. Sinnott, S. Smarzty.
This was a major horticulturally oriented expedition. A great amount of seed was collected from such genera as *Androsace, Berberis, Gentiana, Lilium, Meconopsis* and *Primula*. The seeds were distributed to many botanical gardens, nurseries and private growers throughout the world.

1991 Edinburgh Expedition to Makalu and Milke Dunda. (EMAK)
Personnel: D.G. Long*, R.J.D. McBeath*, D.R. McKean*, D.A.H. Rae*
This expedition was primarily horticultural with funding from a number of Charitable Trusts, SRGC, AGS, the Göteburg Botanical garden, and a number of nurseries including Ardfearn, Christie's, Edrom, Holden Clough and Inshriach. The seed collections covered such genera as *Arisaema, Corydalis, Cremanthodium, Gentiana, Meconopsis, Primula* and *Saussurea*.

Rodgersia nepalensis and *Spiraea hemicryptophyta* were introduced to cultivation.

BHUTAN
1975, 1979, 1982 Personnel: A.J.C. Grierson* and D. Long*

1984 Personnel: D. Long*, I.W.J. Sinclair* All these Bhutanese expeditions were for general botanical collecting to provide information for "The Flora of Bhutan".

SIKKIM
1992 Edinburgh Expedition. (ESIK)
Personnel: D. Long*, R. J. D. McBeath*, H.J. Noltie*, M.F. Watson*

This summary does not exhaust the list but it is sufficient to demonstrate that the RBG Edinburgh includes a number of experienced collectors of the Himalayan flora among its staff, both past and present, who have enriched the diversity of Sino-Himalayan plants in cultivation. Most of them have been concerned with the general flora, some like David Chamberlain with an overriding interest in the taxonomy of the rhododendrons. But one of their number, Ron McBeath, has always had a keen eye for plants of horticultural merit or potential on his many expeditions which have not been confined to the Himalayas. Since 1967, in addition to the expeditions to Yunnan, Sichuan and Sikkim already noted, he has collected in the Himachal Pradesh of India six times as well as in Iceland, Norway, the Pyrenees, the Picos de Europa, southern Spain, Cyprus and Mallorca. He combines unrivalled experience of the natural environment of the Himalayan and other alpine species with practical familiarity of their cultural needs. He bridges the gap between the scientific botanist and the rock garden enthusiast since he is also a long term member and former Convener of the Edinburgh Group of the SRGC and has acted as judge at many of the SRGC Shows. His lively, descriptive articles in the SRGC Journal convey the fascination of plant hunting in the high mountains. Since retiring from RBGE he has established an alpine plant nursery at Lamberton in Berwickshire.

Another name to note in the list of Scottish Himalayan collectors is that of Robert Mitchell who was the British leader of the historically important Cangshan Sino-British Expedition in 1981 which was the first post-war Sino-Himalayan expedition and also the one which inaugurated the practical and fruitful collaboration with the Kunming Botanical Institute. Mitchell is a man of many parts. During the 1970s he was the Curator of the St Andrews Botanical Garden, noted later. He has a wide experience of the floras of different parts of the world and is well known for botanical articles and his monographic treatment of plant groups like the trilliums.

It would be quite wrong to conclude that the exploration of the Sino-Himalayan flora was the sole preoccupation of the RBGE. Especially in the 1960s and 1970s a number of botanists associated with the Garden worked extensively in the Middle East and South West Asia. Pre-eminent amongst these was Peter Hadland Davis who, although a member of the Botany Dept. of the University of Edinburgh, worked closely with the Garden. Davis was born in Weston-super-Mare in 1918 and educated mostly at Reading. In 1937 he was apprenticed to Will Ingwersen's Alpine Plant Nursery at East Grinstead where his consuming passion for plants became manifest. He made a few trips to the regions he was to study later before the War rudely interrupted his apprenticeship. He served in the Armed Forces until 1945, the last two years on special duties in Cairo, where he managed to fit in some botanising. After the War he went to the Botany Dept. at the University of Edinburgh, where he remained for the rest of his career, first as a student and ultimately professor. As soon as he graduated he started on his life-long study of the flora of Turkey and the eastern Mediterranean, which culminated in the nine volume 'Flora of Turkey and the Aegean Islands' which is one of the botanical landmarks of the 20th century.

To mention Peter Davis immediately suggests the name of Ian Hedge who was Curator of the Herbarium of the RBG, Edinburgh for some 20 years, where he built up contacts with botanists throughout the world. He also has wide practical experience of the flora of South West Asia, including Afghanistan and collaborated with Davis. He is particularly known for his encyclopaedic knowledge of the families which used to be the Cruciferae, the Umbelliferae and the Labiatae.

§ CHAPTER 2 §

Private Collectors

We must now consider briefly the latter-day role of private persons in the increase in the rock garden flora. Contemporary collecting expeditions are brief concentrated affairs compared with the early Sino-Himalayan explorations. That has become possible chiefly on account of the convenience of modern travel which has made it easy for private persons to travel to distant places. The advent of cheap air travel via package tours has made it possible for many professional men, rarely women, to take extended holidays in the mountains to search for plants and bring them back for cultivation in the garden. Oleg Polunin could be regarded as a role model in this respect. He was a master at Charterhouse School who was able to use his vacations for plant hunting and publishing a number of excellent floras of regions as far apart as the Mediterranean and the Himalayas. These floras, based on first hand experience in the field as well as detailed library and herbarium studies, became essential reference books for the new generation of plant hunters. No traveller looking for plants in the Himalayas would dream of going there without Polunin and Stainton's two volume work: 'Flowers of the Himalaya', published in 1984 and 1988.

CATEGORIES
Private collectors of alpine plants fall roughly into four categories:

1. Keen growers who go on package holidays to see alpine plants in the wild and bring back some living specimens for their own gardens.
2. Persons, usually botanists or dedicated gardeners and often retired, who lead flower treks to regions with good alpine plants and who collect specimens at the same time.
3. Persons who organise flower collecting treks which they finance by selling shares to participants guaranteeing seed at the end of the trek.
4. Nurserymen and seedsmen who go out collecting specimens for commercial sale.

Before 1970 there was little concern about wholesale removal of plants from the wild so that collectors would openly mention that they had dug up clumps of rare plants in the Alps or bagfuls of primulas in the Himalayas to grow at home. But in the last 30 years there has been much greater awareness of the need to conserve wild plants so that nowadays most expeditions concentrate on finding and photographing wild plants in situ, not digging them up, and only collecting seed on a limited scale. Partly on account of the tremendous loss of species in the wild and partly because of the realisation of the potential of genetic exploitation, countries have recently become aware of their need to safeguard their native plants, many of which may be of interest to international breeding and pharmaceutical companies. This topic is considered in more detail in Chapter 6.

Throughout the century there has been control of the import of wild plants into the UK so that people returning from holidays have had to declare their plants and seeds and have them ready for inspection by plant inspectors at a later date. Such controls have, however, been laxly applied to private individuals by Customs Officers and, with the general relaxation of Customs inspections in recent years and the almost total abolition of import controls within the EC, one suspects that a great many people bring in plants illegally. Having said that, the general impression is that most people who bring in plants are aware of the CITES Conventions on prohibited plants and of the need to avoid bringing in diseased or pest-infected specimens.

In any review of the private collectors who have contributed significantly to the introduction of new plants we can naturally take no note of the keen gardeners who went abroad and came back with a few species which might be for the collector's own benefit or that of friends, since only rarely do such plants get into cultivation. If they do it is generally impossible to trace their provenance. With respect to the rest it is surprising how few of such serious, private collectors have been Scottish, unlike those connected with official or semi-official expeditions.

Also, even for the relatively well known private collectors it is amazing how few of the species collected that have been unusual in cultivation have appeared under a Collector's Number in the Plant Finder. Perhaps the greatest contribution of such collectors has been the refurbishment of stocks of seeds of species such as primulas which rely heavily on the injection of fresh seed to maintain them in cultivation.

We can now consider some of the collectors who have made significant contributions.

PETER BARR

The early years of this century call to mind collectors such as George Forrest but there were also others who travelled abroad, mainly in Europe, to bring back plants. One of the most colourful was that outstanding plantsman Peter Barr from Govan who had such a passion for narcissi that he earned the title of "Daffodil King". Most of his career was at the end of the 19th century but he continued into the 20th. He travelled in search of species of *Narcissus* in France, Spain and Portugal and, in a way we think remiss today, brought home sackfuls of bulbs, often lamenting that in some areas the bulb population was somewhat denuded. At the age of 81 he developed a passion for primulas and built up a collection of several thousand plants.

EUAN COX
Euan Cox's interest in plants developed from a chance meeting with the renowned Reginald Farrer which led to his joining forces in a collecting expedition to Upper Burma in 1919. One year out there with Farrer was enough for Euan but it fired his enthusiasm for plants which led to a career in horticultural journalism and the laying out of a garden in the family home at Glendoick near Perth. While running the family jute business in Dundee he devoted a great deal of energy to developing a magnificent rhododendron garden. In 1954 he established a nursery at Glendoick in collaboration with his son Peter. As a journalist he was gardening editor of Country Life and also founded and edited The New Flora and Silva in 1928. In 1926 he published 'Farrer's Last Journey' and, in 1945, 'Plant Hunting in China' which was an excellent account of botanical expeditions in China and Tibet. In collaboration with Peter Cox, three books were published: 'Modern Rhododendrons', 'Modern Shrubs' and 'Modern Trees'. In a rather different context he also published in 1935 'A History of Gardening in Scotland'.

PETER COX V.M.H.
After his father's death Peter Cox continued his interest in rhododendrons and soon the nursery at Glendoick was among the top nurseries for that genus in the whole of the UK. With his wife Patricia, the splendid garden centre was established with rhododendrons again to the fore. Either as sole author or in collaboration with his father or his son Kenneth he has written a number of definitive books on rhododendrons, culminating in 'The Encyclopedia of Rhododendrons' in 1997.

Peter Cox began his collecting career in 1962 with a visit to Turkey followed by expeditions to India, Nepal, Bhutan and, most importantly, to China which he visited twelve times between 1981 and 1999. He was among the first Westerners to be allowed back into China after the War The main collections were naturally of rhododendrons but he also collected primulas, gentians and meconopsis. He had a wide range of partners on these expeditions including such well known plantsmen as Lancaster, Mitchell, Chamberlain and Hutchison as well as his wife Patricia and his son Kenneth. In addition to many choice plants brought back as seed from these expeditions he also recorded several unusual and desirable forms which could not be collected. These included a white form of the normally blue *Primula sonchifolia* in Yunnan, a crimson-throated form of the normally clear yellow *Rhododendron wardii* in south east Tibet and a single clump of a deep red *Caltha* sp. which is normally bright yellow. The nursery has marketed at least 40 new hybrid dwarf rhododendrons since its inception, cultivars recognisable by their 'bird names' such as 'Curlew', 'Egret', Phalarope and 'Ptarmigan', many receiving R.H.S. Awards. Glendoick also raises large numbers of rhododendron species and must market a bigger range than any other nursery.

KENNETH COX

Kenneth Cox has in recent years played a major role in the further development of the nursery He has now taken over most of the hybridizing including evergreen azaleas and many are still to be launched on the market after strict selection. Kenneth Cox has also become a major tour leader to China and Tibet and is now a recognised expert on their rhododendrons and other plants. His father quotes him as saying "primulas are best left in their own homes as the mass of flower can only ever be insultingly imitated at home" and adds "he may be right but there is always the challenge of succeeding with a so-called impossible plant". Even with these views he must have been sorely tried when he came across the rare *Primula falcifolia* on the Doshong La in Tibet in flower but with no seed. It would have been wonderful to establish this plant in cultivation; previous introductions of seed by Kingdon Ward in 1924 and Ludlow and Sherriff in 1938 failed to become established.

The Cox family occupy a unique position in Scottish horticulture, having done more than any others to develop dwarf rhododendrons as plants suitable for small suburban gardens.

ALASTAIR MCKELVIE

In mentioning Alastair McKelvie it would be wrong not to bring in the name of Chris Chadwell who, although not a Scot, was instrumental in introducing him to plant collecting. Chadwell has been a Himalayan collector since the early 1980s, financing his treks, up to 13 by the end of the century, either by subscription or by selling collected seed through his Seed Catalogue. He set up the Himalayan Plant Association, later named the Sino-Himalayan Plant Association, in the early 1990s and has run it more or less single handed ever since. The Association which has been instrumental in bringing together people interested in Himalayan plants, publishes a magazine, holds meetings and runs a Seed Exchange.

In 1990 Chris Chadwell was looking for a companion for a trek to India and it was by sheer chance that Alastair McKelvie heard of this and was enrolled. This trek to Himachal Pradesh was the first of ten collecting trips he made in the 1990s, usually around four weeks duration, some with Chadwell but most as a tour leader of a flower trek or as organiser of a seed-collecting expedition. Alastair McKelvie is a botanist trained at the RBGE and a keen rock gardener so he was quickly able to identify plants in the wild. The ability to know your plants and where they grow is essential for a short expedition. Forrest could afford to spend a fruitless month exploring a barren area but not so your modern collector who relies on detailed homework before arriving in the field.

McKelvie has collected in Himachal Pradesh, Central Nepal and Sikkim, up to altitudes of 4000m and brought back well over 1000 different seed lots.

Many of his collections are in gardens throughout Scotland. Thirty eight of his collections with Chris Chadwell (CC&McK) are listed in the Plant Finder as being in commerce while material from his later expeditions with Ian Christie and Fred Carrie to Nepal (Gosainkund 1995: GOS and Langtang 1997: MECC) is being evaluated at Carrie's and Christie's Nurseries for future sale. McKelvie and Chadwell, together with various collaborators, have brought back seed of some very desirable species and forms. Of particular merit have been good forms of *Rhododendron anthopogon* and *R. lepidotum*, and also many desirable primulas such as *P. buryana* from Dhaulagiri in Central Nepal. This looked a real winner but was short-lived and sadly has now almost certainly passed out of cultivation. More permanent have been an excellent pink form of *P. nana* (*edgeworthii*) and a white *P. sikkimensis* var. *hopeana*. Several monocarpic meconopsis proved good garden plants, especially a dark red form of *M. napaulensis* and a fine pale yellow *M. gracilipes* which are in cultivation.

In the company of Fred Carrie and Ian Christie, Alastair McKelvie has explored the Gosainkund and Langtang areas of Central Nepal, finding excellent forms of *Gentiana depressa* and *G. ornata* which Christie is now growing in his Nursery at Kirriemuir. Possible hybrids between *Primula aureata* and *P. deuteronana* were also brought back and are being evaluated at Carrie's Nursery at Tough in Aberdeenshire. Other species brought back have belonged to the genera *Ligularia*, *Rosa*, *Cremanthodium*, *Geranium* and *Clematis*. Disappointingly several most desirable species from the high passes of Ladakh failed to survive Scottish winters in spite of coming from such frozen regions.

Another collector who should be mentioned in connection with Chris Chadwell is Magnus Ramsay, who formerly worked at Threave Gardens in Galloway and who accompanied Chadwell on several expeditions between 1985 and 1989 and brought back interesting seeds from Himachal Pradesh and Kashmir. Chadwell found Ramsay a wonderful companion as he was a tall, strong climber who was able to reach plants which would otherwise have been inaccessible.

MARGARET AND HENRY TAYLOR

The Taylors from Dundee are one of a number of husband and wife teams who have done so much for the SRGC and for rock gardening in general. They have roamed the world and brought into cultivation much good, new material. To their great credit they never sought outside funding. They have never used expedition initials so that it is not often possible to recognise plants which they introduced. They have been wisely selective so what they decided to introduce proved first rate plants. The pages of the SRGC Journal and the AGS Bulletin bear testimony to their assiduous collecting as well being a joy to any hard-pressed editor. From 1968 they explored the mountains of Europe including Spain, France, Italy, Austria and Yugoslavia and then, in 1987, they turned their attention to the Himalayas and continued their explorations there to the end of the century.

They have introduced around 15 good, new plants into cultivation from the mountains of Europe including *Allium narcissiflorum* (the true pale pink form) from France, *Androsace cantabrica, Narcissus* x *christopheri* and *Ranunculus parnassifolius* 'Nuria' from Spain, *Daphne hendersonii* 'Rose Bud' from Italy and *Dianthus scardicus* from Yugoslavia. They are especially known for their informed familiarity with the genera *Narcissus* and *Ranunculus* from the European mountains. Their 'Nuria' form of *Ranunculus parnassifolius*, first described in 1978, has been a frequent winner at Club Shows ever since.

Their Himalayan exploits have been well documented in the pages of the SRGC Journal. Covering much of the same ground in Himachal Pradesh as Chadwell and McKelvie, they have amassed an unrivalled knowledge of the flora of that region, especially the Rohtang and Hampta Passes. They have been particularly successful in bringing back seed of primulas and androsaces. One of their finest plants from Himachal Pradesh is *Androsace studiosorum* 'Doksa'. As well as collecting in the mountains the Taylors have brought several new plants into cultivation through their own breeding programmes. At least five new hybrids are in cultivation and in the Plant Finder. They include such splendid plants as *Corydalis solida* 'Highland Mist', raised by crossing *C. transsilvanica* x *C. solida, Gentiana* 'Margaret', a three-way cross raised in 1988 by crossing *G. sino-ornata* x *G. farreri* x *G. ternifolia, Narcissus* 'Camoro', raised in 1975 by crossing *N. cantabricus monophyllus* x *N. romieuxii, Ranunculus* 'Gowrie', raised in 1981 by crossing *R. parnassifolius* x *R. amplexicaulis* and *Primula* 'Tantallon', raised in 1977 by crossing *P. bhutanica* x P. *edgeworthii*. Also in 1983 they raised *Clematis cartmanii* 'Joe' from a batch of *C. marmoraria* seed sent by Joe Cartman of New Zealand.

As well as distributing their own introductions, the Taylors have helped to bring introductions from John and Brenda Anderson of Wester Balruddery, Dundee, into cultivation. The Andersons collected widely in South Africa, Argentina and Chile between 1970 and 1990 and brought back some excellent plants. Among those propagated and given to nurserymen by the Taylors are *Androcymbium striatum* from Lesotho, *Romulea thodei* from the Drakensburg, *Oxalis adenophylla* 'Brenda Anderson' from Argentina and *Sisyrinchium arenarium humile* also from Argentina

MIKE AND POLLY STONE
'Scottish' in the sense that they have been domiciled at Fort Augustus in Inverness-shire since 1963, the Stones are another husband and wife team. They are possibly unique among collectors in the sheer number of plants they have introduced since they started travelling in the mountains in 1984. Even before their travelling days they were obtaining seed from wild plants suitable

for the rock or wild garden from as many places as possible, averaging 500 or more taxa per year. They sow all of this plus about 200 packets from their own garden seeds. As a result they estimate that, after 25 years at 'Askival', their home in Fort Augustus, they have almost 12,000 taxa established. Since 1984 the Stones have been on 15 expeditions mainly to North America to study the local flora and bring back seed amounting to several hundred different plants. Since they raise most of their own plants from the collected seed accessions rarely appear in the Plant Finder directly although they probably do so indirectly from people who have obtained material initially from the Stones.

As time passes it becomes increasingly difficult to bring back truly new introductions but much of what they have brought back is quite new to cultivation in Scotland. They have actually discovered previously unknown species of *Penstemon* and *Dodecatheon*, a hybrid primula which American botanists claimed not to exist as well as a new taxon in the genus *Arnica*. It would be invidious to select particular plants which they have brought back since they extend over 100 genera, but of particular importance are species of *Penstemon, Trillium, Erythronium, Primula, Calochortus, Phlox* and a whole host of woodland genera.

They have established an international reputation as collectors and botanists and have been accompanied in the field by distinguished botanists, both European, like Kazbal and Kummert from the Czech Republic and Austria respectively, and American, including Case, Lowry, Ratco and Russell while various University botanists have provided access to herbaria and members of the US Forest Service have provided valuable assistance. Plants collected by the Stones have spread widely through the rock garden plant community either directly or through nurserymen. The Stones now run their own wholesale nursery, 'Askival Alpines'. So in several respects they have exerted a tremendous influence on the development of gardening this century. Much of the accumulated wisdom derived from the Stone's expeditions and their gardening experience have been distilled in the twice yearly 'Stone Column', written by Mike Stone and brilliantly illustrated with Polly Stone's photographs. These highly readable and lively articles have been appearing for the last 17 years in 'The Rock Garden', the SRGC Journal, and have provided the rock garden community with a great deal of valuable advice and critical comment.

JIM ARCHIBALD
Among contemporary plant collectors few can match Jim Archibald who from 1962 to the present day has made 16,000 collections, mostly seed, and whose career as a collector, nurseryman and hybridiser is quite outstanding. It is difficult to summarise the career of this Scot from the east of Scotland who has spent most of his working life in south west England and in Wales. In the latest edition of the Plant Finder there are at least 180 plants listed as

collected by Archibald, accompanied at times by his wife Jenny and by other botanists and gardeners. The areas visited range from North America to North Africa, Europe and Turkey. To illustrate his abilities, his expedition to Iran in 1966 along with his wife, resulted in the collection of twelve species of *Dionysia*, a genus then fairly new to gardening, one of which proved to be a new species which was later called after him, *D. archibaldii*. As with all his expeditions, the Iran trip was meticulously prepared and researched in advance so that once in the field he could move swiftly to his chosen destination. His expedition to Morocco was written up fully for the AGS Bulletin in 1963 and is a model of how to write in a clear and interesting manner for a non-technical readership.

Jim Archibald ran 'The Plantsman Nursery' at Buckshaw in Dorset from 1967 to 1975 in partnership with that great plantsman Eric Smith. Together they grew a wide range of interesting and unusual plants. His work with the genus *Helleborus* epitomises his practical skills. At Buckshaw he bred many new hellebore cultivars, using some of the species and varieties he had collected mostly in the Balkans. Other breeders have also used his hellebore collections as the basis for developing new cultivars. Many clones of *H. foetidus* and *H. orientalis* hybrids were bred at the nursery as well as 'seed strains' such as the Galaxy and Midnight Blue Strains, which were constantly evolving but which the nursery kept as true to type as possible.

When Eric Smith left the nursery, The Plantsman Nursery was succeeded by Buckshaw Gardens and Archibald more or less gave up selling named clones and concentrated instead on seed strains, largely for wholesale purpose. He had realised that many named clones gave rise to superior progeny rather negating the point of exclusive preoccupation with their maintenance. Although based in the south of UK he corresponded regularly with Scottish growers such as Harold Esslemont on the growing of dionysias and is on record as having visited Jack Crosland to take a seedling plant of the then rare *Dicentra peregrina* back to that skilled plantsman Peter Edwards, who turned it into a show plant within a twelvemonth.

RUTH TWEEDIE

Most of the private collectors of renown concentrated their efforts on North America or the Himalaya but Ruth Tweedie from East Lothian did her collecting in South America, where the family had a sheep farm in Patagonia only 225km north of the Straits of Magellan. She collected many outstanding plants in the 1950s from an inhospitable area where Charles Darwin had been a hundred years previously. She recorded magnificent flowering bushes of *Embothrium coccineum* growing rather surprisingly at 400m on dry hillsides exposed to the full force of the westerly gales. She is perhaps best known for her introduction of that first class garden plant *Oxalis laciniata* but she also introduced such charming plants as *Cruckshankia gracilis*, grown for many years by Alex Duguid at Edrom until it was stolen. The equally beautiful *C.*

hymenodon which she introduced, is also no longer with us. She also brought into cultivation *Symphostemon lyckholmii*, *Nardophyllum bryoides*, *Anarthophyllum desideratum* and *Pernettya mucronata* T173, a very fine seedling of which was propagated at Inshriach Nursery and given the name 'Stag River,' after her property in Patagonia. It is still in cultivation.

JACK DRAKE
The Nursery at Inshriach will always be remembered for that pioneering plantsman Jack Drake who undoubtedly started many a rock gardener on the road. Jack Crosland recalled going to Jack Drake's Nursery in the 1950s and coming away with a dozen alpines and much good advice which started him on his illustrious rock gardening career. Eminent plantsmen such as Ron McBeath, Jim Jermyn, Magnus Ramsay, Brian Mathew and Jim Archibald all worked for a time at Inshriach. Jack Drake also collected, especially in New Zealand where the cool, wet climate of South Island is comparable to that of Inshriach, so New Zealand alpines have always done well there. His most outstanding New Zealand introduction was probably the hybrid *Raoulia* x *loganii* which the Nursery still sells. He also brought back seed of some of the New Zealand celmisias and they formed the basis of the excellent 'Inshriach Hybrids' which germinate better than almost any other celmisias.

OTHER COLLECTORS
The foregoing list of private collectors inevitably omits many distinguished growers who, during a lifetime of gardening, have collected seed periodically on trips abroad to study the local flora. Usually they return with a few choice items which have probably stayed in cultivation if not in commerce so there is little record of them. The simplest form of seed collecting is that quoted in 1985 by Wilf Holmes from Banchory. He prevailed upon a non-botanical friend who was going on a trekking trip to Nepal to slip a handful of seed into his pocket of anything that took his fancy. The resulting mishmash of material was difficult to identify but was distributed by Holmes among rock gardeners and, as a result, there are now many gardens with splendid flowering specimens of rhododendrons and meconopsis, all from this miscellaneous seed. Interestingly enough, the seed was collected in much the same area as the AGS Sikkim Expedition so that it was possible to identify some plants from the AGS notes. This a good example of interaction between the amateur and the official approach.

The Himalayas and China have become the focal point for much small-scale collecting as an increasing number of people trek there. Some of them, like Peter Burnett, have collected seed of many primulas in Nepal and these have flourished in the late Bobby Masterton's garden at Cluny in Perthshire. Skilled growers such as Anne Chambers, Fred Hunt, Richard Lilley and Heather Salzen have regularly trekked in these regions and have brought back seed which has been distributed throughout the SRGC and the species concerned are often in commerce, even if not listed with a collection number in the Plant Finder. Many first-class rock gardeners and field botanists such as Michael and Lynn Almond have travelled extensively in the European Alps and in Turkey but have never been collectors although their knowledge has been of great value to plant hunters who followed in their footsteps. Henry Tod was an early explorer who visited the Rocky Mountains in the company of the distinguished American plantsman Dr Henry Worth. Tod also became known for being the first to grow many of the plants collected by Peter Davis in Turkey.

Nurserymen have been regular plant hunters, bringing back small quantities of seed but, perhaps more importantly, building up a knowledge of rock plants and their ecology of inestimable value in developing their business. Jim Jermyn, formerly from Edrom Nursery, has travelled extensively in Europe and Japan. Jim Sutherland of Ardfearn has trekked widely in China and Tibet while Bill Chudziak of Moffat has travelled in Nepal in search of meconopsis of which he held a NCCPG National Collection.

Even before the days of fast air travel, many members of the SRGC and AGS travelled abroad in search of plants notably to the Swiss and Austrian Alps and to the Greek Islands. Collecting was not the main aim of such trips but there was always the odd bit of seed collecting and, perhaps unfortunately, some digging up of plants. But those were the days before we all became so conservation minded. Names which come to mind include Harold Esslemont, Jack Crosland and Sheila Maule, who re-introduced the lovely *Narcissus rupicola* ssp. *watieri* into cultivation from North Africa. But probably of greatest benefit to rock gardening was the way these people used their energies and skills in propagating and distributing material brought back from both official and commercial expeditions. Often they developed expertise in the growing of particular groups of plants unmatched even by botanical gardens. One recalls the remarkable way in which Harold Esslemont grew tiny plants of *Dionysia* brought in from the Middle East or propagated and worked out the growing requirements of the difficult *Crocus scardicus*. Similarly seeds and plants from the great expeditions of Ludlow and Sherriff and others were regularly sent to such growers as the Knox Finlays at Keillour, the Rentons at Branklyn and the Mastertons at Cluny who grew them on with great skill. Liaison between private grower and institutions has been one of the strengths of gardening in Scotland although naturally there are problems when botanical gardens are asked to give away rarities to all and sundry. Seed from many a private expedition found its way into Botanic Gardens which did a useful job in recording and cataloguing material which might otherwise have disappeared into private gardens without trace.

THE EXPLORATION FUND

The Exploration Fund was set up by the SRGC in 1985 to award grants to help finance projects or trips pertaining to rock garden plants. Feedback by way of seeds, articles or photographs was not essential but desirable and hoped for. Recipients of grants did not have to be members of the SRGC. Since 1987, when the first grants were made, until 1998 there were 46 applications of which 24 were successful. In some years there were no applications while, at the other extreme, in 1993 there were seven applications of which only one succeeded. In other years there may have been three or four applications which were all approved.

Although the Fund was designed to help young people who were interested in gardening or in plants generally many older people have been given awards and even staff of publicly funded bodies have received grants. It was hoped that the SRGC would benefit from the expeditions by receiving seeds for the Seed Exchange, by articles and/or photographs for the Journal or by talks to SRGC Groups. It must be conceded that these hopes have not been realised. Even the required reports on expeditions have not been particularly illuminating if written at all. More than 50% of the expeditions were to the Himalayas or to China to study the local flora, but more often than not simply to finance a holiday. Other areas visited included New Zealand, the Alps, Sweden, Africa and North America. Only about five expeditions collected seed. Thus very little new information has been derived from the expeditions either with respect to rock gardening, growing conditions or the local floras visited. Where seed was gathered it referred to species of primula, gentian, or meconopsis, which rely on accessions of fresh seed to keep uncommon species in cultivation. Articles in the Journal have dealt with such topics as primulas in the wild, the alpine flora of the Cantabrian Mountains and trekking in the Himalayas.

Although the initial objectives of the Fund have hardly been realised it has enabled keen growers to go on trips which would otherwise have proved prohibitively expensive and bring back information which has no doubt been of some benefit to other Club members.

§ CHAPTER 3 §

The History of the Scottish Rock Garden Club

Most of the private collectors just noted, who have contributed to the rock garden flora, have been members of the SRGC which has been the mainstay of alpine gardening in Scotland and whose history we must now consider. But first we must take note of the origins of the Alpine Garden Society in England since it was the launching pad for the Scottish Club.

In October 1929 a meeting was held in London to consider a proposal by Sir William Lawrence for a Rock Garden Society. It was agreed to set up a Society dedicated to rock gardens and rock garden plants. It is of historical interest that a proposal was mooted to have two sections in the Society, one for those interested in growing alpine plants and another for those who appreciated rocks for their beauty in a grass setting. However, feeling was strongly against having what was described as "a species of horticultural rock society........devoid of plants". So the word Rock was dropped and the Alpine Garden Society was born. The title has not been without its problems over the years. The AGS can not be said to be either an Alpine Garden Society or a Rock Garden Society, in the strict sense. The SRGC has also faced this problem since, as well as rock plants, both Societies are also concerned with shrubs, particularly rhododendrons, herbaceous perennials and bog and woodland plants. Nowadays there are also other garden societies such as the Hardy Plant Society with which there is considerable overlap. Nevertheless both the AGS and the SRGC seem unconcerned about defining the limits of their interests very precisely and proceed happily on their ways.

From the early days of the AGS it was clearly felt that Scotland should be included in the Society's remit and John Renton of Branklyn, Perth, was appointed Committee member for Scotland. He held that post long after the SRGC was established but the position seems to have slipped into abeyance some time in the 1940s. The idea of a Scottish Society was given a real fillip in the 1930s by the influx of a large number of plants from collecting expeditions, especially those of George Forrest, Kingdon Ward and others in the Himalayas. Interest and encouragement from the Royal Botanic Garden, Edinburgh led to a meeting to consider the formation of a Society.

The first meeting, held in the Rutland Bar, Edinburgh on 27 July 1933, resulted in a decision to form a "Club to be known as 'The Scottish Rock Garden Club' for the purpose of creating an interest in Rock Garden Plants, to encourage their cultivation and to hold Meetings and Exhibitions for this purpose". A second meeting in August agreed a Constitution and Office-bearers were elected with Andrew Harley as first President, Mr. E. P. Laird as Secretary and Mr. F. Glass as Treasurer. Mr Glass soon had to retire and the post was filled by Bill MacKenzie of the RBGE who continued as an active member of the Club for many years and was elected Honorary President in 1994. The members of the first Committee came from a wide geographical area but were already known for their skill and interest in rock gardening (MacKenzie,1983). Some of the gardens of the Committee members are still in existence but it is a pity that some, such as the huge and magnificent natural rock slopes of Glassel House, Aberdeenshire, which belonged then to Miss Robinson, are now overgrown and neglected, although happily there are moves afoot to restore it..

In the early years the Club set up Committees to organise shows and lectures and agreed to affiliate with the Royal Caledonian Horticultural Society. With the agreement of Mrs Forrest, the widow of George Forrest, the "George Forrest Memorial Prize Fund" was set up and bronze medals were struck. It was agreed that these medals would be awarded at the Club's Shows at Edinburgh and Glasgow for the best plant in the Show. A single silver medal was also struck and this was presented to Mrs Forrest. At this time Roland Cooper of the RBGE wrote an article about George Forrest and this was distributed to members of different societies together with a printed slip for the return of donations. It was also agreed to publish a book on the "Life and Work of the Late George Forrest" and Roland Cooper agreed to write it. The cost of producing 1000 copies would be £100; members would receive a free copy. By the start of the 1936 season the Club had enrolled 442 members. It was agreed to enlarge the Annual report of the Club, a move which lasted only two issues.

A proposal to amalgamate with the AGS was defeated. One might question the need for two more or less identical societies within the UK but the SRGC has always been proudly independent. It was also agreed to publish an Annual Bulletin and the first issue appeared in 1936. Only two issues were produced before the War stopped publication and it was not until 1946 that it reappeared after a lapse of six years, unlike the AGS Bulletin which continued throughout the War years. The SRGC Bulletin or Journal then became a bi-annual publication in 1951, in which form it has continued to the present day. In 1982 the title was changed from the 'Journal of the Scottish Rock Garden Club' to 'The Rock Garden'.

At the outset of the War in 1939, the Club was still being run centrally without the more or less independent local Groups which exist now. There were still just two Shows, in Edinburgh and Glasgow, some held to raise money for the Red Cross, although there had been some local exhibitions such as those held in Aberdeen in the Botany Dept. of the University under Professor Matthews. A resolution to suspend the activities of the Club at the outset of the War was defeated so that it continued, albeit on a much reduced scale throughout the War.

After the War, a meeting was held in Glasgow in 1946 at which it was agreed to resuscitate the Club. Membership was thought to be around 300 but records had not been kept very well in the inter-regnum. A new set of Office

Bearers soon got the Club going again, notably with Major Walmsley as President, Archie Campbell as Treasurer, David Livingstone as Secretary and Kenneth Corsar as Editor. A Seed Exchange was set up in 1948 by Bobby Masterton of Cluny, Aberfeldy, a vet who had transformed an area of hillside above the River Tay into a wonderful, woodland garden. In 1949 he recorded that there were 36 seed donors and that 70 people had asked for seed. From such early beginnings has grown the magnificent Seed Exchange, renowned worldwide for the range of seeds offered and for its swift despatch of seeds. After Masterton retired from the scheme in 1965 there were several managers until Joyce Halley took over in 1973 and continued for 17 years until 1990. Since then the Seed Exchange has been run by Jean Wyllie with the aid of an army of helpers. There are now more than 5000 items listed in the Exchange with 800 donors, 1500 applicants and 60,000 packets of seed sent out.

The Journal has continued to grow in size and quality from the early days of black and white photographs to full colour throughout and from typewriters and cold metal type to computers, digital colour and off-set litho printing which allows it to be prepared in-house and sent camera-ready to the printer. The Club has been lucky in having had a succession of excellent editors who have remained in post for long periods of time. It has always been an onerous task so that it is worth-while mentioning those who undertook the job. They were Kenneth Corsar (1937-1950), John Mowat (1951-1967), Alfred Evans (1968-1969), Peter Kilpatrick (1970-1976), Robert Mitchell (1977-1982), Ian and Carole Bainbridge (1990-1994) and Alastair McKelvie (1983-1989 and 1995-2000).

Shows have always been the life blood of the Club. After the War the system of holding the two major Shows in Edinburgh and Glasgow continued and they were very successful, even though they were rather formal affairs. For example, in Edinburgh in 1949, the Show was opened by Lady Elphinstone and there were 2800 paying visitors. Gradually, regular Shows were held at venues throughout Scotland. By the mid 1950s there were seven Shows held annually in places such as Dundee, Dunfermline, Dumfries, Penicuik, Aberdeen as well as Edinburgh and Glasgow, most of them two or even three-day events and often held in mid-week. Obviously this arrangement was inconvenient for people who had to travel outwith their own area or for people with full-time jobs. Those two great stalwarts of showing in the 1960s and 70s, Harold Esslemont and Jack Crosland used to sweep the boards because they had hit on the system of taking the back seat out of Harold's car which he would then drive down to the Show, install the plants and then drive home to Aberdeen. Jack would then drive down at the end of the Show, two or three days later, and bring the plants back. Clearly few could manage what they did.

By the mid-1970s the Shows were declining in appeal and quality and it was decided to change them to one day events to be held on a Saturday. This obviously limited the number of hours the Shows were open but it did generate much more interest, with more members entering plants. However, there is no doubt that much of the greatly increased vitality of Shows since the mid 1980s has been due to the inauguration of the AGS Salver, presented by the AGS in 1983 to mark the Golden Jubilee of the SRGC, for the highest aggregate of First Prize Points in Section 1 of Club Shows. This immediately led to enormous competition among the top growers with the result that exhibitors who for example had regularly declined to drive to Aberdeen for early staging at 8.00am suddenly found they could manage to do so. Thus all the top growers were going to all the six major competitive Shows in Scotland plus the one in the north of England.

Discussion Weekends are now very much part of the Club scene. From the first one in Edinburgh in 1957 they have become an annual event. In the early years they were held in hotels but with increasing cost they were switched to University and College Halls of Residence which were much cheaper. However, over the years the cost of such accomodation has risen rapidly while hotels are now prepared to offer excellent weekend deals so that there is now a switch back to them. From Friday night to Sunday afternoon, over 100 members listen to talks, inspect the Show, buy plants at the Trade Stands and generally meet old friends.

From time to time since 1950 the Club has mounted displays at the Royal Highland Show in June and has regularly been awarded a Gold Medal. At first the Shows perambulated around Scotland but later settled down at Ingliston, near Edinburgh. Such Shows are hard work to set up and man so they have never been mounted very regularly. The latest and most successful display of this nature was in 1997 at the first RHS "Scotland's National Gardening Show" where the Club won a Gold Medal with a display of planted troughs, made out of polystyrene fish boxes, a success which was repeated in 1998 and 1999. In this last year, the SRGC was runner-up for the Best Exhibit in the Show (Figs.6 and 7).

Prize monies at Shows have always been derisory compared to those of many horticultural societies. Away back in 1960, three shillings (15p) was given for First Prize in a one pan class; by 1988 that had risen to 30p, hardly in line with inflation. But prize money has never been regarded as more than a token and has very often been just given back to the Club by the winner. There are a great number of trophies awarded at Shows, again often regarded by the constant winners as simply something to be kept clean. The Shows, which are run by local Groups for the main Club, epitomise the relationship between them and the Club. In the early days there was only the Central Club but over the years local Groups have been set up, and disbanded, so that by 1998 there were 18 such Groups, three of them in the north of England. The groups are autonomous bodies with their own accounts and rules; members pay a subscription to the main Club which entitles them to the Journal, entrance to all the Shows and participation in the Seed Exchange. Local groups often levy their own subscriptions and run lecture programmes, garden visits and Shows.

The SRGC has long been a member of the Royal Horticultural Society's Joint Rock Garden Plant Committee along with the AGS. The Committee meets at Shows, usually four times a year in Scotland, to give First Class Certificates, Awards of Merit, Certificates of Preliminary Commendation and Certificates of Cultural Commendation to plants submitted to it. The Committee deals with all rock and alpine house genera other than irises, rhododendrons, narcissi and tulips, although it deals with dwarf members of these genera when the specialist committees are not meeting. This system allows meritorious plants to be recognised as such and brought into general cultivation.

Since its foundation the SRGC, together with the AGS, has achieved a great deal in fostering the growing of rock plants in the widest sense of the term. The main Botanic Gardens in the UK have clearly been in the forefront of growing new plants and developing new techniques of growing them but, over the years, most collecting expeditions have ensured that their seeds were sent to amateur growers of note who, in many cases, have been more successful than the institutions. Seeds collected by Forrest, Kingdon Ward, Ludlow and Sherriff etc were distributed widely to amateur growers. Also there have been many private expeditions, as described in Chapter 2, to which members have subscribed and had success with the seed they received. The collaboration since its inception with the RBGE has been of value to both parties. Many plants raised by amateur growers have ended up at "The Botanics" while, in reverse, the RBGE has been good at distributing rare plants to keen growers. Harold Fletcher, Regius Keeper, deserves particular mention as he was a keen supporter of the Club. Roland Cooper, Curator, distributed his personally collected Himalayan seed to Club members and wrote the book on George Forrest. Finally the Club owes a great debt of gratitude to Alf Evans, author of the definitive book on the peat garden, who played a prominent role in the post-war history of the Club as both President and Honorary President. He was an Assistant Curator at the RBGE for many years and combined this with an active involvement with the Club. After his retirement from the the Botanics he became an almost full-time writer, lecturer and tour guide, travelling all over the world leading flower tours.

PLANTS AT THE SHOWS

With the passage of time there is no doubt that the standard of the exhibits has improved immensely. Plants which would formerly have won Forrest Medals easily would now have difficulty in winning a First Prize. For example it is doubtful if that regular winner *Telesonix jamesii* would ever win a Forrest Medal nowadays. There has also been a change in the types of plants being shown and these will be considered later. Gone are the days when judges would be heard to say that they would only give a Forrest Medal to a bulb if they were completely stuck. But then judges are funny creatures with whims which obey no laws. Judges at Vegetable Shows have to consider a huge number of characters and tot up points before awarding a prize but SRGC judges have no such constraints. Where else would the judges be people who were actively showing themselves, who know who has submitted which plant and who have been known to say that they would never give a prize to a crucifer? But having said that Shows are fun days and contribute enormously to the esprit de corps of the Club.

Periodically since the Club was founded there has been concern about growing plants in pots as opposed to the open garden. Back in 1954 Major Walmsley stated that "a pot should never be regarded as a permanent home for a plant whereas the open ground may well prove to be. The alpine house is not altogether out of vogue but one finds it more widely used for propagation purposes" And, at the 1961 Discussion Weekend, a Brains Trust hotly debated "whether plants grown in alpine house should be allowed to compete in our Shows with those grown in the open. There is a danger of non hardy plants having an advantage". Such arguments still rage but only in regard to Shows where there is concern that plants which need some winter warmth are receiving the top prizes. But since there can never be any correct definition of what is hardy, a laissez-faire attitude may be the only one to take. Judges will always be divided as to whether *Cyclamen persicum* is a hardy alpine. A further problem arises as to what plants qualify as 'rock plants'. Judges would not quibble at allowing hellebores or pulsatillas on to the bench, although they are not rock plants, but would turn up their noses at a splendid pan of annual lobelia. It is just as well that most rock gardeners do not take the Shows too seriously.

As noted earlier, the pattern of Club Shows has changed greatly since 1938 with one-day, five-hour shows taking the place of the two- or even three-day shows of the early days. Equally striking has been the change in the species and cultivars exhibited and awarded prizes. It is not feasible to quantify these changes in tabular form since such a wide variety of plants is involved. Perhaps the best way is to make comparisons at 10-yearly intervals from 1938 to 1998 and consider what has changed even if they are not really quantifiable. One factor which prevents accurate comparisons between then and now is that until the mid 1950s there were only two Shows, usually held around mid-April or early May but nowadays the Shows run from early March until late May, followed by one or two autumn Shows so that the range of plants is bound to be much greater. For example, an old favourite such as *Primula* 'Linda Pope' was winning the top prizes in 1938 and is still doing so today but by 1998, sixty years after the first Show, we have plants like *Rhododendron degronianum* var. *yakushimanum*, *Primula aureata* and *Clematis marmoraria* which were either not known in the wild or were not in cultivation in 1938. Apart from inevitable changes due to new introductions there have also been huge changes in fashion. Probably the biggest difference between the early shows and today is the greatly increased emphasis on bulbs. They were conspicuously uncommon in the early days but now make up a large proportion of any Show.

EARLY SHOWS

The prize-winning plants at the earliest Shows in Edinburgh and Glasgow in 1938 would be familiar to present-day exhibitors. Lewisias, saxifrages, dwarf rhododendrons, primulas and gentians predominated while the species in each of these genera would have been much the same as today. By the time the Shows resumed in 1948, the range of plants was similar but during the interval a number of new plants had arrived on the scene and were being grown and exhibited by keen growers. Prominent among them was *Primula aureata* which had been found as a seedling at the RBGE among a pan of swertias. Also shortias from Japan were on the benches for the first time. Cushion plants such as androsaces were beginning to appear but their heyday was yet to come.

By 1958 the picture was changing fast. Species of *Cassiope, Kalmiopsis* and *Shortia* were now common together with European primulas but there was still only one species of *Dionysia* in cultivation at that time, *Dionysia curviflora*. The excitingly new *Kelseya uniflora* from Montana still wins prizes but is no longer the sure-fire winner it once was. Bulbs were coming to the fore with species of *Narcissus, Tulipa* and *Erythronium* commonly exhibited. Pleiones were also appearing although many eminent growers regarded them as 'stove plants' and unsuitable for rock garden benches. The argument about what is hardy or not and whether a plant which needs winter protection should be eligible is still a matter of contention and is perhaps even more acute nowadays when growers are attempting to grow exotic species from all over the globe.

CUSHION PLANTS ARRIVE

It was, however, not until 1968 that we see the beginning of the age of the cushion plants. Dionysias, androsaces, raoulias, haastias and kabschia saxifrages were now exhibited in great profusion. It is interesting that kabschia saxifrages were out of fashion for a long time, many species dying out in World War II, but they made their come back by the late 60s when Valerie Finnis built up her collection at Waterperry, only to fall rather out of favour again by the 90s. The raoulias and haastias marked a surge in the popularity of New Zealand species which included good show plants such as *Leucogenes grandiceps* and *L. leontopodium*. The cushion plant era produced many magnificent specimens from a number of expert growers. Raising their drabas, androsaces and dionysias from seed they took from five to ten years to produce show specimens which then appeared at shows for years to come and were immediately recognised by other growers and, of course, the judges. One of the most famous was Harold Esslemont's pan of *Draba mollissima* which reached a mammoth diameter of 30cm and won innumerable prizes before it was honourably retired from show and presented to the RBGE to mark the opening of their new Alpine House. It was about this time that a practice arose for judges to be appointed from among the keenest exhibitors so that it often happened that they were judging plants in the same class they were competing in, so reserve judges had to be called in to adjudicate.

AGE OF THE BULBS

By 1978 things had settled down and there were not many changes from the earlier decade. Dionysias were the big hit then but the biggest change was the increase in bulbs, especially with many more species of *Fritillaria* while dwarf irises such as *Iris winogradowii* were becoming popular. With an increase in the number of plant-hunting expeditions, often by amateur gardeners, plants began to flood in especially from Himalayan regions. Asiatic primulas became increasingly popular exhibits. As already noted, the institution in 1983 of the Alpine Garden Society's Salver for the Plantsman of the Year was probably the biggest single factor in the explosion of exhibiting at shows, with a dramatic increase in the number and range of species and cultivars. Instead of one or two keen growers there were now many. Their rivalry had a major impact on the range of new and unusual plants.

By 1988, plants from Japan, South America, North America and New Zealand were vying with those from the traditional areas of Europe and the Middle and Far East. Orchids such as *Dactylorhiza*, *Pleione*, and *Cypripedium* displayed a wide range of variation while ericaceous plants were becoming fashionable with genera such as *Cassiope*, *Kalmiopsis*, *Phyllodoce*, *Arcterica* and *Andromeda* among the exhibits.

TO FEED OR NOT

There was an increasing trend for plants to become bigger and blowsier. Whereas in the early days it was thought that alpines did not really need feeding, the new generation of growers fed their plants at fortnightly intervals with half strength liquid fertiliser to produce cabbage-like plants. Contention arose. Could enormous potfuls of lush *Lewisia brachycalyx* or *Primula forrestii* be 'in character' as required in the Show Schedules? Judges had increasing difficulty in adjudicating in a single class between a dwarf *Ranunculus* in a six inch pot and a massive giant of *Clematis marmoraria* reaching a metre high. This would soon be followed by an even larger cultivar *C. cartmanii* 'Joe.'

FASHIONS

As time passes, fashions in plants change. By 1988 the range of particularly popular plants included *Erigeron* 'Canary Bird', *Pulsatilla vernalis*, *Trillium grandiflorum*, *Cypripedium calceolus* and lewisias. In particular *Lewisia cotyledon* now came in a wide range of colours ranging from the original pink to deep red, yellow, orange and white — a colour spectrum which just did not exist in 1938. By 1998, the 65th year of the Club the range and diversity of exhibits continued to expand. The old arguments as to whether exhibits should only comprise plants lifted from the open ground or whether plants kept permanently in pots should be allowed had been cast aside. In 1968 it was estimated that 60% of plants exhibited were lifted from the open ground but by 1998 the vast majority of plants shown were grown in pots. Rare and delicate plants were rarely lifted. Dwarf rhododendrons and other shrubs with shallow root systems were perhaps exceptions to this rule. Bulbs continued to increase; fritillaries were now one of the 'in' categories with up to 50 entries per class at some Shows; trilliums and crocuses ran them close for popularity while regular 'rare' entries such as *Tecophilaea cyanocrocus* from South America could always be relied on to take the top prizes. Cushion plants were now less conspicuous but there was still a plea in the Journal for judges to see beyond dionysias and to give awards to less fashionable genera. A new genus on the show scene was *Corydalis* with many new species, often from the collection at the Göteborg Botanical Garden in Sweden. Ericaceous entries had declined dramatically and dwarf rhododendrons were becoming almost endangered species.

THE AGE OF THE COMMON PLANT
In the 1930s hybrids were looked down on but by the end of the century an increasing number of hybrids from deliberate crosses were being exhibited especially among *Narcissus, Ranunculus, Lewisia* and *Primula* and were accepted on an equal basis with true species. No longer were prizes going to tiny cushions with only a few flowers just because they were rare while magnificent specimens of common species were ignored. The trend seemed to be to accept the dictum laid down in Show Schedules that 60% of points when judging should go for condition, 30% for skill in cultivation and only 10% for rarity. But as usual, the individual idiosyncracies of judges often determined a different weighting.

FORREST MEDALS
By 1998 Forrest Medals were being awarded to what the judges considered 'the best plant in the Show', regardless of how common it might be whereas in the early days rarity and difficulty were paramount. Harold Esslemont used to recount how he won Forrest Medals with a *Jankaea* with only three flowers, a tiny seedling *Dionysia aretioides* and a small *Haastia pulvinaris* which was probably dead. Forrest Medals were rarely given to bulbs in the early days although Harold Esslemont did win with a *Fritillaria gibbosa* in 1969. By the end of the century, however, bulbous plants stood an equal chance of winning. By that time too, large plants of common species when at their spectacular best, and fortified by regular feeding, seemed to stand the best chance of winning a Forrest Medal so that auriculas, pulsatillas and

gentians now appeared in the list of winners. Up until 1965 no members of the Amaryllidaceae, Cruciferae, Labiatae or Leguminosae families had won a Forrest Medal. The trend to more familiar plants was exemplified by the decision in the 1990s to allow 'polyanthus' type primulas to appear on the benches. Up until then they were strictly forbidden

NEW INTRODUCTIONS

Another innovation about then was the introduction of classes for three or more pans of plants all from one continent. This attracted good entries as the enthusiasm for new introductions increased. Whereas before World War II, most introductions were from large expeditions financed by wealthy landowners or business men, by the end of the century new introductions or re-introductions were increasingly derived from seed-collecting expeditions mounted by Botanical Gardens, and by private persons who offered a share of seeds collected in return for a suitable contribution to the cost of the trip. There was therefore great interest in new species from all over the world which led to a wider range of species on the Show benches. Growers now took a keen interest in growing plants from particular regions of the world. For example, South American species of *Ourisia, Tropaeolum, Nassauvia* and *Nototriche* were appearing in the classes for 'new, rare or difficult'. Bizarre arisaemas from Asia were becoming fashionable, although far removed from what the founding members of the Club would have regarded as an alpine plant. The Club Seed Exchange has further contributed to the variety with almost 5000 plants to choose from, many of them otherwise unobtainable. It is therefore no surprise that many prize winning plants have been raised from this source.

TRADE STANDS

As interesting as the changes in plants have been the changes in the Trade Stands. Up until the 70s there would only be one or at most two Trade Stands at a Show, selling a small range of species, mainly easily grown plants aimed at the general public who had paid to come in but by the 90s demand for space was such that a rota system operated. The sale plants were now much more unusual and aimed at the keen Club members who were looking for the rare and difficult. Nurseries had recognised that such customers worried less about price than about availability. Rock garden nurseries were now much commoner with a trend for experienced amateur growers to start selling plants on a small scale on their retirement, making the task of the full time specialist alpine nurseryman much more difficult. A controversial move was made by the Club in the 90s when it allowed members to sell plants at the Shows and to keep 50% of the sale money. The regular nurserymen who had built up impressive stocks of good and unusual species over a long time regarded this as unfair competition, although perhaps illogically they did not mind members donating plants for nothing to be sold on the Club stands.

§ CHAPTER 4 §

Growers of Note

Although Botanical Gardens, Universities, Museums and Research Institutes have been and will remain at the forefront of advances in botany and horticulture, in gardening there has been a tradition of the gifted amateur who has developed garden design, introduced new plants, often by financially supporting plant collectors, and worked out new techniques for growing plants. Even for a genus like *Primula* which has been extensively researched in Botanic Gardens and Universities, many advances in how to grow and propagate them have been due to amateur gardeners.

Unfortunately, many plant collectors encounter a lack of feedback from gardeners who have received seed or plants from expeditions. Even a simple note of germination success would be a great help; additional information about growth, flowering and garden-worthiness is almost wholly lacking. Organisations such as the Sino-Himalayan Plant Association would seem to be a way forward but, even here, it is always the same few who respond. But amateur gardeners constitute a vast reservoir of expertise and access to plant material which needs to be tapped. It is here that bodies such as the SRGC, the AGS and the Hardy Plant Society and perhaps the NCCPG can play an important role. As Jim Archibald has aptly observed "some accepted channel is necessary for interchange of plants between the professional, botanical world and the amateur gardener" and also "our main enemies are ignorance, over-confidence and selfishness". Indeed there has always been a flow of plant material between gardeners and Botanic Gardens but it has been on a one-to-one basis of personal contact and respect.

As we have seen, the development of rock gardening in Scotland has been closely associated with the growth of the SRGC. Edinburgh and, shortly after, Glasgow were the centres of interest and expertise before World War II, followed after the War by the emergence of groups of dedicated growers at Aberdeen, Perth and Dundee followed by the almost meteoric appearance of Stirling on the rock gardening scene. As the Shows became more extensive and competition became more intense, growers appeared from all over the country often not associated with any particular centre. Indeed, by the end of the century, Edinburgh and Glasgow which had set the ball rolling, could no longer be regarded as the main centres of advances in rock gardening in Scotland.

In this general context we must now consider the private growers who have contributed so much to our understanding of how to grow and display so many alpine and rock plants. Any survey of this nature is bound to be selective and based largely on the accounts and descriptions published over the years in the pages of the SRGC Journal and the AGS Bulletin. It is most convenient to deal with growers of greater or lesser note on a regional basis, generally in association with the local SRGC Group.

Aberdeen
HAROLD ESSLEMONT

Although he did not appear on the rock garden scene until 1950, Harold Esslemont of Aberdeen must be regarded as one of the father figures of the SRGC. He died in 1992 aged 91 when the Journal noted that "his skill in cultivating rare and difficult plants to superb standards and his generosity and sage advice encouraged many members of the Club to grow and show their plants as he had done for well on 40 years, often vying for the Forrest Medal with Jack Crosland. Surely no one will ever match Harold's Show achievements". In his career as a plantsman, Esslemont won 43 Forrest Medals, 5FCCs, 9AMs, 11PCs and 37CCs, an astounding record never surpassed.

He started his first rock garden in 1937 but the War intervened and he spent five years in the RAF where, in his spare time, he grew tomatoes in old petrol tins. After the War he joined the SRGC and soon began showing, gaining his first FM in 1956 with *Shortia uniflora* grown under the greenhouse staging. He was prepared to travel long distances to show his plants. On one occasion he took six plants in boxes on the night train to London and the next day was his most successful ever since he won the Farrer Medal for the best plant in the Show as well as three PCs and four CCs.

He grew a variety of plants in his alpine house but his greatest successes were with cushion plants which he always grew hard, often in tufa, with very little feeding and watered sparsely in a plunge bed. Asked towards the end of his life which plants he liked best he listed *Eritrichium nanum*, *Dionysia aretioides*, *Anchusa caespitosa*, *Kelseya uniflora*, *Daphne petraea* *Campanula morettiana*, *Jankaea heldreichii*, *Draba mollissima*, *Fritillaria gibbosa*, *Kalmiopsis leachiana* 'M. le Piniec', *Phlox triovulata*, *Cassiope wardii* and *Raoulia eximia*. Anyone who frequented SRGC shows in those days will recognise the names and remember the plants. He always had a good laugh about the raoulia for which he received a FM when it was already dead or, at least, well on its way out. As well as these plants he grew crocuses and fritillaries to perfection and was one of the first to grow *Primula aureata* well in his alpine house. He would bring out his huge cushion plants to all the Shows; they were like pedigree cattle winning awards from year to year. He formed a close friendship with Jack Crosland. They showed together, went on plant collecting trips to Europe together and regularly swapped plants. Crosland had a frost-free alpine house, unlike Esslemont, so plants would be shipped out from Aberdeen to Crosland's house at Torphins for the winter. Between them Esslemont and Crosland raised the standard of showing at SRGC Shows in a way no one had done before or has done since.

One of Esslemont's fortes was his nurturing of up-and-coming rock gardeners to whom he would give first class plants which were bound to win a prize in a year or two and he passed on to them the wisdom of his many years of experience. Top growers such as Maxwell, Leven, Hunt, and the Youngs could all be regarded as his protégés.

JACK CROSLAND

A Yorkshire man who moved to Scotland as boy, Jack Crosland travelled widely for Paton & Baldwin, the wool firm, and his travels often took him past Inshriach Nursery where he would buy alpine plants to grow in his cold garden at Torphins, Aberdeenshire. His garden was full of species and cultivars of all manner of attractive plants while his frames were crammed with seedlings and cuttings into which he would delve to present a plant to an interested visitor. He always seemed to have a pot of unusual plants which many other growers had never heard of, such as *Hormathophylla reverchonii*, a shrubby alyssum. He had an uncanny knack of growing plants in pots tucked away and forgotten in odd corners but which he would more or less discover, resuscitate, bring to a Show and win a top prize. He was a superb grower so that plants from both his garden and alpine house were regular winners at the Shows. He won 30 FMs, a total unbeaten by anyone except his friend Esslemont. His first win was in 1961 with *Rhododendron hanceanum* and his last was *Cassiope selaginoides* in 1985. He was especially renowned for growing pleiones in his shaded alpine house. His success with this genus meant that much newly collected material was sent to him to grow and/or propagate. He was one of the first to grow such star plants as *Pleione humilis* 'Frank Kingdon Ward' as well as the true form of *Pleione forrestii*. He was among the earliest to grow *Rhododendron degronianum* ssp. *yakushimanum* in his woodland garden, as well as trilliums and omphalogrammas of which he was particularly fond.

As might be expected of a Group with Harold Esslemont and Jack Crosland among its most active members there has been no dearth of top growers in the Aberdeen area. During the 1980s and 90s growers from Aberdeen were such regular recipients of Forrest Medals at the Shows that the term 'Aberdeen Mafia' was coined.

IAN and MARGARET YOUNG

They are one of the several husband and wife teams which have contributed so effectively to the activities of the SRGC to which they have come fairly recently, having started their gardening careers in areas other than rock plants. They started showing in the late 1980s and soon rose to the top, winning Forrest Medals and Plantsman of the Year Awards regularly for the rest of the century. In Aberdeen they took over the mantle of Harold Esslemont who tutored them in the skills of growing alpines and gave them many a good plant. They belong to the new generation of growers and exhibitors who grow and show a wide range of plants and are well versed botanically. They are particularly successful with trilliums, fritillaries, irises, pulsatillas, dionysias, and their favourite ericaceous plants like kalmiopsis.

As well as having a flair for showing, the Youngs have a fine garden and alpine house in Aberdeen, which often appear on television where the ebullient Margaret has proved to be a great hit, while Ian is well known as a successful public speaker. The garden includes many rhododendrons which provide shelter for bulbs and herbaceous species, including trilliums and arisaemas. They have constructed a number of enormous raised beds in which they grow dwarf alpines, many from New Zealand (Fig.8). In the alpine house spring bulbs are an early feature, profiting by the extent to which both temperature and humidity are controlled to a precision unknown to earlier growers. In the bulb frame dwarf narcissi and fritillaries are the chief items. The Youngs have been very scientific in calculating the precise needs of the different species so they know exactly when they should start watering them. As a result of the control of humidity, especially in winter, they are able to grow plants like *Eriophyton wallichii* from the high Himalayas which would otherwise rot in our unpredictable winters. Although not collectors, the Youngs grow many species from the seed collected by different expeditions.

OTHER GROWERS
Other growers and exhibitors in the Aberdeen Group include Bob Maxwell from Lumphanan, Aberdeenshire, who fell heir to many of Esslemont's plants and continues to show them. Maureen and Brian Wilson from Aberdeen regularly win prizes with plants not often seen at Shows such as gesneriaceous species. Wilfred Holmes from Banchory, Aberdeenshire, probably sows more seeds of alpines annually than anyone else and is the only member of the SRGC to have a genus of orchids named after him, by Philip Cribb, (*Holmesia*, now changed to *Microholmesia*) which he discovered in East Africa. Fred Carrie at his nursery at Tough, Aberdeenshire, has won many prizes with his cushion plants which seem to thrive in his harsh climate at just over 300m, including *Paraquilegia anemonoides*. He has introduced many Himalayan plants into commerce, some from expeditions with Alastair McKelvie from Aberdeen who specialises in growing Himalayan plants, mainly from his own collecting. John Aitken of Parkhill, Aberdeenshire, was a great grower of gentians, heathers and, by way of contrast, show auriculas. He and his son David, built what must be one of the longest raised beds ever made, for his alpines (Fig.9). Heather Salzen from Aberdeen has created a very fine collection of water colours of alpine plants, many of which she grows or has found on her expeditions to such distant places as Mongolia and Patagonia. Another water colour artist from this area is Mary McMurtrie of Balbithan, Aberdeenshire, now in her 90s, who formerly ran an alpine plant nursery but now concentrates on painting and on travel, especially to the Algarve, to obtain material for her illustrated books of the local flora.

A noted Aberdeen figure, not a rock gardener until his retirement, but the Honorary President of the SRGC until his death in 1978 and an expert on the Scottish flora, was Professor J.R. Matthews, Professor of Botany at Aberdeen University from 1934-1959. He devoted a life-time to the study of plant distributions and floristic associations. He was one of the last botany professors who had a deep interest in growing plants and, perhaps prophetically wrote in the SRGC Journal in 1966: "It might be assumed that a botanist, by virtue of his profession, would have an interest in the growing of plants, but in many cases the assumption could well be wrong. Fashions in botany have changed, as in many things, since the days when the late Professor Bower of Glasgow University was wont to declare that every botanist should spend at least three months in the potting shed. In my early years I served a longer apprentice and have never regretted the experience".

Borders

EDROM NURSERY: Miss Edith and Miss Mollie Logan Home, Alex Duguid and Jim Jermyn.

The Misses Logan Home were among the founder members of the SRGC. They began gardening near Duns, soon began showing and in 1936 set up their own nursery at Edrom near Coldingham. They were an imposing pair of ladies, both about six feet tall. Starting his working life as a shepherd on the Royal Estate at Balmoral, Alex Duguid began his gardening career at Edrom. Armed with a love of plants in his native Deeside and a deep knowledge of Farrer's books, he set about building a rock garden for the ladies. He then had a lengthy spell with Sir William Milner in Yorkshire but returned in 1947 to Edrom which soon became a plant hunter's paradise. He remained there until he retired to Deeside in 1978. Seeds and plants were received from all over the world and the ladies were soon exhibiting at Shows throughout the country. Duguid's main role was that of propagation at which he became very skilful. He pioneered the use of materials such as pumice and sphagnum which are still used today. With the benefit of his 'green fingers' he was able to grow such species as *Calceolaria uniflora* var. *darwinii*, *Primula dryadifolia*, *P. kingii*, *P. sherriffae*, *Gentiana farreri* and many species of *Meconopsis*. He also developed the use of stone troughs for alpines and became a master of the art.

After the Misses Logan Home and Alex Duguid the nursery passed into the hands of Jim Jermyn who had been trained at the Royal Botanic Garden, Edinburgh, Inshriach Nursery and the Schacht Alpine Nursery near Munich, so he was well equipped to take over. Under his control the nursery continued its tradition of exhibiting at shows so the name of Edrom is now well known at Chelsea and at the RHS Halls in London. Jermyn has travelled widely in search of plants and is especially familiar with the Japanese flora. The Edrom Nursery has recently been taken over by Cath Davis and Terry Hunt.

JOHN MCWATT
John McWatt, a GP from Duns in Berwickshire, was an eminent grower of primulas in the first half of this century in his one hectare garden, with two rock gardens and several greenhouses. Between 1911 and 1933 he was awarded 24 Silver or Gold medals by the RHS in London, mainly at Chelsea, plus many awards within Scotland. He is particularly remembered for his excellent book "Primulas of Europe" published by Country Life Library in 1923 and for the three primulas he bred – 'McWatts's Blue', now very scarce and difficult to grow, 'McWatt's Crimson', now also rare, and 'Mc Watts's Cream', still widely grown and admired.

Dundee, Fife and Angus
GEORGE and BETTY SHERRIFF
An early garden in Scotland devoted to alpine plants was that of the Sherriff's at Ascreavie in Angus. George Sherriff has already been considered as a Himalayan collector but the garden at Ascreavie deserves mention in its own right. The site is 290m above sea level and well inland so winters are cold and long which may be one reason why Himalayan plants did so well there. The Sherriffs bought Ascreavie in 1950 on their return from India, with many of the early plantings from established gardens such as Keillour and Branklyn. By the time Betty Sherriff died in 1978 the garden was a treasure house of rare plants with rhododendrons, primulas, saxifrages, and meconopsis predominant. Several Himalayan plants were named after the Sherriffs. A few of many examples include *Rhododendron sherriffii*, named after its finder George Sherriff, *Primula sherriffae*, named after Sherriff's mother and *Lilium sherriffiae*, named after Betty Sherriff. Among the rare primulas at Ascreavie, *P. kingii* flourished by the stream, with its roots in the water, but grew nowhere else in Scotland. *P. flaccida* and *P .reidii williamsii* grew without winter protection. *Meconopsis* was a special feature with such gems as the pink *M. sherriffii*, now rarely in cultivation, the purple *M. delavayi*, unfortunately stolen from its trough on one of the last garden open days, and two good forms of *M. grandis* – 'GS600' and 'Betty's Dream Poppy', a splendid blue form which Betty Sherriff found in the wild after hearing instructions in a dream.

Since 1978 Ascreavie has changed hands several times and the garden now shows little trace of what it once was.

CYRIL LAFONG
When Cyril Lafong from Glenrothes, Fife, appeared on the Show scene in the early 1990s, unlike most newcomers, he did not just produce a few nicely grown plants but created a sensation by showing an impressive range of immaculate pans of alpines which won him many prizes. Since those days he has continued to produce plants of quality. It is surely one of the strengths of

the SRGC how often newcomers can win spectacularly without spending time in the apprenticeship stakes.

Dr Lafong grows a wide range of alpines but specialises in cushion plants such as Aretian androsaces which he grows in lean composts in clay pots plunged in sand in a well-ventilated greenhouse fitted with fans. He grows his bulbs in plastic pots in a richer compost but his basic compost comprises equal parts of JI No. 3 and a mix of Edzell grit, fine bark and peat in the ratio 1:1:1. It is interesting how modern growers are now making up their own composts rather than just using JI – almost a return to the old days of special composts for particular kinds of plants.

HENRY and MARGARET TAYLOR

The Taylors have already been mentioned in the section dealing with collectors, but as very successful growers they earn notice here as well. They are first class exhibitors, rivalling that other Dundee grower Fred Hunt in the quality and variety of plants they exhibit. They grow almost every alpine imaginable but will always be remembered for their pans of New Zealand clematis such as *C. marmoraria*, for magnificent forms of *Ranunculus parnassifolius* and bulbs, especially fritillaries. They have won many Medals and Certificates at SRGC Shows throughout the latter part of the century and have been an inspiration to budding exhibitors. The surprising variety of alpines grown in their small garden at Invergowrie always astonishes visitors

MICHAEL and LYNN ALMOND

The Almonds from Dundee must have scoured more hillsides looking for plants than anyone other than the Stones and the Taylors. They have spread their net from the European Alps through to Turkey. Their descriptive articles in the Club Journal are lessons in how to write interesting and informative guides to anyone who wishes to follow in their footsteps. They insist they are not collectors; they hardly need to be, given the beauty and precision of Michael and Lynn Almond's photographs. The information they have gleaned has been of great value to those who grow the plants they describe. They are also able growers and have established a rock garden complete with raised beds planted with a rich assortment of alpines on a rich but stiff clay in the Carse of Gowrie.

BRENDA and JOHN ANDERSON

The Andersons of Wester Balruddery, Dundee, were unique in that one bank of their garden was in Perthshire and the other in Angus. It was in 1964 that they started work on their marvellous site, a steep-faced valley with rich, moist soil on either side of a small stream. Their garden soon became famous for drifts of meconopsis and primulas together with extensive plantings of rhododendrons. In early spring *Primula bhutanica* made a carpet of blue on the east-facing bank. The Andersons spent much of each winter in the southern hemisphere collecting hardy plants so that their garden was soon full of species from the Drakensberg, Australia, Tasmania, Argentina and Chile. The hardy yellow cactus *Maihuenia poeppigeii* from Chile flowered on the sunny rock garden while mutisias flourished on the walls of the house. John Anderson died in 1985 and Brenda in 1994 but it is pleasant to record that many of their plants were distributed by their descendants among Scottish Botanic gardens.

JAMES COBB

Most rock gardeners choose a few plants they like and attempt to grow them to the best of their ability. Not so James Cobb from Kingsbarn, Fife, who takes an interest in a wide range of plants including irises, cypripediums, lilies and, more recently in the 1990s, penstemons. His methods for growing lilies are not to be found in any text-book but they work very well. Probably to most people he is known as 'Mr. Meconopsis' on account of the book he published in 1989 in which he made the authoritative text on the genus by Sir George Taylor accessible to ordinary gardeners. This genus is a minefield for taxonomists so Cobb had quite a job in hand to disentangle the complexities and clarify the situation, in the course of which he was not afraid to tread on a few toes by slating the taxonomists whenever he felt they merited it. By 1994 he seemed to have decided in an article in the Journal entitled 'Goodbye Meconopsis' that enough was enough. He proposed that "on the first of January 1995 all plants should stick with names they have at that moment for ever. If anyone wanted to communicate with the taxonomists, who would be free to go on changing things, then one could simply feed the name into a computer network.......and get the latest update from taxonomists. Like this, taxonomists could mess about to their heart's content and the rest of science plus bewildered gardeners would have their own immutable system". It is interesting that, at the turn of the century, something like Cobb's proposal seems nearer than was at one time imaginable.

Apart from his philosophising, his book and articles on meconopsis are excellent examples of just what a gardener needs to know. Apart from elucidating the vexed questions of taxonomy he recommended ways to germinate seed and described his growing regimes in simple terms. He has dealt lucidly with the knotty problem of *Meconopsis* x *sheldonii* forms, especially the new, fertile strains. The 'Kingsbarns Hybrids' were produced by Cobb but even into the sixth generation he could not arrive at a true blue. He is a professional biologist but wrote that "a prodder is a scientist who does not have green fingers and the corollary is that someone with green fingers is a scientist who is so intuitively sure of the facts that he does not need to prod. Actually.... I'm glad I'm a prodder".

FRED HUNT

Fred Hunt from Invergowrie, near Dundee, began his garden career as a grower and exhibitor of chrysanthemums but switched to alpines under the tutelage of his next door neighbours, Henry and Margaret Taylor. His name regularly appeared in the list of prize winners in the early 1980s and it was not long before he was sweeping the boards with his immaculate plants. His trademark is magnificent presentation with not a blemish on a single flower or leaf and attention to detail. He was one of the first of the modern exhibitors to feed their plants regularly so they appeared in superb condition and larger than ever before. Medals, certificates and trophies abounded as Hunt continued his amazing career right up to the end of the century. He has exhibited a remarkably wide range of plants, many obtaining RHS awards, including FCCs for *Calluna vulgaris* 'Kinlochruel', *Clematis marmoraria*, *Edraianthus serpyllifolius* 'Major' and *Pleione* Shantung 'Ducat' It is hardly possible to identify which he grows best but he is renowned for his European primulas, cypripediums and an imposing rage of fritillaries like *FF. conica, crassifolia* and *tubiformis*. Perhaps his trademark plant is the rare and possibly extinct Chilean bulb *Tecophilaea cyanocrocus* shown to perfection, while his six- and three-pan entries are works of art, all produced in a small, village garden and alpine house. In the 1990s he travelled widely in China and Tibet in search of primulas and rhododendrons.

JOYCE HALLEY

Joyce Halley from Broughty Ferry, Dundee, was a keen grower, who will be especially remembered for the 17 years she spent running the SRGC Seed Exchange. She was tireless in her zeal and expected her helpers to emulate her, any mistakes being met with sharp comment but just as readily with praise when it was earned. She took a close interest in the Rock Garden run by Dundee Parks Department which she helped to develop. One incident is worth recalling: she had 30 good seed donors from Czechoslovakia but one January she received no requests from them. On enquiry she found that the seed lists had been held up by Government officials so, on her own initiative, she looked up the previous year's records to see what the Czechs were interested in and sent them an appropriate selection together with some particularly choice species — result – happy Czech donors.

Edinburgh

The Edinburgh Group members were inevitably front runners from the beginning. Their close proximity to the Royal Botanic Garden, Edinburgh and their historical associations were key factors. Before World War II the Club did not achieve much but immediately afterwards it blossomed.

ALAN WALMSLEY

One of the stalwarts who got the Club going again was Major Alan Walmsley who was President from 1947 to 1951 during which time he saw the membership increase from 500 to 2000. He and his wife created a beautiful garden at Culderry in Wigtonshire, recognised as one of the best in south west Scotland. He assembled a good collection of rare and interesting plants many of which he collected abroad, including ericaceous species and bulbs which were his particular interests. He was especially remembered for a huge pot of *Phyllodoce nipponica* whch won a FCC and a Farrer Medal at the AGS London Show in 1946, and, in the same week, a FM at the SRGC Show in Glasgow where it was judged to be the most outstanding plant of the year. The same plant was recorded as still alive in 1969 with a diameter of at least 60cm.

KENNETH CORSAR

One of the earliest members of the Club, he was Editor of the Journal from 1937 to 1950 and later President. Apart from his notable services to the Club he was well known for his skill with auriculas which he grew with great success at the top of Braid Avenue in Edinburgh. He later moved to Milton Bridge in Midlothian where he grew some rare primulas like *Primula cusickeana* which he brought to perfect flowering, one of the few occasions this has been achieved in this country. As Richards has observed in his book on primulas, this is one of the most intractable species in cultivation. Corsar also wrote an excellent little book 'Primulas for the Garden'.

HENRY TOD

An Edinburgh agricultural soil scientist, Henry Tod applied his professional skills to rock gardening particularly with respect to the response of ericaceous plants to lime. His detailed studies demonstrated the complex nature of the responses which involved interaction between calcium and magnesium such that excess calcium can suppress the availability of magnesium (see also p.102). Tod helped to revive the SRGC after World War II and was President from 1960 to 1963.

Apart from his sterling work for the Club and his work on rhododendron nutrition he was a very able grower who grew many of the plants which Peter Davis had collected in the Middle East. He also collected alpines in the Rockies and Wyoming with Dr Carleton Worth. He won FMs with *Kelseya uniflora* and *Douglasia laevigata*. Henry Tod also supplemented his valuable work for the Club by acting as a Judge at Shows. When once asked how one became a Show Judge he simply replied "just read as much as you can about plants and go on reading and if in doubt read it all again".

SHEILA MAULE

An eminent plantswoman and SRGC office-bearer Sheila Maule became well known for her 'garden in a quarry' at Balerno outside Edinburgh, which she started in 1947 and was still looking after when she died in 1996. Here she assembled a great variety of plants many raised from seed she had collected in the mountains of Europe. She was instrumental in bringing *Narcissus rupicola* ssp. *watieri* into cultivation and was among the first to grow Japanese plants of which she had a large collection. As her health and sight failed she concentrated on bulbs in her alpine house.

IAN and KATHLEEN SIMSON-HALL
The Simson-Halls built up an excellent collection of plants at their house at Cramond on the outskirts of Edinburgh. They were particularly good with ericaceous species and had a fine collection of rhododendrons. Theirs was a real plantsman's garden where visitors were always welcome to see some of the potential of rock gardening.

HARLEY MILNE
Amont the stalwart members of the Edinburgh group in the latter part of the century is Harley Milne. A grower and exhibitor, he has been noted for his administrative roles in the Club, being at different times Group Convenor, Show Secretary and Club President. He is an Honorary Vice-President of the Club and Vice-Chairman of the RHS Joint Rock Garden Plant Committee.

OTHER GROWERS
Other prominent Club members in the Edinburgh area included David and Isobel Simpson who were Club librarians for many years while Isobel Simpson was Secretary from 1975 to 1982. Their contribution to rock gardening was very much by way of promoting the Club, plants and gardens in as many ways as possible. James (Jimmy) Aitken of Cramond is another person who is remembered for his contribution to gardening rather than as grower of particular plants. He was particularly interested in the life and exploits of plant collectors. He was an active office-bearer of several gardening societies and was the first Secretary of the Friends of the Royal Botanic Garden Edinburgh.

Outside Edinburgh, down the East Lothian coast at Boonslie lived Squadron-Leader John Boyd-Harvey and his wife Christina. He was Secretary of the Club from 1951 until just before his death in 1966 and was followed by his wife who took over and remained in post until she died in 1974. In the late 1920s and 30s they were International Motor Cycle drivers and it was in the course of their driving trips in Europe that they developed their interest in plants and gardens. After the War they established a fine garden at Boonslie well endowed with interesting plants and shrubs, many of them raised from seed by Mrs Boyd-Harvey who was also noted for her impressive pans of cyclamen at Shows, especially *C. hederifolium*. The Boyd-Harveys also grew many plants collected by Ruth Tweedie in Patagonia such as *Oxalis laciniata*. They contributed a great deal to the Club and were assiduous in writing articles and giving lectures.

Fig. 1 Sir Isaac Bayley Balfour (p.3)

Fig. 2 J. McNab's Rock Garden 1880 (p.65)

Fig. 3 George Sherriff (p.10)   Fig. 4 Map of George Forrest's Travels (p

Fig. 5 George Forrest on horseback (p.6)

Fig. 6 Sandy Leven with Caithness Glass Trophy (p.33)

Fig. 7 Winning exhibits at Strathclyde 1999 (p.33)

Fig. 8 Modern Rock Garden Layout 1999 (p.43)

Fig. 9 The Great Wall (p.43)

Fig. 10 Sales Area in Garden Centre 1999 (p.61)

Fig. 11 Display Area in Garden Centre 1999 (p.61)

Fig. 12 Rock Garden at RBGE 1995 (p.65)

Fig. 13 Rock Garden at Leith Hall (p.75)

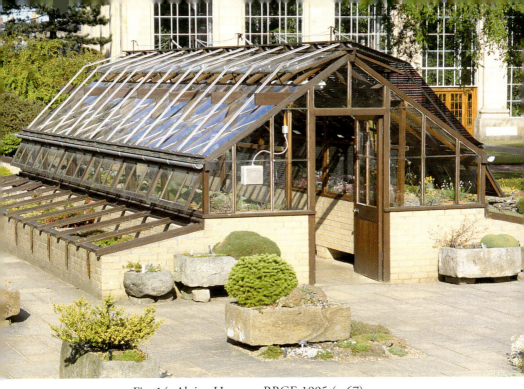

Fig. 14 Alpine House at RBGE 1995 (p.67)

Fig. 15 Ron McBeath in RBGE Alpine House (p.67)

Fig. 16 Four types of 'stone' trough (p.79)

        Cement   Concrete
Reconstituted stone   Real sandstone
              Polystyrene fish box

Fig. 18 Painting stages (lower painted: upper paint smoothed out) (p.79)

Fig. 17 Polystyrene box being roughened by heat gun (p.79)

Fig. 19 Pile of six completed boxes (p.79)

Fig. 20 *Saussurea laniceps* (p.97)

Fig. 21 *Draba oreades* (p.98)

Fig. 22 *Incarvillea compacta* (p.98)

Fig. 23 *Cremanthodium ellisii* (p.97) Fig. 24 *Cassiope fastigiata* (p.99)

Fig. 25 *Cassiope selaginoides* (p.100)　　　Fig. 26 *Cassiope wardii* (p.100)

Fig. 27 *Rhododendron laudandum* (p.103)　　　Fig. 28 *Rhododendron primuliflorum* (p.101)

Fig. 29 *Rhododendron ciliatum* (p.105)

Fig. 30 *Rhododendron lepidotum* (p.105)

Fig. 31 *Rhododendron racemosum* (p.106)

Fig. 32 *Gentiana georgei* (p.111)

Fig. 33 *Gentiana hexaphylla* (p.111)

Fig. 34 *Gentiana sino-ornata* (p.109)

Fig. 35 *Gentiana veitchiorum* (p.109)

Fig. 37 *Meconopsis horridula* (p.116)

Fig. 36 *Corydalis cashmeriana* (p.112)

Fig. 38 *Meconopsis grandis* (p.116)   Fig. 39 *Meconopsis integrifolia* (p.115)

Fig. 40 *Meconopsis paniculata* (p.114)

Fig. 41 *Meconopsis pseudointegrifolia* (p.115)   Fig. 42 *Meconopsis quintuplinervia* (p.115)

Fig. 43 *Meconopsis villosa* (p.113)

Fig. 44 *Primula aureata* (p.124)

Fig. 45 *Primula strumosa* (p.123)

Fig. 46 *Primula ioessa* (p.125)

Fig. 47 *Primula calderiana* (p.123)

Fig. 48 *Primula forrestii* (p.119)

Fig. 49 *Primula sikkimensis* (p.125)

Fig. 50 *Primula tanneri tsariensis* (p.124)

Fig. 51 *Primula whitei* (p.125)

Fig. 52 *Primula macrophylla* (p.123)

Fig. 53 *Primula chionantha* (p.123)

Fig. 54 *Primula minutissima* (p.122)

Fig. 55 *Primula reidii* (p.126)

Fig. 56 *Primula gracilipes* (p.124)

Fig. 57 *Primula rosea* (p.122)

Fig. 58 *Androsace delavayi* (p.117)

Fig. 59 *Omphalogramma elwesiana* (p.118)

Fig. 60 *Anemone rupicola* (p.127)   Fig. 61 *Anemone obtusiloba* (p.127)

Fig. 62 *Paraquilegia anemonoides* (p.127)

Fig. 63 *Trollius pumilus* (p.128)

Fig. 64 *Potentilla cuneata* (p.128)　　　　Fig. 65 *Delphinium tatsienense* (p.127)

Fig. 66 *Potentilla eriocarpa* (p.128)

Fig. 67 *Saxifraga hypostoma* (p.128)

Fig. 68 *Arisaema candidissimum* (p.129)   Fig. 69 *Arisaema nepenthoides* (p.129)

Fig. 70 *Arisaema flavum* var. *tibeticum* (p.129)

Fig. 71 *Arisaema triphyllum* (p.185)

Fig. 72 *Lilium flavidum* (p.130)

Fig. 73 *Lilium nanum* (p.130)

Fig. 74 *Lilium lophophorum* (p.130)

Fig. 75 *Lilium sherriffiae* (p.130)

Fig. 76 *Lilium souliei* (p.130)

Fig. 77 *Nomocharis aperta* (p.131)

Fig. 78 *Nomocharis pardanthina* (p.131)

Fig. 79 *Daiswa polyphylla* (p.130)

Fig. 80 *Achillea ageratifolia* (p.151)

Fig. 81 *Arabis caucasica* (p.135)　　　　Fig. 82 *Draba polytricha* (p.135)

Fig. 83 *Campanula aucheri/tridentata aff.* (p.136)

Fig. 84 *Campanula betulifolia* (p.136)

Fig. 85 *Campanula versicolor* (p.153)

Fig. 86 *Edraianthus graminifolius* (p.15

Glasgow and West of Scotland
WILLIAM C. BUCHANAN

Perhaps the greatest Scottish rock gardener in the early part of the century was William (Willie) Buchanan, a farmer at Garscadden Mains near Glasgow. Not many farmers have been renowned as gardeners, which makes him especially notable. When his farm was bought for housing he moved to Bearsden, Glasgow where he created a second wonderful garden. As early as 1910, when he was aged only about 20, he became excited by the plant introductions of Farrer, Forrest and Kingdon Ward and was soon growing them at Garscadden. He was particularly friendly with Farrer who visited him at the farm while Buchanan contributed to Farrer's 1913-14 expedition. By the time the seeds arrived he was away in the army so his sister sowed them and grew the plants on until he returned home. He also grew plants from Sherriff's expeditions and was one of the few to be successful with *Saxifraga sherriffii*. Buchanan donated a photograph of it to the SRGC slide library where it still exits. Ludlow publicly acknowledged Buchanan's skill as a grower of Himalayan rarities.

Buchanan was one of those master growers and propagators who seemed to be successful with anything which took his fancy. He had truly catholic tastes and would grow anything he reckoned was a good garden plant, except that he was reputed to detest lewisias and refused to grow them. He was especially successful with ericaceous species and raised a number of hybrids such as *Daboecia* x *scotica* 'William Buchanan' and 'William Buchanan Gold' as well as *Pieris japonica* 'William Buchanan' and *Astilbe* 'William Buchanan'. Although a stern judge at Shows he rarely exhibited but was always ready to show his garden to other growers and was most generous in giving plants to visitors. He corresponded widely and was altogether a man ahead of his times in rock gardening. The William Buchanan Lecture on the topic of growing plants was established in his honour at the SRGC Discussion Weekend. He continued his long career as a grower until he died in 1963. It is a pity that he was so reluctant to commit his knowledge to paper. But at least his collection of slides, mostly taken by Professor Pontecorvo, formerly of the Genetics Dept. of the University of Glasgow and an enthusiastic alpine gardener, are part of the SRGC Slide Collection.

DAVID LIVINGSTONE

An interest in plants arose when David Livingstone had access to his grandfather's nursery at Carluke in Lanarkshire. He started showing dahlias but was coming to SRGC Shows as early as 1938. During the War he served with the RAF in Iceland and then returned to the BBC where he worked for 32 years. He was an active member of the SRGC before the War and he soon settled down again to writing his many articles for the Journal and the AGS Bulletin. He was Secretary and later President of the SRGC. He helped greatly in setting up the Joint Rock Garden Plant Committee of which he was a member for over 20 years. Primulas were his great interest, both European and Asiatic and he travelled extensively to collect them. Like many Club members he received plants from collecting expeditions which he grew on and propagated with great success. In 1950 he published a long article in the Club Journal based on his experience of growing all the species and cultivars then available. This article eventually reached Kingdon Ward who wrote to Livingstone saying what a joy it was to learn that someone was growing the plants which he and others had laboured to collect.

Livingstone devised all sorts of special composts for his primulas; one for petiolarids had 3 parts light loam, 2 parts peat, 1 part well rotted cow manure, the straw chopped by scissors, and 1 part coarse sand, sieved through a flour sifter. He disagreed with John Richard's new classification of these primulas, complaining that he was confused as to what names he should attach to the 17 kinds of petiolarids he had in his alpine house and that he was not alone in his confusion.

DON and JOAN STEAD

No one in the west of Scotland could quite compete with the famous Willie Buchanan in breaking new ground, but Don and Joan Stead at their garden in Thorntonhall near Glasgow designed two outstanding gardens, each to suit their individual tastes, where they demonstrated what a wide range of alpines could be grown on their intractable, clay soil. They also gardened in entirely different conditions at their cottage in Ardnamurchan in Argyll, exposed to Atlantic gales and storms on a light sandy soil. They were keen exhibitors. Joan Stead was Club President in 1979 while Don Stead was Publications Manager for 10 years.

OTHER GROWERS

Anne Chambers of the West of Scotland Group is a noted painter of plants in water colour and an expert photographer, who went on several expeditions to the Himalayas and China from the 1970s onwards and was among the first European botanists to visit Bhutan. Consequentially she knows the Sino-Himalayan flora very well and has grown many of the plants, especially pleiones. Lyn Bezzant established a rock garden in Bearsden, Glasgow before moving in the 1980s to the Lake of Menteith in Perthshire where she has specialised in dwarf shrubs, especially Ericaceae and also dwarf bulbs, especially crocus. She also regularly hunts for plants in southern Europe. Bette Ivey is another person who has moved garden, beginning in Ayr then going to Kirkmichael in Perthshire in 1988 and later to Cupar, Fife. She is noted for her first class show plants and for a lifetime's service to the SRGC of which she was President in 1991.

Inverness-shire and Highlands
JACK DRAKE and JOHN LAWSON
As well as being collectors and introducers of plants, Drake and Lawson were expert growers at their nursery at Inshriach near Aviemore which Lawson continued to run until 1999. The cool, moist conditions there provide ideal conditions for moisture-loving plants such as primulas, meconopsis, gentians, nomocharis, trilliums and celmisias, while the long, cold winters ensure an uninterrupted dormant period. But even at Inshriach there could be dry years when the light soil dried out alarmingly and there was need for much watering.

Drake and Lawson occupy an important place in Scottish rock gardening since they were among the first nurserymen to specialise in alpines and provide a much needed source of plants for gardeners after World War II. Because of their expertise, many rare plants from expeditions were sent to Inshriach for propagation in the knowledge that they were as likely to survive there as any where. *Meconopsis grandis* 'GS600' probably owes its existence today to its rescue at Inshriach. Among the many new plants raised there *Dianthus* 'Inshriach Dazzler', a seedling from *D. neglectus*, is especially worth noting. It produces carmine-pink flowers in profusion for a long time in early summer. Inshriach was also well known for its alpine phloxes such as 'Crackerjack' and 'Red Admiral' and gentians such as 'Drake's Strain', 'Blue Heaven' and 'Darkness'. In the early 1950s *Primula* x *pubescens* and *P. auricula* were popular plants and Inshriach came up with several good hybrids such as 'Christine'. 'Dianne Hybrids' were produced from *P.* x *forsteri* and several good hybrids were bred from *P. marginata*, such as 'Drake's Form'. Candelabra primulas hybridise freely and, from their close proximity at Inshriach several cultivars arose such as 'Inshriach Hybrids', 'Bonfire' and 'Inverewe'. Inshriach was one of the first nurseries to develop new strains of *Lewisia cotyledon*, the finest being the 'Sunset Strain', with outstanding self-coloured flowers. The nursery also helped to develop Buchanan's new *Daboecia* hybrids;as well as 'Willie Buchanan' one was named 'Jack Drake'. The nursery was well known for its New Zealand plants, especially celmisias. The Inshriach cultivars seem endless. How better to sum it all up than in the words of Jim Archibald when he wrote in 1960 "Inshriach is a garden for the enthusiast and ..... embraces alpines from every continent, combined in one great harmony of colour and form, a vast concerto in which there are many soloists but one in which almost everyone can have in his own rock garden with a little skill and a little more patience".

MIKE and POLLY STONE
The remarkable achievements of the Stones in growing an immense number of species of alpines have already been noted. Since they began rock gardening in the 1960s they have created a notable garden at 'Askival' which is widely recognised as exceptional both aesthetically, in the structural

features of the rocky landscape, and in the scientific importance of the immense number of species which grow there. The Stones would accept that one additional respect in which 'Askival' is unique lies in the historical record of its evolution, warts and all, chronicled in the twice yearly 'Stone Column'. The Stones do not exhibit but garden purely for pleasure, although latterly they grafted a small wholesale nursery onto the garden to finance the garden and trips abroad after Mike Stone retired, although the garden remains personal and private as always.

It is easier to say what the Stones do not grow rather than what they do. Whatever it is it must be hardy down to −20°C, which eliminates what they term 'MRWs' i.e. Mediterranean Roadside Weeds which can masquerade as alpines or qualify for bulb classes at Shows as well as lower altitude species from elsewhere. Their high humidity does not suit plants like dionysias from very arid areas. That leaves the Arctic, the higher European mountains, Turkey, the Caucasus, Central and Eastern Asia and America. It is an indication of how much they grow that a visit to the garden can take 7-8 hours to complete even though it is only 0.67ha and parts are still undeveloped.

DICK TROTTER

Dick Trotter retired from the post of Treasurer of the Royal Horticulatural Society, London to set up a rock and wild garden at Brin between Inverness and Fort Augustus. In the 1960s he raised the Brin form of *Gentiana sino-ornata* and also two hellebore cultivars. 'Trotter's Wheel' was a pure white form of *Helleborus niger* which flowered for 10 months a year. It was marketed by Jack Drake at Inshriach. He also bred 'Trotter's Spotted', an orientalis hybrid with pure white flowers and purple spots which was marketed by his daughter, Elizabeth Parker-Jervis. Another hellebore raised in Scotland, not in Inverness-shire but in Fife, was *Helleborus foetidus* 'Wester Flisk' which was discovered by Mamie Walker when she moved to an old rectory garden at Wester Flisk near Newburgh in Fife. This delightful red-stemmed form breeds more or less true and has been in cultivation since 1980.

OTHER GROWERS

Other prominent members up in the north of Scotland include Jim Sutherland who, almost single-handed ran the Inverness Group and Show for many years and, since his retirement, has developed Ardfearn Nursery described elsewher in this book.

Another development in the north was the setting-up of a Morayshire Group in the 1990s which under the initial guidance of Ian Smith soon grew into a splendid band of keen growers of rock plants.

Perthshire
JOHN and DOROTHY RENTON

The one hectare garden at Branklyn, Perth, so lovingly constructed by the Rentons must be one of the finest gardens of its kind anywhere. From the early 1930s until their deaths in the late 1960s, they were active, indeed founder members of the SRGC, winning a Forrest Medal as long ago as 1934. John Renton was the designer while Dorothy was grower and 'plantsman'.

The layout is quite superb with pleasing vistas at frequent intervals and, although there are thousands of plants, it never looks crowded and is surprisingly well protected from the main road which passes close by. Because the Rentons were such excellent gardeners they received plants from many expeditions, especially those of Ludlow and Sherriff. Many good plants are in cultivation because the Rentons not only propagated rare species but were very generous in distributing them to other gardeners. Of all the plants they raised, the accolade must go to the meconopsis of which they raised at least 26 varieties. Best known, of course is *M.* 'Branklyn', which received a FCC in 1963. Primulas also did well at Branklyn including *P. reidii* and *P. forrestii* both of which grew outside with only cloche protection during winter. *Corydalis cashmeriana* seeds itself happily at Branklyn and likewise that statuesque crucifer *Megacarpaea polyandra* but probably the greatest achievement at Branklyn was the growing outside in a trough of that difficult Himalayan crevice plant *Paraquilegia anemonoides*. The Rentons showed how to grow and propagate it successfully so that nowadays it is a fairly common, although difficult plant, sold by many nurseries. But it was the Rentons who showed the way.

Another great feature of Branklyn is the rhododendrons which have been skilfully blended into the grand design, to make a spectacular display in spring and early summer. From time to time the garden has suffered from gales and late frosts which have required some replanting but each time the garden has been restored to its original design. Fortunately Branklyn Garden was bequeathed to the National Trust for Scotland when John Renton died so, unlike so many gardens both the design and many of the plants have been preserved.

MAJOR GEORGE and MRS KNOX FINLAY

The Finlays came to Keillour Castle in Perthshire in 1938 and between them created a garden of renown from an area which had been allowed to fall into neglect. It was not until after World War II that work on the garden could proceed but 10ha were eventually fenced in and made rabbit proof before planting could be carried out. Much of the spade work was done by the Major in spite of having broken his neck in the army in 1945.

The deep gorges of the Keillour and Horn burns which flow through the garden made an ideal home for many species of rhododendron and other trees and shrubs. They planted up the rock and woodland garden with a huge collection of plants while they devoted the water garden to primulas and other moisture-loving plants. The success of their garden can be assessed by the way plants from expeditions were regularly sent to Keillour where they could be assured of skilled hands to grow and propagate them. Plants from the Ludlow and Sherriff expeditions were sent to them as soon as they were unpacked. They were also instrumental in saving many valuable plants from the late Andrew Harley's garden at Devonhall by bringing them to Keillour.

The Knox Finlays were skilled in growing Himalayan plants, not just singly but in huge clumps. Liliaceous species such as liliums, nomocharis and notholirions were favourites as well as meconopsis, petiolarid primulas, gentians, corydalis, cassiopes, rhododendrons, paraquilegias and cyananthus to name but a few. *Meconopsis* was a favourite genus and they grew many to perfection including 'Betty's Dream Poppy' of which they were particularly fond. It was a source of pride to them when a spontaneous hybrid at Keillour between *Meconopsis integrifolia* and *M. quintuplinervia* was named *M.* x *finlayorum* by Sir George Taylor. Over many years they successfully presented plants to the Rock Garden Plant Committee. Major Finlay was a member of the RHS Lily Committee and was awarded the RHS highest award, the Victoria Medal of Honour, in 1969. When he died in 1970 his wife continued the work they had started together for a further 17 years. Latterly, although frail, she still managed to tend her garden and show visitors around. Like her husband she also received the Victoria Medal of Honour, an award which at the time had been given to only one other woman in Britain, Her Majesty, the Queen Mother. Sadly Keillour is now but a shadow of its former glory.

BOBBY MASTERTON

In 1950, working as a vet in Aberfeldy, Perthshire, Bobby Masterton together with his wife Betty, set about making a garden at Cluny on a steep slope overlooking the River Tay. The derelict site was mainly deciduous woodland on a rich leafy soil which Masterton soon tamed and planted up with a huge range of rhododendrons and other shrubs of such genera as *Acer*, which gave a glorious autumn colour. In spite of the spring riot of colour Masterton used to say that he preferred the autumn glory. As well as its shrubs, Cluny is known for the fine collection of herbaceous plants, mainly Himalayan primulas which Masterton grew to perfection without protection. To see drifts of *Primula sonchifolia* sprawling down the banks of a stream in April in the company of *P. bhutanica* is breath-taking. Meconopsis, cardiocrinums, notholirions, lilies and trilliums grow to perfection in the moist woodland soil. In the outstanding collection of shrubs perhaps pride of place should go to *Embothrium coccineum* which, however, is not fully hardy in such a cold site and has suffered badly from time to time. Many a gardener, after seeing Cluny, has been inspired to go home and try to emulate something of what he or she has seen.

Masterton undoubtedly showed gardeners the way forward in the growing of petiolarid primulas in which he was an acknowledged Scottish expert. He pioneered their propagation by leaf cuttings. He was also responsible for setting up the SRGC Seed Exchange which has achieved great success, very much in his original form. On his death and that of his wife in 1980 the garden has continued in the capable hands of their daughter Wendy and her husband John Mattingley and is now open all year to the public.

Many new species, especially primulas, continued to arrive at Cluny after 1980, often from the Himalayan expeditions of Peter Burnett, a colleague of Mattingley. With short-lived plants like primulas the collections are always in a state of flux so the present aim of the garden is to build up collections of species whose numbers have declined to critical levels and make them available for general circulation. The garden currently holds the NCCPG national collection of Asiatic primulas.

D.M. MURRAY-LYON

After a distinguished War record when he commanded the 11th Indian Division in Malaya, Major-General D.M. Murray-Lyon, always known as 'Murray' in the Club retired in 1946 to Pitlochry, Perthshire, where his garden at Ardcuil became widely known. He specialised in Himalayan plants, especially those collected by George Forrest. Plants which he regarded as hardy growers included *Iris forrestii*, *Pieris formosa* var. *forrestii*, *Paraquilegia anemonoides*, *Anemone rupicola*, *Androsace spinulifera* and *Omphalogramma vinciflorum*. His secret for most of these was a humus-rich soil which did not dry out. He devised his own methods for dealing with the cold winters which were common at nearly 200m at Ardcuil. To avoid the shoots of his pieris being blasted by late spring frost he would either plant them where they could not catch the early morning sun or get up at the crack of dawn on frosty mornings to spray the new, red growth with cold water before the sun reached it – a technique actually used by orchard growers to protect blossom. He made much use of retaining walls or dykes in which all sorts of marginally hardy plants seemed to thrive. He was fond of quoting a letter from the Convener of a group which had visited the garden: "I think it was the ease of examining plants high up on the walls which they found most impressive."

OTHER GROWERS

A notable alpine grower from Perthshire was John Duff who, for a long time gardened at Glenfarg in what he described as a frost pocket. He died in 1997 at the age of 92 after a long and distinguished career in rock gardening. In spite of the harsh winter climate at Glenfarg he created one of the finest rock gardens in Scotland with a host of rare and unusual plants grown supremely well, especially cushion species grown outside with no protection. He had an enviable record of prizes and trophies and was noted for the interest he took in new and younger members of the Club who never lacked for practical advice.

James R. Aitken is a nurseryman in Perth who has developed an interest in the native Scottish flora, travelling about the country to photograph native plants and writing about them. His garden at Perth, right next to Branklyn Garden, is home to a fine collection of alpines.

Dr Chris North from Newmill of Napp, Perthshire, has an extensive woodland garden full of desirable, shade-loving species although prey to wild pests of all sorts. In his earlier days it was one of the show-piece gardens of the region. But his main interests have been in the many new varieties of lilies which he bred at the Scottish Crop Research Institute, Dundee. He developed new methods for growing the most difficult species. During much of his spare time he has travelled the length and breadth of the Mediterranean finding and recording plants. He has incorporated the results of these travels in articles in the SRGC Journal and in 1997 produced an extremely useful book on the flora of the Mediterranean which is an essential guide for anyone who goes plant hunting there.

Stirling

When the Stirling Group organised its first Show in 1980 it saw the beginning of a remarkable development in which a number of skilled growers appeared almost simultaneously on the scene so that the Group is now the centre of innovative expertise and the cultivation of new plants. Much that is new and progressive in Scottish rock gardening had its origin here. Although many of the group live in Dunblane, which is in Perthshire, it is expedient to discuss their activities under the heading of Stirling since this is the Group to which they are attached.

SANDY LEVEN

One of the prime movers in this scene is Sandy Leven (Fig.6) who is another of those rock gardeners who began their gardening career with dahlias and chrysanthemums. Working in Inverness he stocked up with plants from Inshriach and moved to Stirling in 1977 where he soon developed his garden and alpine house. A keen exhibitor with many FMs and certificates to his credit he soon made his name in the SRGC and acted as President from 1997 to 2000. His garden reflects his catholic tastes but he specialises in bulbs of which he grows many new and unusual species. Fritillaries are his forte. He has noted that many of them produce powerful aromas which can be disconcerting if confined in the space of a car. In his Journal articles he has noted that "fritillaries are very handy plants, especially in multi-pan classes. They always complement each other's colours, never clashing like brightly coloured flowers.......the trick is to get them flowering at the same time."

GLASSFORD SPRUNT

Another Stirling stalwart and perfectionist, perhaps like all successful exhibitors, Glassford Sprunt specialises in dwarf bulbs, especially crocus and cyclamen. Indeed it is through the interests and activities of the Stirling Group members that the SRGC Dwarf Bulb Group has been set up. His alpine house which houses his crocuses and cyclamen is a model of precise planning. To illustrate his attention to detail we can refer to an article he wrote about exhibiting *Dionysia aretioides*. He obtained the plant in 1982. In 1992 he exhibited it at the Morecambe Show where it was having "one of its less good years and some of the foliage is still visible". Like most top growers he removes the flowers immediately after the Show to stop seed developing; in 1982 he removed more than 1700 flowers. In 1993, however, he could record the removal of 2856 flowers on the 36cm cushion after it won its second FM. Sprunt goes on to say "it is important to start the preparation for next year's show as soon as the flowers have been removed in the current year. Perhaps the most important single act is the turning of the pot. During the summer it is only turned once a month by a quarter turn. From January onwards when the flower buds start forming the turning process is stepped up in frequency; by then it becomes a quarter turn every week. Failure to turn the pot resulted in the south side flowering about two weeks before the north side" Such are the demands of competition.

OTHER GROWERS

On a frosty, wind-swept site near Dunblane, Stirlingshire, at 250m above sea level, Evelyn Stevens has created a garden with the emphasis on the creation of shelter belts and specimen trees and shrubs for both interest and visual effect. But her main claim to fame must lie in her collection of meconopsis and snowdrops. She has thoroughly investigated the nomenclature of *Meconopsis grandis* cultivars, especially the many forms travelling under the name 'GS600' and has amassed a collection of them in the hopes of bringing some order out of chaos. She has named a fine *M.* x *sheldonii* 'Jimmy Bayne', after the builder who gave it to her from his garden and has also brought some order to the naming of the various fertile cultivars related to *M.* x *sheldonii* which abound in the nursery trade. Another meconopsis Dr Stevens has been successful with is *M. punicea* which she has propagated and from which she has obtained seed so that it is now well established in cultivation.

Jean Wyllie of Dunblane inherited the perennial problem of distinguishing between the seed of *Lewisia nevadensis* and *L. brachycalyx*, when she became Manager of the Seed Exchange after Joyce Halley but since she is, herself, an enthusiastic grower of lewisias, which she exhibits at the Shows, she was able to sort out this problem by reference to her own plants.

§ CHAPTER 5 §

Alpine Nurseries and Gardens

NURSERIES

We have already made some mention of the long established nurseries like Inshriach, Edrom and Glendoick but we also have to make a few general comments on the history of alpine nurseries in Scotland. Without the support of nurserymen who specialise in the sale of alpine and rock plants rock gardening would not have developed the way it has. All rock gardeners will tell you of the hundreds of plants they have killed and of the need to re-stock from time to time. The plant stalls at the Shows illustrate the great demand for alpines, particularly those that are rare in cultivation or difficult to grow. Many alpines, like primulas for example, are inherently short lived and must be periodically raised from seed. Elsewhere in this book we have described the role of plant collectors in obtaining fresh stocks of plants for our gardens. Very often it is the alpine nursery which bulks up the new introductions and makes them available to the public. Only relatively few rock gardeners subscribed to the 1990 ACE expeditions to China but plants from the expeditions became widely available through the trade shortly thereafter.

In the early years of the 20th century few people had cars so there was a great postal trade in plants, for which small alpines were especially suitable. Jack Drake's nursery, for example, at the relatively isolated location of Aviemore, relied heavily on the postal trade. Shows provided another outlet for nurseries but they were few and far between and did not generate much revenue. Later, when more people had cars, the remoteness of a nursery was a secondary consideration for the enthusiast and so the postal trade diminished, especially with the increasing cost of postage, although it was still important. Alpine nurseries were never at any time exactly gold mines but there were relatively few of them and, with the great increase in interest in rock gardening from the 1930s onwards, most nurseries did fairly well. Up until the early 1980s the alpine nursery trade was mainly in the hands of full-time growers who relied entirely on the business for their livelihood and were able to employ staff, especially during the packing season. However, from then onwards there was a trend for people in a full-time job to produce a few alpines for sale in their spare time. This led, for example, to innovations like the SRGC 50/50 scheme in which people who sold plants at Shows could keep half the proceeds and devote the rest to the Club. Often such small scale initiatives led to early retirement and the investment of lump sums in a nursery business with the hope it would make a profit but without the need to rely on it entirely as a source of income. The proliferation of small nurseries in the 80s and 90s led to increased competition at the Shows and reduced profit all round, in contrast to the early years when there was only a single nursery at Shows.

The advent of the large Garden Centres in the 1990s (Figs.10 and 11), with meals, playparks for children, stalls for bric-a-brac etc meant that people increasingly bought their plants at such centres just as they bought their groceries at Supermarkets rather than the local shop. As a result the full-time alpine nurseries found it more of a struggle to make a living. Customers were loathe to spend an adequate amount on a plant which might have taken years to reach a saleable size. For, example, in 1939 Edrom Nursery was advertising *Primula edgeworthii* at 7/6 (or 37½p) per plant while, by the end of the century, a nursery was only able to charge £2 or so, hardly in line with inflation. The large Garden Centres generally do not propagate plants but buy them in wholesale so a few large wholesale firms appeared on the scene to supply them. By the end of the century the Dutch plant industry, based on a widespread co-operative system, was beginning to propagate alpines on a scale with which Scottish nurserymen could not compete.

EARLY NURSERIES

The specialist alpine nursery did not really appear until the 1930s. Before then rock plants were sold by general nurserymen but the advent of the AGS and then the SRGC undoubtedly provided an impetus for increased trade. Edrom Nursery in Berwickshire was established in 1936, advertised in the AGS and SRGC Journals and set up stands at the major flower shows such as those of the Royal Caledonian Horticultural Society in the Waverley Market, Edinburgh. Edrom was followed by Jack Drake at Inshriach, a nursery which sold itself in 1939 as a 'new nursery in the Highlands' and has traded successfully ever since. The early adverts from Jack Drake are interesting in their special offers of rare plants such as '*Dianthus arboreus* (true) for 2/- for one month only or until stocks run out'. One infers that stocks soon did so. Another nursery was that of Aberchalder gardens on the shores of Loch Ness which offered in 1939 in the AGS Bulletin 'Hardy surplus plants from a Highland Garden'. They continued in business until the 1970s but then disappeared as a nursery. They were unusual in that the nursery was just an adjunct to a magnificent wild garden, full of primulas, meconopsis and gentians. The surplus was planted out in a field and customers went round with the Head Gardener who dug up huge clumps and dumped them in a trug. Aberchalder was well off the beaten track and it was surprising that any customers actually found it. There is a story, from the time when Captain Bethel owned it in the 1960s, of a customer who asked the gardener whether they were kept busy. "Michty me" said he, "We're real busy. There's hardly a day goes by but someone doesn't come in".

Before World War II the SRGC Journal was full of adverts from firms such as Bannatyne and Jackson, offering rock plants in any quantity, Dobbie & Co. of Edinburgh who offered to construct rock gardens and Donald

Wintergill of Thornliebank, Glasgow who sold a wide range of alpines. After the War, prominent among the several alpine nurseries which appeared, were the Castlefield Nurseries at Kippen, near Stirling, run by Miss Jenny and Miss Helen Clark. The Clark Memorial Lecture, which is given annually at the AGM of the SRGC, was set up in memory of Miss Jenny who, besides running the nursery, was a staunch supporter of the SRGC. This nursery was later taken over by Miss Mary Guthrie Smith but no longer trades. Mrs J. Laing ran a nursery at Hawick from 1938 to 1953, trading in primulas, gentians, hepaticas and lithospermums but this has now disappeared. One post-war nursery which has survived until the end of the century is that of J.R. Aitken of Perth who advertised the complete design and layout of alpine gardens. An excellent photographer, he delighted many SRGC meetings with his wonderful accounts of Scottish native alpines of which he had a real fund of knowledge. Among the adverts of those days were those of Grants of West Calder, Midlothian, who could supply any kind of peat, sand and gravel as well as composts which were widely used.

Other notable post-war nurseries included J. R. Ponton of Kirknewton and later of Earlston who regularly had stands at the Shows, Miss Izat of Grovemount Nursery at Auchterarder, Lt. Col. Stitt of Blairgowrie, who specialised in gentians, and the Lyles of Maryfield Nursery in Fife, also gentian specialists, and King & Paton of Dalbeattie who sold a wide range of alpines. Mary McMurtrie appeared in the early 1960s at Balbithan with her double primulas and old laced pinks while Jim Archibald was advertising rare South African bulbs for sale. Sadly most of these nurseries have disappeared.

Although alpine nurseries came and went over the years several have survived and are still going strong into the 21st century. This is particularly true of Glendoick Nursery which has followed the trend and has developed into one of the foremost garden centres in Scotland, complete with the obligatory tea-room, and an unsurpassed reputation for rhododendrons. The 1980s saw the start of Ardfearn Nursery near Inverness where Jim and Alasdair Sutherland have developed a centre for rare alpines and where they do all their own propagating. Their nursery is a prime example of a place where rock gardeners can stock up on rarities they have lost or on plants new to cultivation which the Sutherlands have raised. Their Show stands are always thronged with eager buyers. Jim Sutherland was a professional horticultural adviser who has collected in China and is therefore well equipped to run a nursery of this kind.

The early 1980s also saw the beginning of Christie's Nursery at Kirriemuir in Angus where Ian Christie and Ian Martin built up a large collection of interesting plants, especially autumn gentians of which they now look after the National Collection. A nursery such as this epitomises the problems of modest-sized retail nurseries not on main tourist trails which have to rely for their success upon the excellence and range of their products. Ian Christie is a well known lecturer and plantsman who has been on several

Himalayan expeditions. At the other end of the scale there is Tough Alpines at Tough near Alford, Aberdeenshire, where Fred and Monika Carrie produce huge numbers of alpines for the wholesale trade as well as running a retail outlet. The quality of their products has to match the strict requirements of their commercial customers. Their plants, growing in the rigorous climate of upper Aberdeenshire at a height of 330m, are clearly hardy but, like all alpine nurserymen, retail or wholesale, they are entirely dependent on the seasonal demand for their products. A poor spring can be a real blow to business which may not pick up again that year.

In addition to these nurseries there are many people who turn their hand to selling a few alpines, often species and cultivars not obtainable elsewhere. The growth of subscriber-seed collecting expeditions has meant that these growers can obtain interesting plants which they propagate for sale. It must be conceded that such part-timers are not particularly welcome in the commercial alpine nursery trade.

From this account we can conclude that, throughout the century, the specialist alpine nurserymen have provided a valuable service for rock gardeners who really would be rather lost without them. At the end of World War II the AGS and the SRGC appealed to gardeners to stock up with alpine plants so that nurseries could get back on their feet. At the end of the century growers need reminding to support the nurseries to ensure that a full range of alpine plants continues to be available to gardeners. Garden Centres may be good value but, with very few exceptions, they do not supply the range of plants which gardeners seek.

THE ROCK GARDEN AT THE RBGE
Before considering the history of the rock garden at the Royal Botanic Garden, Edinurgh it is worth glancing at the history of the parent body. The garden can be said to have begun in 1670 when Dr Robert Sibbald and his friend Dr Andrew Balfour started to cultivate medicinal plants on a small plot of land 40 x 40ft at Holyrood in Edinburgh. The garden can therefore claim to be the second oldest Botanic Garden in Britain after Oxford which was founded in 1621. The small plot of land at Holyrood soon became too small so Sibbald and Balfour obtained a lease of the garden attached to Trinity Hospital, a site now occupied by the east end of Waverley Station.

Both the gardens were placed in the charge of James Sutherland, a young man of whose origins nothing much seems to be known but who was described as "a youth who by his owne industry had obtained great knowledge of the plants and of the medals". Whatever his antecedents he soon rose to eminence, publishing Hortus Medicus Edinburgensis in 1683, a list of plants in the Physic Garden, appointed Professor of Botany in 1695, King's Botanist in 1699 and Regius Professor of Botany in 1710. Sadly he died in 1719 more interested in medals and coins than in the Physic Garden.

No great progress was made in the Physic Garden until John Hope was appointed Regius Keeper in 1761. He successfully united the Town Garden with the Royal Garden and transferred it to a two hectare site on the road to Leith where Haddington Place now stands. Further progress had to wait until William McNab was persuaded to come from Kew to Edinburgh in 1810 as Principal Gardener at a salary of £50 per year. He, and Robert Graham, who was appointed Regius Keeper in 1820, were instrumental in moving the garden to its present site at Inverleith. The operation took more than three years to complete. McNab invented a transplanting machine which allowed large trees to be moved successfully, including specimens as large as a 43ft tall *Alnus glutinosa*.

John Hutton Balfour succeeded Graham in 1845 and soon expanded the garden to an area of more than 28ha. His son Isaac Bayley Balfour, whom we have met in the opening pages of this book, was appointed in 1888 and immediately set about improving the outdated gardens, the laboratories and administration quarters. In 1889 the garden came wholly under the Crown and Edinburgh became a major centre of taxonomic research particularly in relation to the Sino-Himalayan region. As we have already noted the steady flow of new species from the Far East has been a major aspect of research down to the present day. In 1922 William Wright Smith was appointed Regius Keeper and maintained the research orientation. He also developed the garden, where the woodland and copse took on much of their present form while the rock garden was enlarged and the heath and peat gardens were constructed.

With the death of Smith in 1956 the posts of Regius Keeper and Professor of Botany, which had been joined for nearly 200 years, were separated. Harold Fletcher was appointed Regius Keeper in 1956 and research continued on much the same lines. Important developments took place in the 1960s with the opening of a large new herbarium in 1964 and a whole range of new glasshouse in 1967. The new herbarium was needed to cope with the greatly increased investigations of overseas floras, particularly in the Middle East and Far East. Fletcher was succeeded by Douglas Henderson followed by John McNeil, David Ingram and then, right at the end of the century, Stephen Blackmore. By the year 2000, funding which had been entirely the responsibility of Government, had increasingly to be raised from other sources, such as the research councils and businesses. Joint initiatives such as the Dawson Chinese Garden were becoming increasingly important.

THE PRESENT ROCK GARDEN
The rock garden at Edinburgh covers an area of rather more than one hectare. It is one of the largest in the world and is rightly famed for its size, design, quality of upkeep and range of plants. Naturally it was developed over a period of many years and was reconstructed several times. The first rock garden was constructed by James McNab, eldest son of William McNab, in

1871 but with a layout (Fig.2) quite alien to modern tastes. McNab used squared masonry from a dismantled building and boasted about the many hundreds of little compartments he had constructed with the stones set vertically on edge. In spite of his enthusiasm he came in for much criticism particularly when Bayley Balfour took over. The fuse for Balfour's reconstruction appears to have been lit when Reginald Farrer paid a visit in 1907 and described it as a 'Devil's Lapful'. He went on to say "The plan is simplicity itself. You take a hundred or a thousand cart loads of bald square-faced boulders. You next drop them all about absolutely anyhow, and then you plant things amongst them. The chaotic hideousness of the result is something to be remembered with shudders ever after".

Whether stung by these remarks or not Balfour personally supervised the tearing apart of the old rock garden and saw to a reconstruction using hundreds of tonnes of bold lumps of conglomerate from the Callander area of Perthshire 120km away and also red sandstone from Dumfries 80km away. The new rock garden, which is basically the same as the one we see today (Fig.12), was completed in 1914. It was highly praised by Henri Correvon, the Swiss expert on the cultivation of alpine plants, who exclaimed "Words fail me to express my enthusiasm. Everything is flourishing to an extent I have never found elsewhere. Professor Balfour is an enthusiast and loves plants in a way I have seldom seen ".

Neither type of stone was ideal for building because the bedding planes of the sandstone slabs were much too narrow so that some of the rocks had to be placed on edge. When laid flat they looked just like stone steps and many were used to serve that purpose. The pieces of conglomerate had been obtained by blasting and still bore the drill marks so that it was impossible to lay the rocks along natural lines of strata. It was certainly not possible to build a natural rock garden of the kind envisaged by Simons-Jeune in his classic book 'Natural Rock Gardening' published in 1933 although, with the passage of time, as soil was replaced to improve fertility, attempts were made to realign the blocks in a more natural way. A further disadvantage was that the rocks were too hard for plant roots to penetrate. Despite these limitations the one hectare rock garden was built and soon planted up with an impressive collection of plants. Because the soil in the garden is acid it suited many of the new plants being introduced from the Sino-Himalayan region such as rhododendrons, gentians and primulas but since lime was not applied lime-tolerant species were not so successful.

Good drainage was achieved by skilful orientation of the rocks which provided a cool root run and reflected heat for the benefit of sun-loving species. As Alf Evans, an Assistant Curator in charge of the rock garden, observed in an article in the SRGC Journal in 1976 "Rocky summits, crevices, cracks and ledges are used to hold some species, open sites, south-facing slopes, dry situations and well drained places cater for others, while north-facing rock work furnishes shade, coolness and moisture, essential to the well-being of still more. Sub-arctic plants, high mountain species, pasture plants, dwarf denizens of woodland and shade are in constant battle for survival and the staff at the garden are forever taking sides on the part of the suppressed".

In 1933 a north-facing moraine was constructed across an area of lawn with few rocks but superlative drainage. This feature has been hugely successful and has allowed many rock plants such as kabschia saxifrages to thrive in the gravel bed at the west end of the rock garden. But one has to concede that by today's standard the rock garden as a whole is not especially beautiful although the addition of waterfalls and pools in recent years has helped greatly. There is still too much rock and not enough soil for many of the plants to be successful The introduction of spreading leguminous shrubs has helped to screen some of the more unsightly rocks.

The collection and layout of plants in the rock garden is an attempt to bridge the gap, some might say gulf, between aesthetic, horticultural considerations and botanical research. Space always imposes a limit on how many species can be grown. Even with Asiatic plants it is only possible to grow about 10% of the alpine plants from those regions. The labels on the plants bear testimony to the many plant hunters who have contributed to the collection and to the many parts of the world from which the plants have come. Attempts have been made to grow together plants of a single genus or from a particular part of the world. This is useful for the botanist but also conveys some inkling of taxonomy to the visitor. In the 1990s the Scottish Rare Plants Project was initiated to contribute to the preservation of Scotland's rare plants by cultivating them and, hopefully, propagating them for release into the wild. The aim is laudable and is having some success but it remains to be seen what impact it might have on the wild flora. It is ironic that many of Scotland's native alpines are very difficult to grow; an attempt to grow them in the RBGE rock garden in the 1970s was not a success. There has been some success with *Lychnis viscaria*, a rare plant from Holyrood Park in Edinburgh, which has been propagated and released back into the wild. One person who has had great success with growing Scottish native plants in the late 1990s has been Bill Paton of Aberdeen who has, in a small suburban plot, established more than 100 native flowering montane species and 50 non-flowering species. He has distributed plants to the Botanic Gardens at Edinburgh, St Andrews and Aberdeen and is renowned for his 'fish boxes' planted up with splendid collections of Scottish native plants.

Plants are not immortal and losses have to be replaced. At any one time there are probably around 5000 species growing in the rock garden, all of them recorded on computer with a unique number and, in the garden, with a permanent label if it has not been broken, misplaced or stolen. Theft can be a problem it is sad to say. Cynics have observed that the occasion of important conferences is when rare items are most at risk. This risk is not confined to Botanic Gardens but is something which the top growers of rare and unusual species have to be concerned about when on holiday.

THE PEAT GARDEN

As well as the rock garden there are two adjacent areas which merit attention — the peat garden and the heath garden. The former was constructed in 1939 to accommodate the many plants which like moist, acid conditions. It replaced the ill-fated 'rooteries' which consisted of old tree stumps partially buried beneath a peaty compost. Initially plants grew well but soon succumbed to honey fungus. The peat bed was copied from the one at Logan Garden in Wigtonshire created by the McDouall brothers and has since been adopted all over the world. It was built by using irregularly shaped turves from the top layer of a peat deposit, open and spongy in texture and light brown in colour with a pH of about 4. The plants in this peat bed are mainly dwarf rhododendrons and other ericaceous shrubs such as cassiopes and phyllodoces, autumn gentians, dwarf primulas, trilliums, schizocodons and shortias. The peat garden has undoubtedly been a success but it does need a fair amount of irrigation in summer in Edinburgh while wet seasons encourage the growth of liverworts and polytrichum moss which can be difficult to eradicate. Many growers in wet areas of western Scotland such as the Stones have abandoned peat blocks because of the moss problem.

THE HEATH GARDEN

William McNab in the 1830s had established a splendid collection of South African heaths and had devoted a whole glasshouse to their successful cultivation. By the 1930s they were entirely out of favour, a salutary reminder that there are fashions in botanic as well as private gardens, with obvious problems for conservation. But hardy heaths were becoming popular, especially European species so about 1935 a heath garden was constructed at the east end of the rock garden where most of the European species of *Erica* and *Calluna* and their many cultivars were grown along with dwarf junipers, pernettyas, brooms and small bulbs such as crocus and squills. The heath garden soon became one of the most popular parts of the whole garden. By the end of the 20th century, however, the heath garden had only a limited range of plants and was becoming overgrown with perennial weeds so, in 1997, all the plants were taken out and the whole site reconstructed. The plan was to create the semblance of a Scottish moorland with a ruined croft, — an addition of dubious merit — lochan and peat bogs and to have it ready for the International Rock Garden Conference in 2001. It is to be hoped that no problems are encountered with 'heather sickness' which has affected many heather gardens elsewhere, notably at Ness Garden near Liverpool.

THE ALPINE HOUSE

Following the erection of the new range of glasshouses in 1967 an alpine house was built in the early 1970s (Figs.14 and 15) to house those alpines which did not require heat but needed dry conditions in winter. A constant electric fan ensures a steady flow of air which is of great value in suppressing the incidence of fungal moulds. When the alpine house was opened Harold Esslemont presented the RBGE with a magnificent pan of *Draba mollissima* fully 25 cm across and a winner at many shows. At the end of the century this plant was still going strong although no longer on public display. The Alpine House is a never failing source of interest and delight, especially now that so many new species are appearing in the plunge beds.

THE SPECIALIST GARDENS

In addition to the main site at Inverleith, RBGE has three Specialist Gardens at Dawyck, Benmore and Logan, especially suited for species which are not at their best at Inverleith.

Dawyck

Dawyck Garden near Peebles has been an arboretum since the late 17th century when the Veitch family introduced a variety of exotic species of trees. Successive introductions and plantings by the Naesmyth family established the overall design of the garden. The enthusiasm of Sir John Murray Naesmyth in the 19th century led him to subscribe to many plant hunting expeditions, notably those of David Douglas who sent back many fine conifers. From 1897 the estate became the property of F.R.S. Balfour who extended the collection In 1978 his son Colonel Alastair Balfour gifted the policies to the nation to become part of the Royal Botanic Garden. The garden consists of 24ha along the Scrape Burn rising to about 190m giving it an almost continental climate with moderate rainfall and cold winters. There is no rock garden as such but there are many shrubs introduced by E.H. Wilson from China including many fine rhododendrons. There are also drifts of meconopsis, a berberis collection and a collection of rare Scottish plants.

Benmore

The Younger Botanic garden at Benmore in Argyll north of Dunoon takes its name from the mountain Beinn Mhor and from Harry George Younger who gave the estate to the nation in 1925. In 1929 the policies about the mansion house became part of the RBGE. The garden extends over the mountain's southern spur. With abundant rainfall of over 2500mm a year and its acid soil the garden provides ideal conditions for plants used to a wet climate, especially Asiatic species like rhododendrons. The garden is used for ecological plantings of Bhutanese plants. Although there are extensive plantings of Himalayan primulas and meconopsis there is no rock garden in the strict sense.

Logan

Logan Garden in Wigtownshire was transformed into a haven for exotic species in the 1870s by James and Agnes McDouall whose sons Kenneth and Douglas continued as keen gardeners and introduced many plants from the great plant hunters such as Forrest and Farrer. In 1969 the walled garden and some of the woodland amounting to 10ha were gifted to the nation by the Trustees of the late R. Olaf Hambro and became part of RBGE.

With the sea not far away the influence of the Gulf Stream allows Logan to enjoy an almost sub-tropical climate. Plants from warm temperate regions of the world which elsewhere would need glasshouse protection can flourish outside. More than 40% of the plants in the garden derive from the Southern Hemisphere. There is a splendid rock gully with a range of alpines largely from New Zealand, with celmisias predominant. The famous peat garden constructed by the McDouall brothers was reconstructed by the RBG according to the original design. At Logan there is a great emphasis on material of known wild origin to serve as biological standards for research and conservation. Conifers from Tasmania, Florida and South America abound along with new plantings of the beautifully scented Maddenia rhododendrons. Recently collected material from South Africa, New Zealand and particularly Chile has been planted at Logan as part of the RBGE research programme.

PRIVATE GARDENS

There are a number of other gardens in Scotland which are or have been well known for their alpine plant collections. Most of the ones mentioned here are open to the public. Some are privately owned while others are owned and run by Institutions such as Universities or commercial firms. No doubt there are many others which are not open to the public and therefore largely escape notice.

Kildrummy Castle Gardens

This splendid garden is situated right beside the ruined Kildrummy Castle near Alford, Aberdeenshire. The 'New Castle', located across from the ruins, was built in 1900 by Col James Ogston, known locally as 'Soapy Ogston' because he owned a soap works in Aberdeen.

The garden was started about the same time in an old quarry from which the stone for the old castle had been taken. It was known as the Back Den of Kildrummy. A Japanese firm constructed the water garden while Messrs Backhouse of York sent David Peary for six months to lay the foundations of the garden up against the quarry face. The estate was sold in 1945 and the new castle let as Kildrummy Castle Hotel. The garden was offered to the Ministry of Works who declined it so, in 1968, a Charitable Trust was set up to run the garden and continues to do so.

The enchantment of the garden centres round the small burn which has formed pools and falls in the water garden where Asiatic primulas, skunk cabbages (*Lysichiton*) and *Gunnera* flourish. At an altitude of 300m and situated in a hollow the garden can experience severe frost so that many shrubs such as eucryphias suffer but *Pieris formosa* var. *forrestii* does well while the *Embothrium coccineum* 'Norquinco Valley Form' at the side of the picturesque bridge, which is a copy of the Brig o' Balgownie in Old Aberdeen, makes an exceptional specimen, flowering in great profusion most years unless the frost has been too severe. The quarry has proved a good home for many alpines but the temperatures have proved too low for many species so it is now planted in large measure with dwarf rhododendrons and acers which produce a fine backdrop to the sunken garden.

St Andrews Botanic Garden

This seven hectare garden was originally owned by the University of St. Andrews. In the 1970s Bob Mitchell was the Curator and he constructed, with loving care and an eye for imaginative design, a rock and water garden equal to any in Scotland. Asiatic primulas, meconopsis and dwarf rhododendrons flourish by the stream side. There is also a landscaped glass area for alpines. Nowadays hard pressed Universities are unwilling to spend money on gardens like this so that they risk falling into disrepair. However, fortunately Fife County Council took it over and restored it to its former glory.

Crarae Gardens

This is one of the finest woodland gardens in Scotland which was started in the steep glen of the Crarae Burn on the shores of Loch Fyne in Argyll as long ago as 1904 when Sir Archie Campbell, the 5th Baronet, started the garden round the house, largely with a collection of plants from Reginald Farrer who was a nephew of Sir Archie's wife. In 1925 Sir George Campbell began planting the present glen garden with primulas, magnolias, meconopsis, rhododendrons, a variety of shrubs and a very wide range of trees, especially with more than 20 species of eucalyptus. The garden is really exciting in spring when the primulas and rhododendrons are at their best and then again in autumn when the colour is quite spectacular. The deep glen provides a dramatic setting for this rich collection. It is difficult to avoid superlatives when referring to Crarae. The present Laird, Sir Islay Campbell, maintains the garden in first rate condition almost single-handed with only the assistance of part-time labour.

Cherrybank Garden

The Bell's Cherrybank Garden on the outskirts of Perth was constructed as a heather garden from scratch in the 1980s on the seven hectare grounds of United Distillers. It now is home to some 30,000 plants of 750 cultivars planted in groups of 40 per cultivar, beautifully laid out to a design by Unel Uddleston. The garden now contains the National Collection of *Erica*. One of the most notable cultivars is *Erica carnea* 'Bell's Extra Special' with gold foliage and light heliotrope flowers.

An Cala

The garden of An Cala, on the windswept Isle of Shiel, in Argyll was established by Col Arthur Murray, later Lord Elibank, in the 1920s on what was old, rough sheep pasture on bedrock through which a thin soil from a former raised bed protruded. Hundreds of tons of top soil were brought in by coal puffers as ballast with Lakeland Nurseries of Kendal as contractors. By 1937 there were beautiful striped lawns leading down past rock terraces to a dammed pool with waterfalls tumbling through clefts in the surrounding rocks planted with rhododendrons. The name 'An Cala' in Gaelic means 'haven', an appropriate name for such an oasis of peace.

Kittock Mill
This garden at Carmunnock houses the National Collection of hostas with over 400 cultivars. The owner, Pat Jordan, started the garden in the early 80s and now specialises in the plantaginea types from China with perfumed flowers, including those bred by Mildred Secker and the late Eric Smith. She has also many of the fortunei types which form large clumps with strong, sturdy stems admirably suited for flower arranging. The collection thrives in spite of the fact that hostas do not like cold wet winters and are especially prone to attack by slugs and snails.

Torosay Castle
In 1899 Walter Guthrie and Sir Robert Lorimer connected Torosay Castle on the Isle of Mull with the garden by three descending formal Italianate Terraces. To the west of the terraces was built a water garden which was restored in the 1960s by Col. Miller. The interesting rock garden was restored by Jacquetta James. In addition a Japanese Garden was created in 1980, opening up vistas of Loch Linne to Ben Nevis 60km away. With a mild climate many tender shrubs such as *Embothrium*, *Crinodendron* and *Eucryphia* thrive. In the 1990s the terraces below the house and the woodland and bog gardens were extensively redeveloped by Mike Swift, the head gardener, who had been responsible for propagating *Meconopsis* x *sheldonii* 'Lingholm Strain' and who brought plants of the strain to Torosay when he moved from Lingholm.

Kilmory Castle
The gardens at Kilmory Castle at Lochgilphead in Argyll had been neglected until Argyll & Bute District Council took over the 12ha around the castle. The great garden of Kilmory was started as long ago as 1770 with many different rhododendrons. The garden supplied plants for Kew and contained a collection of hardy ferns and alpines which were said to rank along with the collections in the Royal Botanic Garden, Edinburgh as among the finest in Britain. The reconstruction has focused on the restoration of the herbaceous borders and the rock and water gardens.

Stonefield Castle Hotel
The house at Stonefield was built by Sir William Playfair in 1837 on a promontory beside Loch Fyne. It does not have a rock garden but is

nevertheless of interest because many of the rhododendrons are as much as 150 years old and were raised from seed collected Sir Joseph Hooker during his pioneering expeditions to Sikkim in 1850.

Cruickshank Botanic Garden
This garden in Old Aberdeen is partly funded by the University of Aberdeen, partly by the Cruickshank Botanic Garden Trust and is also supported by The Friends of the Cruickshank Botanic Garden. It was founded in 1898 by the bequest of Miss Anne Cruickshank whose father had been Professor of Mathematics in the University. The garden of four hectares is on a light, sandy soil, less than two kilometres from the North Sea and with a rainfall of about 750mm per year.
The first rock garden was constructed at the end of World War II by the head gardener, James Robb, under the guidance of Professor Matthews, the Professor of Botany and, as already noted, Honorary President of the SRGC for many years. They made use of an old sunken garden although it was never satisfactory so that it later became an alpine lawn and dwarf shrub area. In the 1960s a new rock garden was built using 250 tons of Old Red Sandstone. By 1970 through the hard work of the head gardener Fred Sutherland and his staff, it had become the home of an excellent collection of alpines of all sorts, especially bulbs. At one time it housed the National Collection of autumn gentians but the dry soil and low rainfall were not ideal so the collection was moved to the RBGE which in turn faced the same problems. The latest home for the collection is Christie's Nursery at Kirriemuir. At the Cruickshank, however, the dry conditions and long hours of summer sun are just what dwarf bulbs need. It is strange how such a wonderful garden, beautifully maintained by Bob Rutherford and his small staff, is relatively unknown even within the city boundary.

Mount Stewart Gardens
The gardens of Mount Stuart at Rothesay on the Isle of Bute date back as far as 1717 when the 2nd Earl of Bute ordered plants from William Miller, the Quaker seedsman at Holyrood Palace. A survey of the 120ha of garden in 1759 showed parterres, a bowling green, a kitchen garden and a lime tree avenue in different parts of the garden. By the 20th century the gardens were divided into four main areas: Kitchen garden, Rock garden, the Wee garden and the Policies. The one hectare rock garden was designed at the turn of the century by Thomas Mawson and greatly developed after World War II by Eileen, wife of the 5th Marquess of Bute and later by Jennifer, wife of the 6th Marquess. The rock work is enhanced by tumbling water from a burn almost two kilometres away. The emphasis in the garden is on Asiatic species of which Jennifer has collected over 1500 species and cultivars, including many primulas, meconopsis and rhododendrons. The Wee garden, which is located in the mildest part of the garden, is chiefly devoted to plants from the

Southern Hemisphere, landscaped by Thomas Mawson with paths, waterfalls and pools.

As well as the gardens mentioned above, Scotland is rich in gardens which the public can visit but which generally do not have specialised rock gardens. The emphasis tends to be on woodland policies with rhododendrons and other shrubs which are well sited to the mild, moist climate of much of the country, especially the north and west but it is interesting that here are a number of east coast gardens which are able to cope with the relatively low rainfall.

GARDENS OF THE NATIONAL TRUST FOR SCOTLAND

The National Trust for Scotland (NTS) was set up in 1931. Since then it has acquired or now administers more than 100 properties. In addition more than 40,000ha of countryside are in the care of the Trust comprising farms, forests, mountains, moorland, waterfalls, islands, cliffs, and, of course, many beautiful gardens. Not all the properties run by the Trust have gardens but many do and these have been sensitively developed over the years in an attempt to recreate or maintain the aims of the people who originally planted them. Most of the gardens are large and were often initially planted up as wild rather than formal gardens. Thus shrub gardens abound, often full of rhododendrons, but deliberately designed rock gardens are conspicuous by their almost complete absence. It would not be Trust policy to design such a garden on a site where there was not one when the garden was handed over.

It is not intended to describe Trust gardens in any detail but merely to mention those which have some form of rock garden, whether as a natural feature or man-made, as well as those wild gardens containing species which have traditionally fallen within the interests of the SRGC such as meconopsis, gentians, primulas and dwarf rhododendrons.

Inverewe
Of all the gardens of the Trust, that at Inverewe, in what used to be called Wester Ross, is probably the most famous. The founder, Osgood Mackenzie, bought the estate in 1862 and immediately started to develop the bleak headland into a sheltered garden full of exotic species. He carried out this task until he died in 1922 when his daughter, Mrs Mairi Sawyer, continued the work. In 1952, a year before she died, she handed it over to the Trust together with an endowment for its upkeep. Since then the gardens have been developed largely under the guidance of two ex-members of staff of the Royal Botanic Garden, Edinburgh, Dr McQueen Cowan, ex Assistant Regius Keeper and Professor Douglas Henderson, ex Regius Keeper, so that by the end of the century there are well over 2500 different species of flowering plant in te collection.

The site at first hardly looked an inviting place to start a garden, since it was windswept with an acid peaty soil but Mackenzie realised that the Gulf

Stream provided the necessary warmth and absence of frosts to grow a wide range of plants many of which could only be grown under glass even at places like Kew. Because of the dearth of decent soil he had to import innumerable creels of topsoil to make pockets in which to plant. Windbreaks were an immediate need so Mackenzie planted dense belts of Corsican and Scots pine on the outside with thick hedges of *Rhododendron ponticum* throughout the garden. Mrs Sawyer agreed, in her fascinating account of the garden written in 1953, that the rhododendron was a mistake on account of its aggressive spread and that it would have been better to have planted more of species like *Griselinia littoralis* and *Escallonia macrantha*.

Mackenzie built a large rock garden below the house in what was a fairly exposed spot which he planted up with dwarf phlox, campanulas, lewisias, saxifrages and gentians among others. In later years there has been quite an emphasis on New Zealand species which thrive here. The Chatham Island forget-me-not, *Myosotidium hortensia*, does well and always attracts visitors in spring; celmisias also flourish. The Torridonian Sandstone on which the garden is situated is easily broken up so that rock plants can send their roots down into the rocky substrate and benefit from the perfect drainage they need. West of the formal rock garden is Creag a Lios, a natural rock garden which contains a wide range of species which prefer some shade and plenty of moisture. They include ourisias which grow well here; a delicate pink hybrid between *Ourisia coccinea* and *O. macrophylla* called 'Loch Ewe' was raised at Inverewe and is widely grown.

Just north of Creag a Lios are peat banks and a pond where the masses of candelabra primulas give a breath-taking display of riotous colour in late spring. These primulas have hybridised to a great extent over the years so now there is an immense range of colour and form. One called 'Inverewe' is especially attractive and has been in the trade for many years. In these damp, shaded areas the meconopsis produce huge, blue blooms on tall stalks in early summer, complementing the azaleas which are also in flower. And there we must leave Inverewe which is one of the show pieces of the north west.

Branklyn
John and Dorothy Renton built Branklyn House in 1922 and from then until John Renton's death in 1967, his wife having died the previous year, they built up his one hectare garden into one of Scotland's finest. In 1967 it was bequeathed to the Trust. We have already written about the Rentons as growers so we can confine our attention to particular features of the garden. Among the notable features of Branklyn are the scree beds built by the Rentons to the recipe of Reginald Farrer consisting of five parts of River Tay gravel to one part of leaf soil loam with a surface of stone chips, a rather spartan mixture but one which supported many alpines. Among the choicer scree plants the difficult *Paraquilegia anemonoides* and *Stellera chamaejasme* grew happily outside with only a pane of glass over them

during winter. They always maintained it was easier to grow them that way than in a pot in a cold greenhouse. Among herbaceous plants Branklyn was famous for the collection of meconopsis including *Meconopsis grandis* 'Branklyn', *MM betonicifolia*, x *sheldonii*, *quintuplinervia*, *dhwojii*, *integrifolia*, *aculeata*, *horridula*, *napaulensis* and *regia*.

With the addition of leaf mould and peat many primulas were grown by the Rentons including ten species of petiolarids. They even managed *P. forrestii* outside under a cloche. Altogether about 120 species of *Primula* were grown. Branklyn was and still is noted for its North American plants, including trilliums, of which seven species were grown by the Rentons together with kalmias, sanguinarias, lysichitons, erythroniums and aquilegias. The garden is especially suited to lilies and other members of the same family. Although it contains thousands of plants Branklyn never seems crowded. The Trust is to be congratulated on maintaining the spirit of the garden as the Rentons would have wished. Successive overseers such as Stewart Annan, Robert Mitchell and David Tattersfield must be credited with doing just that.

Leith Hall

The last male representative of the Leith Hay family, which dates back to 1789, died in action in September 1939. The Hall, in Aberdeenshire, together with 500ha of farm, woodland and garden was presented to the Trust in 1945. The grounds are full of old and interesting trees while the garden, which is largely enclosed, contains a variety of shrubs and herbaceous plants. Of particular interest is the rock garden which was designed and built by the late Charles Edward Norman Leith Hay. It is situated on a natural slope with a stream but had been neglected for many years until, in 1985, Eric Robson, the Trust's then Garden Adviser, approached the Aberdeen Group of the SRGC with a request for advice. The Group agreed, as part of the Club's Jubilee Celebrations, to assist with reconstructing and restocking the rock garden. They assembled an interesting collection of hardy, rock plants from members and then planted them out. The result was a colourful display of dwarf alpines (Fig.13) which has continued to thrive ever since and has been a regular visitor attraction. The western side of the garden was reopened in 1991, after being completely smothered in weeds and shrub, to provide a site for a collection of ferns and other shade-living plants.

Crathes Castle

The Burnetts lived in Crathes Castle near Banchory, Aberdeenshire, for over 350 years until in 1952 the 13th Baronet made over the Castle and part of the estate to the Trust. The style of the garden is rather more English than Scottish, due to the influence of William Robinson and Gertrude Jekyll, at the end of the nineteenth century, in creating a more informal style than hitherto. Gertrude Jekyll visited Crathes about 1895 when she was greatly impressed by the "brilliancy of the colour masses" as well as the size and quality of the gooseberries. But it was not until 1926 that Sir James and Lady Sybil Burnett of Leys began to develop the garden into the outstanding horticultural showpiece it is today.

There are eight individual gardens within the two hectares of the walled garden at Crathes. The soil is an excellent loam and slightly acid with a rainfall of about 750mm. Although it is 25km inland from Aberdeen and could be expected to suffer from severe frosts many plants such as eucryphias grow happily at Crathes within the shelter of the walls. Every effort is made to keep the garden very much as Sybil Burnett planned it in the 1930s as an informal garden full of shrubs and herbaceous perennials. There is no rock garden as such but a number of plants of interest to rock gardeners are scattered about the garden. There is a good collection of dwarf rhododendrons near the Doocot while a number of meconopsis and candelabra primulas grow in the herbaceous borders.

Brodick Castle

Brodick Castle Garden on the Island of Arran in Bute is like Inverewe since it enjoys a mild, moist climate which suits many Asiatic plants to perfection. The 25ha garden was started in 1923 by the Duchess of Hamilton who quickly established a large collection of plants from the Himalayas, China and Chile, principally rhododendrons, so it now ranks among the finest rhododendron gardens to be found anywhere in the world. The large-leaved *Rhododendron falconeri* and *R. sino-grande* thrive in a way which would be impossible in the east of Scotland. The collection of camellias is also quite outstanding. Like Crathes it does not have a rock garden but there are many rocky outcrops where dwarf rhododendrons are at home while candelabra primulas and meconopsis abound about the various streams and ponds, but it is not a garden where one looks for rare or difficult alpines. The formal garden dates from 1710 and has now been restored as a Victorian garden but it holds little of interest to the rock gardener.

Brodick Castle provides a home for the Horlick collection of rhododendrons which was created by Sir James Horlick on the island of Gigha off the coast of Kintyre in Argyll. On this exposed, little island he devised a system of windbreaks which enabled him to plant up 20ha of shrubs, mostly rhododendrons. On his death he left the collection at Gigha to the Trust who propagated material for growing at other Trust properties, especially Brodick.

Arduaine

In 1897 James Campbell bought Asknish Farm on Loch Melfort south of Oban in Aryll and immediately named it Arduaine from the Gaelic Ard (headland) and Uaine (green). In 1903 he and his wife started the garden in a sheltered spot on the windy headland, having learnt a lot from their friend

Osgood Mackenzie of Inverewe. Their first move was to plant 2,000 Japanese larch seedlings to provide protection. In 1905 they built the imposing Arduaine House overlooking Loch Melfort. James Campbell planted many of the trees which are mature today and after he died his son Bruce continued the work. But after the War it was a struggle to maintain the eight hectare garden with a greatly reduced labour force. Severe gales added to the problems by bringing down many of the large trees, while the house had been sold to become a hotel. Happily in 1971 the brothers Edmund and Harry Wright from Essex bought the garden and set about restoring it. They renovated the paths and borders and soon built up the rhododendron collection for which the garden is now famous. By the 1990s the garden was in prime condition and, to safeguard its future, the Wrights handed it over in 1991 to the Trust which accepted it for its plant collection and its aesthetic quality. Some unfortunate dissension between the former owners and the Trust ensued but the maintenance of the garden continued.

For the rock gardener Arduaine is worth visiting for its splendid collection of dwarf rhododendrons such as *R. degronianum* ssp. *yakushimanum* and its many hybrids. 'Miss Yule's Rockery' contains little of merit but the garden abounds in fine candelabra primulas, meconopsis and other moisture-loving species.

Threave
This garden in Dumfries and Galloway is yet another west coast garden where Himalayan plants thrive. The estate and gardens, now amounting to over 800ha were given to the Trust in 1948 by Major A. F. Gordon together with an endowment. There are extensive rocky out-crops where alpines flourish while the fine primulas and meconopsis are a special feature. The beds of the monocarpic species of the former such as *M. napaulensis* and *M. paniculata* and their hybrids make an imposing display in early summer. There are many perennials at Threave which were brought back from the Himalayas by Magnus Ramsay who collected extensively in the 1980s with Chris Chadwell. For example he brought back from Kashmir seed of the difficult *Incarvillea arguta* which grew for many years at Threave. In the spring there is a delightful display of more than 200 cultivars of daffodils. Brodie Castle at Forres in Inverness-shire, is another Trust garden with an excellent collection of daffodils, many of them bred by Brodie of Brodie himself.

Other Trust Gardens
The Trust has many other gardens of great interest to the discerning gardener but perhaps less so to the rock gardener than the ones mentioned above. They include Balmacara, Broughton House, Castle Fraser, Culross Palace, Falkland Palace, Fyvie Castle, Greenbank, Haddo House, The Hill House, Hill of Tarvit, House of Dun, Inveresk Lodge, Kellie Castle, Malleny, Pitmedden and Priorwood.

§ CHAPTER 6 §

Technical Advances and Conservation

ROCKS
At the beginning of the century the emphasis was very much on rock work, often to the detriment of the plants which at times seemed to be a secondary consideration. Even as late as 1930 this attitude was evident when, as already noted, at the inception of the AGS, there was a serious proposal that a section of the Society should be devoted to rock construction and also that the name should be the Rock Garden Society. In the days when a garden of any note employed at least one gardener there was no problem about installing massive stonework. Indeed most Flower Shows had separate categories for exhibitors who employed a gardener and those who did not.

Reginald Farrer at the turn of the century was one of the first people to ridicule the current random disposition of rocks and to advocate arranging them in a more natural way.

Farrer was quite adamant about how to proceed. Never use artificial stone nor architectural rubbish, nor granite, flint, slate or porphry but use your local stone provided it is of a suitable kind such as sandstone, limestone or whinstone. He enunciated the imperative building rules: use as few rocks as possible, bury them deeply in the ground, lay them on their broadest face and slope them steeply into the ground. He then laid down the rules for constructing screes and moraines, the latter with quite elaborate equipment for automatic watering.

By the time rock gardening began to take off in Scotland in the 1930s Farrer's detailed rules were largely forgotten and fairly simple natural designs such as that of the RBGE rock garden were being copied, although on a smaller scale. The larger Scottish estate gardens often had natural features which were turned into rock gardens but the average gardener had to make do with a small suburban garden and the use of a few local rocks. There was, however, still an emphasis on very free drainage and the formation of a natural appearance of which Farrer would have approved. Screes were much in fashion and usually consisted of a deep sump filled with Farrer's recipe of old bricks, clinkers and coke-blocks which he said was the "alpha and omega of success". By the end of the century Scottish rock gardens were generally modest affairs usually consisting of a few strategically placed rocks in the middle of a mound of well-drained compost and grit, but the majority of rock plants were now being grown in raised beds and troughs.

RAISED BEDS
Raised beds were known as far back as the 16th century, often to grow herbs, or on a grander scale to complement the architectural style of the adjacent

house, but it is only in the latter part of the 20th century that rock gardeners fully appreciated the splendid results which can be achieved by growing alpines in raised beds. There is now a huge literature on how to construct and maintain them but one of the best books is 'Growing Alpines in Raised Beds, Troughs and Tufa' by Duncan Lowe (1991). The principal merits of raised beds are accessibility to plants at a convenient height, growing conditions which provide good drainage and a good free root run for the plants. The aesthetic gain lies in the ability to look at and smell plants more easily in raised beds. The size of such beds can vary greatly, ranging from less than a metre to the length of one built by David and John Aitken in the 1980s in their garden near Aberdeen which was 36m long and 75cm high (Fig.9). They constructed it from granite setts from the old cobbled streets of Aberdeen. Whatever the size of a raised bed it should not be less than 25cm deep to allow sufficient root run and it should not be more than 1.5m wide so that one can reach across it comfortably. They can vary in size from small informal affairs with a few rocks, to elaborate slab-construction beds while winter protection can be achieved with something as simple as small panes of glass to elaborate pergola structures to keep out rain and snow.

TROUGHS
To the early rock gardeners old stone troughs, hewn from a boulder and often found lying around a farm steading, must have seemed ideal and inexpensive receptacles in which to grow their plants, provided they could be moved. Time has proved them right. They could provide a garden in miniature and did away with the need for a rock garden as such. By the end of World War II, however, such troughs were expensive and hard to come by. Whereas in the old days troughs were made slowly by hand, a job usually given to the apprentice, nowadays powerful, abrasive wheel cutters can do the job in a fraction of the time so stone troughs can still be made. However, not everyone has the ability to do this and such troughs are very heavy so, in the 1970s a way was found to make pseudo-troughs out of 'hyper-tufa', a mixture of cement, coarse sand and riddled moss peat which has the advantage of being much lighter than stone and just as good for growing plants. So today many troughs are made of hyper-tufa.

A later development, in the 1990s was the use of expanded polystyrene boxes, usually obtained from the fish trade, in the construction of troughs (Figs.16-19). However, they do look too much what they really are, fish boxes, unless treated with a coat of masonry paint. Ian Young of Aberdeen is credited with the idea of further enhancing their appearance by roughening the outside with a heatgun to give a very natural semblance of stone. Boxes of this sort rose to fame at the Scottish Garden Exhibition in 1998 when, as already noted, the SRGC won a Gold Medal for a display of them planted up with alpines.

TUFA

Tufa is not a rock but a mineral deposit which is formed by calcium-rich water emerging from the ground and depositing its calcium on the surface to form a hard sponge-like structure. When such deposits have accumulated in layers over centuries, they form a rock-like substance which can be cut up and into which plant roots can penetrate and absorb the various minerals present in the tufa. It is thus a self-contained growing medium which can be used in different ways, either using several blocks to form an outcrop or even a cliff as Roy Elliott has done so successfully. It is very light so it is easy to move the blocks around, use a single block as a garden feature or install several blocks in a trough. It is very useful in the alpine house; Harold Esslemont latterly grew most of his cushion plants in holes bored in a piece of tufa. Growth tended to be slow but it led to the production of a good, tight cushion. He also used for a time crushed tufa as a top dressing on his pots but stopped this when he discovered that the tufa held too much moisture around the neck of the plants. Most plants grow well enough in tufa other than lime-hating species, such as some Aretian androsaces which simply curl up and die. In the UK, tufa is only found in any quantity in a few places in the west of the country and is therefore expensive. The softer the tufa the easier it is to carve and bore holes in it but it tends to crumble quickly if left outside. Really hard tufa weathers slowly but is more difficult to work and plant roots can not penetrate so readily.

SOILS

At the beginning of the century gardeners had their own secret soil and fertiliser recipes for their plants so that the tyro gardener was often at a loss to know what to do and how to evaluate the various recipes on offer. These would refer to mixtures of loam, sand, peat, leaf mould, animal manure, limestone chips, grit, bonemeal, superphosphate, compound fertilisers, burnt clay and coke cinders. The real breakthrough was the development of simple reliable formulae at the John Innes Institute in the early 1930s. These replaced the chaotic mixtures with a combination of loam, sand, peat, lime and compound fertiliser. The three formulations, JI, JI2 and JI3, differing in nitrogen content, have been the basis for soil composts right up to the end of the century. Two drawbacks to the use of John Innes composts were the variable nature of 'loam' and the difficulty of obtaining a good quality version. Hence formulations which required only peat and sand, but no loam, were devised at the University of California in the 1950s and these have been used world-wide ever since. Such soilless composts have the advantage of being much lighter than loam-based composts but they require more care in watering and the supply of supplementary fertiliser.

Top rock gardeners are divided as to what type of compost to use and it appears that either loam based or soilless composts are excellent if properly handled. For growing ericaceous plants special JI composts were devised, omitting lime which is often replaced with sulphur. The question of lime and the growth of ericaceous plants has been examined by many people but no wholly satisfactory answer has emerged, although Ca/Mg ratios seem to be important in determining whether lime is harmful (see p.101). It is interesting that, by the end of the century, there has been a trend back to more complex mixtures partly because of the politically correct aversion to the use of peat and its replacement by materials like coconut coir, cocoa shell, perlite, expanded vermiculite, glass wool and composted bark. The last of these when finely pulverised has proved an excellent medium for rooting and growing plants. Gardeners appear increasingly likely to experiment with new substances in their composts but nobody in Scotland so far seems to have adopted the Japanese recipe of 50% ground pumice and 50% dried seaweed which certainly gives excellent results.

One of the great boons to the rock gardeners in the 1980s was the availability of slow-release fertilisers which yields its nutrients gradually over a long period. The addition of such fertilisers allows plants to be grown in pots for a whole season without the need for regular feeding.

POTS

In the first half of the century all pots were made of fired clay. Gardeners had no choice but to use these heavy, porous containers which dried out quickly. The accepted practice was to place layers of broken crocks, at the base of the pot to encourage good drainage. Latterly the need for crocking was challenged when it was realised that if the compost was free-draining and the pot porous, extra crocks were unnecessary so nowadays few clay pots are heavily crocked. The life of clay pots is short, especially if plunged outside over winter, when they simply crumble.

With the advent of plastic pots in the second half of the century the scene changed. These light weight receptacles could be easily handled and stacked and soon proved to be as good a clay pots if the correct procedure was followed. They obviously needed less water and care had to be taken to avoid over-watering, especially in winter. Crocks are not normally used but it is essential that the compost is well drained with a high proportion of grit or coarse sand. The top growers remain divided over the merits of the two kinds of pot. Many do very well with either although there are staunch protagonists of one or other system. The growers who win prizes at shows tend to use clay pots for reasons of appearance — sometimes going so far as to polish them with vegetable oil — but one hopes there are now few SRGC judges around who down-point plants because they are in plastic pots. By the end of the century most people were using plastic pots for raising seed because of the ease of handling hundreds of pots. Thankfully the days of sowing seed in old polystyrene coffee cups seems to be over. They were not aesthetic and took up more space than the current small square pots.

WATERING

The most notable growers appear to have their own systems of watering. For example, Harold Esslemont would very rarely water a pot of alpines from above but would either water the sand in the plunge bed or stand the pot in a few inches of water for a short time. He judged the need for water by lifting a pot and feeling its weight. On the other hand, Eric Watson, an ex-President of the SRGC, grew dionysias with enviable success but watered round the edges of the pot with a watering can. He judged the need for water by checking whether the gravel staging beneath a pot was moist or not. Both men were brilliantly successful in growing perfect specimens.

Once it was realised that most rock plants in pots did not like to be watered ad lib overhead with a watering can, especially if they were cushion plants, various systems were devised to solve the problem. The commonest one from the 1950s onwards was to water the plunge bed of sharp sand in which clay pots were sunk rather than the pots. Obviously for this system the porous clay pots were obligatory. Another way to reduce the frequency of watering and allow people to go off on holiday was to use the capillary method devised, in the 1960s, whereby pots were allowed to take up water from an irrigated sand bed or irrigation mat; this could be linked to a ball-cock and cistern to provide an automatic watering system. This method could be made to work with both clay and plastic pots provided the latter were not crocked so as to interrupt the capillary action. Mike and Polly Stone were early proponents of the capillary system. It is of some interest that they tried to follow Eric Watson's watering system of standing pots on gravel but soon found that the pots became too wet because the gravel broke the vital capillary flow. What they had not realised initially was that Watson used only clay pots since the system does not work with plastic ones.

Obviously raised beds and troughs have to be watered in dry weather. At the height of the growing season there is probably little harm in overhead watering since the plants are being rained on from above anyway. The danger is usually too much water in winter so many beds and troughs need winter protection by a pane of glass or other suitable cover. Himalayan plants from monsoon areas certainly need plenty of water in the growing season and really can hardly get enough. Ron McBeath's philosophy was to recommed emptying a can of water over such plants whenever he passed by.

ALPINE HOUSES AND FRAMES

The people who set up the AGS and the SRGC in the 1930s felt quite strongly that rock plants should be grown outside, even when they were destined for shows, when they could be lifted and potted up for display. Right until the 1960s most of the plants which won Forrest Medals for their owners were lifted from the open ground. The idea of alpine houses devoted to cushion plants did not really appear until the 1950s. Even the RBGE did not have a custom-built alpine house until the 1970s. However, the success of such people as Jack Drake, Harold Esslemont and Jack Crosland in growing and exhibiting superb specimens of cushion plants raised in an alpine house encouraged others to follow suit, especially the band of younger exhibitors who appeared from the 1970s onwards.

The methods used in alpine houses vary. Some growers use plunge beds filled with sand, others simply use benches topped with gravel. But all demand free ventilation; an alpine house should feel buoyant at all times. A good example is the alpine house at RBGE with fan-assisted ventilation which is particularly important in autumn in reducing the risk of attack by botrytis. For a large alpine house automatic ventilation is essential. Alpine houses do not normally have any heating. Growers of plants like cyclamen which need a slight degree of cold protection will normally install a small lean-to structure or frame to keep temperatures just above freezing. Alpine houses entail a lot of work which is why many top growers do not possess one. Cushion plants need constant attention to prevent drying out or attack by moulds and must be rotated a few degrees daily to ensure even development of flowers all over the cushion.

Even if growers do not have an alpine house they will almost certainly possess some frames in which to bring on propagating material or pots for shows. Even those with an alpine house will also have frames in which they keep pots of plants which have finished flowering and are now making growth. The numerous frames beside the alpine house at the RBGE are used to store pots of plants like kabschia saxifrages after flowering. Like alpine houses, frames come in all sizes, shapes and design but should all have such common features as adjustable ventilation and a degree of optional shading. They may be provided with plastic covers or even Dutch lights in glass but it is important to avoid over- damp conditions in winter.

Bulbs have become an increasingly important part of the rock gardener's interests and the bulb frame was developed in the 1970s to meet the needs of those bulbs which need a certain amount of winter protection plus summer baking. Elaborate designs have been suggested but all share the essential features of extremely free drainage, wire mesh above and below ground to keep rodents at bay, together with glass or plastic lights which serve both to keep rain off in winter and allow the plants, many of which are from hot, dry regions, to experience the summer warmth necessary for the formation of next season's flowers. As well as the need for a bulb frame it was realised that such plants benefit by feeding if they are to realise their potential. Regular feeding with mineral fertilisers have wrought a transformation in the size and quality of the flowers of bulbous species in recent years.

HORTICULTURAL CHEMICALS
The 20th century saw a tremendous rise in the amount of chemicals used by gardeners followed by a sharp decline towards the end of the century, as people became aware of the hazards to man and the environment from their

indiscriminate use. As so often, however, the pendulum has perhaps gone too far in the blanket disapproval of all things chemical. Books published at the very beginning of the century make horrifying reading with recommendations for the use of such noxious substances as arsenic, strychnine, nicotine and mercury to control pests and diseases. Apart from notorious murder trials one might speculate as to what extent their use led to accidental deaths or at least unreported long-term suffering among those who used them with greatest abandon. Following the development of hormone weedkillers in the early 1950s the pesticide industry developed apace firstly with systemic insecticides, followed by fungicides and then, as ecological consciences were smitten, the introduction of biological control by natural predators.

Of all the many branches of horticulture, rock gardening probably uses less chemicals than most. Chemical weedkillers are rarely used except on paths since selective herbicides are of little use and much danger among choice alpines. Neither are fungicides used much except for the control of damping-off in seedlings or mildew on rhododendrons. Insecticides are more widely used in the alpine house and frame to control aphids, red spider mites and mealybugs. Perhaps the biggest pest facing the rock gardener is vine weevil which can decimate whole beds of primulas. Initially there was success in controlling it with deadly chemicals such as lindane but this was withdrawn so, by the end of the century, gardeners had no really effective chemicals to deal with this pest in the cool damp conditions usually found in Scotland. In the 1990s biological control of wine weevil with nematodes or specially prepared composts incorporating control ingredients appeared to offer promising solutions but it remains to be seen how effective they will be under Scottish conditions.

Chemicals based on hormones have been used extensively since the 1950s to encourage root formation in cuttings; these substances can speed up rooting but rarely cause cuttings to root which would not otherwise do so. Compounds to promote germination have been used for many years with only minor success. The one which has received the most publicity is gibberellic acid (GA), a naturally occurring plant hormone which has been shown to replace the cold requirement of many seeds and can be remarkably effective (Abdalla and McKelvie, 1980). Norman Deno in the 1990s in the USA carried out a vast number of experiments using GA and produced recipes for germinating large numbers of species. However, the expense of the chemical, the hassle of applying it, the unreliability of its effect and the fact that most seeds germinate reasonably well without chemical aids has prevented the general use of GA except as a laboratory tool.

PROPAGATION

Great strides have been made over the century in the propagation of rock plants both from seed and by vegetative means. One of the greatest innovations has been the introduction of plastics of all kinds, especially polythene which has allowed moisture retention coupled with the penetration of light and the flow of carbon dioxide to create ideal conditions for rooting and germination. Improvements in our knowledge of the germination process has led to better and faster germination. An understanding of the principles of stratification, dormancy, double dormancy (as in trilliums and lilies), light requirements, age of seed, and, for orchids, mycorrhizal associations has greatly helped the average rock gardener to achieve consistently better results, even if the scientific reasons which underlie the practice may be only partly understood. The growth of seed exchange schemes such as that of the SRGC has led to an increase in practical experience as gardeners cope with the vagaries of unfamiliar species.

Vegetative propagation has also improved immeasurably over the century with the growth of scientific understanding of the physiology of rooting and its relevance to everyday practice. The exposure of cuttings to a permanently moist atmosphere by means of mist beds has made it possible to propagate hitherto impossible species on a large scale. This has led to the use of thin polythene or clingfilm to create similar conditions for rooting, something the average gardener can readily use. Expert rock gardeners can now propagate dwarf daphnes, eritrichiums and tiny androsaces with an ease which would have been the envy of earlier generations. Advances in the propagation of bulbs by simple techniques such as twin-scaling have allowed stocks of rare bulbs to be bulked up by the amateur — a rewarding experience.

In the second half of the century micro-propagation has enabled the horticultural industry to mass produce clones for sale at an unprecedented rate. By growing meristem material from the tips of plants in test-tubes of chemical nutrients and hormones it has become possible to propagate on a vast scale. With such methods, newly bred cultivars can reach the market years before it would have been possible by conventional methods. Such meristem tip material offers the additional bonus that it is usually free from virus so the technique is also valuable for ridding stock of virus disease. These methods are expensive and recipes have to be devised for each new species and even new cultivar so that only material which is likely to be sold on a large scale will be micro-propagated. Nevertheless several botanic gardens have successfully used these techniques to propagate rare or endangered species and that surely will be in the interests of the rock gardener. The successful micro-propagation of *Primula aureata* for example augers well for the future.

GENETIC ADVANCES

It is worth recalling that it was not until the opening years of the 20th century that the rules of inheritance, discovered by Mendel and published in 1866 and 1869, were rediscovered and confirmed. Since then the science of genetics has developed with accelerating tempo to impinge on almost every aspect of biology and its applications. But as far as rock gardeners are concerned breeding practice is still largely at the pre-Mendelian level of sophistication. Crossing two likely parents and hoping for the best just about sums it. A few enterprising persons may have proceeded to a back-cross but that was the limit. Of course the commercial breeders of crops and ornamentals moved with the times and exploited techniques such as polyploidy and the use of F1 hybrids etc but rock plants were not included in their sights since the financial reward would have been trivial.

There was a fair degree of snobbery in the early days of the AGS and the SRGC about hybrids which were looked upon with disdain, especially in the rhododendron world. That attitude took a knock when Peter and Kenneth Cox demonstrated out in China just how much inter-specific hybridisation takes place in the wild. Not everyone approves of the *Clematis marmoraria* hybrids produced by people like the Youngs, describing them as blowsy compared with delicate alpines. But that is a matter of taste. From the 1980s onwards named cultivars appeared increasingly among the RHS Awards for rock plants in place of species and natural varieties and this trend was very evident in the many cultivars on the show benches. Many of these new cultivars were named without reference to Registration Authorities or to the official Nomenclature Codes and often were never published, so the naming was sometimes technically incorrect. The trend to new cultivars has led to renewed interest in the correct naming of plants by the amateur together with increased interest in their naming among plant taxonomists. Disputes arise as to whether, say, *Pulsatilla* 'Budapest', can be used as a name for plants which agree precisely with the original description although they are descendants of several seed-raised generations. Some growers will argue that plants can not be given an existing clonal name if they have been grown from seed while others will reply that commercial growers have been doing just that for years when they sell named cultivars of cross-pollinated species

There has also been interest at the end of the century in the correct naming of vegetatively propagated rock plants in an effort to bring some order out of a confused situation. A good example is the Meconopsis Group set up by Evelyn Stevens and Mervyn Kessels in the 1990s to identify and propagate the true cultivars of the tall, blue *Meconopsis* species.

We can end by recognising that the advent of genetic engineering has the potential to introduce undreamt of novelties of form and colour among rock plants but is unlikely to do so in the near future because the financial return will not justify the cost.

CONSERVATION

The ethics of conservation and the collecting of plants have undergone enormous changes during the course of the 20th century. One has only to look at how botanists and gardeners used to regard plant collecting to appreciate that what was once accepted as the norm is now quite beyond the pale.

Consider for a moment the way botanists behaved at the beginning of the century. The Botanical Exchange Club swapped herbarium sheets like postage stamps — like the stamps the rarer the better. Here is what Professor Dickie of the University of Aberdeen wrote about the rare *Saxifraga cespitosa* in his 'Botanist's Guide' published in 1860 –"Mr McNab of the Edinburgh Botanic Garden found at the base of the precipice (east of Ben-a-Buird) a tuft of *S. cespitosa*, portions of which he gave to me, as I was near him when he happened to find it". Or Francis White, in 'The Flora of Perthshire' in 1898 who wrote about the rare *Saxifraga cernua*, "It is to be hoped that botanists, when taking specimens, will bear in mind that the limited station on Ben Lawers is the only place in Britain for this plant." Even as late as the middle of the century a crocodile of 50 or so First Year Edinburgh University students, under the leadership of J.L. Smith, could be seen on a Saturday morning in May marching across Aberlady Bay, east of Edinburgh, picking up plants, common or otherwise, for Smith to identify before they were stuffed into a vasculum and thence into the herbarium collection of 50 plants which every student had to hand in at the end of the term. Thankfully such activities are a thing of the past.

Collectors too have been just as heedless of the effects of their collecting on the local plant communities. For example, Frank Kingdon Ward was so struck by the beauty of the new lily he had found, later named *Lilium mackliniae*, that he dug up 300 bulbs which he packed in moss and sent off to England by air. But then, although the plant only appeared to grow on one particular hillside, it was there in such quantities that Ward was bound to feel that removal of a few hundred bulbs would make little difference. Such wholesale collecting would not be accepted as ethical today. This lily produces masses of seed which germinates readily and hence offers the preferred way to collect the species.

Ward's activities pale into significance when compared with those of the professional bulb hunters of the Middle East who devastated whole hillsides of their bulbs in order to sell them to wholesale bulb merchants in Europe and America. Many readers will remember a chain store in the 1960s which sold large quantities of what was purported to be *Cyclamen hederifolium* but which was, in fact, the fairly rare *C. mirabile* which had been stripped from a Turkish mountainside. After World War II when travel to Europe became possible again the pages of the AGS and SRGC publications frequently bore accounts of members, who, with some degree of pride it must be said, dug up *Daphne petraea* or *Eritrichium nanum* out of crevices with their ice axes to bring home in triumph. It was the done thing and few seemed to object to the practice. By the 1970s the climate of public opinion was changing and wholesale collecting was no longer approved of. Alerted by books such as Rachel Carson's 'Silent Spring', which identified the dangers of the over- and indiscriminate use of chemicals, people began to move away from protests about nuclear power to concern about the environment. Buzz words such as pollution, ecosystems, conservation and ecology became fashionable. It was gradually realised over the last 30 years of the century that genetic variation in plants and animals was to be valued for biological, economic and aesthetic reasons and that this applied not just to the rare and beautiful but to all species. The more rational protagonists soon realised that it was not possible to try to conserve everything so that some species had to be privileged because of their special value or rarity.

By 1980 the IUCN (Institute for Conservation of Nature and Natural Resources) came out with the statement that "conservation is the management of human resources so that it may yield the greatest sustainable benefit to present generations while maintaining the potential to meet the needs and aspirations of future generations". From this it became apparent that the world needed sensible polices for the conservation of the world's biological diversity. In terms of plant conservation, a series of Red Books was produced listing the species which were extinct, endangered, vulnerable or rare. Such statistics have to be taken with a pinch of salt since people tend to extract figures which suit their own purpose. For example, reports for FAO in the 1990s on deforestation in Nepal, could, according to which of the many alternative values were chosen for the various parameters, predict either that all the forest would have vanished by the end of the century or that the mountains would be sinking under the weight of trees.

How then can rock gardening contribute to conservation? There are two alternative approaches to the preservation of rare plants, the *in situ* or the *ex situ* approach. *In situ* refers to the conservation of plants in their natural ecosystems by establishing Nature Reserves and for many species that must be the best method. For example many cultivated primulas can only survive in the garden by replenishment from wild stock. Although hardly a raison d'être for conservation it is necessary if we are to continue to grow such plants. Nowadays there are thousands of nature Reserves and National Parks across the world, especially in under developed countries where it is not possible to conserve all the threatened species and it is here that the *ex situ* becomes relevant. Botanic Gardens, Research Institutes, Universities and even private gardeners through such organisations as NCCPG, dealt with below, can conserve species by growing and propagating them and, wherever possible, by saving seed in Seed Banks at temperatures of $-20°C$. Micro-propagation has also been used widely to conserve material. The trouble with these approaches is that frequently only a very limited degree of genetic variability is preserved in a given species, stocks may become infected with virus diseases or simply die from unknown causes. The increased concern about conservation in the latter decades of the century is laudable but it is doubtful how far gardeners are able to play a significant role in this respect, for the simple reason that fashions come and go in horticulture as in all things so that, before it is realised, particular species and cultivars just vanish. There are many plants which were commonly grown early this century which are no longer in cultivation. The genus *Primula* is a good example since many species have come into our gardens only to vanish later unless fresh importations from the wild have replenished the stocks.

The average rock gardener can make a practical contribution by trying to avoid buying plants which have been collected from the wild, although this may be a counsel of perfection. It is also important to make sure that plants are correctly named and to distribute especially rare and unusual plants among the gardening community. For the expert growers, liaison with Botanic Gardens is a useful way to conserve species. Especially in rock gardening, the amateur grower often has greater knowledge of particular groups of plants than the professionals. During the century the SRGC has played a major part in conserving plants since the Shows and Seed Exchange serve to keep good plants in cultivation, apart from changes in fashion.

Whatever the approach, most rock gardeners would doubtless readily accept that plants suitable for the rock garden, frame or alpine house should be neither damaged by collection nor disturbed by over zealous handling in their wild habitat. Of course, they will always want to introduce selected material from the wild to extend the range of cultivated species although there is no general agreement how this should be done. There is a risk of a 'holier than thou' attitude whereby Institutions and 'experts' take unto themselves the sole right to introduce new material from the wild and condemn amateurs for attempting to do likewise. As in all things a sensible, balanced approach is called for. In many parts of the world it is now illegal to dig up any plant without the owner's permission. Governments are now becoming quite strict about this because they have realised that species may carry genes which may be of commercial value. This attitude is likely to be strengthened now that genetic engineering is in full swing, genes can be patented and the raw material is increasingly seen to be of potential economic value.

It is generally agreed that plant collecting by expeditions or by individuals should not take place but that a limited amount of seed collecting is permissible if done with the consent of the local authorities. At the official level, plant collecting of any kind is hedged around by a vast number of Regulations, the most relevant of which to collectors are CITES (Convention on International Trade in Endangered Species of Wild Fauna and Flora) and EC Regulations which implement it (McGough,1993). Under CITES, trade in a wide range of endangered species is forbidden. Even for plants which are in no way endangered, the Regulations, if followed to the letter, are fearsome and, for many overseas countries, involve an amount of paper work which can never be completed in a month of Sundays. One suspects that rock gardeners out in the wilds on plant-hunting holidays will continue to collect small amounts of seed discretely without going through the rigmarole of the necessary paper work. What is to stop them? They may even countenance the removal of the odd cutting since there can be little harm in doing so. Even plant hunting expeditions to which gardeners can subscribe and receive collected seed in return probably have negligible effects on plant numbers.

NCCPG

The National Council for the Conservation of Plants and Gardens was established in 1978 under the auspices of the Royal Horticultural Society. Its principal aim was to establish a central bank of information about rare plants and collections, which gardens and gardeners held, and to encourage and preserve collections of particular genera. By the end of the 20th century there were about 600 collections of genera (National Collections) of which only about 40 were in Scotland. Of these less than 20 genera were of genera commonly regarded as 'rock plants' so as far as alpines are concerned the NCCPG has had limited success in Scotland.

The original aim was to compile a master list of all plants which were rare and in danger of disappearing from cultivation for one reason or another. As that information became available National Collections would be set up either in private hands or under the auspices of an Institution. The holder would maintain and propagate the plants in the collection and act as a centre for their dissemination, preferably through the Nursery Trade so that plants, as George Bernard Shaw once said "shall be given to all men who offer an honest price for them, without respect of person or principles". The Council accepted that in exceptional cases, especially in the early stages of the scheme, distribution might be entrusted to amateurs.

In an article in the AGS Bulletin in September 1982 Joy Hulme summed up the objectives of the Council and how the AGS might co-operate in implementing them. She wrote "the remaining floral regions of the world [are] increasingly inaccessible to a present-day George Forrest. It behoves us all to play our part in retaining the treasures that he and countless others have brought us and ensure that they have a firm footing both in our public and private gardens. The Society hopes that every member will endeavour to co-operate with it and the NCCPG in this worthwhile task."

How then has the Council succeeded in its principal objectives in the 20 years or so since it was set up? There is no doubt that for many genera the holders have done an excellent job in assembling a wide range of species and extended our knowledge of the genera as witnessed by many erudite articles in the 'New Plantsman'. There is no doubt that by the end of the century there is a far bigger range of plants than there was in, say, the 1960s. The advent of many small specialist nurseries has helped greatly in the process of spreading rare and unusual species and cultivars. So at least some of the objectives of the NCCPG are being satisfactorily met.

However, when we come to rock plants the picture is neither so clear nor so rosy. Of the many genera which rock gardeners would regard as at the core of their hobby hardly any have a satisfactory National Collection. Some have been set up and either quickly folded or have lingered on in a rather desultory fashion. Autumn gentians are a case in point. Originally the collection was held at the Cruickshank Garden in Old Aberdeen but dry soil and climate were not conducive to its maintenance nor was funding adequate. The Collection then moved to RBG Edinburgh but met undefined problems there. The latest move at the end of the century is to Christie's Nursery at Kirriemuir where, it is hoped, it will have a stable future. Of the Collections of alpines in Scotland only for the Cassiope Collection at Branklyn is there a list of its contents in the Plant Finder Reference Library. For the others this rather essential information is lacking.

Not everyone has accepted the unqualified value of the NCCPG scheme. The main objection apparently refers to the dangers of assembling all representatives of one genus in one or two Collections because of the risk of virus or fungal disease spreading quickly through a collection of closely related species or simply general death over a period of time. Not every species of a genus may be suited to the particular site where a Collection is located. For example, the Asiatic Primula Collection at Cluny contains many difficult species which grow very well but *Primula vialii* poses problems there, although it is a species which many who cannot grow the rarities find relatively easy. Also, interest among Collection holders may wane so that what starts out as a representative collection fades away with time. But there is another more general caveat. There has always been a great emphasis on the preservation of all available cultivars. Graham Pattison of the NCCPG wrote in the AGS Bulletin in 1993 "A more frightening figure is that of *Paeonia* with some 800 cultivars recorded but only 300 available commercially today, with only 70 available from one nursery. In 1986, however, there were only 152 commercially available. Most of the new additions will be modern cultivars". But does it really matter that we lose many old cultivars? Many are not even as good as ones that were bred but never reached commerce. Who would seriously suggest trying to resuscitate all the many short-lived dianthus cultivars which were bred in the early years of this century? What is really important is the preservation of genetic variability in cultivated species. As an organisation, the NCCPG appears unaware of the principles of population genetics which point to the need for much greater emphasis on broadening the genetic base of cultivated species and thereby increasing the scope for selection and the appearance of new and improved cultivars. The NCCPG scheme needs to be supplemented by additional means of preserving rare and endangered species.

The Hardy Plant Society has performed a valuable service in locating and propagating rare plants. As already noted the SRGC itself has been responsible for spreading rare and unusual plants among its members through its Seed Exchange which like other similar schemes throughout the world provide an immense range of species and cultivars.

Preamble to Chapters 7-12

We now come to the survey of rock plants introduced from different parts of the world other than western Europe. There is a practical limit to how many species can be noted so we have tried to include those which are most highly regarded and accessible as well as those which may be of interest on other counts. A specialist in any group will regret the absence of some favourite, or the latest species to be introduced, or some star item which is so difficult to grow but this account caters for the general membership of the Club, most of whom are not specialists and may prefer broader perspectives. Any other dissatisfaction with the choice of species selected for comment can be put down to idiosyncracy, to a modicum of which we are all entitled.

The species have been chosen to be representative of the introductions from different regions. In the interests of readability, authorities and synonyms are omitted from the text but included in the index. We have adopted the new names for plant families, admittedly with an ill grace. We bear with the taxonomists when they clear up confusion between synonyms or between species and varieties. But when they decide to jettison landmarks which have been with us for a life-time we detect more than a whiff of arrogant pedantry. However, we are stuck with these names, so for those who find them unfamiliar, the new family names, followed by the old, familiar ones in brackets, are as follows: Apiaceae (Umbelliferae), Asteraceae (Compositae), Brassicaceae (Cruciferae), Fabaceae (Leguminosae), Clusiaceae (Hypericaceae), Lamiaceae (Labiatae).

Comparison of where different species of plants are to be found is bound to illustrate some of the tenets of plant geography. This is hardly a topic we can pursue here but it is worth noting some of the principal ideas since they set the evidence for differences in distribution in a wider context. The most fundamental concept is that of the floristic region. Plant geographers have divided the surface of the earth into some three dozen such regions, distinguished by location, physical conditions and a characteristic flora. Within such regions a variable number of sub-regions have been distinguished which, although they may have much in common, nevertheless significantly differ in the array of associated species. Often the correlated occurrence of particular species is so marked that having found one of the species in the field we confidently expect to find the others. Members of such an association are adapted to similar climatic and edaphic conditions which may provide a guide to their cultivation. The many travellers' accounts of the Himalayan flora at different elevations amply illustrate the phenomenon.

Once the distribution of a given species is known we might wonder how it got there. Some may have arisen *in situ* but that will not be so for others which have originated elsewhere and arrived at the present site by migration. Climates change over time. For survival and effective reproduction any species is constrained within physiological limits peculiar to that species.

Given genetic variation plants can and do adapt to altered conditions but the rate at which they can do so often cannot match the rate of change in climate and other factors, so they have to migrate or perish. By various methods of dispersal plant populations can spread to new areas more congenial to their needs. Given the periods of time available, species which originated far apart may end up in the same floristic association.

To take the discussion of distribution a little further, if we plot on a map where a given species is to be found we often find it occurs very locally in a single region and so we label it an endemic species. Other species may have a wide and continuous distribution or be more or less cosmopolitan while still others may turn up in widely separated sites, with no occupation in-between, or related species may occur on different continents separated by vast oceans.

Endemics may be so for different reasons. An endemic species may have arisen recently and had insufficient time to spread or, more likely, may be a relict which has had to retreat in the face of changed conditions to make a final stand in the now infrequent sites to which it is sufficiently adapted. On the other hand, topographical and climate change may have split a previously continuous population into isolated segments which are free to adapt to their particular conditions and evolve into local races or separate species. The occurrence of geographical races in very widespread species is virtually a rule. Such differences may be partly due to adaptation and partly due to chance fixation of novel gene combinations, derived from a genetically variable source. The widespread, cosmopolitan species have achieved a versatile combination of adaptations which confer a greater degree of independence of habitat, compared with specialised species. Clearly, it requires a great deal of information about distribution, frequency and variation in growth and development within and between related taxa to determine the probable status of the members of a floristic association, although simple information about exact distribution and relative frequency has great pragmatic value.

Knowledge of the distribution of chromosome number can provide clues to past history. Thus in taxa which display difference in the degrees of polyploidy, i.e. differences in the number of sets of chromosomes above the primary diploid number, there is a tendency for higher levels of polyploidy to be associated with successful colonisation of new territory, adding a directional element to the situation. Not a great deal is known about rock plants in this respect but the Himalayan rhododendrons appear to provide an example since there is a considerable range in chromosome number among the species of the region, suggesting a successful and comparatively recent colonisation of the new habitats provided by the development and erosion of the mountain chain they occupy.

Instances of disjunct distribution are particularly informative. Rock gardeners will be familiar with the number of more or less circumpolar species which turn up on mountain tops in southern temperate regions. Especially in the northern hemisphere, this situation can be related to the effects of glaciation whereby previously widespread tundra species were left occupying the habitats to which they were adapted when the ice retreated. If the ice returns we can visualise an expansion of their distribution down the mountain side, although with the advent of global warming the converse may be anticipated.

More dramatic examples of disjunct distribution occur when oceans separate species of the same genus. This situation most notably refers to such taxa which occur in two or more isolated land masses which include Antarctica, New Zealand, Australia, South Africa or South America. It is a beguiling thought that such apparently odd distributions may be in some way related to the consequences of plate tectonics and continental drift which led to the break-up of the former Gondwanaland. To entertain such a speculation it is necessary to reconcile the timing of the separation of the continental land masses with the time at which the relevant genera were established. The break-up of Gondwanaland started some 135 million years ago, about 35 million years before the appearance of flowering plants. But the separation of the land masses took place in stages. Thus, South America appears to have separated very early from Antarctica and the other regions, while both Australia and New Zealand were separated from each other when both were still attached to Antarctica at a time when South America had not drifted far from the latter. It has been estimated that the southern land masses were at least much closer together or even in contact up to the early Tertiary, about 45 million years ago, by which time angiosperm evolution was well under way. So even if these disjunct distributions were attributed entirely to dispersal, especially by wind and sea, as many would argue, such dispersal would have been easier when the continents were closer together than they are now.

The flora of islands is always interesting. In general, the further an island is from the nearest land mass the greater the proportion of endemic species peculiar to that island. One has only to think of New Zealand, the Galapagos or Hawaii to agree. Such oceanic islands often provide examples of adaptive radiation whereby a number of closely related taxa have evolved from a common origin to colonise a variety of ecological niches, accompanied by correlated changes in growth and development, as in New Zealand celmisias and hebes. Less isolated islands like Tasmania or the Falkland Islands, where there have been former land connections with the nearest continent, share much of their flora with climatically similar regions of the mainland. But they also boast a few endemic species as evidence of the effectiveness of their separation in allowing evolutionary divergence. As might be expected all degrees of floristic difference occur according to the degree of isolation of islands.

These brief comments are offered as general background to the various observations about distribution in the following survey of introduced species of rock plants.

§ CHAPTER 7 §

The Sino-Himalayan Region

The Himalayas comprise one of the world's youngest mountain chains which owes its elevation to the thrust of the Indian tectonic plate below the immense Tibetan plateau. The comparatively short period of roughly 20 million years covers the main phase of elevation, especially in the Karakoram. The sources of the larger rivers of both India and Pakistan were established before the Himalayan range developed on the north east frontier of Kashmir so that they rise north of the watershed. As the mountains rose the rivers eroded their way southward to create spectacular gorges. The process still continues so, in geological terms, this immense region is an area of surface instability and change and this has implications for the flora. A number of genera like *Rhododendron, Primula* and *Gentiana* have their centres of distribution in the Himalayan region, characterised by a great wealth of species and often a reticulate pattern in the distribution of characters used for classification. There are plenty of instances where clear-cut taxonomic distinctions may be hard to come by since populations which appear distinct in part of their ranges may intergrade where they come into contact. They carry the imprint of evolution in action.

In such a complex situation it is difficult to perceive the main attributes of the flora. Two approaches help in this respect, namely the geographical and the ecological. Grierson and Long (1983) have shed light on the former. Starting from the long recognised affinity of the Himalayan flora with that of China and Japan and the likelihood that the alpine flora of the Chinese mountains has been the source of the developing flora of the Himalaya, they have recognised six elements of the Himalayan flora according to distribution as follows:

1. Taxa which range from the north west Himalayas (Kashmir and West Nepal) to Japan e.g. *Cardiocrinum, Cornus macrophylla, Hypoxis aurea.*
2. Taxa distributed from the north west Himalayas to China e.g. *Anemone rupicola, Cremanthodium, Cyanathus lobatus.*
3. Taxa which are endemic and range from the north west to the eastern Himalayas, but do not extend to China and Japan e.g. *Delphinium brunonianum, Potentilla atrosanguinea, Rhododendron anthopogon.*
4. Taxa distributed from the eastern Himalayas to Japan but absent from the western Himalayas e.g. *Enkianthus, Rodgersia, Tiarella polyphylla.*
5. Taxa distributed from the eastern Himalayas to China but absent from both the west Himalayas and Japan e.g. *Adonis brevistyla, Cassiope selaginoides, Primula sikkimensis.*
6. Taxa restricted to the eastern Himalayas (East Nepal, Sikkim, Bhutan, north Assam and south east Tibet) e.g. *Meconopsis superba, Primula whitei,*

Rhododendron glaucophyllum. Within this group there are a number of species which, on present evidence, appear confined to Bhutan e.g. *Lilium sherriffiae, Saxifraga flavida, Viola bhutanica.*

In addition to this series there are several other elements i.e. the Tibetan, the Euro-Siberian and the Arctic Alpine. The Tibetan plateau is dominated largely by xerophytic species adapted to its lower rainfall and high altitude. In places throughout the Himalayas sheltered from the monsoon, especially on elevated northern slopes, the conditions are sufficiently similar to accommodate typical Tibetan species e.g. *Paraquilegia microphylla, Potentilla multifida, Saussurea gossypiphora.* By some workers, the Tibetan flora itself is regarded as related to the steppe and desert vegetation of Iran, Afghanistan and both east and west Pakistan. The Euro-Siberian region extends from Western Europe through Northern Eurasia to Siberia. Although the Himalayan region is separated from it by the Tibetan and Central Asian Plateau, a number of typical Euro-Siberian species contribute to its flora e.g. *Euphrasia officinalis agg., Potentilla anserina, Viola biflora.* The Arctic Alpine species have a wide, often circumpolar distribution in the Arctic and often turn up at the highest elevations in the mountains of Europe and Asia, frequently with a very disjunct distribution. Examples of such species, which occur in Bhutan, Sikkim and elsewhere in the Himalayas, include *Androsace chamaejasme, Myosotis alpestris* and *Thalictrum alpinum.*

The other, ecological method of bringing conceptual order to floristic complexity is presently handicapped by lack of sufficiently detailed information about associations of species according to habitat. Gross changes in the dominant species and growth form are, of course, obvious as one passes from sub-tropical lowland forest upward through zones of broad-leaved or pine forest through evergreen oak, blue pine, spruce and hemlock to reach the *Abies* fir zone where the species with which we are concerned start appearing. Beneath the fir forest there is a rich ground flora of shrubs, including rhododendrons and small herbs, as well as primulas, growing on the mossy floor of the forest. At elevations of 3600–3800m the trees become more stunted as the tree-line is approached and juniper and various rhododendrons become increasingly frequent, to dominate the scene above the tree-line. During the monsoon season there is a rich flora of herbs, including many of the more familiar primulas. No doubt as a consequence, in part at least, of centuries of grazing at these altitudes, damp, grassy meadows occur and these are often ablaze with primulas and gentians. At higher elevations still we encounter the typical alpine flora, growing in scree and rock crevices, buried beneath snow from October to March and generally with abundant moisture, although, on sheltered, well drained sites on northern slopes more xerophytic conditions may prevail.

With this brief introduction we can now consider a sample of the Sino-Himalayan species which have featured most prominently among the introductions of the 20th century.

Dicots
Asteraceae
Cremanthodium   This genus includes about 50 generally rather small Himalayan and Chinese herbaceous species. The basal leaves are long-stalked and often kidney shaped. In most species the fragrant flowers are yellow, with the general appearance of little sunflowers, but in some they are orange brown or pink. They are solitary, nodding, appear late in the season and often large, even up to a diameter of 7cm in *C. ellisii*, with often short stalks. They are true alpines, from about 3500m upwards, adapted to cool, moist, peaty conditions, often in scree and with a reputation for being difficult to grow, especially if they are from the highest altitudes. Nevertheless nine species are listed in recent SRGC seed lists, including several unnamed species from recent expeditions. To mention a few: *C. delavayi* is one of the larger species, growing to about 90 cm with cob-webby hairs on the young leaves; *C. ellisii* (Fig.23) grows to about 20cm with large, bright yellow flower heads; *C. nepalense* is a little shorter with 2-3cm wide yellow flowers with broad, prominently veined basal leaves; *C. rhodocephalum* is pink flowered. They are often regarded as difficult but are not particularly so in the cooler conditions of Scotland while in Norway they are grown with considerable success. However, some species have a tendency to die back in the first year of germination while still at the cotyledon stage. They will come up the next year so pots should not be discarded.

Saussurea   From our point of view the most interesting members of this large and widespread, northern genus are the high alpines from the Himalayas, including more than 30 species, in which the flower stem is protected either with large, papery bracts, as in *S. longibracteata*, or narrower bracts which are richly provided with long hairs. In extreme cases the whole plant may be wholly invested in a woolly coat, which creates a bizarre appearance. Their success in colonising cold, wet, exposed and endlessly windy sites must depend largely on this remarkable adaptation. *S. longibracteata* is well worth growing for its striking appearance but, in spite of several attempts, it does not seem to have become established. The best known species is *S. gossypiphora*, one of the 'snowball' series in which the flowers are all at the top of the stalk, with an apical hole in the "wool" to allow entry of pollinating insects in search of nectar. As noted by Grierson (1991) this species has been confused with the similar *S. laniceps* (Fig.20) in which the flower heads are also near the tip of the shoot but placed laterally, with several lateral, entry points for the insects. These species are found in the western Himalayas, Nepal and Bhutan. The woolly species are almost impossible to grow even in a greenhouse unless special precautions are taken to maintain a cold, dry environment throughout the winter, probably with the aid of electric fans. Among the most impressive of the papery bract series is the robust *S. obvallata* which has been successfully grown in a sharply drained, raised bed of humus-rich compost at Inshriach Nursery, confirming

Ron McBeath's view that these intriguing plants are not impossible to grow.

Bignoniaceae
Incarvillea This genus is divided into two groups with either tall, leafy stems or with leaves which are tufted or in the form of a rosette at ground level. It is these acaulescent species which are suited to the rock-garden. *I. compacta* (Fig.22) is a small species, growing to about 15cm or less. The inflorescence is so compressed that, in some forms, the flowers look as if they arise individually from the crown. According to Grey-Wilson (1994), the corolla which is either rose or a paler shade, is flushed with yellow while the throat is lined with purple. It is a native of Tibet, western Sichuan and north west Yunnan, on moist, stony slopes at 3000-4500m. *I. delavayi*, introduced by Forrest, grows to about 40cm with long pinnate leaves. The flowers, carried on a strong peduncle, are similar to those of *I. compacta*, although more purple. This hardy species from south west China is probably better placed in the border rather than the rock garden. *I. mairei*, another Forrest introduction, has basal pinnate leaves, in which the terminal leaflet is longer and broader than the rest. The stout stem carries solitary or several flowers which are pink, purple or crimson with yellow, grey or white in the throat. The variety *grandiflora*, with larger flowers, was introduced to cultivation by Ludlow and Sherriff. Ludlow found it in south east Tibet where it "plastered the rock faces and the stony hill slopes with its flat rosettes of dark green pinnate leaves and with its great gloxinia-like reddish-pink, white striped flowers". *I. mairei* can be relied upon to flower regularly and thrive provided it grows on a particularly well drained site.

Brassicaceae
Draba The usual cushion or mat-forming habit of this northern genus makes them attractive rock plants, especially when the numerous, little short-stemmed flowers, which are usually white or yellow, combine to make a splash of colour against a rock face. Among the humbler members of the genus *D. oreades* (Fig.21), widespread across the Himalayas, forms tiny mats with rounded clusters of flowers.

Campanulaceae
Codonopsis Many of the species of this genus have a twining or climbing habit with more or less bell-shaped or open, starry flowers which may be white, yellow or greenish-blue to purple. Many are very handsome although marred by a foxy smell, especially when bruised. Fifteen species appear in the SRGC seed lists, of which more than half are twiners. Among the non-climbers we can note *C. clematidea* and *C. ovata*, the two most familiar species which are often confused with each other. *C. clematidea* is the taller of the two, with many branching stems rising to 60cm or more, generally less in cultivation, with ovate leaves. The bell-shaped corolla, which is reflexed at

the tip, is pale blue with dark veins, especially within and often with an orange ring round the base of the stamens. *C. ovata* grows only to about half the height of *C. clematidea*, with many sterile stems. The corolla is more distinctly blue, purple-veined within, almost black at the base, funnel-shaped but not reflexed at the tip. Both occur in Kashmir, but *C. clematidea* extends to northern India and *C. ovata* to the western Himalaya. *C. meleagris* grows to about 40cm. The leaves are mostly basal. The stem carries a single, nodding, rather cylindrical corolla which is yellow-green or pale blue without, beautifully marked with purple veins, and rich purple within. It is a woodlander from Yunnan. *C. vinciflora*, from south west China and the northern Himalayas, closely related to the much more vigorous *C. convolvulacea*, is a rather delicate species with charming, campanulate, starry, blue flowers, which climbs modestly or trails along the ground. *C. thalictrifolia* is an attractive tall herb which has been sometimes in cultivation and was reintroduced in the late 1990s by the MECC Expedition to the Langtang in Nepal.

Cyananthus This is a small Sino-Himalayan genus of mostly late flowering species of which the best known species is *C. lobatus*, with a prostrate, radiating habit, toothed or lobed leaves and large, funnel-shaped flowers which come in many shades of purple to blue, as well as white. A form sent back by Sherriff, 'Sherriff's Variety' has large, lavender blue flowers. *C. microphyllus* has small, narrow, unlobed leaves and rather periwinkle-like blue flowers. *C. delavayi*, with thyme-like leaves, mat-like growth, and smaller violet flowers, was introduced by both Forrest, Ward and later collectors. All these species prefer, cool, moist peaty conditions.

Crassulaceae
Sedum Only a few Himalayan members of the Crassulaceae are commonly grown. *S. fastigiata* is a herbaceous, dioecious species which grows to about 15cm, with narrow, lanceolate, shiny leaves. The clustered male flowers are dark purple. It occurs around 4000m in the Himalayas, Tibet and western Yunnan. *S. kirilowii* is also dioecious but reaches twice the height or more with a stout, erect stem and narrow, crowded leaves, toothed towards their tips. The numerous, clustered flowers are typically yellow-green but may also be orange in var. *aurantiacum* or brown-red in var. *rubrum*. *S. primuloides* is another high altitude species, from western China. It spreads by rhizomes and forms low hummocks of rosetted leaves. The attractive one centimetre flowers on short stalks vary between white and pink.

Ericaceae
Cassiope These small, evergreen shrubs occur in high mountains or the northern tundra and are well known for their charming, bell-shaped flowers. They are at home in the peat garden, provided the drainage is satisfactory and they are not short of water during the growing period. *C. fastigiata* (Fig.24)

grows on the forest floor at lower elevations, on open moorland beyond the tree-line or in rock crevices on drier slopes. It has been introduced several times from the central Himalayas, including one collection by Ludlow and Sherriff in 1949. This species tends to be slow growing and is not always easily grown outside. *C. selaginoides* (Fig.25) grows usually as a small bush to a height of about 25cm. It also occurs in different forms but the best is that collected by Ludlow and Sherriff (LS 13284). A miniature form var. *nana* has been recently introduced by Ron McBeath. *C. wardii* (Fig.26) is a larger, stoloniferous species with stout four-angled stems, white flowers and not easily propagated. A number of good cassiope hybrids are widely grown, including crosses to non-Himalayan species, e.g. 'Bearsden' (*C. lycopodioides* x *C. fastigiata*) and the particularly floriferous, 'Muirhead' (*C. wardii* x *C. lycopodioides*). The Stones at Fort Augustus in the 1990s raised a splendid range of 'Askival' hybrids between various Himalayan and other species, described in the AGS Bulletin in 1998.

Gaultheria There are several Chinese species suitable for the peat garden, although some are stoloniferous and invasive. *G. cuneata* is just such a one, spreading to form a wide mat of hard, dark green leaves. The white, urn-shaped flowers occur in clusters in spring, followed in August by white, globular fruits. *G. nummularioides* is a completely prostrate, trailing little shrub with bristly stems. The urn-shaped flowers are contracted at the mouth, white, sometimes tinged pink or brownish, followed by blue-black fruits. There is a minute variety, (*G. n. minuta*), collected by Forrest, in which the leaves are tiny. *G. thymifolia* and *G. trichophylla* are closely related small species. The former, from northern Burma and Yunnan, has a slender, creeping habit. *G. trichophylla*, from the Himalaya and western China, forms mats of fine, wiry branches. The small bell-shaped flowers vary between red, pink and white, succeeded by pale blue berries.

Rhododendron The smaller rhododendrons, which span a range of size from small, prostrate species to compact bushes of a metre or more in height, are among the most important members of the rock garden. They provide structure and texture in shape and leaf form while a judicious selection of species and hybrids will bring colour from late winter to August. Many are hardy in Scotland although gardens in western areas can enjoy a greater range of species. The first influx of Asiatic species resulted from Sir Joseph Hooker's Himalayan explorations of 1848–1851, followed, later in the century, by the introductions by French missionaries from south east Tibet, Sichuan and north west Yunnan. Early in the 20th century Wilson introduced several species from west China but the major influx was due to George Forrest from his successive expeditions to Sichuan and Yunnan between 1904 and 1932. About the same time, Kingdon Ward, Rock and Farrer and, later, Ludlow and Sherriff, contributed new species to our garden flora. Since then many expeditions of all sorts have brought back rhododendron seed, many species have been re-introduced, often as different forms or sub-species, and there is no apparent end to the process nor of the new clones produced by hybridisation.

The greatest diversity of species is to be found in western China and the Himalayas, growing at elevations of 2500–5000m, where they experience high rainfall, a humid, temperate climate and grow on organic soils generally minerally deficient. Cox (1985) has noted that at the altitudinal zone preferred by rhododendrons, at about 3700m, there are five months of rain and seven months of snow. In alpine Upper Burma at the same altitude, July and August are cooler than an average English summer. Most of the alpine rhododendrons are exposed to the South West Monsoon from June to September. It is hardly surprising therefore that Asiatic rhododendrons do not establish themselves naturally in Britain, except in shaded, moist, peaty conditions. Compared with their native habitat the British climate is too dry and the soils are often too heavy and alkaline, although recognition of their needs can overcome such obstacles by attention to site and soil composition. Although some of the dwarf species grow under tree cover, generally they prefer open sites such as forest clearings, rocky outcrops or treeless moorland. Many collectors have commented on the vast areas of moorland covered by a dense, continuous growth of dwarf rhododendrons, to the exclusion of other plants and playing much the same ecological role in the Himalayas as *Calluna* heath does in the Highlands. The traditionally recognised intolerance of rhododendrons to alkaline soils may seem rather paradoxical because, in western China and the Himalayas, a great many species grow on limestone mountains, as Forrest repeatedly reported. The apparent contradiction between native habitat and garden experience has been recently studied by Kinsman (1998, 1999) who determined the pH of the shallow soil overlying limestone at several sites favoured by rhododendrons in north west Yunnan. At almost all sites the soil samples had pH values less than 6. Only one species, *R. primuliflorum* (Fig.28), was shown to be growing in alkaline soil at pH 7.4–7.9. In the high summer rainfall in Yunnan the flux of acid precipitation and acid soil water is downward throughout the active growing season, and possibly at all seasons of the year, so that even on the thinnest soils overlying limestone the physiological requirements of rhododendrons are met. On this hypothesis, in Britain, except in the wettest areas, net water deficit develops in soils during late spring, summer and autumn so that there is an upward flux of water and where the underlying rocks are alkaline the roots are exposed to a high pH. But this kind of situation appears to be only one of several and can hardly be the whole story. Thus, McAleese, Rankin and Hang (1999) have carried out an extensive survey of the pH of soils in which rhododendrons were growing in north west Yunnan, in both pre-monsoon and monsoon periods. They have also collected numerous samples of soil from about the roots for analysis of organic content and also the concentrations of calcium, magnesium, iron and manganese. The evidence showed that many species of rhododendron thrive with their roots in contact with limestone soil of high pH. Their success in this respect cannot be attributed to the presence of high magnesium content, since the underlying rocks are not dolomitic, nor can deficiency of either iron or manganese be identified as limiting at either high or low pH. The ultimate interpretation may turn out to be quite complex and involve the adverse effects of bicarbonate and chloride ions (Leake and Read, 1989), the unusual capacity of rhododendrons and other ericaceous species to accumulate high concentrations of manganese in their foliage (Korcak, 1988) as well as the role of their fungal mycorrhiza (Leake and Read, 1989).

Many of the rhododendron species are very widespread and give rise to geographical races which may differ to some extent in size, growth form, leaf size and often colour of the flowers. Natural hybrids are not infrequent and sometimes locally abundant. Attempts to bring conceptual order to such a huge assemblage of species, sub-species, varieties etc. has proved difficult. To quote Peter Cox (1985): " Few species are really distinct; the genus is really a botanist's nightmare and no two botanists would come out with anything like a similar classification". The primary classification based on the early collections of Hooker, Forrest and others was due to Sir Isaac Bayley Balfour, Professor of Botany at Edinburgh. His successors, also based in the Royal Botanic Garden Edinburgh, have built two edifices, dissimilar in some respects, on these foundations, and this is currently a source of confusion to those uncertain which scheme they should follow. The attempt to apply a hierarchical scheme of classification to a dynamic, evolving assemblage of populations always proves frustrating, since it will encounter so many instances of border-line cases and gaps in the information about distributions.

The clones introduced to cultivation and familiar to horticulturists, have very often been derived from a few individuals or perhaps only one and may be unrepresentative of the population from which they were collected. Traditionally such clones or types were the raw material of the taxonomist but to-day the emphasis is on the distribution of variation within and between populations, defined not only by morphological criteria but also by evidence from chromosome number, biochemical differences etc. As a consequence the status of forms is often down-graded taxonomically when they are seen as variants of a wider assemblage. It appears that difference in emphasis between the older and the newer taxonomic criteria underlies the difference between respectively Davidian's scheme and the Edinburgh Revision of Cullen, Chamberlain and Philipson. The most practical approach to this dilemma is that adopted by Peter Cox (1985) who is familiar with the taxonomy, has participated in and led many Himalayan expeditions to collect rhododendrons and has also unrivalled experience both as grower and hybridiser. Pragmatically he recognises particular, named clones for their garden value, whatever status the taxonomists finally decide to accord them. This approach to plant naming for a whole range of taxa became increasingly common towards the end of the century as growers and hybridisers became weary of the endless wrangling of taxonomists.

The following selection of the most important rock garden species is based on the recommendations in the SRGC Journal of E.H.M. Cox (1953), H.H. Davidian (1963) and A.D. Reid (1969), of A. Evans (1974) and, especially, the definitive publication by P.A. Cox (1985), who adopted the Revised Edinburgh Classification which is the one used here.

Pogonanthum Section   A distinct group often with tubular flowers in little heads at the ends of the shoots. Although they prefer some shade, too much promotes lanky growth and they will not thrive in hot, dry situations. *R. anthopogon* has a widespread distribution from east Nepal through Bhutan, north west Arunachal Pradesh and south east Tibet at 2700–4800m. The flowers vary from white to pink. The leaves are large and aromatic, serving as incense in Tibetan monasteries. It grows to nearly 60cm. The flowers tend to appear at the top rather than the sides. Ludlow and Sherriff collected seeds in the vicinity of the Tibet–Bhutan border in 1934 and these germinated successfully, one of them, grown by the Coxes of Glendoick Nursery, receiving an AM from RHS in 1969 under the name 'Betty Graham'. In 1938, in south east Tibet Ludlow and Sherriff encountered north facing hillsides clothed with this species in all shades of pink. In the sub-species *hypenanthum* the forms with small dark leaves are the most desirable. 'Annapurna 1974' with pale yellow flowers is one of the best. *R. laudandum* (Fig.27), from south east Tibet, forms a compact bush up to a metre in height. The undersides of the leaves are covered in scales, which may be dark red or green according to variety. The flowers vary between white and pale pink, with a hairy corolla. Apparently, only the variety *temoense*, with green leaf scales, is in cultivation. *R. trichostomum*, one of Forrest's finds in Yunnan, is an attractive, upright shrub with small grey-green leaves and large globular heads of tubular flowers which are white, pale rose or intermediate. All are equally eligible for the rock garden. *R. sargentianum* was introduced by Ernest Wilson from western Sichuan in 1903, where it has a very local distribution. It grows to about 30cm with a dense habit. The tubular flowers are yellow to white in colour. The leaves are aromatic. It is a hardy plant which makes a fine show.

Rhododendron Section
Boothia Subsection   The members of this subsection are very attractive but should only be grown in mild conditions. *R. leucaspis*, introduced by Kingdon Ward from the Tsangpo Gorge, Tibet, at 3000m, is considered by Evans as one of the most ornamental of the dwarf rhododendrons for which he recommends a sheltered site, shaded from early morning sun, where the large white flowers with chocolate stamens can realise their potential. *R. megeratum* is another fine species with chocolate stamens and yellow flowers in single or paired clusters. It has a wide Himalayan distribution and is also a

tender species worth a little effort in finding sheltered sites.

Campylogynum Subsection In this group there is only one variable species, *R. campylogynum*, discovered by Delavay in 1893 in western Yunnan and introduced by Forrest in 1912. It encompasses a great diversity of forms, consistent with its wide distribution from Arunachal Pradesh, south east Tibet, Upper Burma to south west Yunnan. Neat in growth to about 60cm, with leaves that are dark green above, glaucous on the under side, the thimble-like flowers nod on long pedicels above the evergreen foliage. They are immensely variable in colour, ranging from cream or pinkish through salmon to red and black-purple. The variety *myrtilloides*, a Kingdon Ward discovery from Upper Burma, with tiny flowers, includes the dwarfest forms within this group. Although some forms are tender, in general this is a first class, hardy species, considered by Peter Cox (1973) as among the finest of the dwarf rhododendrons. It keeps its compact shape, is easily grown and is quite charming when in flower. A collection of different colour forms growing together can hardly fail to excite attention.

Glauca Subsection Extending from east Nepal, south east Tibet through Sikkim to Bhutan, *R. glaucophyllum* was first found by Hooker in 1850. Evans recommends this as a foliage plant; the undersides of the leaves are intensely blue. With age it can become rather spreading in habit and can grow well over a metre, although some clones are much smaller. The bell-shaped flowers vary between pink-purple, rose to pale pink or creamy white. The variety *tubiforme* has a stiffer habit and rose pink campanulate flowers. *R. charitopes*, found by Farrer in Upper Burma in 1920, is less hardy although a beautiful shrub with apple-blossom pink flowers decorated with red spotting.

Lapponica Subsection This group includes a large number of dwarf rhododendrons. With one exception they are unlikely to exceed 1.5m in cultivation. The evergreen foliage is aromatic to varying degree. The flowers, usually of an open funnel shape, are produced in terminal trusses or are solitary. Colours include purple and purple-blue shades, sometimes yellow and very rarely white. About a dozen species are suited to the rock garden in Scotland. *R. lapponicum* is circumpolar in distribution, with geographical races in North America, Siberia and Japan. *R. impeditum*, discovered by Forrest in Yunnan in 1910, must be familiar to all rock gardeners. Neat in habit, growing to 30–40cm, with mauve to purple-blue flowers it is a hardy stand-by. *R. hippophaeoides*, found by Kingdon Ward in 1913 in Yunnan, is quite a different plant, upright in shape and growing to a metre or more, although generally less in cultivation. This is another very hardy and easy species with clusters of deep violet-blue flowers. Cox (1985) notes that the many introductions since 1913 are remarkably uniform for such a widespread species. *R. orthocladum* var. *microleucum*, another Forrest introduction, makes a very compact, hardy little plant especially notable for its white flowers in April and May. *R. rupicola* has perhaps the deepest coloured blue to purple flowers of this section. The variety *chryseum* is variable in habit but has attractive cream to yellow flowers and is perfectly hardy.

The closely related *R. flavidum* has large flowers which are also yellow. *R. fastigiatum*, in spite of its name, is not fastigiate, but forms dense, hummocks which, after many years growth may only attain some 25cm (Evans 1974). The flowers are various shades of light to dark purple. It is quite similar to *R. impeditum*, equally hardy but differs in the colour of the scales on the underside of the leaf which are darker in *impeditum*, with a translucent golden margin. *R. polycladum*, native to Yunnan, is a more straggling plant than the species already considered but is outstanding for its flower colour which ranges from lavender to blue-purple. Cox (1985) noted that the best forms are the nearest one can get to pure blue in the Lapponica Section.

Lepidota Subsection The species in this section vary in habit from low to upright and straggly. The open, campanulate flowers are borne on slender pedicels longer than the corolla and vary in colour, including white, yellow and pink to purple. Their distribution is widespread, from different altitudes and different ecological associations. They include common species in the Himalayas and Yunnan, tolerating drier sites in their native habitat. *R. lepidotum* (Fig.30), in cultivation since 1850, is a rather straggly species, growing to 60–90cm with pink, crimson, yellow or white flowers. *R. lowndesii* found by D.G. Lowndes in Nepal in 1950, is stoloniferous, forming a dense creeping mat, with yellow, red marked flowers. It is tender and better grown in a pan in the alpine house.

Maddenia Subsection *R. ciliatum* (Fig.29) grows 1-2 metres high with a fairly compact habit. The white or pinkish flowers are bell shaped, often narrowly so, while the calyx is conspicuously fringed with hairs. It occurs between 2500 and 3000m in Nepal, Sikkim, Bhutan and south east Tibet. It has often been introduced and has proved the parent of many cultivars.

Saluenensia Subsection includes small, evergreen, creeping to erect hardy species which can attain 1.5m. The flowers although funnel-shaped are so open as to appear almost flat. The calyx is usually large, coloured and hairy. Flower colour spans the range from pink to purple but no whites have been reported. The distinctions between the species are not well defined. *R. calostrotum*, discovered by Kingdon Ward in north east Burma, varies in habit from compact to upright. The distinctive young foliage is blue-green in colour and the large flowers crimson-purple. *R. calostrotum* ssp. *keleticum* is an old favourite, perfectly hardy and so easy that it is sometimes used as ground cover. Although not very freely produced in many of the available clones, the flat flowers are deep purple with red spots in the lower part of the corolla. *R. radicans* is smaller than ssp. *keleticum*, forming a 5–10cm layer of leaves, rooting as it spreads along the ground. Best grown on a peaty slope with a little shade it will reward with its display of usually solitary, flat purple flowers.

Scabrifolia Subsection   *R. racemosum* (Fig.31) is one of the hardiest of the dwarf species. It readily produces self-sown seedlings and can flourish under quite spartan conditions in the open. The flowers vary from various shades of pink to white. This is one of the species which clothes whole hillsides in its native habitat of Yunnan and south west Sichuan. The best horticultural form is Forrest's Number 19404. There are other clones which will grow to an unwelcome height and should be avoided.

Trichoclada Subsection   This includes another of Forrest's finds in western Yunnan at 3500m. *R. lepidostylum* grows to about a metre, carries yellow flowers, singly or in pairs, but is mainly valued for its evergreen, bluish-green leaves which make an attractive show from spring well into the late summer. *R. cowanianum* is "one of the least spectacular rhododendrons and only of interest to the keen collector" according to the Coxes in "The Encylopedia of Rhododendron Species", but it has a certain delicate charm and is easy to grow. First introduced in 1954 it was re-introduced in 1991 by Chadwell and McKelvie.

Triflora Subsection   *R. hanceanum* may vary between clones, from compact and low-growing to tall and sprawling. The white to yellow funnel-shaped flowers are held in elongated trusses of 5–15. Some clones like 'Nanum', which is very dwarf, produce yellow flowers in great abundance and is much more attractive than the type.

Uniflora Subsection   *R. ludlowii* was discovered by Ludlow in south east Tibet in 1936. He found it growing to about 30cm with large, flattish flowers with long pedicels, of primrose-yellow colour, spotted with reddish brown at the base. It grows slowly and is regarded as rather difficult but it has played an important role as parent of a number of valuable, yellow flowered hybrids such as 'Chikor' and 'Curlew'. *R. pemakoense* found by Kingdon Ward in the Tsangpo Gorge, south east Tibet is another compact shrub growing to about 60cm. This has the reputation of hiding its foliage below a mass of large pink-purple flowers, even at an early age. It is easily grown and will spread by suckers if well suited to its site. *R. pumilum* was introduced by Hooker in the mid-nineteenth century. It is a prostrate species growing up to 15cm. Although attractive with pink, thimble-like flowers, it appears to be not too easy to satisfy, at least in eastern Scotland. Ludlow and Sherriff came across a small group of albino plants.

Ponticum Section

Neriiflora Subsection Within this Subsection is a group of species which form small, prostrate creeping shrubs. The most famous species is *R. forrestii*, with large, fleshy, tubular, campanulate flowers which are scarlet to crimson in colour. Cox reports that the best specimens he has seen were growing up or down north facing walls or rocks. Since the type is reluctant to flower in cultivation it is better to grow either var. *repens* or var. *tumescens* which are less so. It is important to keep the plant free of moss and weeds, and protect young growth with a cloche — extra effort but worth making for such impressive flowers.

Williamsiana Subsection *R. williamsianum* was discovered by Wilson in west Sichuan in 1908. It has a compact habit but grows from 60cm to 1.5m. The large bell-like flowers range from pale pink to rose. It is hardy, provided it is not sited in a frost pocket where it is likely to suffer damage to its handsome bronze, spring foliage.

Vaccinium These are peat bed species. *V. delavayi*, from south west China and Upper Burma, forms an evergreen shrub about 40cm tall but sometimes very much larger. It is grown chiefly for its bronzy young foliage, since the white or pink tinged, urn-shaped flowers are rarely seen. The crimson or purplish fruit is about half a centimetre wide. *V. nummularia* has quite a different form since it produces a stiff, branched, bristly, prostrate evergreen mat. The light pink flowers are succeeded by globular fruits, which are at first red then turn black. In the wild it usually behaves as an epiphyte with pendulous habit.

Gentianaceae
Gentiana Along with the primulas and rhodendrons, the Asiatic gentians include some of the most important Sino-Himalayan species introduced this century. Among the nine sections into which the genus is divided, Section Frigida includes most of the cultivated species, which have a tufted or lax growth form, with linear or linear lanceolate basal leaves and stem leaves with a cartilaginous margin. Both calyx and corolla are 4-5 lobed. The naming and distinctions among the Ornata group of autumn gentians have given rise to confusion. For example *G. sino-ornata* was discovered by Forrest in 1904 in north west Yunnan and later in the Lichiang range in 1910. Seed from the later collection was flowered at Ness and the Royal Botanic Garden, Edinburgh under the name *G. ornata* and was only later recognised as distinct from *ornata* which has also been confused with *G. veitchiorum*. It is not surprising that such mix-ups should occur since these gentians have a very similar growth form and general appearance and many natural populations are very variable in corolla colour and leaf shape and size. Sporadic collecting from different sites focuses attention on such differences, rather than the

inter-grading continuities which more representative collecting often reveals.

A perceptive approach to the taxonomic problems was summarised in the SRGC Journal by James Cullen (1978). The Ornata group of gentians has a very wide distribution in eastern Asia which extends from central Nepal in the west, eastwards through the Himalaya into Sikkim, Bhutan, Tibet, Assam, North Burma and the mountains of mid-west Sichuan into Kansu and beyond Tsinghai. Apart from a small area in Tibet the distribution is continuous. The ecological requirements of all members of the group are very similar — damp pasture land at 2750–4500m. In cultivation they thrive under cool acid conditions. Cross pollination appears to be the rule. Pollen is released shortly after the flowers open while the style lengthens above the anthers, to open a few days later to reveal the stigmatic surfaces. According to Ian McNaughton (1996), who has grown a great range of species and cultivars of these Himalayan gentians, a variety of pollinators visit the flowers, especially hover flies in search of pollen and small bumble bees in search of the nectar which is located at the base of the corolla. Within the complex of populations there is a reticulate pattern of variation, in the sense that a few diagnostic characters used for identification turn up in different combinations in different parts of the geographical range of the group, ruling out a simple, hierarchical classification. As a contrast, however, there is a gradient or cline in corolla length from west to east of the range, from an average of 34mm in Nepal to 63mm in Kansu. Many hybrids have been produced in cultivation and occasionally reported from the wild.

Faced with this kind of situation botanists tend to recognise a few broad categories or attempt to identify and give names to as many as possible of the various combinations of characters i.e. the 'lumper' versus the 'splitter' approach. However, Cullen adopts the more sophisticated concept of the 'aggregate species' within which one can recognise a number of micro-species. On this scheme the Ornata Series of the Frigida Section comprises a single aggregate species, *Gentiana ornata* Wallich sensu-lato, and a number of micro-species, which correspond well enough with the species recognised by gardeners, as well as intermediates. Better understanding of the situation will come from information about chromosome number across the range. It is already known that in populations of *G. sino-ornata*, *G. farreri* and *G. veitchiorum* which have been examined cytologically, the plants are tetraploid in *sino-ornata* and *farreri* and diploid in *veitchiorum*. Where adjacent populations differ in this way the likelihood of effective crossing between them is greatly diminished because of the high degree of sterility of hybrids. Although such a difference in chromosome number apparently validates the taxonomic distinctions between *G. veitchiorum* and the other two species, before this evidence can be taken at face value we need to know how far it is consistent across the range of relevant populations. Bearing these qualifications in mind we can note the more important members of the Frigida Section.

G. ornata, from Nepal and Sikkim, was the first member of the group to be discovered by Wallich in 1820 but it was not brought into cultivation until 1930 by T. Hay. The plants are small, with a terminal rosette of narrow leaves which are fully expanded at flowering time. The flowers are sessile. The corolla, which expands immediately above the calyx into a tubby shape, can be of various shades of blue, or even white with yellow-green stripes, bordered in darker blue or purple. *G. prolata* was discovered by Cooper in Bhutan in 1914. Its distribution overlaps that of *G. ornata* in Nepal and Sikkim but spreads further east into Bhutan, Tibet and Assam. Although a smaller plant it is so similar to *G. ornata* that it was not separated until 1918. Unlike *ornata*, the corolla does not expand above the calyx but is smoothly tapered. Since the flowers are smaller it has been neglected although it has the advantage of flowering a little earlier than *G. ornata*. *G. veitchiorum* (Fig.35), found in 1915 in Sichuan by Wilson, produces larger plants with a persistent basal rosette of broad, blunt leaves. The flowers are sessile. The corolla is narrowly funnel-shaped with reflexed lobes, 40–45mm long. Both the lobes and inside of the tube are deep purple-blue; outside there are five broad greenish-yellow bands. McNaughton (1996) has noted that the original species is very scarce and that a later introduction by Ludlow and Sherriff in 1942 was kept at Inshriach Nursery for some years. New introductions have been made recently by the CLD 1990 and ACE 1994 expeditions and made more widely available by the Askival Alpine Nursery. *G. sino-ornata* (Fig.34) forms robust plants which tend to form mats. The basal rosette is in bud at the time of flowering. The lanceolate leaves taper gradually to the sharp apex. The sessile or almost sessile flowers are funnel-shaped and of various shades of blue within and deeper blue with greenish-yellow stripes without. An albino form was discovered by Forrest.

G. depressa from Nepal has proved to be a difficult species in cultivation in spite of Wilkie's (1950) comment that "it appears to be quite hardy and a good grower". There is an immense range of variation in this species, described by Christie in the SRGC Journal in 1996, following the 1995 GOS Expedition to central Nepal.

Cullen notes that plants which manifest various combinations of the traits used to separate *sino-ornata* and *veitchiorum* occur in different parts of Yunnan and south west Sichuan. They present the general appearance of *G. veitchiorum* but lack the basal rosette and may be hybrids. *G. sino-ornata* is a favourite in Scottish gardens and is easily maintained in damp, cool, peaty conditions but should be divided and replanted every few years for best results. *G. farreri* was discovered by Farrer in Kansu. Cullen restricts the name to the uniform and distinct plants from this region, although it has been applied by others to populations from Sichuan. Typically they form strong growing plants, with a basal rosette in bud at flowering time and a mat-forming habit. The flowers have a distinct peduncle. The corolla is of a pale 'Cambridge' blue with a clear white throat – a very distinct combination which, along with the narrow, grass-like leaves makes this species easily recognisable. McNaughton doubts whether the original *G. farreri* is still in existence and suggests that what commonly passes for it may be hybrids with a partial resemblance to the real thing. Cullen attaches the name *G. oreodoxa* to specimens collected in mid-Yunnan and adjacent Burma, which resemble *sino-ornata* but the corolla tends to swell as it emerges above the calyx in a manner reminiscent of *ornata*. Although fairly distinct in parts of the distribution there are evidently intermediates elsewhere, grading into *G. sino-ornata* to the north and east. Different samples have been given names which obscure rather than reveal the biological reality of the inter-grading populations. The most recent addition to the garden-worthy species is *G. coelestis* which was collected at 4200m by the Chengtu, Lijang, Dali (CLD) expedition in 1992. According to Ian Christie (1995), who has successfully grown and described the species, the flowers recall those of *G. ornata*, with small, tubby-shaped, sky-blue trumpets which face upwards. The inside of the corolla is striped deep blue and even more darkly spotted.

A number of hybrids have been produced, which are often more widely grown and more vigorous than their parents. To mention a few: *G.* x *macaulayi* refers to hybrids between *farreri* and *sino-ornata*. According to Cullen the name embraces seedlings from both the second generation and back-crosses. A number of recognisably different forms are in cultivation. The cross between *G. farreri* and *G. ornata* has been made in both directions. 'Devonhall' refers to the cross with *ornata* as seed parent while the reverse cross is called 'Farorna'. They are similar, with pale flowers which are somewhat expanded above the calyx, like *ornata*. The cross between *G. farreri* and *G. lawrencei* was made by Macaulay of the Royal Botanic Garden, Edinburgh and acquired the name x *caroli*. The plant is very like *G. farreri* in appearance, with slightly smaller flowers and is more easily grown than *G. lawrencei*. The hybrid 'Inverleith' was produced at RBGE in 1938 from the cross *G. farreri* x *G. veitchiorum*. It is intermediate between the parents and has become a popular rock-garden plant although the consistency of origin of plants with this name is suspect. The cross between *G. veitchiorum* and *G. sino-ornata* probably occurs naturally. The artificial cross has been made both ways. With *G. sino-ornata* as seed parent the hybrid is known as x. *stevenagensis* and the reciprocal as x. *bernardii*. Both are intermediate between the parents, with basal rosettes rather like those of *G. veitchiorum* and purplish leaves and flowers. Hybrids have also been produced between *G. veitchiorum* and both *G. ornata* and *G. prolata*. This list does not nearly exhaust the total kinds of hybridisations, which have been fully documented by Ian McNaughton in his 1996 article in the SRGC Journal. The upshot of all this is that an indefinite number of cultivars of similar general habit but with subtle differences of hue, according to the origin of the parents, are available and will doubtless continue to increase in number.

Propagation of these gentians is generally from rooted offsets which are teased apart in February or March, although not all kinds produce them with the vigour of *G. sino-ornata*. According to McNaughton some forms root well enough from stem nodes while others may be increased by 2-3cm cuttings from stem tips. After insertion into a peat and sand mixture or equivalent they are kept cool and moist. Increase by seed is likely to be most effective in non-hybrid plants since hybrids are so often sterile. It should be sown on a well drained peat based seed compost and exposed to frost to promote germination.

Among other members of the Frigida Section we can note *G. georgei* (Fig.32), first found by Forrest in north west Yunnan in alpine meadows at 3400-3700m. Referred to by Wilkie (1950) as "one of the aristocrats of the genus", it forms basal rosettes from which spring 10cm stems carrying a single flower of deep blue, purplish flowers of variable hue. It is uncertain whether it is in cultivation. Known from the end of the nineteenth century, *S. hexaphylla* (Fig.33) was introduced to Britain from Kansu by Farrer in 1914, although most of the seed was sent back by Kingdon Ward. As the name signifies, it is at once recognisable by the leaves which are in whorls of six and by the six lobes to the corolla which is pale blue with six broad blue bands on the outside. It is an attractive plant growing to about 15cm. It is easily grown in lime free conditions but should be lifted, divided and planted in a new site or at least with fresh soil every two years. *G. sikkimensis* was first collected in the nineteenth century but was rediscovered and introduced by Forrest from north west Yunnan in 1904. The shoots, which may grow to 15cm, form a mat, and carry the flowers in terminal groups above a cluster of leaves. The blue, white-throated corolla is tubular to funnel-shaped. Easy to grow, given a damp site, it is not in the first flight of gentians and is not often seen. *G. stragulata* is another Forrest discovery in Yunnan in 1914. It is rather like a larger version of *sikkimensis*, although the corolla, one to three per stem, is contracted at the mouth. The colour is blue within, purple-blue without. *G. trichotoma* has also been known since the late nineteenth but the introduction to Britain was from Sichuan, near the Tibetan border, by Kingdon Ward. It grows more or less erect to 60cm or more. There are generally three flowers per stalk in the leaf axils as well as at the end of the stem. They are deep blue, with a whitish, blue-spotted interior, occasionally white. This is a handsome plant which grows well enough in Scotland provided the soil is not too dry.

In the Section Aptera, *G. gracilipes* from Kansu has been in Britain since 1914. From the rosette of fairly long (15cm) narrow leaves arise several stems carrying paired leaves which closely invest the stems. The corolla of about 4cm is bell-shaped, deep purple-blue inside and greenish outside. It is easily grown and readily increased by seed. *G. kuroo* is a native of the alpine regions of Kashmir and the north west Himalaya. Known since Royle found it in 1835, it was not until 1929 that a substantial importation of seed from Kashmir brought it to the notice of gardeners. The more or less decumbent stems grow to 25cm with a rosette of numerous basal leaves. The terminal flowers are solitary or occasionally two or more on short stalks. The narrowly bell-shaped corolla, about 4cm long and almost as wide when fully open, is blue with greenish spots and a pale, whitish throat. The flowers do not appear until September or October. It prefers deep loam in the sunniest part of the garden. The true species is now rare in cultivation although impostors abound.

Finally we have a couple of closely related species worth noting in the Section Isomeria, *G. cachemirica* and *G. loderi*. *G. cachemirica* is perennial with lax, ascending habit and basal, oval leaves. The ovate, or ovate-rounded, stem leaves are in pairs. The calyx is partly hidden by the uppermost leaves. The bell-shaped corolla is at least 2.5cm long and about half as wide and of a fine blue colour. *G. loderi*, a native of Kashmir, has been confused with *G. cachemirica* from which, according to Wilkie, it differs chiefly in having a more tubular corolla with larger lobes and fringed, erect folds. These are both very desirable, scree plants.

Lamiaceae (Labiatae)

Dracocephalum In this widely distributed genus the opposite leaves are entire or toothed. The tubular and distinctly two-lipped flowers are in terminal whorls. There are several Sino-Himalayan rock-garden species. *D. calophyllum*, introduced by Forrest from Yunnan, grows to about 30cm or more with deep purple-blue flowers in a terminal raceme. The closely related *D. forrestii*, with abundant, finely divided leaves grows to about the same size. The outstandingly beautiful *D. isabellae*, with clusters of large (4cm), violet flowers, was found by Forrest on the Chungtien Plateau and dedicated to his sister, who acted as his agent on his first expedition. It is rarely seen. *D. nutans* spreads by rhizomes, and grows to between 15 and 30cm, with smaller, blue to lilac flowers. The attractive *D. wallichii* from Himachal Pradesh is now in cultivation following several introductions in the 1990s. Moist, well drained sunny sites suit all these species.

Fabaceae (Leguminosae)

Although leguminous plants abound in the Himalayas very few have remained in cultivation for long except a number of shrubs. The genera *Oxytropis* and *Astragalus* contain many beautiful species but their deep tap root systems present difficulties in cultivation.

Papaveraceae

Corydalis Both the Sino-Himalaya species noted here require moist, organic-rich, well drained conditions. *C. cashmeriana* (Fig.36) grows from small, ovoid tubers which produce flowers generally labelled as sky-blue. Ranging widely from Kashmir to south east Tibet this is one of the species sent home in quantity by Ludlow and Sherriff but at first only a few growers, especially the Knox Finlays, succeeded in keeping it. Gradually as its requirements became better known, and perhaps as a consequence of unconscious selection for adaptation to Scottish conditions, it became well established. Fairly recently *C. flexuosa* has been introduced from Sichuan by Compton, D'Arcy and Rix and this has proved an instant success in cool, shady sites. The wild species has turquoise blue flowers, but there are other cultivars with different shades of blue e.g. 'Blue Panda, 'China Blue' and 'Père David'. *Corydalis* is one of the genera which are becoming very fashionable towards the end of the century. Many more species are coming into cultivation largely as a result of the pioneering work undertaken at the Göteborg Botanic Garden in Sweden.

Meconopsis Although the earliest introduction of seed from species of *Meconopsis* dates from Hooker's mid-nineteenth century expedition to Sikkim, followed by sundry introductions during the rest of the century, the main introductions were during the 20th century. This genus is centred in the Sino-Himalayan region. The most wide ranging species, *M. horridula*, has a distribution which extends from Upper Kansu, north west Yunnan, Upper Burma, along the Himalayan chain to Nepal. With the exception of the yellow European *M. cambrica*, all the other 40 or so species occur within the *M. horridula* range, but generally with a much more restricted, often quite local, distribution. They are true alpines which grow in woods, meadows and scree slopes from 2000m upwards. Taylor, whose monograph (1934) on the genus is our authority and source, notes that several species occur at 5000m while *horridula* has been recorded at an upper limit of about 6000m. Although many of the species grow to a large size and are hardly rock garden plants, they are companions of the alpine rhododendrons and primulas and must be included in our survey. The genus is divided by Taylor into a number of Sections, Sub-sections and Series. The species selected for comment are listed by Series and this is sufficient to indicate closeness of relationship.

Chelidonifolia *M. chelidonifolia* is polycarpic with rather small 4-petalled yellow flowers and a branching habit. In cultivation the purple-black stems may ascend to 1.75m but, according to Wilson, who collected and introduced it, wild specimens were smaller with clear yellow flowers about 6.5cm across. Since seed is hard to come by propagation is by vegetative buds which appear in the axils of the upper stem leaves. Like most meconopsis it prefers cool, damp, shady sites to realise its potential, which is perhaps under-rated.

Villosae *M. villosa* (Fig.43) is also polycarpic but differs from the preceding species in its unbranched stem. Also, the flowers arise singly in the axils of the uppermost leaves. This species was first recorded by Hooker in 1849 but collected again in Bhutan in 1913 by Cooper. The basal leaves have long bristly petioles. The 4-petalled flowers are yellow. According to Evans (loc. cit.) *M. villosa* resents disturbance and should be propagated by seed which is readily produced.

Superbae   This series includes the two closely related, monocarpic species *MM. superba* and *regia*. The leaves are toothed along the margins and provided with a dense pubescence which makes them easily recognisable. In *M. regia* the flowers on a branched inflorescence are yellow, while in *M. superba* they are white and spring singly from the axils of the upper leaves. *M. regia* was first introduced from Nepal in 1928 and several times since from the same country. The basal leaves form a large golden coloured rosette. It is hardy, given the usual preferred conditions of moisture and a cool site during its growing season and rich feeding. According to James Cobb, who published a valuable account of cultural methods for different species of the genus in the SRGC Journal (1994), and in his comprehensive book 'Meconopsis' (1989), at the time of writing it appeared not to be in cultivation since what passes as the species is the result of hybridisation with *M. napaulensis*. Although grown in Britain since the late nineteenth century from seed obtained by a native collector from Tibet, it was Ludlow and Sherriff's 1933 introductions of *M. superba* from west Bhutan which are of most importance. *M. superba* appears not quite so easy to maintain as *regia*. Cobb emphasises the need for organic feed, deep, rich soil, some winter protection and a regular supply of water to the roots to protect from summer drought.

Robustae   In this series all the species have deeply lobed leaves. The three species mentioned here are monocarpic and readily hybridise with one another to produce sterile progeny. The flowers are either yellow or some shade of red, blue or purple or rarely white. *M. dhwojii* was first flowered in Britain in 1932. This species is essentially a woodland plant with finely divided leaves. The numerous 4-petalled yellow or cream-yellow flowers are carried on axillary branches to form a conical mass. The leaves are marked with dark purple spots at the base of the bristles. It readily hybridises with *M. paniculata* and *M. napaulensis* to produce sterile progeny. The closely related *M. gracilipes* was collected in central Nepal in the late 1990s by Carrie, Christie and McKelvie. It is a delicate and delightful species which is now in cultivation.

M. paniculata (Fig.40) was first introduced by Hooker in 1849 from Sikkim but Cooper found it in Bhutan in 1914-15 and Kingdon Ward in north east Assam in 1928, so it has a wide distribution. It is easily recognised by the pendulous, yellow or white flowers which arise singly in the axils of the uppermost leaves and in several-flowered sprays from the lower leaves. Taylor notes that in some forms the flowers are too small to warrant horticultural notice but, in others, they may be 5cm across and worth growing. It is very similar in appearance to *M. napaulensis* although smaller. Cobb notes that two forms are in cultivation: a lime green form from Sikkim and a grey-green

Fig. 87 *Dianthus scardicus* (p.154) Fig. 88 *Ramonda serbica* (p.157)

Fig. 89 *Corydalis bulbosa* (p.157) Fig. 90 *Corydalis ochroleuca* (p.157)

Fig. 91 *Acantholimon sp.* (p.139)

Fig. 92 *Androsace hedraeantha* (p.158)

Fig. 93 *Androsace villosa* (p.158)

Fig. 94 *Cyclamen cilicium* (p.140)

Fig. 95 *Cyclamen parviflorum* (p.140)

Fig. 96 *Primula amoena* (p.141)

Fig. 97 *Trollius ranunculinus* (p.142)   Fig. 98 *Saxifraga sempervivum* (p.159)

Fig. 99 *Saxifraga marginata* (p.159)

100 *Daphne oleoides/Helleborus cyclophyllus* (pp.159/158)

Fig. 101 *Viola graeca* (p.159)

Fig. 102 *Crocus abantensis* (p.144)

Fig. 103 *Crocus biflorus* ssp. *isauricus* (p.144)

Fig. 104 *Crocus chrysanthus* (p.144)

Fig. 105 *Crocus cancellatus* ssp. *mazzaricus* (p.143)

Fig. 106 *Crocus fleischeri* (p.144)

Fig. 107 *Crocus pallasii* ssp. *pallasii* (p.160)   Fig. 108 *Crocus sieberi* ssp. *sublimis* (p.161)

Fig. 109 *Crocus sieberi* ssp. *atticus* (p.161)

Fig. 110 *Iris afghanica* (p.145)

Fig. 111 *Iris attica* (p.145)

Fig. 112 *Iris unguicularis* (p.161)

Fig. 113 *Iris winogradowii* (p.146)

Fig. 114 *Fritillaria acmopetala* (p.146)   Fig. 115 *Fritillaria bithynica* (p.146)

Fig. 116 *Fritillaria crassifolia* ssp. *kurdica* (p.147)   Fig. 117 *Fritillaria davisii* (p.162)

Fig. 118 *Fritillaria latifolia* var. *nobilis* (p.147)

Fig. 119 *Muscari macrocarpum* (p.148)   Fig. 120 *Ornithogalum oligophyllum* (p.1

Fig. 121 *Scilla sibirica* ssp. *armena* (p.148)

Fig. 122 *Sternbergia candida* (p.149) Fig. 123 *Sternbergia sicula* (p.148)

Fig. 124 *Sternbergia lutea* (p.148)   Fig. 125 *Tulipa biflora* (p.149)

Fig. 126 *Erigeron aureus* (p.167)   Fig. 127 *Erigeron compositus* (p.167)

Fig. 128 *Erigeron pinnatisectus* (p.167)   Fig. 129 *Hymenoxis acaulis caespitosa* (p.168)

Fig. 130 *Townsendia condensata* (p.168)   Fig. 131 *Townsendia exscapa* (p.168)

Fig. 132 *Townsendia montana* (p.168)

Fig. 133 *Cornus canadensis* (p.170)

Fig. 134 *Kalmia polifolia* (p.171)

Fig. 135 *Phyllodoce empetriformis* (p.17

Fig. 136 *Gentiana algida* (p.172)

Fig. 137 *Phlox adsurgens* (p.173)

Fig. 138 *Phacelia sericea* (p.172)

Fig. 139 *Phlox diffusa* (p.174)

Fig. 140 *Phlox hendersonii* (p.174)

Fig. 141 *Phlox hirsuta* (p.174)

one from Bhutan. *M. napaulensis* is very variable so introductions from different regions have led to taxonomic confusion. To quote Taylor "there is a flux of forms which so intergrade as to make any precise definition impossible". The flower colour may be red, purple or, less often, white in Nepal while blue colours turn up in parts of Sikkim and west Sichuan. This hardy, border plant, easily raised from seed, can grow to 2m or more and carry up to 300 flowers. The monocarpic rosettes, which often persist for several years before the flower spike appears, are extremely handsome and merit a place in the garden for their appearance alone. *M. napaulensis* and *M. paniculata* differ in stigma colour which is green in the former and purple in the latter. Cobb (1988) notes that purple appears to be recessive to green, a distinction to be borne in mind when examining putative hybrids.

Simplicifolia   In this series the species are "potentially polycarpic". The entire or slightly lobed leaves are gathered into a basal rosette with persistent leaf bases. The solitary flowers on long scapes arise from the rosettes. According to Taylor there are two strains of *M. simplicifolia* – one, usually polycarpic with blue-purple flowers and the other, usually monocarpic and rather rare in cultivation, with light blue flowers. It prefers good drainage, an open soil and a shady site and seed is set freely although Cobb rates this one of the more difficult species to keep going. *M. quintuplinervia* (Fig.42) is a polycarpic species discovered by Przewalski in 1880, but it was effectively introduced to Britain in 1914-1915 by Farrer who was greatly attached to its elegant, blue-purple flowers. Unlike the other species considered it is stoloniferous. Given a cool, moist spot it will spread to form a mat which may be either of the preferred, compact form or more straggly, decked with an array of pendulous flowers held on 25cm scapes. It is hardy and easily propagated by division in spring.

Grandis   The three species in this Series selected for comment are distinguished by the presence of a false whorl of stem leaves from which the flower stalks arise. The monocarpic *M. integrifolia* (Fig.39) was first introduced to Europe by the French missionary Abbé Farges but the effective introduction to Britain was by Wilson in 1904. In its natural habitat it grows to about a metre and may carry as many as 18 yellow flowers which can be an impressive 20–25cm in diameter. It produces seed freely and prefers a cool, moist, well drained site with some shade. *M. pseudointegrifolia* (Fig.41) is closely related to *M. integrifolia* from which it chiefly differs in carrying its flowers on basal scapes and by its long style, in contrast to the lobed, sessile stigmas of *M. integrifolia*. The hybrid between *M. integrifolia* and *M. simplicifolia*, which occurs in nature is Kingdon Ward's 'Ivory Poppy', which was called *M. harleyana*, after R.L. Harley who first encountered the plant in cultivation. *M. betonicifolia*, the well known border plant, may be either mono- or polycarpic. First found by Delavay in Yunnan in 1886, Forrest,

Rock and Kingdon Ward later sent back seed. Within the species there may be two geographic races, one of which acquired the name *M. baileyi*. The few flowers are semi-pendulous and succeed one another from the axils of the uppermost leaves. The flowers vary between rose to shades of blue. *M. grandis* (Fig.38) is polycarpic and native to eastern Nepal, through south east Tibet to Sikkim and Bhutan. A number of introductions were made in the 19th century and it was first flowered in Britain at the Royal Botanic Garden Edinburgh in 1895. Forms vary in quality, but the best is that discovered by Sherriff in 1933 in Bhutan, known as Sherriff 600' or 'GS 600', which was found growing to over a metre in height on hillsides among small bushes. This well known species with the rich blue flowers is quite hardy in many parts of Scotland, provided it is given the usual cool, moist root-run and rich organic feeding. It can be distinguished from the other blue poppy, *M. betonicifolia*, by its simple, unlobed leaves. There are a number of different forms of what are called *M. grandis* in the trade, some fertile and others quite sterile and suspected to be of hybrid origin. Evelyn Stevens has taken the lead in sorting out the confusion among the many cultivars which are called 'GS 600'. The most famous hybrid, of course, is x *sheldonii*, the result of crossing *M. grandis* with *M. betonicifolia*. In the late 1990s, as already noted, a Meconopsis Group was set up under the auspices of the SRGC to try to bring some order into the naming of the various perennial, blue poppies which are grown in many gardens. This group is but one of many devoted to the study of individual genera.

<u>Aculeatae</u>   The species in this series are monocarpic and are generally provided with stout bristles or pungent spines. *M. latifolia* is native to Kashmir from where it was introduced by Appleton in 1908. This is one of the hardier species which can tolerate comparatively dry conditions, provided the soil is open and well drained. Growing to about a metre in height the numerous flowers, borne singly in the axils of the upper stem leaves or sometimes along the length of the stem, are pale blue or occasionally white and borne on pedicels which are covered with spreading spines. In favourable conditions self-sown seedlings are regularly produced so propagation is easy.

Finally, we have *M. horridula* (Fig.37) which earns its name from the armoury of pungent spines which protect the base and rest of the stem as well as both sides of the leaves. As noted earlier it has the widest distribution of all the species. Established in Britain since about 1904, it has been re-introduced a number of times, so forms vary a great deal. The Mount Everest expedition in 1921 collected *M. horridula* at about 6000m, in the form of a small, basal rosette and scapes only a few centimetres high, compared with the normal growth to about a metre. It is not difficult to grow given sharp drainage.

In his account of cultural methods Cobb repeatedly emphasises the need for rich feeding for these poppies, with protection from summer drought by root watering and care to minimise risk of fungal infection. Many growers in Scotland lost meconopsis plants in the dry summers of 1996 and 1997. Contrary to what most people felt about the wet summer of 1998, meconopsis growers revelled in the 'pseudo' Himalayan conditions. Although survival does not appear to be influenced by soil pH, acid conditions favour the development of blue colour in species like *M. betonicifolia* and *M. grandis*. Conditions for effective seed germination are critical. Cobb advises that seed should be sown in early to mid-February in warmth and reasonable light. Day temperature should not exceed 13-15°C or fall below 7°C at night. High humidity should be maintained, preferably with mist, before and after germination.

Primulaceae
Androsace A number of Sino-Himalayan species of this large genus have become established. They share the same general growth form, with spreading stolons, which establish a mat of variable size or a hummock in some species. They generally have a wide natural distribution, favouring screes and rocky open situations. *A. delavayi* (Fig.58) is a cushion forming species which may become mat-like with age. The almost sessile, fragrant flowers are white or of shades of pink with a yellow eye. A high elevation scree species from Nepal to north Burma and Tibet, used to the protection of heavy winter snow cover, it is best grown in the alpine house to escape the frost. *A. himalaica* grows to about 6cm with relatively large pale pink to purple flowers with a yellow eye, carried up to a dozen at a time in a compact umbel. *A. lanuginosa* is an easily grown, rather sprawling species with lilac flowers with a greenish-yellow eye, also in umbels. It is best grown in well drained, rather sparse conditions. *A. muscoidea* is another stoloniferous species which forms small, tight mats. The white, green-eyed flowers, are borne singly or as small umbels. There is a form *longiscapa* which rather resembles *A. sarmentosa*, noted below. *A. sempervivoides*, from the north-west Himalaya, produces stolons, like *A. sarmentosa*, but is smaller, with glabrous leaves. *A. sarmentosa* is a larger species with red stolons which spread to form a mat. The pink to carmine flowers, with a green-yellow eye, are arranged in tight umbels. With a wide range from Kashmir to western China it is an admirable plant for the scree or raised bed. *A strigillosa* from the central Himalayas is rather different. It forms open clumps which carry large, loose umbels of pinkish-white flowers, with a deep purple-red reverse, borne on stalks up to 20cm. It needs winter cover. Several of these species of similar appearance are often confused. Margaret and Henry Taylor have made a notable contribution by naming and bringing into cultivation many of the androsace species of northern India. Only a few of these Himalayan species will grow in conventional rock gardens. Most need the specialised conditions of alpine house, frame or raised bed.

Omphalogramma This genus closely resembles *Primula* in which genus it was formerly included. However, the solitary, funnel-shaped, long tubed flowers generally have 6 and sometimes 7 or 8 petals and are carried horizontally. They are plants of great beauty, found wild on moist alpine slopes and are generally regarded as rather difficult to maintain. Moist, organic-rich soil and a sunny, sheltered site offer the best chance of success. In *O. delavayi* the flower is in the form of an open funnel with deep purple, fringed or toothed petals and borne on 10 to 20cm stems. *O. elegans*, a Forrest plant, is one of the easier species. The flowers are bluish-purple with white hairs on the upper surface. *O. elwesiana* (Fig.59), discovered in Sikkim in 1878, with violet-purple flowers, is smaller and grows to about 15cm. *O. vinciflorum*, according to Evans, is the species which flowers best. It is tall and completely dies down in winter to survive as a large resting bud, which is easily displaced. The flowers are indigo blue to deep purple.

Primula The greatest diversity, amounting to nearly 50% of the species in the genus, occurs in the eastern Himalayas, within the mountain regions of Sichuan, Yunnan, Upper Burma, Assam and south east Tibet. According to Richards (1993) if we include central and western Himalayas the total rises to just under 70%, compared with the 6.8% for Europe. They are comparative newcomers which have evolved during the geologically recent formation of the Himalayan mountains which are still developing. It has been suggested that dispersal from this region to other northern zones, including northern Asia, Europe and beyond may have taken place during the successive glacial eras.

In keeping with their montane origins, at 3500-4500m, primulas are essentially plants of cool, moist habitats, generally requiring good drainage, shade and often a rich substrate of humus. More than 300 species have been recorded from the Himalayan Region. Although in their native habitats many of the species grow in immense abundance, often by the hectare, many are notoriously difficult to maintain in cultivation, either because of winter rot, failure to set seed or inherent short longevity. Scotland is fortunate in providing some of the most generally favourable conditions for garden culture although, as the Stones (1983) have noted, the flowers of quite a number of them are often spoiled by late spring frosts. Where this is likely frame culture is advised. Also many are short-lived in cultivation and need to be maintained from seed. The most consistent early successes were recorded by the staff of RBGE and skilled growers like Major and Mrs Knox Finlay of Keillour Castle and Mr and Mrs John Renton of Branklyn, both of Perthshire. Later Jack Drake at Inshriach Nursery made a wide range of Asiatic species commercially available. It is interesting that plants do well in many locations for a number of years then all die about the same time. It is uncertain whether weather conditions are responsible but it is certain that almost all Himalayan primulas need to be replenished from fresh imports of seed from time to time.

The species selected for notice here include those most widely grown as well as others which are kept by only a few growers or have survived in the past for at least a time and therefore merit renewed attention. Mostly, but not exclusively, we are dealing with species which were either originally discovered or rediscovered and introduced to cultivation by Forrest, Cooper or Ludlow and Sherriff and their associates, Taylor, Hicks and Elliot, especially by Sherriff who pioneered the importation of live plants by air. We have paid particular attention to R.S. Masterton's SRGC Journal (1975) review of species grown in Scotland.

In such a large genus it is no surprise that the taxonomy is sometimes complex and there have been differences of opinion as to whether particular accessions are to be accorded specific or sub-specific status. Wright Smith and Fletcher laid the foundations for classifying members of the genus into a number of Sections based on such characters as type of inflorescence, structure of the leaf hairs, degree of development of the bracts etc. in a long series of papers in the Transactions of the Royal Society of Edinburgh and also the Transactions and Proceedings of the Botanical Society of Edinburgh between 1941 and 1948. Richards (1993) has recently reviewed the taxonomy, including additional characters, and has ended up with a scheme which, while basically similar to that of Wright and Fletcher, differs to some extent in what is included in some of the Sections and in their names. Since Wright Smith and Fletcher's nomenclature is the one currently followed in trade catalogues etc. we have used it in the following survey of the Sections.

Amethystina   There are a dozen species and sub-species in this section with only *P. kingii* represented in a few gardens, including, at one time, Ascreavie, Kirriemuir, where Mrs Elizabeth Sherriff grew an impressive array of Himalayan plants, some of which she had collected with her husband. This species, like the rest of this section, is restricted to the eastern Himalaya and north west China, and has been found in Bhutan, Assam and south east Tibet growing in moist pastures at 3500–5300m. The umbel of campanulate crimson flowers is borne on a scape of variable length, not exceeding 20cm and often a good deal less. Ludlow and Sherriff recorded it from Bhutan in 1933, on their first expedition, and found it later in the Ha valley and also in south east Tibet in large quantity. Sherriff introduced it into cultivation but it has always proved difficult requiring fresh importation of seed to keep it going.

Bullatae   These are sub-shrubby primulas with thick stems and a preference for dry sites between stones or with the protection of an over-hanging rock. The most famous one is *P. forrestii* (Fig.48), introduced in 1909 from Yunnan by Forrest. The rootstock is robust and woody, covered with wrinkly leaves, and supporting a strong flower stalk carrying an umbel of large orange-yellow, fragrant flowers. Masterton was of the opinion that the plant can live up to half a century. Under favourable conditions it can be grown outside in Scotland, but it is safer to keep it in the alpine house. Propagation is by seed.

Candelabra   From the cluster of leaves like those of the common primrose arise tall scapes bearing at intervals whorls of brightly coloured flowers. They are generally easily grown plants of moist meadows and streams, from the length of the Himalaya and extending into west China. Flowering in May and June they can be readily propagated by seed or division. *P. anisodora*, found first by Forrest in 1922 in Yunnan, grows to about 60cm with several whorls of brownish purple flowers. It is aromatic, smelling of aniseed. *P. aurantiaca*, also found by Forrest in west China at about 3000m, is a small, easily grown species of some 30cm with red-orange flowers. It can be easily propagated by pegging down the terminal bud which forms at the end of the scape. It hybridises readily with *P. pulverulenta. P. beesiana* was found by Forrest in north west China. The rose-crimson flowers with a yellow eye are borne on a mealy 60cm scape. Like so many of the candelabra primulas it readily hybridises and is really a plant for bogs and stream-sides. *P. bulleyana*, another Forrest discovery from Yunnan and another sturdy plant of 70–80cm, has 5-6 tiers of crimson buds which open to orange flowers. *P. burmanica*, found by Kingdon Ward in Upper Burma, is very like *P. beesiana* but with golden-eyed, purple flowers. *P. cockburniana*, introduced by Wilson from south west Sichuan, grows to about 30cm with dark orange-red flowers. It is more at home in the rock garden, but is short lived and must be propagated regularly from seed. *P. prolifera* was found by Forrest in 1916 in Yunnan. It grows to some 90cm with golden-yellow flowers. *P. poissonii*, was found by Delavay in 1891 in Yunnan. It grows to about 50cm with yellow-eyed, purple-crimson flowers and is soundly perennial in a moist habitat and, unlike many of the other species in the Section, it does not hybridise. *P. pulverulenta*, one of Wilson's plants from north west China, is another species which is really too big for the rock garden, but worth a notice since it is so easily grown, widely available and attractive, with flowers which vary from dark pink to red, often with a purple eye. *P. serratifolia*, was found first by Delavay in Yunnan in 1884, but has been collected from other parts of the Himalayas and was among the accessions from the 1990 RBGE Chungtien, Lijiang and Dali Expedition. The scape grows to about 30cm, with yellow flowers with bars of orange-yellow from the mouth of the tube to the edge of the corolla. According to Masterton it may flower a second time in the autumn and rarely sets seed. Many of these candelabras hybridise freely so that mixed beds are likely to contain a great mixture of forms.

Capitata   The very short stalked flowers are gathered into a tight, flattened or conical head in which the individual flowers open in succession from below upwards. *P. capitata* is a widespread species from the Himalayas, Tibet and west China introduced by Hooker in 1849. The leaves are like the common primrose but covered in white farina. Since it accepts comparatively dry conditions it is well suited to the rock garden but tends to be short-lived. The heads of violet flowers stand on 25cm scapes. There are three sub-species or varieties in cultivation: var. *capitata*, which lacks farina and was discovered by Cooper in Sikkim; var. *mooreana*, also from Sikkim, but larger in size and very late flowering and var. *sphaerocephala*, found by Forrest in Yunnan, without farina and with funnel-shaped flowers in a globose head.

Cortusoides   The large, crinkled leaves, heavily veined and with a well defined petiole confer an attractive appearance to the plants in this section. The species from which the section derives its name is not Himalayan but is native to west Siberia. The magenta-red *P. geraniifolia*, with lobed leaves, found by Sherriff in 1937 in Central Bhutan, growing alongside *Androsace geraniifolia*, is a sound perennial in gritty soil and regularly sets seed. *P. heucherifolia* is closely related. It is a small, hairy leaved plant with light purple flowers, first found in 1869 by Abbé David in western Sichuan. The only other Himalayan in this group worth noting is *P. polyneura* which has an immense distribution through north west China. A vigorous plant with rose-purple flowers it is best suited to the dappled shade of a woodland garden.

Denticulata   The type species, *denticulata*, found in Nepal, Sikkim, Bhutan, Tibet, and Assam was introduced to cultivation in 1840 and needs no further comment, except to make the point that most of the plants found in the field have flowers which are delicate both in form and hue compared with the brightly coloured, almost blowsy cultivars which are currently grown. This phenomenon is true of many species which have been long in cultivation. *P. atrodentata* is like a smaller version of *denticulata*. Ludlow and Sherriff frequently found it growing in open meadows at 3600-4900m in south east Tibet and elsewhere, sometimes in the company of *P. macrophylla* and in such numbers that the hillsides were painted a velvet purple colour. However, it is uncommon in cultivation, perhaps because it is shorter lived than *denticulata*. *P. glomerata* from Nepal and southern Tibet is very similar to *P. capitata* but, although often collected, it sets little seed and soon dies out.

Farinosae   This is the largest section in the genus, covering a very wide distribution. *P. clarkei*, although known from Kashmir since 1876, was not in cultivation until the late 1930s. It has been placed in several different sections but it is convenient to deal with it here. Small in size, without farina and with rich pink flowers, it forms a rhizomatous mat with leaves which recall those of a violet. It is widely cultivated but short-lived although division and replanting extends its life. *P. involucrata*, was discovered by Wallich in 1825 and encountered in north east and central Bhutan by Ludlow and Sherriff, often in great numbers. It has white or pinkish drooping flowers with a yellow eye and a pleasant fragrance. It grows in moist meadows and by streams. In cultivation it needs frequent division. Seed is often produced. *P. rosea* (Fig.57), known since 1831 from the north west Himalaya, with its colour forms, is well known and commonly grown in moist soil. Less familiar is *P. yargongensis*, now regarded as a ssp. of *P. involucrata* but with pink-purple flowers.

Floribundae   This is a small section in which the edges of the leaves are turned inward and the inflorescence is in the form of superimposed whorls of yellow flowers. *P. floribunda*, widespread in north west Himalaya and found by Wallich in 1825, with 15cm leaves and a scape of up to 25cm, is only for the alpine house in Scotland where it needs some degree of frost protection since it grows in the wild between 500 and 2700m.

Minutissimae   The inflorescence in this section, which is distributed over the Himalayas and Tibet, is greatly reduced, often to a single flower on a very short scape. *P. reptans* is a tiny plant grown in shaded pans in the alpine house. It spreads by stolons to make a close mat and can easily be multiplied by division but is not long-lived. The large single flowers are violet with a white eye. The even smaller species *P. minutissima* (Fig.54) is often collected and grown but is never long lived.

Muscarioides   Natives of the eastern Himalayas, Tibet and parts of West China they usually have hairy leaves which grow in distinct rosettes. The flowers are in tight heads or spikes with negligible pedicels. *P. bellidifolia*, found in 1877 in Sikkim, was rediscovered and introduced by Cooper in 1915. The firm of Bees Ltd. gained an Award of Merit for it under the name *P. menziesiana*. Ludlow and Sherriff found it in East Bhutan and again in south east Tibet on grassy sites. The inflorescence is in the form of a short spire of purple-blue pendant bells. According to Masterton it is generally short lived in cultivation and needs to be grown – rather unexpectedly – in a dry situation or in a pot. *P. muscarioides*, with deep purple flowers, was first found in south east Tibet in 1904. It grows rather large, is best accommodated in the greenhouse or frame and, although not the easiest to please, is widely available. *P. viallii* was discovered by Delavay in Yunnan but introduced to cultivation by Forrest. It is the easiest and most popular primula of this section although many top growers find it rather difficult. It escapes the hazards of winter wet by hiding underground, unlike other members of the section which usually form resting buds above ground. Under favourable conditions the scape can reach over 50cm with a dense spike of blue-violet flowers preceded by buds with crimson calyces. Forrest wanted to call this species *littoniana* after his friend and companion Litton, who introduced him to travel in Yunnan and who later died of blackwater fever. It is sad that the inexorable rules of taxonomic precedence have robbed him of such a fitting memorial.

Nivales   This section has many beautiful species although not many are in cultivation. The thick, fleshy leaves are ribbon-shaped and generally covered with meal. The fairly large, open flower heads are followed by cylindrical capsules. They do best in fertile soil under shade and do not require such moist conditions as most of the Asiatic primulas. Propagation is by seed. *P. chionantha* (Fig.53), found by Forrest in 1913 in North Yunnan, grows to about 50cm with large white, yellow eyed and scented corollas. It is easily grown and widely available. The closely related *P. melanops*, now regarded by Richards as a sub-species of *chionantha* and found by Kingdon Ward in Sichuwan in 1922, has a deep purple flower with a black eye. Although rather short lived it is easily raised from seed. *P. macrophylla* (Fig.52), first found by Wallich in Nepal in 1820, is a very variable species. Although it can form large clumps it needs to be kept going from seed in the long term. Ludlow and Sherriff found it, both in Bhutan and south east Tibet, often in vast numbers. Both *P. sinoplantaginea* and *P. sinopurpurea*, also regarded by some as sub-species of *P. chionantha*, have more or less purple flowers, the latter with a paler eye. The former, the smaller of the two, was first found and introduced by Forrest while the latter was found by Delavay in Yunnan but introduced from Tibet by Forrest.

Petiolares   This section contains some of the most attractive primulas, many of which were collected by Ludlow, Sherriff and their associates and often sent home by air by Sherriff. According to Masterton they do best where the annual rainfall is about 1000 mm although they can be successfully grown in much drier conditions. Scottish climatic conditions favour them. The Ludlow and Sherriff field notes generally refer to moist situations with good drainage such as grassy slopes or stream sides as their natural habitat. The flat seed capsule is covered by a thin membrane which ruptures when the seed is still green. If sown at once the seed will germinate within 10 days. This section has been further classified into a number of sub-sections of which two i.e. Griffithii and Sonchifolia include species in cultivation. Members of the former are the easier to maintain because they over-winter underground. They are native to the eastern Himalayas and south and south east Tibet. *P. calderiana* (Fig.47), discovered by Hooker in 1849, was introduced by Ludlow and Sherriff. The flowers are purple with a yellow eye. The whole plant has an unpleasant fishy smell which can be detected at 100 metres in the wild when the plants are growing in mass. There is a sub-species, *strumosa* (Fig.45), with yellow flowers and a golden-yellow eye, first found by Cooper in 1915. Crosses with the type yield a wide range of colours. *P. griffithii* from south east Tibet and Bhutan was introduced by Ludlow and Sherriff. Although generally like *calderiana* it is more robust, with yellow-eyed purple flowers on a 45cm scape and without the unpleasant smell. Found in the wild growing in the shade of abies or rhododendron forest it does best in rich loam and shade. It is often confused with the more vigorous hybrid derived from the cross with the *strumosa* sub-species of *calderiana*. *P. tanneri* apparently embraces both the yellow flowered *nepalensis* and the purple form of *tsariensis* (Fig.50) with a yellow eye, which was introduced by Ludlow and Sherriff in 1937, from central Bhutan and Tibet. The taxonomy of these forms is not entirely clear.

Sonchifolia   In the Sonchifolia section, *P. gracilipes* (Fig.56) from Nepal and Sikkim to Bhutan and south Tibet, is a common species in the wild. Indeed it was the first plant recorded by Ludlow and Sherriff on their first expedition in 1933 on their way to Chengdu. With bright magenta to purple-pink flowers, and orange-yellow eye with a white margin this species grows well in Scotland, given a moist soil with humus, some shade and preferably winter protection but it tends to flower sporadically throughout the winter and does not produce the spectacular display of its native habitat as the snows melt and the flowers all burst open. It is widely available, includes a number of named cultivars and has probably been reintroduced many times. *P. petiolaris*, with a wide Himalayan distribution, is very close to *gracilipes*. It is a small plant, without farina, with a loose rosette leaves, pink flowers with a white bordered yellow eye and similar cultural needs.

P. aureata (Fig.44) is an attractive plant with a cluster of cream-yellow flowers and a darker, almost orange centre which does best under alpine house conditions. It originated as a rogue in a germinated batch of *Swertia* seed from Sikkim in RBGE in 1935. The broad leaves have farina on both sides. The gold-centred cream flowers are borne on a short scape. The species occurs in two forms, the type and the form *fimbriata* with smaller flowers and dissected petals. In the wild, *P. aureata* produces many interesting hybrids of uncertain parentage. Carrie, Christie and McKelvie collected a range of such hybrids at Gossainkund in central Nepal in 1995. *P. bracteosa*, discovered in Bhutan by Griffith in 1838 and found again by Cooper in 1916, was introduced to cultivation by Sherriff in 1937. The flowers are pink with a margined yellow eye. The end of the scape develops a vegetative bud which may be pegged down to produce another plant. *P. nana (*syn *edgeworthii*) is a woodland plant from the north west Himalayas. It loses some of its outer leaves during winter but the tight packed flower buds are closely invested by farina coated leaves. The flowers open early. Plants in the western Himalayas tend to have blue or lilac flowers while those in Nepal and further east have pink flowers. For many years a good pink form 'Ghose Strain' was grown, very similar to the form introduced by McKelvie and Chadwell in 1990 from Annapurna and which is still in cultivation. There is also a cream-white variety called *alba*.

P. sonchifolia loses all the old leaves in autumn and produces a large resting, scale-covered bud, about the size of a hen's egg, which sits above ground. This species is regarded as one of the most beautiful of the primulas, with yellow-eyed, blue violet flowers. Found by Delavay in Yunnan in 1884 it occurs also in Sichuan, Bhutan and Tibet. It is not difficult, given cool, moist conditions. *P. whitei* (Fig.51), found in 1905 by Sir Claude White in Bhutan, was also collected by Ludlow and Sherriff in southern Tibet. At first this accession was named *P. bhutanica*, which, however, turns out to be a very closely related species. It appears that what is commonly taken as *P. whitei* in cultivation is really the more vigorous hybrid with *bhutanica*. As in *sonchifolia* there is a tight winter resting bud. Typical *whitei* has pale to dark lilac flowers with a white or greenish-white eye.

Rotundifolia   *P. rotundifolia* with long stalked, orbicular leaves, from the Nepal and Sikkim, was discovered by Hooker in 1841 in Nepal. The undersurface of the leaf is covered with farina. The yellow-eyed pink flowers are arranged in umbels. It requires rich, moist, well drained soil and is difficult to keep so seed should be sown annually. In the wild it is always found in the shelter of a rock and seems to need a degree of protection in the garden.

Sikkimensis   This large section contains a number of popular species, distinguished by long, toothed leaves and umbels of handsome drooping flowers. The available species are hardy and prefer moist and/or shady conditions. *P. alpicola* is a fine plant which grows to about 50cm. It was found many times by Ludlow and Sherriff who were impressed by the range of colour forms, including white (*alba*), pale yellow (*luna*) and violet (*violacea*). Propagation is by seed and division. *P. ioessa* (Fig.46) is a particularly attractive species discovered by Ludlow and Sherriff in south east Tibet in 1936. The violet flowers are funnel-shaped. The plant grows to about 30cm, sets seed readily, is easily grown and must be regarded as one of Ludlow and Sherriff's most successful introductions. *P. sikkimensis* (Fig.49) is a larger species with pendant, fragrant yellow flowers which shares the preference of candelabras for moist conditions, although, in the wild, colonies can be found on dry, rocky ledges. Such a form was introduced by the MECC expedition to the Langtang in Nepal in 1997. The smaller form, *hopeana*, with pale yellow flowers was found first by Cooper in 1914-15, again by Ludlow and Sherriff in central Bhutan and also by more recent collectors. *P. waltonii* has been collected from many parts of Tibet and Bhutan. It is very similar to *P. sikkimensis* but with rich, deep red, sweetly scented flowers covered within with white farina. It is often represented in gardens by hybrids which are easier to grow.

Soldanelloides   This section includes exquisite species which are very difficult to maintain. The hairy, long-stalked leaves are finely toothed. The long, slender scapes carry tight heads or spikes of flowers. All are alpine house subjects except *P. flaccida* which was introduced by Forrest in 1914. According to Masterton it is commonly believed to be monocarpic although this is not so in Scotland. The narrow leaves lack farina. The scape grows to some 35cm and carries a head of nodding, deep lavender flowers. A moist sloping stance with plenty of humus and shade suits it best. *P. reidii* (Fig.55), with its very hairy leaves, is best treated as a short-lived alpine house plant. Its variety var. *williamsii*, found in Nepal in 1954 by Stainton, Sykes and Williams, is a great deal hardier and will survive outside in the right conditions in Scotland. The fragrant flowers vary from white to blue. *P. wattii* from Sikkim, Assam and the Burma-Tibet border was discovered by King in 1877. It is another fine plant with large, violet campanulate flowers. It has been grown with great success by Jack Drake at the Inshriach Nursery. *P. buryana* is another species which has only been fleetingly in cultivation. Its large, white, heavily scented flowers are impressive but the plant behaves almost as an annual. The latest introduction was from central Nepal in 1990 by Chadwell and McKelvie but in spite of setting seed for a few years it soon died out.

P. sherriffae is the last of our selection of Asiatic primulas, named after the mother of the man who, more than any other, with the exception of Forrest, enriched our gardens with some of the gems of the Himalaya. This species was found by him growing on cliffs in south east Bhutan in 1934. The pale, long tubed violet flowers, dusted with farina, are carried on a short scape. A difficult species, it has been grown with great success by the staff of RBGE and by Mrs Elizabeth Sherriff at Ascreavie.

Ranunculaceae

Aconitum A number of the low-growing monk's hoods would make valuable additions to the rock garden. They are generally rare in cultivation. Seed has been brought back by recent expeditions so such species as *A. pulchellum* and *A. violaceum* may become less so. *A. hookeri* which grows only to about 10cm, with dark blue or purple-blue flowers, is in cultivation. It is a true alpine, occurring at about 4000m from Nepal to south west China. Ludlow and Sherriff encountered many species of aconitum during their travels, none more admired than one given the name of *A. fletcherianum*, which was included in Sherriff's last consignment by air of the choicest of their finds in 1949, but alas, as so often, to no avail.

Adonis Of the three Himalayan species in this genus *A. chrysocyathus* is the gem with terminal, golden yellow flowers up to 5cm across. Collected by Chadwell it proved difficult to flower except when grown outside by Martin Carter at Kinlochard Youth Hostel in Stirlingshire where the wet almost monsoon conditions seemed to suit it.

Anemone There are several attractive anemones from damp, upland pastures and hillsides, with a preference in cultivation for moist, organically rich, well drained conditions. Probably the most familiar is *A. obtusiloba* (Fig.61) which is a variable species with white, pink or blue flowers and also a rare yellow form from Himachal Pradesh and Kashmir at high elevations. Sherriff met with it in central Bhutan in 1937 in immense numbers in different colours in the same population. *A. rivularis* is a hardy species, which grows to about 50cm, with a reputation for spreading its seedlings too generously. Several flowers, usually white or, less often, blue on the reverse of the petals, are carried in a loose umbel. *A. rupestris* is an attractive, small species with glossy, dark green leaves and many white flowers, recently introduced by the 1990 CLD and the CC&McK 1990 expeditions. *A. rupicola* (Fig.60), from south west China to Afghanistan, has rather a different habit. The stalked basal leaves are three-lobed and toothed and the solitary white flowers, tinted with pink or violet on the reverse, are sessile or almost so. It has a wide distribution and is suited either to the alpine house or a sheltered scree. *A. trullifolia* is another recent introduction. It is a robust species which produces clumps of cool blue flowers on 20cm stems during early summer.

Aquilegia *A. fragrans*, widespread in west Himalayan pastures, grows between 40 and 80cm. The basal leaves are biternate with toothed, shiny leaflets. The white, fragrant flowers are pendant or horizontal. *A. viridiflora* with the typical aquilegia-type flowers has greenish sepals and a corolla which varies in colour from green or reddish to almost black, while, from western China there is a form var. *atrorubens* with dark purple flowers. This species, which is so different from what we expect in an aquilegia, is easily grown in cool, well drained conditions.

Delphinium *D. brunonianum* from Himalayan screes at 4000–5000m grows between 15 and 40cm, with deeply lobed and toothed basal leaves, many stems and a flattish group of flowers with a dark, blue-purple hood and even darker petals. *D. cashmerianum* is closely related but with less of a hood so the dark petals are more obvious. *D. muscosum* was discovered in Bhutan in 1937 and later introduced to cultivation by Sherriff. It is a high alpine from 4500–5500m which grows from 5 to 15cm, with solitary flowers of deep violet colour, white bearded in the throat, making an attractive display above the lacy, divided, hairy foliage. It needs to be propagated from seed since it is short-lived but worth the effort. There are several other charming species like *D. pylzowii* with hairy, dark violet flowers and *D. tatsienense* (Fig.65), with blue to mauve flowers, which is long-lived and readily sets seed. These species are best grown on moist scree which will check a tendency of some of them to grow taller than the preferred height of about 10cm, which is just right for maximum effect.

Paraquilegia The beautiful lilac flowers and deeply cut blue-green leaves of *P. anemonoides* (Fig.62) can be found in rock crevices right across the Himalayas. Following the initial success outdoors at Branklyn this attractive species is now widely grown and seems hardy although a pane of glass during winter is often beneficial.

Trollius The members of this genus of globe flowers are best suited to the bog garden and are similar in form to our native *Trollius*. *T. pumilus* (Fig.63), from Uttar Pradesh to south west China, grows to about 30cm with solitary, yellow flowers which open flat. The closely related *T. yunnanensis*, from western China and Yunnan, grows to about twice the height and the flowers are more golden but otherwise similar.

Rosaceae
Potentilla Three species of this immense genus are worth noting in the present context. *P. arbuscula* has the general appearance of the familiar European *P. fruticosa* but is generally smaller with dark veined stipules and three, usually broader leaflets. The flowers are deep yellow. There are several varieties like *albicans* and *bulleyana*, with white hairs and *beesiana* which forms attractive, silvery hummocks. *P. cuneata* (Fig.64) is a low, creeping species with leaves split into three, small toothed leaflets. It spreads by runners, often with such abandon as to be a nuisance in the garden. The yellow petals are slightly notched. It occurs under scree conditions from Kashmir to south west China. *P. eriocarpa* (Fig.66) has a similar creeping habit although the lower parts of the rather woody stems are sheathed in silky scales and the lemon yellow flowers are larger. It requires the same gritty conditions as the preceding species, and being less aggressive, is preferable but both are attractive species for the rock garden.

Saxifragaceae
Saxifraga A small number of species of this genus have been introduced at various times from the Sino-Himalayan region but not many have become established in cultivation, although their number will probably increase as a result of recent expeditions. The genus has been divided into 15 Sections, two of which include the species worth noting. In Ciliatae the plants form mats with simple, deciduous leaves and sprays of yellow to orange flowers. In *S. brunonis* native to Tibet, northern India, Sikkim, Nepal and Yunnan, the plants spread by crimson runners which form rosettes at their tips. The yellow flowers are borne above the mat of radiating branches on 8cm stems. According to Evans the plants do best in a moist site near the front of the peat bed. *S. diversifolia* is from Upper Burma, Sichuan and Yunnan. The stems are taller, reaching to 40cm, with clusters of golden flowers. In nature the leaf shape and size is very variable. It prefers, moist acid humus-rich conditions. The other species noted are classified in Porphyrion, which includes the Kabschia saxifrages, characterised by a dense, often cushion-like growth form of simple leaves and relatively large flowers which are either borne singly or in panicles. In *S. andersonii*, from lime-encrusted cushions of oblong leaves, rise short, 3cm stems carrying one or several relatively large white flowers. A widespread species found in Tibet, Bhutan, south west China and Nepal, it grows best on neutral, moist scree. *S. matta-florida* produces a close mat of

small rosettes on which rest the solitary, white sessile flowers. Its distribution overlaps much of the areas occupied by the other species mentioned. *S. stolitzkae*, from Nepal and Bhutan, is a hummock forming species with clusters of white flowers carried on 3cm stems. It grows best on well drained, moist scree and, according to the Encylopaedia of Alpines is one of the best of the recent Himalayan introductions. *S. hypostoma* (Fig.67), recently introduced from central Nepal, for the alpine house or protected trough, forms light green, compact cushions embellished with many, open, nearly sessile white flowers.

Thymelaeaceae
Daphne This is a predominantly European and Asiatic genus but one species of Sino-Himalayan origin, *D. retusa*, is a valuable, hardy, evergreen shrub which grows slowly to 60cm or more. The relatively large, fragrant, bright purple and white centred flowers are borne on the tips of the stems in spring and are followed by shining red fruits, the seeds of which readily germinate. It was first introduced by Wilson from west China in 1901 and on several occasions since then. Unlike most daphnes it can be easily propagated from stem cuttings. It is very similar to the slightly taller *D. tangutica*.
Stellera An intractable but most desirable species is *S. chamaejasme* from dry slopes in the Tibetan borderlands, a herbaceous plant with leafy stems and sweet-scented yellow- pink flowers. This charming species has been collected by Ron McBeath and grown with a certain degree of success at RBG Edinburgh. John Good reported in the AGS Bulletin that in China he packed fresh seed of *Stellera* into a poly bag inside his dirty socks. When he got home the seeds were already germinating. Hence the moral – to germinate these seeds, "place inside dirty socks".

Monocots
Araceae
Arisaema Interest in these intriguing monocots is on the increase. Recent expeditions have brought back new species which are being assessed for garden worth and a dozen or more species are being grown in the Royal Botanic Garden, Edinburgh. Relatives of our familiar *Arum*, with a spathe and spadix, the tip of either of which may be extended like a tail. The spathe is often mottled or streaked to produce striking patterns. They are plants of cool, shady places. Ludlow and Sherriff seemed to ignore this genus. *A. candidissimum* (Fig.68), discovered by Forrest in Yunnan, is an easily grown, fragrant species which appears able to withstand drier conditions than most. The spathe, which usually precedes the trifoliate leaf, is white, with green stripes, and often a wash of pink which deepens with age. *A. flavum* (Fig.70) has a small, sulphur yellow "pot-bellied" spathe and is hardy in cultivation. In *A. nepenthoides* (Fig.69) the spathe is about 15cm long, with a tubular base and three lobes, of which the central one arches forward, and is of green or

red-brown colour. These are just a few of the growing list of species which have been brought back in recent years from almost every Himalayan expedition..

Liliaceae
Cardiocrinum *Cardiocrinum giganteum* which was once included in *Lilium*, is a common woodland plant from Kashmir to south west China. Its 2-4m tall stems with large, white, drooping flowers form an impressive backdrop in woodland gardens. Easily grown, it is a favourite food of slugs.

Daiswa This is a small genus with a wide distribution which includes northern Europe and Asia. The best known Himalayan species, formerly known as *Paris polyphylla* (Fig.79), has been transferred into the genus *Daiswa* These are plants of moist, shady places, spreading by rhizomes which send up single, erect stems provided with a whorl of four or more leaves just below the terminal flower of 4-6 narrow sepals and a similar number of narrower petals. The anther filaments carry long, thread-like tips. The species appear in late spring, or early summer, usually when the gardener has concluded they must have died. *D. polyphylla* is a widespread, often abundant species in which a number of varieties have been collected and introduced by Robert Mitchell, British leader of the 1981 Cang Shan Sino-British expedition. These include the varieties *thibetica, delavayi* and *yunannensis*, in which there is a striking form *alba*, with a white ovary. *D. violacea* was also found on this expedition in deep, woodland shade, in the company of ferns.

Lilium The best known Sino-Himalayan species in cultivation are low growing, with the appearance of a *Nomocharis* or a *Fritillaria*. Only more recently have they been located in *Lilium*. They have a broadly similar distribution from western China to Tibet. *L. lophophorum* (Fig.74) has solitary, bell-shaped, yellow or greenish-yellow flowers with long, pointed tepals. It generally grows to between 10 and 15cm. *L. nanum* (Fig.73), which grows to about 10cm, was first found in 1845, locality unknown. The solitary, bell-shaped pendulous flowers are deep purple and scented. There is also a larger variety, *flavidum* (Fig.72), which has pale yellow, fragrant flowers. Both forms have a similar distribution and may be found growing together at about 4000m in the Himalaya and western China.

In *L. sherriffiae* (Fig.75) the 30-90cm stem is tinted purple. The 1-2 funnel-shaped recurved flowers were described as "maroon with inside chequered with gold" by Betty Sherriff who found a specimen two months before her husband came across large colonies in central Bhutan. The species was named after her. *L. souliei* (Fig.76) is very similar to *L. nanum*, slightly larger and with deep pink-purple, glossy flowers. This was one of the species sent back by air by Sherriff in 1947 and was successfully flowered in several gardens.

Nomocharis This genus includes some of the most beautiful of garden plants. They are closely related to lilies from which they are distinguished by their wide open, saucer-shaped flowers with two whorls of tepals, of which the inner has at the base little ridges about a central channel, while the outer whorl is flat without the channel. The filaments are swollen with a pointed awn at the tip. Eight species are recognised, distributed through the mountains of China, Tibet and Burma. Five or six are regularly grown. They are plants which require well drained, humus-rich soil. Half the art in maintaining them seems to lie in reconciling an open, sunny site with a cool root run. They have been grown to perfection by Alf Evans in the Royal Botanic Garden, Edinburgh and by the Stones in their garden of Askival at the south end of Loch Ness. *N. aperta* (Fig.77) from western China, grows to about 60cm with about half a dozen rosy purple flowers on long pedicels, with moderate, central, purple spotting. *N. farreri* can be regarded as a variety of *N. pardanthina*. It is a larger plant, growing to 90cm, hardy and long-lived in the right situation. There are more flowers per stem than in *N. aperta*. They are a delicate shade of pink, with crimson basal spotting, and a fringed edge to the inner row of tepals. *N. mairei* from western China, is the brash member of the series with purple spotting across both whorls of tepals, on a white to pink background, and a strongly fringed margin at the edge of the inner whorl – an eye-catching plant in which the flowers may be as much as 10cm across. In *N. pardanthina* (Fig.78) the colour varies from pink to almost white with delicate spotting in the interior. *N. saluenensis* is another tall species, which is closer to *N. aperta*. The flower colour varies from pale rose-purple, to white or yellow, with very fine coloured dots, and a distinct central, green zone. Its range includes western China, northern Burma and south west Tibet. Propagation is by seed which is best sown in a frame either in autumn or spring.

Notholirion This is another genus close to *Lilium* with a wide distribution from western China and Tibet, along the Himalayas. The plants are monocarpic and grow from bulbs which consist of a few white scales covered by ribbed brown scales which form an onion-like tunic. Many small bulbils are left round the withered bulbs and these should be used to maintain the stock. Although not the easiest of plants they were grown very successfully in Perthshire by R.S. Masterton who described his methods in a SRGC Journal article in 1979. He provided his plants with plenty of leaf mould and peat, with moisture about the roots. He noted that the plants withstood frost well. *N. bulbiferum* was introduced to cultivation in 1878. Although too big for the average rock garden, it is a plant of great presence, since it grows to about 180cm with about 30 wide open flowers with green tips. The colour varies from pale lavender to the dark purple-mauve flowers encountered by Ludlow and Sherriff.

N. campanulatum was first introduced by Cox and Farrer in 1919 from Upper Burma. It differs from *N. bulbiferum* in being smaller, growing to about 120cm, in having about 20 pendant flowers, which do not open out to *macrophyllum* was first found by Wallich in 1819 in Nepal, but has since been found a number of times in Tibet, Sikkim and Bhutan. This is more of rock garden dimensions, although safer in the alpine house. It grows to 30-40cm with a slender stem and usually 3 to 5 bell-shaped flowers, described as pale mauve or lavender but lacking the green tips to the petals of the other two species. There is also *N. thompsonianum* with racemes of beautiful scented, rose flowers rising to some 90cm and regarded by some as the most attractive members of the genus. Found wild at moderate elevations of about or less than 2000m on rather dry slopes it prefers open, sunny sites in the garden.

Orchidaceae
Pleione A genus of about 16 species found from Nepal to China, Burma and Taiwan. They grow well in Scotland in cool summers in a glasshouse with plenty of feeding followed by dry, winter dormancy just above freezing. The following species are the ones which are grown most readily. *P. praecox*, with lilac-purple, scented flowers is the earliest to bloom in September. *P. humilis* is the earliest of the spring flowering species, producing white flowers from January onwards. The cultivar 'Frank Kingdon Ward' is particularly striking; it used to be grown to perfection by Jack Crosland, that master of pleione culture. He was also an expert with *P.* x *confusa*, collected in 1924 by George Forrest as *P. forrestii* but now recognised as a hybrid between *P. forrestii* and *P. albiflora*. The commonest pleione is *P. bulbocodoides* which encompasses *P. formosana*, *P. limprichtii* and *P. speciosa*, all of which are sometimes accorded specific status. With their pink flowers, they are the easiest grown of all the pleiones with many cultivars. The inter-specific 'Shantung ' hybrids raised by David Harberd are particularly striking..

Zingiberaceae
Roscoea These members of the Ginger family, from western China and the Himalayas, are adapted to humus-rich soil and shade. The tubular flowers expand into three lobes, of which the uppermost is erect and conspicuous or hooded, and with a petal-like staminode reminiscent of an orchid labellum. Most of the species in cultivation were introduced by Forrest. In *R. alpina*, which Forrest found in Yunnan, the pink flowers appear singly in succession on 10-20cm stems. In *R. auriculata* the bright purple flowers are borne on taller stems of about 40cm. *R. cautleoides* is the best known species. Here the flowers are yellow although purple and white forms occur naturally. In *R. humeana*, another Forrest species, named after a young Edinburgh gardener who fell during the first World War, several flowers open at the same time before the leaves mature. They are purple, lilac or white in colour while there is also a wild yellow form. *R. purpurea* grows to about 40cm with long leaves. Several flowers which are pale pink or white with purple markings are hidden in the leaf sheaths. It occurs from Uttar Pradesh to south east Tibet.

§ CHAPTER 8

South West Asia and the Balkans

South West Asia

This region includes the countries of Turkey, Iran and Afghanistan whose floras have been regarded as sufficiently similar to merit recognition as the Turano-Iranian Region. Some qualification is necessary. Turkey represents a three-way bridge between Europe, Asia and Africa in geological terms. The climate of the coast is Mediterranean, while the interior of the country experiences an arid, continental steppe climate of hot summers and cold winters. On the Black Sea Coast the climate is temperate and humid with year round rainfall. The major part of Iran is occupied by the Central Plateau with a continental desert climate. In the north, the territory is bounded by high mountains which represent a northern branch of the Alpine-Himalayan orogenic system, separating the Caspian area from the Central Plateau, which is also bordered by mountains in the south west and the east. In Afghanistan the climate is generally arid as a result of the distance from the sea and the rain shadow effects of the very mountainous terrain. Rainfall is low, irregular and subject to extreme annual variation. Consequently the vegetation is dominated by xerophytes adapted to such rigorous conditions. The most notable feature of the region as a whole is the continental climate with extremes of temperature, both diurnal and annual, low rainfall and two periods of plant rest, in the hot, dry summer and the cold winter. Many plant genera have evolved and have their centres of distribution in the region.

Earlier generalisations about similarity of the vegetation throughout the region have required modification. On the basis of a comprehensive study of diversity and distribution in the family *Lamiaceae*, which includes some 1100 species in South West Asia and can be regarded as fairly representative of the flora as a whole, Hedge (1986) noted that only 16% of the species are common to Turkey and Iran, that there are few examples of species which are widespread throughout Iran and Afghanistan and fewer still which occur in both Turkey and Afghanistan. Such differences stem largely from the high incidence of endemism in south west Turkey where the flora shows a distinct Mediterranean influence which becomes progressively less evident eastwards through Iran and Afghanistan. Even within Turkey there are three climatic zones: Mediterranean for much of the country, continental for the north and north east and more or less oceanic in the vicinity of the Black Sea, with correlated differences in the distribution and composition of the flora. The Turkish flora also overlaps that of the Balkans with strong indications that migration has been from east to west. Thus for many species it is rather arbitrary as to whether they should be considered under the heading of the

Balkans or South West Asia. Also, at the other end of the region, the flora of Afghanistan and Iran has been enriched by species whose origins are in Central Asia. It has even been suggested that the flora of Iran has more in common with that of Central Asia than that of Turkey and that the floristic region should be redefined as Irano-Turkestanian.

One of the characteristic features of the sub-alpine regions of the mountains of South West Asia is the evolution of the 'Thorn Cushion' habit in which the rather shrubby plants form densely tufted cushions or mats with needle-like, spine tipped leaves. Their compact form and spiny leaves are recognised as adaptations to life on arid slopes and hilltops where wind pressure is the major threat to survival by way of mechanical destruction and desiccation. Such adaptations are especially well developed in species of *Acantholimon, Astragalus,* and *Onobrychis* but also occur in some species of genera like *Dianthus, Gypsophila* and *Minuartia*. It is an interesting observation that the same kind of adaptive growth form turns up in South America among entirely unrelated genera.

From this brief survey it might be guessed that the rock plants from south west Asia are likely to be best suited to sharply drained scree or raised bed and, where it is essential to simulate the annual cycles of growth and rest by control of watering, the alpine house or bulb frame will be preferred. Our knowledge of the flora of Turkey is chiefly due to Peter Davis. Many expeditions established the representative herbarium collection which formed the basis of Davis' many-volumed Flora of Turkey. We can now consider representative species, starting with the dicots as usual.

Dicots
Boraginaceae
Anchusa Most of the species of this genus are too big for the rock garden but there is one species from Turkey and south-east Europe, *A. leptophylla,* growing to 40 –70 cm, which is very acceptable. The dense spikes of flowers are purple to blue with a white eye. The typical form is biennial but there is a sub-species, *A. l. incana,* which is perennial, shorter, with the incomparable, bright blue anchusa colour.

Brassicaceae
Aethionema This genus of about 70 species is particularly well represented in Turkey and a little less so in the wider Mediterranean region. They are ideal plants for a wall, raised bed or scree with a high pH since they are plants of limestone rocks and slopes. The habit is sub-shrubby. *A. armenum* grows as a compact 10cm bush with pointed blue-green leaves, another common feature of the genus. The flowers are pale pink with veins. *A cordifolium* is taller, growing to about 20cm, with ascending stems. It is very close to the familiar *A. grandiflorum,* which is rather woody, loosely branched with many erect stems to 30 cm or more, also with pink flowers and also from Turkey

although it spreads further east into Iran and Iraq. *A. iberideum* has a rather different habit since it branches from the base to form trailing stems with close packed leaves from which arise the scapes bearing white, scented flowers. It is very much a limestone species which occurs in Turkey, eastern Greece and eastwards to the Caucasus. *A. oppositifolium*, from the mountains of Turkey, is an attractive dwarf of some 5cm with a tufted habit and short, springy stems carrying opposite, fleshy leaves in pairs. The terminal clusters of flowers are lilac-pink. *A. saxatile* includes varieties which may be annual, biennial or perennial. The habit is rather lax with white or pink flowers in dense, terminal clusters. It is a mountain plant of dry, rocky places with a wide distribution including Turkey, the Balkans and Crete. All these species are attractive rock plants, none more so than x *warleyense* or 'Warley Rose', which may be a hybrid between. *A. armenum* and *A. grandiflorum*. The flowers are a rich pink, contrasting with the blue-green leaves. There is also a darker form, 'Warley Purple'.

Arabis *A. androsacea* is confined to Turkey where it ascends to 3000m. It forms hummocks from which arise the 6cm stems bearing white flowers. *A. caucasica* (Fig.81), with a wide distribution from the Balkans to Iran, is the familiar, rampant, white garden arabis, with several varieties which include double flowers as well as one with variegated leaves.

Aubrieta This is a small genus predominantly from the Balkans and Greece but with several Turkish species worth noting. Everyone is familiar with the more or less evergreen, tufted mats of the numerous cultivars of complex hybrid origin. The wild species have a similar habit with comparatively large, generally purple or violet, rarely white flowers. They all do best in well drained, limey soil in full sun. *A. canescens*, from the mountains of Turkey has violet flowers. In *A. libanotica* from Syria and Lebanon the flowers vary but are most often lilac in colour. *A. parviflora*, with smaller flowers, which may be white, lilac or pink has a wider range through Turkey, Iran and Iraq. *A. pinardii*, with larger, purple flowers, is from Turkey.

Draba Typically the species of this genus are adapted to stony well drained sites, often at high altitudes. They generally grow as small mounds or hummocks with yellow or white flowers. Among the South West Asian species we can note *D. cappadocica*, endemic to the Turkish mountains, a low cushion plant with short racemes of yellow flowers. *D. longisiliqua*, also forms cushions, sometimes quite large, with 2–14 comparatively large, bright yellow flowers in a loose raceme. In *D. mollissima* the cushions of hoary leaves are only about 5cm high but may grow up to 20–30cm in width. *D. polytricha* (Fig.82) is of similar growth form but the hairy leaves impart a silvery appearance to the low mound. The clustered flowers are also yellow. It is native to Turkey and Transcaucasia. *D. rigida*, from Turkish Armenia and the Caucasus, makes even smaller cushions which are only 2-3cm high. The flowers on 5cm scapes are clustered and yellow in colour. *D. rosularis*, from the Turkish mountains, is yet another cushion type with yellow flowers. All these species can be grown in pans in the alpine house and most will thrive in the raised bed.

Campanulaceae
Campanula With some 300 species this is a large genus which is particularly well represented in Europe. They do not demand such sharp drainage as the species considered so far but they are all plants suited to the raised bed or scree and, occasionally, the alpine house. There are quite a number of first class south west Asian species. *C. aucheri* (Fig.83) is a familiar, tufted plant with short, upright stems. Their solitary, widely open bells are violet blue. It is a native of Turkey, Iran and the Caucasus, a true Turano–Iranian. *C. betulifolia* (Fig.84) from the rocky slopes of Anatolia, produces low growing, leafy shoots with petiolate, dentate leaves and open bell-like flowers which are generally white, less often pale pink, with attractive, pink or red buds. *C. cashmeriana* develops prostrate or semi-prostrate, branching stems. The numerous pendant flowers per stem are a bright blue colour. It is an upland species from Afghanistan to India. *C. collina* from the Caucasus to Turkey although attractive with pendant purple-blue bells, has a reputation for being too exuberant for small gardens. *C. coriacea* is a Turkish limestone species with pubescent, curved stems and open lilac-blue flowers. *C. hagielia*, another Turkish limestone species, grows to about 30cm with spikes of relatively large violet-blue flowers. *C. petrophilia*, from the Caucasus at elevations up to 3500m, has semi-prostrate stems and erect, solitary violet-blue bell-shaped flowers with reflexed lobes. *C. raddeana* is a graceful, upright plant growing up to 40cm, although generally less. The nodding, widely open flowers are amethyst-blue. It is a limestone species from the Caucasus. The flowers of *C. tridentata*, from the Anatolian mountains and upland meadows, are very similar to those of *C. aucheri* although it has a more tufted, compact form. According to the Encyclopaedia of Alpines it travels under several nurserymen's names i.e. *C. bellidifolia, ardonensis, saxifraga* and *tridens* var. *aratica*.

Caryophyllaceae
Dianthus As already noted this genus includes members of the pin-cushion fraternity. *D. anatolicus*, as its name implies, occurs in Turkey but spreads far eastwards. It forms mats with rosettes of basal leaves. The small flowers are borne on short stalks and are white. *D. brevicaulis* forms low mounds, about 5-8cm high, with large solitary flowers in various shades of purple and red. It is a most attractive Turkish endemic. *D. pinifolius*, from Turkey and the Balkans, is very much a pin-cushion type with stiff, linear leaves. The flowers, in compact heads, are pink-purple to pale violet in colour. *D. squarrosus* really belongs outside our region since it is found in Kazakhstan and the Ukraine, but it is so attractive that we can slip it in here. It forms mats or mounds with linear, pointed leaves and relatively large, white, fragrant

flowers. There is a dwarf variety called 'Nanus'. Finally we can note the upland Turkish endemic *D. zederbaueri*, another cushion type with white or pink flowers.

Gypsophila This large genus, with a world-wide distribution provides a few choice South West Asian species, all of which like the same kind of conditions as aubrieta — well drained, calcareous soil in full sun. *G. aretioides*, with tiny, thick hairy, densely packed leaves, forms a cushion of rosettes on which sit the stemless, "pearly" white flowers. This is a high alpine from Iran and the Caucasus. *G. briquetiana* also produces cushions with small, rough edged, fleshy, pointed leaves. The inflorescence of several white or pink, purple-veined flowers are carried on many springy stems. This is a limestone endemic from the mountains of Turkish Armenia where it grows on exposed slopes and ridges. *G. tenuifolia*, from mountain slopes and meadows of the Caucasus and north east Turkey, produces more open, tufted mats. The comparatively large, white to pink flowers are grouped in panicles.

Clusiaceae
Hypericum This large genus which includes so many trees and shrubs from around the world, includes a few, small shrubby species from our region. *H. cerastioides*, from north western Turkey and south east Balkans is a hardy and easily grown species which forms moderate sized mats, with masses of fairly large flowers. *H. linarioides* grows erect to about 17cm. The leaf margins are deflexed. The yellow flowers often have a reddish tint or red lines. It has a wide distribution through Turkey, Caucasus, Iran and parts of the Balkans. *H. olympicum* is the hardy little bush with the large yellow flowers, which seeds itself about with abandon. It is a very variable species from the Balkans and south and west Turkey, with a number of regional variants which have been named and sold by nurserymen, including *H. polyphyllum* which chiefly differs in the presence of black glands on the petals. *H. pallens* is a limestone species which ranges from Turkey to Syria. It is a tough, little evergreen with yellow flowers which are preceded by red tipped buds.

Crassulaceae
Sedum Although this is a huge and widely distributed genus comparatively few species have been introduced from south west Asia. *S. pachyclados*, a native of Afghanistan, is described in the Encyclopaedia of Alpines as an outstanding specimen plant. The flower scapes arise from tightly packed rosettes and the 5-petalled white flowers are borne on "shaggy" peduncles, which appear twice, in early and also late summer. *S. pilosum* has the general appearance of a sempervivum. The leafy flower stems, varying in height from 3-10cm, carry compact, branching heads of bright pink flowers. According to Heath (1986), who rated it highly as an alpine house plant, it is monocarpic. It is a native of Turkey, Iran and Caucasus. *S. stoloniferum*, with a similar

range to the preceding species, forms loose, fairly large trailing mats. The 10–15cm flower stems carry nearly sessile triplets of comparatively large rose coloured flowers. Unlike many sedums it is partial to a shady, dampish site. It has been often confused with *S. spurium* to which it is preferable.

Rosularia In this small genus we encounter a morphologically different adaptation to arid conditions and temperature extremes. Instead of spines and cushions we have succulent rosettes which generally persist after flowering. They are often found growing in rock crevices. The species suitable for the rock garden or alpine house are particularly well represented in Turkey although only a few of them are currently available. Several of them do well outside, given the absolute need for protection from winter wet. In *R. aizoon* the 7-8cm stems carry panicles of pale yellow flowers. It is a limestone species from Turkey and Russian Armenia. *R. alpestris*, from Afghanistan to Central Asia, has clustered rosettes and terminal heads of white to purple flowers. *R. chrysantha*, a Turkish limestone endemic, produces 15cm stems with yellow to white flowers. *R. rechingeri*, named after the author of the monumental Flora Iranica, produces five centimetre stems with a spike of pale pink flowers. It is found in Turkey and Iraq. *R. sempervivum* forms a woody stem base from which arise the persistent rosettes which carry the flower stems with their panicles of dark pink flowers. It has an immense distribution from Turkey to Iran, Caucasus and Georgia. *R. serpentinica* is often regarded as a sub-species of *R. chrysantha*. The rosettes are monocarpic and the short stems carry panicles of red-lined white flowers.

Geraniaceae
Geranium Only a few of the geraniums earn a place in the rock garden since they are often too big or invasive but there are a few candidates. *G. libani* grows to about 40cm with 5-7 partite leaves which are glossy on their upper surface. The notched petals of its 3cm flowers are in shades of violet. As befits its origin in Turkey, Syria and Lebanon, it is dormant in summer. *G. tuberosum* has leaves which are 3-partite to their base and further divided into many lobes. The rose-purple petals are deeply notched and veined in dark purple. This species ranges from the Mediterranean to Iran, often as a cornfield weed. The tubers are eaten in Turkey. Although it is an attractive species many would shun it for its mundane associations. *G. renardii* is a low growing, trailing species with a woody rootstock. The leaves are palmate with 5-7 broad divisions. The white petals are notched with striking violet veins – a handsome combination. This native of Caucasus was discovered in 1935 by Walter Ingerwersen. Finally there is the border-line hardy *G. wallichianum* with trailing stems, 5-partite leaves and purple-blue flowers, generally with a white eye, from north east Afghanistan to Kashmir. Its preferred form is 'Buxton's Variety', with bluer flowers and more compact habit.

Pelargonium *P. endlicherianum* is interesting because it occurs in Turkey and Syria whereas the numerous majority of the other members of the genus occur in South Africa, with a few species scattered further afield in Australia, New Zealand and some Atlantic islands. It spreads by rhizomes, grows to about 30cm with mostly basal, rounded, shallow-lobed leaves and bright purple-pink, fragrant flowers. It is fairly hardy and may be grown outside, where it will survive the average winter with a pane of glass to keep off the winter rain. It flourishes in the alpine house. *P. quercetorum* from northern Iraq is very similar in habit but of larger size and known to have tolerated temperatures as low as -10^0C at the Royal Botanic Garden, Edinburgh.

Lamiaceae
Scutellaria There are several attractive skull caps from our region, generally with a mat-forming habit, from upland or montane localities, often in open woodland. Many of the skull caps have axillary flowers but in the ones noted here they are in terminal, often dense spikes and span a wide range of colours. Three of the Turkish species, *S. diffusa, S. pontica* and *S. salviifolia* are very similar in general habit but *P. diffusa* and *P. salviifolia* have very conspicuous foliar venation unlike *S. pontica*. In *S. diffusa* the flowers are of various shades of pink, in *S. pontica* of darker hue, approaching purple while in *S. salviifolia* they are bright yellow. *S. orientalis* is really a complex of sub-species which span an immense range from Spain to China and north west Africa. But among the several Turkish sub-species *S. o. alpina*, which occurs also in Iran and Lebanon, has proved a hardy rock plant. It has oval, wavy edged leaves and a spike of yellow flowers. In another Turkish sub-species, *pectinata*, the flowers are bi- coloured — yellow and purple-red.
Thymus There are several choice thymes to note, one of which *T. polytrichus* has made an outstanding contribution. They all form open mats or hummocks with heads or short spikes of flowers which are generally some shade of purple. *T. cilicicus*, introduced by Peter Davis, is a Turkish endemic with lilac to purple flowers but not entirely hardy outdoors in Scotland. *T. leucotrichus* comes in shades of purple and inhabits rocky slopes over a wide area which includes Turkey, Greece, Lebanon and Crete. *T. polytrichus* forms large mats while the flowers are in short, cylindrical spikes of purple, mauve, or rarely, white flowers. It is widely distributed not only in Turkey, Iran and Caucasus but also in central and southern Europe. As might be expected it is very variable, with regional sub-species and a host of named cultivars in the nurseryman's lists.

Plumbaginaceae
Acantholimon Members of this genus manifest the extreme "pin cushion" habit with very compact, spiny cushions especially at higher altitudes. At lower elevations, and where wind exposure is less, the cushions becomes less compact. All the introduced species (Fig.91) can be grown in the alpine house and several can be grown outside in a warm, sheltered site with sharp drainage or in a wall where water cannot collect. All the species mentioned

here have flowers of various shades of pink. *A. armenum*, from Turkey, Syria and Russian Armenia has three-angled leaves and a whitish, purple veined calyx. *A. glumaceum*, with a rather similar distribution, is reported as the easiest to grow outside. *A. ulicinum* is also comparatively hardy. Heath (1981) regarded *A. venustum* as the best of the available species, with rose pink flowers on 15cm stalks and a hairy calyx which persists during the winter.

Primulaceae
Androsace Most androsaces are European, Himalayan or American but there are a couple from South West Asia worth noting. *A. albana* is a hairy annual or biennial with a dense rosette of oblong leaves. The numerous white or pink flowers, with a green-yellow eye, are carried on 10-25cm stipes in tight umbels. This is a mountain species from Turkey, Caucasus and Turkish Armenia. *A. armeniaca* from Turkey, western Iran and beyond also has umbels of variously coloured flowers on stalks of variable height. A variety, *macrantha*, with larger flowers, is a Turkish, limestone endemic.
Cyclamen The genus consists of about 20 species with a distribution centred in the Mediterranean, but extending eastwards through Turkey to the Caucasus and hence adapted to hot, dry summers. They are often to be found in open woodland and sheltered, rocky places. *C. cilicium* (Fig.94) is native to the mountains of south west Turkey, especially the Cilician Taurus. The pale pink, fragrant corolla carries, a deep magenta, irregular blotch at the base of each petal lobe. This is a comparatively hardy species which can be grown outside with variable success.

Closely related is *C. intaminatum*, which was discovered in Turkey in 1934 by E.K. Balls and at first taken as a variety of *C. cilicium* from which it chiefly differs by its smaller flowers of pale pink, with grey veins and without the basal blotches. Although its distribution overlaps that of *C. cilicium* it extends further north. The third closely related member of this trio of Turkish endemics is *C. mirabile*, whose range partly overlaps that of *C. intaminatum*. The young leaves often have a red tint. The corolla is of various shades of pink with a magenta blotch at the base of each lobe, like *C. cilicium*. These species are hardy enough to try outside but do well in the bulb frame or alpine house.

C. parviflorum (Fig.95) is the smallest member of the genus and has the overall appearance of a small *C. coum*. The pinkish corolla carries a purple blotch on each lobe. It flowers from April to June and is found in north east Turkey. Although quite hardy it is usually grown in frames or the alpine house where it must be kept moist to match its damp habitats which are snow covered in winter. *C. trochopteranthum* is immediately recognisable by the arrangement of the corolla lobes, which, unlike the other species, are only partly reflexed so they stand out laterally to give the flowers a bizarre, propeller-like appearance. It is native to south west Anatolia, growing beneath conifers and in rocky scrub. It is probably best in a cool alpine house but can be tried outside where it is about as hardy as *C. cilicium*.

Dionysia In 'The English Rock Garden', Farrer listed 13 species of *Dionysia* from Turkey east to Afghanistan but it was not until 1932 that Professor Guiseppi introduced the genus into cultivation with seed of *D. curviflora, bryoides, michauxii* and *diapensifolia* from Iran. Further expeditions in the 1960s by Admiral Paul Furse and his wife, followed by Jim and Jenny Archibald led to the introduction of 40 species in total with more than 20 in cultivation at the end of the century.

All the species are tufted or cushion-forming plants, with yellow, pink or purple heteromorphic flowers. Coming as they do from areas with long dry periods they need to be kept dry except when in active growth and are therefore best in the alpine house. They are often double-potted or grown in tufa and make excellent cushion plants, being exhibited regularly at Shows.

The following species are the ones most frequently found in cultivation: *aretioides* (probably the easiest species to grow), *bryoides, curviflora, freitagii, tapetodes, viscidula, afghanica* and *lamingtonii. D. involucrata* is a recently introduced species from the Pamirs where it grows on limestone. It produces deep green clusters of oblong leaves with very evident veins. The flowers are in little umbels of three to five, at first lilac with a white eye but darkening with age. Unlike most of its relatives it is not difficult to grow. It attracts immediate interest because it is neither pin- nor thrum-eyed so that even an isolated plant will set seed by self-fertilisation.

There is now a wide range of hybrids available Many of these hybrids began spontaneously in 1990 in the Wurzburg garden of Michael Kammerlander where he grew most of the species currently in cultivation. Since then the number of hybrids has expanded greatly which may not please the purists but needs to be accepted as a fact of life in any popular genus containing a wide range of species

Primula *P. algida* (Section Farinosa) is a true Turano-Iranian species since it occurs in the mountains of eastern and north eastern Turkey, northern Iran and the Caucasus. It can grow to 20cm although is often less, with oblong, toothed leaves which are sometimes farinose. The several to a dozen violet to purple flowers are in terminal umbels. It ascends to 7000m. *P. amoena* (Fig.96) has been considered a sub-species *meyeri* of the wide ranging oxlip, *P. elatior*. It is a real charmer from Turkey and the Caucasus with violet to purple flowers with a yellow eye and the occasional albino.

Ranunculaceae

Anemone *A. blanda* is among the earliest of spring flowers. Spreading by tuberous rhizomes, the long-stalked, basal, tri-lobed leaves are hairless on the underside, unlike its more western relative *A. appenina*. The solitary many-petalled flowers come in a variety of colours — white, pink and all shades of blue to purple, with many named cultivars. It is a mountain plant from western Turkey, the Balkans and Cyprus.

Trollius *T. ranunculinus* (Fig.97) is a globe flower with a difference. It grows to between 20 and 50cm with the basal leaves divided into several segments which are deeply divided and toothed to produce a feathery, ferny effect. The rich yellow flowers are 4-5cm across with many petals. It occurs in moist, upland sites in Turkey, Iran and Caucasus.

Rubiaceae
Asperula These are dwarf plants with four-angled stems and the leaves in whorls of four or six. The small flowers are white or pink. Apparently only a small proportion of the potential rock garden accessions have been introduced, all suited to raised bed, scree or alpine house pans. *A. daphneola* is a Turkish, limestone species which forms large cushions with rough, grey-green leaves and several pink, cylindrical flowers borne in the leaf axils. *A. lilaciflora* is a small, tufted plant growing up to 30 cm, generally less, with clusters of relatively large, pale violet to pink flowers. This is another Turkish limestone species, with several sub-species, including *A. l. lilaciflora*, the one most commonly grown. *A. nitida* is yet another limestone species from Turkey and Greece. The habit is cushion or mat-like with clusters of pink flowers appearing among the overlapping leaves. According to the Encyclopaedia of Alpines the plant referred to often in the commercial lists as *A. n. puberula* is really *A. n.* ssp. *hirtella*.

Scrophulariaceae
Veronica There are a number of good rock plants from Turkey and neighbouring regions in this genus, often found in dry stony places among rocks at moderate elevations and mostly for sheltered sites in the garden. They appeal to connoisseurs of shades of blue, violet and lilac. *V. armena* is a small tufted plant growing to about 10 cm, often less, with trailing stems. The flowers are in loose sprays of bright blue. It occurs in Turkey but reaches also Russian Armenia and Georgia. *V. austriaca* is very much larger since the stems may reach 50-60cm. The inflorescence consists of many flowered racemes of blue flowers which vary in hue and intensity, including gentian blue, in different sub-species and varieties. It occurs in Turkey, Caucasus as well as Central and Eastern Europe. The sub-species *teucrium* has larger leaves and long clusters of flowers. *V. bombycina*, from Turkey and Lebanon, forms open cushions which are densely felted with hairs which cover the leaves and stems. The flowers, in terminal racemes, are described as milky blue by Heath (1986) who valued it highly for the alpine house. To keep it in character he recommended cutting hard back after flowering. *V. caespitosa* forms mats or rounded cushions, which may be quite large. The short spikes of flowers come in a wide range of colours from pale blue to violet. This is another species from Turkey and Lebanon. *V. gentianoides*, which spreads by rhizomes, is really a border plant although there are cultivars from high altitudes of smaller stature. *V. pectinata* is prostrate, rooting at the nodes, and

covered in white pubescence. The elongated, axillary racemes carry many violet to blue flowers. *V. peduncularis*, from Turkey, Caucasus and further afield, produces branched clumps of more or less erect stems to 10-15cm. Loose racemes arise from the upper leaf axils and the flowers are white, veined pink or various shades of blue. The plants sold under this name form mats and have blue flowers. *V. telephiifolia*, from Turkey and the Caucasus, forms low-growing, loose mats from which arise short racemes of pale blue flowers. It is reported to prefer damp crevices

Monocots
Amaryllidaceae
Crocus There are some 30 species of crocus, many of them with several to many sub-species in South West Asia and most commonly found on rocky slopes, in open woodland or upland pastures at moderate elevations. They are distinguished by such characters as time of flowering, whether the leaves appear after or at the same time as the flowers, the external appearance of the corms, the colour of the throat, styles and anthers, the degree of division of the styles etc. Many of them are easily grown in the garden although others are best in the bulb frame or alpine house. It is convenient to group them into those which flower either in the autumn, winter and early spring or later spring. Since flowering time varies according to local conditions the last two categories are not so well defined as the autumn flowering group.

Autumn Flowering. *C. cancellatus* (Fig.105) consists of five sub-species from different localites in Turkey, Lebanon and Syria. The leaves appear after the flowers which are white, lilac or mauve. The best known and most easily grown sub-species is *C.c. cilicicus* which flowers in October–November. *C. karduchorum* is endemic to south east Turkey. The flowers are very pale lilac with a white throat and a noticeably divided style. The plant often given this name should really refer to *C. kotschyanus* var. *leucopharynx* according to the Encyclopaedia of Alpines. *C. kotschyanus* is a large, pale lilac species with two orange spots at the base of the inside of each petal. There are four sub-species which together range from Turkey to Syria, Caucasus and Lebanon. The variety mentioned above lacks the basal orange spots, is known only in cultivation and is the easiest to grow. *C. pulchellus* is a tall species with lilac to pale blue flowers, a deep yellow throat and white or cream anthers. It is native to Turkey, Greece and parts of the Balkans. The leaves appear long after the flowers. It is easily grown, flowering from September to October. *C. scharojanii*, from Turkey, Caucasus and adjacent regions, is worth noting because it is the only yellow flowering autumn species. It is not so easy to keep as many of the species just noted and is rather unusual in preferring damp sites, consistent with its habitat in moist, upland grassland. *C. speciosus* is a hardy, rapidly multiplying species from Turkey, Iran, Caucasus and southern Russia. The leaves appear long after the flowers. There are several sub-species. The typical form has tall, purple veined lilac flowers with a light yellow throat and branched, light orange styles.

Winter and Spring Flowering. *C. ancyrensis* from Turkey, is a small species with rich yellow flowers. There is a robust variety called 'Golden Bunch'. *C. flavus*, from Turkey and the Balkans, is of particular interest since it gave rise to the 'Dutch Crocus', which has been in cultivation since the sixteenth century during which time it has become sterile. The fertile, wild form is of a deeper yellow and worth growing for that reason. *C. fleischeri* (Fig.106) is a small to medium sized species with white petals which are often striped purple on the outside. The finely divided style is orange scarlet. It is native to Turkey, Rhodes and Chios and is easily grown. *C. korolkowii* is a small species from Afghanistan and Central Asia. The outside of the petals is yellow marked to variable degree with purple or brown, while the interior is polished yellow. This is a more tender species. *C. olivieri* has three sub-species: *C. o. olivieri* is of medium size, orange-yellow or yellow with a 6-partite style, from Turkey, the Balkans and Romania. In *C.o. balansae* the style is more extensively divided and the outside of the petals is marked with brown. It is a Turkish endemic. Both sub-species are worthwhile garden plants. *C. pestalozzae* is a very small species from north west Turkey with white or pale lilac flowers with a black spot at the base of each stamen.

Spring Flowering. *C. abantensis* (Fig.102) is a tender species with flowers in shades of blue or lilac with a yellow throat, from north east Turkey. *C. biflorus* (Fig.103) is intermediate to large flowered. It comprises a complex of sub-species and varieties covering an immense range from Italy to Syria, Turkey, the Balkans and beyond. Typically the petals are pale or white on the outside, feathered or striped with purple, with a yellow throat. It has been grown in British gardens since the early seventeenth century, reputedly introduced from the Crimea. For most of this time it was known as the 'Scotch' crocus; probably some Scottish nurseryman distributed a particularly fine variety. Among the sub-species *C. b. weldenii* is outstanding, with white to blue flowers with a pale blue throat; *C. b. alexandri* is similar but with violet shading on the outside. *C. chrysanthus* (Fig.104) is from Turkey and the Balkans. Typically the flowers are small and light or deep yellow, but it has given rise to an immense number of named forms with a great variety of colours e.g. 'Cream Beauty', 'Zwanenberg Bronze', 'Blue Pearl', 'Snow Bunting' etc. *C. gargaricus* from western Turkey is a small orange yellow species with two sub-species, one of which *C. g. herbertii*, spreads by stolons, which is unusual. It also prefers a moist site, provided it is well drained. *C. reticulatus*, from Turkey and the Caucasus, is a small species for the bulb frame with violet markings on the outside of the petals and tripartite orange styles. There are two sub-species with either yellow or black anthers.

Iridaceae

Iris The Irises have been classified into six sub-genera, some of which are further divided into sections (Mathew 1981). However, only two are represented among the species chosen for comment here. They include: Iris, distinguished by well developed rhizomes and bearded falls, i.e. the outermost three tepals of the corolla and Hermodactyloides, small bulbous species which do not exceed 15cm at flowering and in which both falls and standards are well developed, with one exception. Many of the irises from south west Asia have to be grown in a frame or alpine house, where they are provided with sharp drainage and a summer baking. Others are perfectly hardy, especially among the Hermodactyloides which are spring flowering plants for the rock garden. Most of the irises noted here are very variable in flower colour, even in the same population, so that a description fails to do justice to the subtle hues. Only a few of the alpine house species are mentioned here.

Sub-genus Iris. *I. attica* (Fig.111), with a distribution from Turkey to Greece and Yugoslavia, is a very dwarf species in which the flowers are various shades of purple or yellow, sometimes bi-coloured. According to Mathew (loc.cit) it has a general resemblance to the Eastern European *I. pumila*. *I. sari*, from Turkey, is much taller, growing to 30cm, with flowers which are some shade of pale yellow to pale green with crimson or brown-purple veins. The falls carry a crimson or brown patch. This is easily grown in a bulb frame. *I. suaveolens* is a dwarf species from north west Turkey and Bulgaria. The flowers range in colour between yellow and purple and may be bi-coloured. The beard is usually yellow sometimes with a blue tint. This is well established in gardens. *Iris afghanica* (Fig.110) is a comparative newcomer since it was first described in 1972 (Mathew 1981). It is included among a few species which are closely related to Oncocyclus irises but from which they differ in the usual presence of two flowers per stem and the presence of beards on both falls and standards instead of only on the falls. It grows to between 15 and 35cm, often with only a single flower per stem with white falls, strongly veined purple-brown with a central purple patch. The standards are usually yellow with a greenish beard. It is endemic to Afghanistan and is readily grown in the alpine house.

Sub-genus Hermodactyloides. This includes the popular, spring flowering reticulata types. *I. bakeriana* has the general appearance of *I. reticulata* except that the leaves are almost cylindrical with eight ribs. The pale or whitish flowers are variously marked with violet, with a blue-lilac standard. There is a great deal of regional variation in flower colour. *I danfordiae* is one of the two species in this sub-genus with yellow flowers. The other is *I. winogradowii* but *I. danfordiae* is distinguished by the bristle-like standards. It is a native of Turkey. *I. histrio*, from Turkey, Syria and Lebanon, has large flowers which vary from blue to white and appear in late winter. The leaves become quite elongated after flowering. The typical form is best in the alpine house but the variety *aintabensis* can be grown outside in a sheltered site. *I. histrioides* is very similar to the previous species but with more weather-resistant, wider flowers on shorter stems. There are several cultivars which do not greatly differ. *I. reticulata* grows to 10–15cm with the four angled leaves, as in all the species mentioned here apart from *I. bakeriana*. The scented flowers range in colour from white to various shades of blue to deep purple, generally with a yellow crest on the falls. It is found in Turkey, Iran, Iraq and Russian Armenia. Finally we have *I. winogradowii* (Fig.113), a local and rare species from the Caucasus mountains. Mathew rates it as the best of the reticulatas. It resembles *I. histrioides* in size and general appearance except that the flowers are primrose yellow with green spots on the falls. It is a hardy rock garden plant which resents summer baking so it is well suited to Scottish conditions under which it thrives. It also reproduces by tiny bulblets and is clearly a plant to treasure.

Liliaceae

Fritillaria There are about 40 species from South West Asia which have been brought into cultivation. The majority of these are plants for the bulb frame and alpine house, although there are some good rock garden plants among them. In their native habitat most fritillaries are used to a hot summer. In most of the European and Asiatic species the bulbs consist of 2-3 fleshy scales which easily dry out. If grown from seed it will be at least four years before you see the flowers. In the wild many species are found in stony places, screes or dry scrub at elevations up to about 3000m. The flowers are generally campanulate, often solitary and nodding. Since they can vary in height, according to local conditions, quotes of size are approximate. Only the more readily available species are noted here. *F. acmopetala* (Fig.114) grows to about 30cm, sometimes more, with one to three long-stalked, nodding bells which are pale green with brown markings on the inner tepals and green nectaries within. It occurs on limestone in south west Turkey, Lebanon and Cyprus, sometimes in large numbers. It is easily grown outside. *F. armena*, a smaller species from north east Turkey, growing to about 15 cm or less, has a single, pendant dark purple flower. *F. aurea* is a Turkish limestone species of similar height but easily recognisable by its large yellow flower with fine, red-brown spotting. *F. bithynica* (Fig.115), from western Turkey, has green flowers and, like *F. armena* and *aurea*, is also a bulb frame species. *F. bithynica* grows to 20cm or less. The flowers are narrowly bell-shaped, lime green both without and within, but sometimes with purple marking on the outside. It occurs in west Turkey and the Greek islands of Chios and Samos and is a more tender species for the bulb frame or alpine house. *F. bucharica*, from Afghanistan and Central Asia grows to about 30cm and carries a raceme of white, green veined flowers. *F. caucasica*, from Turkey, Iran and Caucasus, is of intermediate size with solitary, more or less purple pendant flowers. According to Rix (1981) it occurs in peaty soil and is not easy. *F. crassifolia* (Fig.116) is credited with four sub-species of different distribution. They are handsome plants of small stature with generally yellow or greenish flowers with brown patterning and often rather indistinct green stripes. The sub-species *F. c. crassifolia* is a Turkish, limestone endemic. *F. elwesii* is a taller species from south Turkey with several dark purple, heavily green-striped flowers. *F. latifolia* (Fig.118), from Turkey and Caucasus, suggests a short stemmed *F. meleagris*. There are several different colour forms. *F. michailovskyi*, from north east Turkey, has several broadly bell-shaped flowers which are purple with a yellow rim. *F. olivieri*, from western Iran, has 1–4 nodding bells on a robust stem up to 30cm. The flowers are bright green on the outside, with purple-brown patterning, and a lighter green within. Synge (1971) regarded this as one of the finest species for the garden. *F. persica* is found in southern Turkey and western Iran and also Israel and Jordan. It is a striking plant with a raceme of dark flowers, variously described as greyish, black or greenish and egg-shaped bulbs. It has been in cultivation since Parkinson's time. The best known cultivar is called 'Adyaman'. *F. pinardii*, from north western Turkey, Iran and Lebanon is similar to *F. bithynica* in habit and size, also with narrowly bell-shaped flowers which are glaucous grey or purple on the outside, orange, yellow or green on the inside. *F. pontica* is another good garden species, from northern Turkey and Greece, with green flowers overlaid by a brown-purple tint. *F. sibthorpiana* is a smaller species with solitary, bright yellow open bells, from south west Turkey but definitely for the bulb frame. *F. uva-vulpis* has solitary, nodding bells which are greyish without, yellowish within. According to Rix (1981) this species has been widely mistaken for *F. assyriaca* which has a similar appearance and distribution. Only a few of the alpine house species are mentioned here.

Muscari The grape hyacinths are small plants with a raceme of bell or urn-shaped flowers which end in six small lobes. They are well suited to the spring and early summer rock garden and are generally undemanding although one or two species are invasive. *Muscari armenaicum* has bright blue, scented flowers with white lobes. It is a native of Turkey, Yugoslavia and Caucasus. There is a double cultivar called 'Blue Spike'. According to Synge (1981), 'Heavenly Blue', which is grown in such immense numbers, is descended from a mere six bulbs received and then multiplied by Messrs Barr. *M. aucheri* is a small species, flowering in late spring and early summer, with a dense spike of sky-blue, rather globular flowers, also with white tips. It occurs in alpine meadows in Turkey and is not invasive. *M. comosum*, now sometimes known as *Leopoldia comosa*, is a common plant of fields and scrub land in southern Europe, the Balkans, Turkey and southern Russia. It grows to about 45cm and produces racemes of short stalked flowers of two kinds. The upper are blue to violet with long stalks of the same colour and sterile. The lower ones are brown. *M. latifolium* has dark, indigo blue, fragrant, pendant flowers which are more loosely arranged in the spike which grows to about 25cm. It is found in Turkey, the Balkans and southern Russia. *M. macrocarpum* (Fig.119), along with the closely related *M. moschatum*, have been given the new generic name of *Muscarimia*. The former has light yellow, pendant flowers, with a robust growth to about 20cm. The flowers at the top of the raceme are sterile and blue-purple in colour. It is a native of Turkey and Greece. *M. moschatum* earns its specific name from its musky scent. The flowers are purplish-olive, becoming yellowish with age. It is not so visually attractive as the other species but the scent is interesting. It is an endemic from south west Turkey.

Ornithogalum This is a large genus with a number of small species suited to the rock garden although they are not very popular and few nurserymen stock them. The inflorescence is a raceme of several to many 6-petalled white flowers which are often open and star-like with a median green stripe. The best known species is the long established *O. umbellatum*, or 'Star of Bethlehem' which has a wide natural distribution in south and central Europe and the Middle East, but is too vigorous for other than a large rock garden. A more desirable species is *O. lanceolatum*, from Turkey, Syria and Lebanon, in which the leaves rest flat on the ground, since the stems are very short or lacking, and the group of sessile white flowers make an attractive plant for the scree or raised bed. *O. oligophyllum* (Fig.120), from Turkey and the Balkans, grows to about 10cm with clusters of several white flowers per scape. There are other white flowered species of similar habit e.g. *O. sibthorpii* and *sigmoideum*.

Scilla This bulbous, widespread genus includes a number of small species which flower either in the spring or autumn. *S. bithynica* is a spring-flowering species from Turkey and south east Europe. It produces racemes of up to a dozen purple-blue flowers and is easy to grow. In *S. mischtschenkoana*, from northern Iran and Caucasus, the flowers generally appear in early spring before the leaves. The white or very pale blue flowers are borne in few-flowered racemes on approximately 12cm stems. *S. sibirica* (Fig.121), the best known spring flowering species, has an immense distribution from central and southern Europe to Turkey and Caucasus. As might be expected there are a number of regionally distinct sub-species. Typically each bulb produces several stems of about 20cm with drooping, intensely blue flowers. 'Spring Beauty' is the most popular variety; there is also a white form known as 'Alba' and a dark one 'Atropurpurea'.

Sternbergia This is a small genus of some half dozen species with a general distribution in the eastern Mediterranean and south west Asia. At first sight some of them could be mistaken for a yellow crocus, although they have six in place of three stamens. The usually golden yellow flowers are of great beauty, although only *S. lutea* (Fig.123), from the eastern Mediterranean is widely grown. They require a warm, sunny, sheltered site. In Scotland they are subjects for the frame or alpine house where watering can be controlled and they can kept dry in summer. The South West Asian species noted here are mostly autumn flowering. *S. candida* (Fig.122), an endemic from south west Turkey, has white flowers. *S. colchiflora* has yellow flowers which appear in autumn before the leaves. *S. clusiana*, with a clutch of synonyms, from Turkey to Iran and Jordan, has impressive flowers which open widely in the autumn sun before the leaves appear. *S. fischeriana* is a yellow spring flowering species with narrow, wide-spreading tepals and a distribution from Turkey to the Caucasus. *S. sicula* (Fig.124) is a handsome, limestone species, with yellow autumn flowers, to be found in Turkey, Greece and Italy.

Tulipa The tulips are mostly found in western and central Asia but south west Asia is home to a number of small species suitable for the rock garden. The corolla is often suffused with intermediate colours which frequently vary both within and between populations and which are often difficult to describe accurately. Authors differ in their description of a given species, either because they have different variants before them or people see subtle hues rather differently. *T. biflora* (Fig.125) grows to about 20cm and, although it has only two leaves, the stems carry one or two wide open flowers which are white, with a yellow, basal patch at the base of the inside of the tepals. The yellow anthers are purple-tipped. It has a classic Turano-Iranian distribution from Turkey to Caucasus. *T. clusiana* has solitary flowers on comparatively tall stems. The basically white flowers, with purple anthers, are decorated externally with pink–crimson streaks. It ranges from Iran to north west Pakistan and has long been established in our gardens. There are several varieties, formerly treated as species e.g. *T. c. stellata* with yellow stamens and flowers with a pale yellow basal patch within, and *T. c. chrysantha* which is yellow with red tints on the outside of the corolla, except for the yellow tepal margins. *T. kolpakowskiana* has usually solitary yellow flowers with red, orange or dark green tints on the outside, from Afghanistan and Central Asia. *T. linifolia*, from Iran and Afghanistan, is a small, excellent rock-garden species with typically, red flowers with a deep purple patch at the base inside the tepal. It is a variable species in which the flowers may be yellow. There are two closely related sub-species: *batalinii*, with yellow flowers and *maximowiczii*, with a shorter stem and red flowers with a black centre with a white margin. *T. orphanidea* is also very variable. It grows to about 25cm. The stems may carry several, but usually a single orange brown flower which is tinted with green or purple or is yellow, shaded red. There are related species or sub-species like *T. hageri* in which the inside of the tepals are light brown, often with a yellow edged basal patch and *T. whittallii* with orange-bronze flowers. *T. sylvestris* is so widely naturalised in Europe and the Middle East that its true origins are unknown. Typically the flowers are yellow or very pale yellow in colour. There are cultivated varieties which differ in colour, size and time of flowering. *T. urumiensis*, from north west Iran, resembles the familiar Central Asian *T. tarda*, but with fewer flowers per scape and without the white tip to the wide opening tepals.

The Balkans

This area, which, for our purposes includes the Balkan peninsula, Greece and the Aegean Islands, has a rich flora estimated by Turrill at between 6000 and 7000 seed plants. Approximately one quarter of them are endemic and found only in this region, often with quite a local distribution. Several reasons contribute to the origin of both the diversity and the endemism. The broken nature of the land, with its numerous mountain chains and valleys, the numerous islands and the fluctuation in the level of the Mediterranean have been prime factors in causing the break-up of formerly continuous populations into smaller entities which became adapted to local conditions and, being isolated, drifted apart from other similarly isolated populations. In addition to such comparatively recently evolved endemic species there are a number of "old" endemics which represent survivors from the Tertiary period before the successive ice ages. The rest of the non-endemic flora has come overland from other geographically distinct floras, especially the Euro-Siberian, including many transcontinental species, the Mediterranean with lesser but significant contributions from the Black Sea flora, the flora of Western Turkey (Anatolian) and also Central Asia and further east with even a few species from North Africa. Genera which include the largest number of endemic species, and which naturally attract the greatest interest, include *Dianthus, Verbascum, Thymus, Campanula, Silene, Stachys* and *Asperula*, and, to a lesser extent, *Allium, Colchicum, Fritillaria* and *Crocus*.

As might be expected the flora of the Balkans shares many species with that of south west Asia but there are sufficient differences, especially in the numerous endemic species, to justify separate consideration. 'Yugoslavia' here refers to the former political and geographical entity which preceded the recent division into several separate states.

Dicots
Apiaceae
Eryngium The sea hollies, which are adapted to dry, sandy places, are easily recognised by the spiny bracts of their flower heads. *E. amethystinum* grows to about 70cm. The tough, basal leaves are divided into spiny lobes and the petioles winged. The numerous globular, blue–amethyst flower heads are borne on bright blue stems to produce a striking effect. It occurs widely in the Balkans, including Yugoslavia, Albania, Greece and Bulgaria and also turns up in Sicily.

Asteraceae
Achillea. These are plants of well drained, sunny places, especially among rocks, with white or yellow-rayed flowerheads and incised leaves which are usually hairy, often densely so to impart a silvery or woolly appearance. The height varies considerably according to conditions. They include the long established *A. tomentosa* from south west Europe, with mats of ferny leaves

and yellow flowers. *A. ageratifolia* (Fig.80) is found among rocks in the mountains of the Balkans. It forms mounds of narrow woolly grey leaves. The generally solitary white flower heads which vary about 10cm in width are carried on 30 cm stems. It is confined to the Balkans. *A. clavennae* produces broadly incised silvery leaves. It grows to 20 cm or more with sprays of white-rayed flowers and the usual yellow disks. It ranges from the Alps to the Balkans. *A. holosericea* grows to about 30cm as a rough average. The leaves are also incised and silvery but here the rays of the densely clustered flowerheads are yellow. It is another inhabitant of rocky places. *A. umbellata* is a dwarf species of 10-20cm in which the covering of short hairs makes the oval, incised leaves appear white rather than silvery. The yellow rayed flowerheads are densely clustered. It is a native of the mountains of central and southern Greece.

Centaurea *C. triumfettii* is a widespread Balkan cornflower with boldly spreading blue outer and violet inner florets in the solitary flower heads. The well defined margins of the involucral bracts are brown or black. The leaves are typically oblong to lanceolate and woolly, especially when young. In the cultivated sub-species *stricta*, which grows to about 15 cm, the leaves are narrower than in the typical form, entire or with one or two teeth, woolly and grey coloured and of more restricted distribution, especially in the northern Balkans.

Helichrysum *H. orientale* is an almost shrubby, tufted, erect plant which grows to about 30cm from dense, basal leaves to produce, flat-topped clusters of relatively large, yellow flowerheads. It occurs in Greece and the islands, including Crete. Although safest in the alpine house it can be grown in sheltered, well-drained scree or raised bed. *H. heldreicheii* is a rare tufted plant from Crete with linear leaves and a tight cluster of small flowers. It has the distinction of being "among the best of mound-forming, silver foliaged plants for the alpine house and raised bed " (Encyclopaedia of Alpines).

Boraginaceae
Anchusa *A. cespitosa* is found only on limestone in the mountains of Crete. The almost sessile blue flowers sit in the middle of the tuft of coarsely hairy leaves. This is a classic scree, raised bed or trough species.

Brassiceae
Alyssum There are several species of *Alyssum* in the area, typically with yellow flowers. *A. cyclocarpum*, now transferred to the genus *Ptilotrichum* on account of some minor differences in the form of the stamen filaments, occurs on limestone up to 2800m from Italy, the Balkans and Turkey. Tufted and sub-shrubby it grows to some 20cm with narrow, downy-silvery leaves and a tight cluster of white flowers. *A corymbosum* and *A. markgrafii* are rather alike in size, 30–50cm. In the former the inflorescence is flat-topped, less so in the latter which has a more montane distribution. *A. montanum* has a wide

European distribution. The habit can be either erect or more or less prostrate. It includes an attractive Yugoslav endemic, *A.m. brynii* with orange-yellow flowers. *A. murale* has rosettes of basal leaves and is widespread in the region. *A. saxatile*, which has been transferred into the genus *Aurinia* can be quite large, up to 90cm. It ranges from Central Europe to the Balkans and has a number of varieties with lemon rather than the usual yellow flowers and also more compact forms, including the variety 'Tom Thumb', which grows only to about 10 cm. These are all plants for well drained, sunny sites.

Arabis *A. bryoides* forms low cushions of small hairy rosettes which give rise to short stipes with a loose group of relatively, large white flowers. It occurs in rocky places in the mountains of the Balkan peninsula. and makes another excellent scree or trough plant. *A. ferdinandi-coburgi* spreads by stolons to form close and often large mats of dark green leaves in the wild. There are several cultivars attributed to this species such as 'Variegata' with ivory edged, variegated leaves but this appears more likely to have been derived from the very similar species *A. procurrens*.

Aubrieta *A. columnae* is a close growing species with purple-violet flowers. It extends from Yugoslavia and Albania to Italy. *A. deltoidea*, from southern Greece, the Aegean and Sicily, has the familiar aubrieta habit with large violet-purple flowers. This is regarded as the main, but not exclusive, source of many cultivars of this stand-by of the spring scene. *A. gracilis* has flowers of a more violet colour and is found in rocky, mountain sites in Yugoslavia, Greece and Bulgaria.

Campanulaceae

Asyneuma *A. limonifolium* forms clumps of mostly basal, lanceolate leaves of variable width with spikes of violet-blue one centimetre flowers carried on stems of variable height, from 30-100cm or more. This Balkan endemic occurs on rocky ground in limestone country.

Campanula This genus includes plants of different growth form, from slender and glabrous to sturdy and more or less hairy. The inflorescence may take the form of solitary blooms, short, lax clusters or dense terminal heads of flowers. The corolla, although basically bell shaped, can take many forms, narrow or wide open, or with spreading petals which confer a starry appearance. The flowers are blue-purple with shades described as lilac or violet. According to Polunin (1980) there are some 90 species in the Balkans of which more than 50 are endemic, illustrating the importance of this genus in defining the floristic status of the region. *C. abietina* spreads by a creeping rootstock. The leaves are lanceolate and the solitary purple, spreading, star-like flowers are carried on a 25cm stem. It occurs widely in the Balkans and the Carpathians. It is advised to divide it periodically and replant in the preferred, sharply drained compost, otherwise it may prove short lived. *C. alpina* is a low–growing, biennial species of 10-20cm with a rosette of leaves and a cluster of many, blue, bell- shaped flowers, from mountain pastures of

Yugoslavia, Albania and Bulgaria. *C. calaminthifolia* is a rosette-forming, prostrate species, with brittle stems, from the Greek Islands with blue or white funnel- shaped flowers. *C. fenestrellata* is a small, upright or lax species, with oval, petiolate leaves, from Yugoslavia and Albania. There are two subspecies: *C. f. fenestrellata* which is glabrous with double- toothed leaves and *C. f. istriaca* with hairy, single-toothed leaves. Both have blue flowers. *C. garganica* is a commonly grown species from south east Italy and western Greece with the large, wide open blue flowers with a white centre. *C. hawkinsiana* has many spreading, slender leafy stems of 10-20cm with long stalked, blue velvet flowers with spreading lobes. *C. moesiaca* is a hairy biennial which grows to about 40cm with a dense terminal cluster of blue-lilac flowers and also small clusters of flowers in the upper leaf axils. It is very similar in appearance to the common *C. glomerata*. *C. oreadum* is a small, slender, creeping plant which inhabits crevices on Mount Olympus. The few or solitary narrowly, bell-shaped flowers are deep blue. This is an attractive plant for the trough. *C. portenschlagiana* hardly requires further comment beyond noting its origin in western Yugoslavia. *C. rupicola* is a creeping, delicate species adapted to limestone crevices. The erect, purple flowers are narrowly bell-shaped. It is native to south and central Greece. *C. sartorii* strikes a different note. The short stalked, orbicular leaves arise from a stout and fleshy rootstock. The stems are prostrate while the upturned, funnel-shaped flowers with spreading lobes are white or pink. It is a Greek endemic. *C. thessala* is a grey, hairy plant with many more or less prostrate stems which carry several, more or less tubular, blue-violet flowers. It is another endemic from central Greece and is probably more suited to the alpine house. *C. thyrsoides* is a rather different species. It produces dense, erect spikes of tubular yellow flowers – very unusual for the genus. It has a wide distribution from the mountains of the Balkans to the Jura and the Alps, just to remind us that there are plenty of non-endemic species as well. *C. versicolor* (Fig.85) is easily recognised. The straight stems of variable height carry clusters of pale blue or lilac, shallow flowers with spreading tringular lobes and centres of darker blue. It has a wide distribution in Yugoslavia, Albania, Greece and Bulgaria. *C. waldsteiniana* is a delicate, hairless, many-stemmed species from the limestone mountains of western Yugoslavia. The inflorescence consists of short, terminal clusters of small blue-violet flowers with wide-spreading corolla lobes.

Edraianthus This is a small genus, especially well represented in the Balkans, but extending eastward to the Caucasus. Eight of the nine Balkan species are endemic. The flowers are carried in terminal clusters with a leafy involucre of bracts which differ in size and shape between species but, otherwise, the general appearance is rather similar. In *E. dalmaticus*, an endemic from the mountains of west Yugoslavia, the 3-6 violet–blue flowers are in terminal clusters, surrounded by a ring of oval, pointed bracts. It does well on scree or raised bed. *E. graminifolius* (Fig.86) forms rosettes of narrow leaves with unbranched flowering stems of 10cm or less. The violet-blue flowers are surrounded by short involucral bracts. It occurs in Yugoslavia, Albania, Greece and also southern Italy and Sicily. *E. pumilio*, from western Yugoslavia, is the best known and perhaps the most attractive of this group of species, since the solitary flowers, of the usual blue-violet colour, contrast with the silvery leaves, while the involucre of bracts is comparatively small. This makes a superb specimen on a well drained and sheltered scree. *E. serbicus* is close to *E. dalmaticus* in appearance except that the tip of the bracts is short rather than long and tapering. *E. serpyllifolius*, from Albania and western Yugoslavia, is a dwarf, often mat-like species with blunt or notched leaves and several short stems bearing solitary, dark violet flowers – a charming combination. Finally, *E. tenuifolius* is very similar to *E. graminifolius* except that the leaves are narrower and the broad bracts are drawn out into a long point which exceeds the flowers. It is confined to Yugoslavia, Albania and Greece. All these species make excellent subjects for well drained, sunny sites.

Caryophyllaceae

Dianthus This genus also contains many endemics. *D. freynii* forms small hummocks of stiff, grey-green leaves upon which sit the solitary flowers, which are generally pink, but may be white. This is a limestone species from Bulgaria and Yugoslavia; it makes an excellent trough subject In *D. haematocalyx* the flower stems are typically branched and carry several large pink-purple flowers which are yellow on the underside and with a rather red calyx. It is to be found among rocks in Albania, Greece and southern Yugoslavia. The sub-species *pindicola* has short stipes and solitary flowers while the variety *alpinus* from high altitudes is dwarfer still with larger, nearly sessile toothed flowers. *D. microlepis* has a low, cushion habit but also produces long, barren stems and flowering stems which are leafless or with minute, scale-like leaves. This is a non-limestone species from alpine meadows in Bulgaria and Yugoslavia, with purple flowers. *D. myrtinervius* is a dwarf plant, with rather sprawling habit and short stemmed purple flowers from Macedonia, Yugoslavia and Greece. *D. nardiformis* forms cushions of fine, branched rather woody stems. The leaves are narrow, more or less cylindrical and pointed. The solitary flowers on 10cm scapes are pink and the toothed petals are bearded. Its range includes Bulgaria and Romania. *D. petraeus* is a variable species with a wide distribution in Yugoslavia, Albania, Greece and Bulgaria. It has a loosely tufted habit. The petals may be deeply incised, toothed or more or less entire, with or without a beard. The colour is white to pinkish. *D. scardicus* (Fig.87) is a low-growing, compact species with long barren and short flowering shoots, which carry solitary, pink, scented flowers A native of mountain pastures in Yugoslavia it is easily grown. *D. simulans*, from Greece and Bulgaria, has the typical adaptation to arid conditions by way of tight, cushion habit and spiny, grey green leaves. The flowers, on short stems, are rose-red.

Gypsophila   *G. nana* is a dwarf mountain plant of rock crevices from southern Greece and Crete. It grows only to a few centimetres, is sticky haired on leaves and stem with light purple flowers.

Minuartia   *M. juniperina*, from alpine and sub-alpine sites in south west Greece, is an erect, rigid, densely tufted little plant with many stiff, more or less spiny leaves.

Silene   This genus is well represented in the region. The species are often distinguished by relatively small differences. The petals have a characteristic shape, with a narrow basal claw and, usually, a spreading limb. *S. alpestris* is a tufted species, which spreads by rhizomes with rosettes of linear or narrowly oval leaves and cymes of several white flowers, on 10-20cm stems. It occurs in the northern Balkans and the Eastern Alps. There is a narrow leaved double form, known as *S. a.* 'Flore Pleno' which is now believed to belong to the closely related *S. pusilla*. *S. asterias*, with clusters of deep purple flowers, is hairless and perennial. It can grow to about 90cm and occurs in the Balkan Peninsula. *S. lerchenfeldiana*, from Yugoslavia, Greece and Bulgaria, is also hairless or nearly so. It is a slender plant with a rosette of lanceolate leaves and a leafy stem carrying a branched inflorescence of red or purple flowers with deeply incised, lobed petals. *S. parnassica* is probably best regarded as a form of *S. saxifraga* which is widespread in southern Europe. It is distinguished by being smaller and more compact with generally only one flower per scape. The flowers are white or pink, with notched petals. It also occurs on limestone. *S. vallesia* is not confined to the Balkans but occurs also in northern Italy and southern France. It is mat-forming with approximately 15cm scapes which carry 1-3 flowers in which the upper side of the deeply lobed petals is pink and the lower side red. Since the petal tips bend inward the inflorescence presents a parti-coloured appearance. It occurs on siliceous screes up to about 2000m. There is a sub-species, *graminea*, with narrow leaves and white flowers.

Clusiaceae

Hypericum   *H. athoum* is a tufted, softly hairy plant which grows up to 20cm. The flowers are in cylindrical clusters. Both petals and sepals have black glands on their margins. It occurs in shady places in Greece. The closely related, more local *H. delphicum* is very similar but larger overall. *H. fragile* is a small herb with a woody base which grows to about 10cm, living up to its specific name in habit. There are pale glands on the leaf margins; the flowers are yellow with a hint of red. This is a limestone endemic from eastern Greece which is sometimes mistaken for the altogether more robust *H. olympicum*, which has already been noted in the section on south west Asia. In *H. richeri*, a common Balkan species from montane grassland and woods, the 10-40cm stems bear net-veined leaves and black-dotted yellow flowers.

Dipsaceae
Pterocephalus   This genus of about two dozen species ranges from Europe, through Asia into China. *P. perennis* has two sub-species, one from Greece, the other from Albania. This is a prostrate, creeping species with downy, grey or silvery leaves in the Greek and glandular, green leaves in the Albanian form. The scabious-like flower heads, up to 4cm across, are carried on 6cm peduncles.

Ericaceae
Bruckenthalia   There is only one species in this genus, *B. spiculifolia*, which looks like an *Erica* from which it differs in a few minor floral characters. It occurs in mountain grassland and open woods in the northern Balkans and also south of the Black Sea. An erect little shrub of some 10-15cm it produces terminal clusters of pink heather flowers. It grows easily enough in the same acid conditions in which so many heathers thrive.

Gentianaceae
Gentiana   *G. frigida* produces rosettes of narrow leaves of rather variable width and shape, with terminal, solitary, sessile bell-shaped flowers which are white-yellow with blue stripes and blue spots in the throat. It occurs in south west Bulgaria, the Austrian Alps and the Carpathians. *G. pyrenaica* is a small, tufted plant with fairly narrow, basal leaves in rosettes. The stalked, flowers are solitary, terminal, funnel-shaped and violet blue in colour, with 10 equal corolla lobes. Mountain pasture is the usual habitat. The distribution is intriguing for it occurs in the Pyrenees, south west Bulgaria, Turkey and the Caucasus. It seems likely that the separation of the Spanish from the eastern populations was the result of former glacial action. There is apparently no record of any difference between them but perhaps it would be worth looking a little harder.

Geraniaceae
Geranium   *G. dalmaticum* from south west Yugoslavia and Albania is widely grown. Creeping by rhizomes it forms carpets of glossy, hairless, divided leaves about 4cm wide or less. The typically pink flowers are 2-3cm across with the face held vertically; there is also a white variety. This is a hardy and attractive rock garden plant. *G. versicolor* is easily recognised by its large white or pale lilac trumpet-shaped flowers with dark velvet veins and notched petals. It has a low spreading habit with divided, pointed leaves. It is found in Yugoslavia, Albania and Greece as well as central and southern Italy and Sicily. In *G. peloponessiacum*, from Albania and southern Greece, the blue-violet flowers, with darker veins or indistinct markings, are gathered into rather open flat-topped clusters on long stalks. It grows to about 60cm and goes dormant after flowering in spring.

Gesneriaceae

Jankaea Although it taxes the skills of the alpine house devotee we have to mention *J. heldreicheii* from the Mount Olympus limestone on account of its beauty and star rating in the Greek flora. The broad spreading, bell-shaped flowers are lilac blue and the leaves a downy white.

Ramonda There are only three species in this genus, *R. myconi* from the Pyrenees, *R. nathaliae* and *R. serbica* both from southern Yugoslavia. The latter two are very similar at first glance since they both form a rosette of dark green leaves with 3-5 leaflets, with woolly, ginger hairs on the underside and glandular haired flower stems. However, in *R. serbica* (Fig.88) the leaf is rhomboidal, quite sharply toothed and narrowed gradually to a short wide stalk, while in *H. nathaliae* the leaf is more oval, less sharply toothed and tapered to a distinctly narrower stalk. In *R. nathaliae* the flat-faced flower is about 3cm or more across and lilac-violet in colour with an orange or yellow eye. In *R. serbica* the flower is a a little lighter in colour and slightly smaller in size. Both species occur in southern Yugoslavia. *R. nathaliae* also occurs in northern Greece, while *R. serbica*, also in northern Greece, extends to Albania and Bulgaria. Both species grow on limestone cliffs and are safest in the alpine house although both may be grown outside. *R. nathaliae* is reputed to be easier to please than *R. serbica*.

Linaceae

Linum *L. capitatum* has a wide distribution in Yugoslavia, Albania and Greece and also occurs in southern Italy. The yellow flowers, in a dense flat-topped head, rise 10-40cm from a rosette of basal leaves which are sustained by a woody rhizome.

Papaveraceae

Corydalis *C. bulbosa* (Fig.89) is a variable, tuberous, open woodland species with a range from Europe to north west Iran, including the Balkans and the Caucasus. It grows to about 15cm with pale green bipinnate leaves. The tubular, horizontal, down-spurred flowers may be white to purple, according to the sub-species which also differ in the denseness of the racemes. *C. ochroleuca* (Fig.90) is a larger, rhizomatous species, growing to about 40cm with a habit which closely resembles that of the familar *C. lutea*. The pale yellow or greenish flowers are carried in dense racemes which arise from the leaf axils. It is a mountain plant of south east Europe to the Balkans. It is a delightful plant but one which may take over if admitted to the rock garden.

Primulaceae

Androsace As already noted, only a few species of this genus occur in south west Asia and the Balkans. *A. lactea* grows on limestone mountains, spreading by stolons to form loose mats of small, hairless rosettes of narrow leaves. The one to several stems per rosette carry umbels of one centimetre, white flowers with a yellow eye and notched petals. It occurs from the Alps eastwards, including Yugoslavia, Albania and Bulgaria. There is also a related, smaller species, *obtusifolia,* of similar habit and distribution, with white or pink flowers and a very hairy calyx. *A. hedraeantha* (Fig.92) is an attractive scree plant from the central Balkans, which forms tight hummocks of small, narrow narrow leaved rosettes. The generally pink, but occasionally white, flowers are borne in close umbels on short or longer stalks. It is closely related to the more familiar *A. obtusifolia* which has larger rosettes. *A. villosa* (Fig.93) occurs on limestone mountains from Europe eastwards as far as the Indian Himalayas. It forms tufts or mats of small, rounded rosettes of leaves which are finely hairy on the under side. The relatively large flowers are white with a yellow eye or, with age, they may become pink with a red eye. They are carried on 3cm stalks. There are a number of varieties which differ in flower colour, habit or development of the stolons.

Ranunculaceae

Helleborus There are about ten species of this genus in the Balkans, many of which are grown in our gardens. *H. cyclophyllus* (Fig.100), a strong growing deciduous species, grows to about 50cm or more with large leaves divided into 5-9 toothed segments. The inflorescence comprises 3-4 glaucous, green flowers about 6cm across, with free carpels. Quite widespread in the Balkan peninsula it may also extend into Turkey. *H. odorus* is generally similar to *H. cyclophyllus* except that the carpels are generally fused at their base. The flowers are green, but not glaucous and their elder-flower scent is much more evident and the tough, usually single leaf overwinters. It also occurs in open woodland and grassy places with a similar, although more extensive, distribution which also includes southern Romania and southern Italy.

H. niger, the 'Christmas Rose', is a very showy species, widely grown but not easy to keep vigorous and free flowering. It needs an alkaline, humus-rich soil in light shade. It is represented by many named cultivars.

Pulsatilla Some seven species of *Pulsatilla* grow in the Balkans but their nomenclature is debatable.The garden-worthy species include *P. halleri* with densely hairy leaves and large bell-shaped lilac-purple flowers, *P. montana* which is rather similar but less hairy and with smaller flowers, and *P. vernalis,* covered with brown, silky hairs and with white, goblet-like flowers, flushed pink or blue outside. All are easy enough in well drained sunny spots although *P. vernalis* needs winter protection in areas with a variable winter climate.

Saxifragaceae

Saxifraga. There are about 30 species of this genus in our region, of which about a fifth are endemic. *S. federici-august*i comprises two sub-species: *S. f-a.* ssp. *grisebachii,* with greyish rosettes of lime encrusted leaves and 15-

20cm leafy scapes with numerous, pendant flowers with short petals but covered with red-tipped glandular hairs. This a popular trough or alpine house plant; the form 'Wisley' is probably the best known. It is a native of central and southern Macedonia, Albania and northern Greece. The other sub-species *S. f-a.* ssp. *federici-augusti*, from Yugoslavia, Albania and Macedonia, is smaller and of less imposing appearance. *S. marginata* (Fig.99) typically forms low cushions of spade-shaped leaves, from which arise the approximately 10cm scapes carrying panicles of relatively large white flowers. It ranges from southern Italy to the Balkans so there are regional sub-species and varieties which differ in flower colour and/or habit and these have given rise to a number of named cultivars all of which have a preference for limestone. *S. sempervivum* (Fig.98) is a favourite alpine house plant with compact, silvery-green, lime encrusted rosettes. The scapes, of about 10cm or more, carry numerous pink purple flowers; both scape and flowers are covered in red glandular hairs. This species is widespread in the Balkans and also occurs in Turkey. *S. stribryni*, from Greece and Bulgaria, is densely tufted with rather flat, tough rosettes of lime encrusted leaves from which arise the branched scape of petiolated, red-purple flowers with red glandular hairs.

Scrophulariaceae
Digitalis   *D. lanata* is a striking foxglove with a hairy, red-purple stem which grows to about 20cm with a dense spike of 2-3cm long white-yellowish flowers with brown or violet veins. By contrast the oblong or lanceolate leaves are only marginally hairy. It occurs in woods and scrubby places in the Balkans and widely elsewhere in Asia to Siberia.

Thymeleaceae
Daphne   *D. oleoides* (Fig.100) has an immense range from the Mediterranean to the Himalayas. It forms a small shrub to about 50cm with oval or pointed leaves and clusters of usually fragrant flowers which are typically creamy white but may be pink in some froms. It is hardy in our climate, given a sheltered, sunny, well-drained site.

Violaceae
Viola.   Almost half the nearly 60 species of this genus are endemic to the region. *V. aetolica* is rather similar to *V. tricolor*, with yellow flowers, in which the upper petals are occasionally violet. It is found in mountain meadows throughout the Balkans. *V. cenisia* has a wide distribution from the south-west Alps to the Balkans but includes a number of geographical races, sometimes accorded specific rank, which occur in the Balkans e.g. *V. magellensis* with violet or pink flowers in which the upper petals are reddish-violet. In *V. elegantula*, from western Yugoslavia and Albania, with large, unequally divided stipules, the flowers may be violet, pink, or occasionally yellow and at times both violet and yellow or even white. *V. graeca* (Fig.101),

from the mountains of Greece and also Mount Gargano in Italy, has a tufted, spreading habit and flowers which may be pink or violet, occasionally yellow, either alone or combined with one or other of the other colours. *V. orphanidis* is softly hairy, with many stems which may reach 70cm, but generally less. The violet or blue flowers are provided with a slender spur. It occurs widely in the Balkan Peninsula. *V. stojanowii*, from Bulgaria and northern Greece, is a low growing, hairy, tufted plant with yellow flowers, the upper petals sometimes tinged violet, with a stout, curved spur. *V. zoysii*, closely related to the widespread European *V. calcarata*, is distinguished by its very compact habit. The solitary flowers are usually yellow or occasionally violet-purple. It is a limestone species from the Balkan Peninsula and the south eastern Alps. In our gardens both species are beloved by slugs.

Monocots
Amaryllidaceae
Crocus About 27 species are recorded from the Balkans of which half are endemic and most are local. They include attractive species several of which will grow in sheltered sites outside. *C. cvijicii*, from Albania and both Greek and Yugoslav Macedonia grows to about 6-7cm. The flowers range from cream to deep orange-yellow, with orange-yellow anthers and tripartite orange style. This is a rare species, which, however, appears best grown outside in scree or raised bed. *C. dalmaticus* is a spring flowering species, growing to under 10cm, in which the leaves appear after the flowers which are pale to deep lilac with a light exterior with purple lines. This easy and variable species lives in rocky places up to 2000m. *C. hadriaticus* flowers in the autumn when the leaves also appear. The flowers are white, with a yellow, rarely white, throat and variable brownish tints outside. It is an upland species from western and southern Greece. *C. kosaninii* is a lowland, spring flowering species from Yugoslavia. The flowers are lilac-blue with some purple striping outside and a yellow throat. It is a late flowering relative of *C. vernus* and is easily grown. *C. malyi* has 3-5 leaves which appear at flowering time, in spring. The flowers are white, with a yellow throat and a brown blotch at the base of the tepals. This is also easily grown outside. *C. niveus* from southern Greece, grows to 15cm or less. It is white or, less often, pale lilac with a conspicuous yellow throat and orange or red, finely divided styles. It flowers in the autumn. *C. oreocreticus* is an endemic from the mountains of Crete which also flowers in autumn. It produces numerous, thread-like leaves shortly after flowering. The flowers are lilac or purple, with grey or buff tints outside. It is easy in a frame or alpine house and is worth trying outside in a sheltered site. *C. pallasii* (Fig.107) produces many narrow leaves, soon after the flowers, which are 8-17cm long and pale to deep lilac with a red, orange or yellow tripartite style. It occurs widely in rocky places in Yugoslavia, Bulgaria, Romania and further afield in Crimea, Turkey and Israel, with several geographically distinct sub-species. *C. robertianus* from moderate

elevation in open woodland in northern Greece also flowers in autumn. The few leaves appear after the flowers which may grow to a height of 14cm and are pale to deep lilac in colour with a deep orange style. *C. scardicus* flowers in the spring or early summer. The flowers are orange yellow, usually purplish toward the base The anthers are yellow and the stigma divided into three lobes. This species, which occurs by melting snow patches in the wild, is regarded as difficult since it requires cool conditions during summer and control of watering during the period when the flowers are forming. *C. sieberi* (Fig.108) flowers in spring with pale to deep lilac flowers with a deep yellow throat, sometimes with a white band separating the lilac and yellow. In Crete the flowers are white with yellow throat and purple markings. The leaves appear at the time of flowering. It occurs in southern Yugoslavia, Albania, Greece, including Crete. There are several sub-species, some of which like *C. s.* ssp. *atticus* (Fig.109) make excellent garden plants. *C. thomasii*, from Italy and Yugoslavia flowers in autumn. The flowers which grow to about 10cm are lilac with a pale yellow throat and a tripartite orange red style. In the typical wild form of *C. tommasinianus* the flowers, with slender, narrow pointed petals, are lilac to purple with a white throat. This familiar, rapidly multiplying spring crocus has many cultivars of different colour. *C. veluchensis* is generally like *C. sieberi*, already noticed, but the solitary flowers are pale to deep lilac, rarely white, tinted purple- blue at the base and lack the yellow throat. It is widespread in the Balkans and can be readily grown outside.

Iridaceae
Iris *I. cretensis* is closely related to and probably a geographical race of the widespread *I. unguicularis*. The flowers are solitary, short stalked, fragrant with white falls with violet veins and apex and lilac standards. It occurs in the Peloponnese and Crete. It is best confined to the bulb frame. *I. unguicularis* (Fig.112), better known by its synonym *stylosa*, is cherished for its scented, winter-flowering habit. It grows to about 40cm with tough, evergreen leaves, lilac flowers with a yellow zone and dark veining on the falls. It is a plant of rocky scrub from North Africa and the eastern Mediterranean, including south and west Turkey. It varies in the wild and so there are many garden cultivars.

Liliaceae
Colchicum This genus includes about 19 species from the Balkans, of which a third are endemic. In *C. pusillum* the several flowers per scape may be pink, lilac or white. The narrow, thread-like leaves appear at the time of flowering in autumn. It occurs in rocky places in central and southern Greece and at high altitudes in Crete. In *C. turcicum*, from eastern Greece, Bulgaria and Turkey, the leaves are not developed at flowering time which is from August to October in the wild. The deep red, purple flowers have, at most, a faint

chequering. The glaucous leaves have a wavy, ciliate margin. *C. variegatum* has funnel-shaped, strongly chequered flowers with petals which taper and are often twisted at their apex. The one or two flowers are deep red or violet purple. The leaves, which appear after flowering in the autumn, have a hard, flexible, wavy margin.

Fritillaria   The majority of the 20 or so species are endemic or local. *F. conica* has yellow cone-shaped flowers which are not tesselated i.e. marked with darker rectangular patterns. The tepals carry a small green to yellow nectary at their base. The 5-7 leaves are shining green. The native habitat is that of rocky hills in south west Peloponnese. *F. davisii* (Fig.117), also from southern Peloponnese, is a lowland species of approximately 20cm with similarly bright leaves. The flowers are bell-shaped, dark purple-brown outside and chequered yellow-green with purple-brown tints within. *F. ehrhartii* occurs on a few Aegean islands. The leaves are not shiny. The flowers are narrowly bell-shaped, purple brown outside with a yellow tip, green-yellow within. *F. graeca*, from Greece, especially Attica, the Peloponnese and also Crete, has one to three flowers per stalk, and these are typically dark purple or blackish. There is a sub-species, *thessala*, with broader leaves and usually green flowers which are lightly chequered brown or purple. *F. messanensis* is variable in colour, with one broadly bell-shaped pendant flower which is yellow or pale brown outside, usually chequered with purple brown markings and sometimes with a green stripe on the back of each tepal. This species can grow to about 30cm, has a wide distribution in the Balkan peninsula and also occurs in Crete. There is a sub-species *F. g.* ssp. *gracilis* with dark purple flowers.

§ Chapter 9 §

North and South America

North America
Although the eastern United States and Canada have contributed attractive plants for the rock garden it is the mountains and valleys of Western North America, with their immense variety of species, many of them endemic, which excite interest. This vast region is dominated by the Rocky Mountains which stretch some 4800km from Alaska to Colorado, with an average width of 400-500km. There are important other ranges as well, especially the Cascade-Sierra Nevada chain west of the Rockies and, further west, the Coastal Ranges of California. The range of physical conditions, climate and rock type has led to a corresponding diversity of plant habitats. The geological evidence reveals a history of mountain building due to collision between tectonic plates followed by erosion. The Rockies are young mountains, mostly created when the North American Plate overrode the Oceanic Plate, which was pushed down into the depths of the earth, accompanied by a persistent zone of vulcanism. The consequent buckling of the earth's crust was accompanied by extensive faulting as the mountains rose. More recently, between 25 to 5 million years ago, the process was reinforced by a massive uplift of a huge area west of the Mississippi, stretching from Canada to Mexico, as the dynamic forces within the earth established a new equilibrium. In the Colorado Plateau the uplift was as much as 1800m but was not accompanied by faulting.

The nature and chemical composition of the rocks may be very different at different latitudes. In the Canadian Rockies limestone and shale, laid down in ancient seas, were forced upwards over the underlying basement rock of gneiss and granite by the tectonic collision. Subsequent erosion and glacial action fashioned the mountains into their present form. The Northern and Southern United States Rockies are rather different. They are disposed in several parallel chains. Many of the mountains are of volcanic origin while others are made up of the gneiss and granite of the basement rock. Their form has been largely determined by massive faulting of the basement rock, rather than deformation of the upper sedimentary strata which have been extensively eroded to reveal the basement rock. At the south end of the chain there are two major divisions, the East and West Ranges.

The comparative youth of these mountains, exposed to the full rigours of erosion, has implications for plant evolution. But, of more immediate significance, the composition of the present flora has been profoundly influenced by the course of glaciation. During the Pleistocene, some 20,000 years ago, the continental ice sheet and its glaciers covered the entire northern area of the continent down to about the Canada-Montana border. Hence most of the vegetation northward of that line has been established quite recently while the whole region has experienced a changing climate which has contributed to a shifting pattern of plant distribution. Adaptation to different, local and often impermanent, conditions coupled with variable gene flow between populations, promotes the taxonomic complexity so often encountered in the flora and so evident in large genera like *Penstemon*, *Phlox* or *Eriogonum*. Commentators almost invariably enter a note of caution when referring to putative species or subspecies in such genera. Colonisation of a broken terrain across a wide front during a period of climatic change offers scope both for gene exchange between populations, which may have been hitherto physically prevented from doing so, as well as the isolation of other populations which become stranded in the restricted habitats to which they are specially adapted.

To the west of the US Rockies lies a vast band of cool deserts, dissected plateaux and isolated lesser mountain ranges, which provide a home for a diverse array of plants which include outliers of the flora from either side of the Great Divide, heat-tolerant plants from the deserts to the south as well as endemics, known only from their restricted locality (Neese 1986). This area, the Great Basin, includes most of Nevada and the western half of Utah. There is no drainage to the sea so the products of erosion accumulate in the valleys. The nature and properties of the deposits vary from valley to valley depending on the chemical composition of the original rocks. This intermontane region has provided conditions for the evolution of a number of plant genera such as *Astragalus*, *Cryptantha*, *Eriogonum* and *Penstemon* which include many species which differ in minor degree and are often narrowly endemic.

Archibald (1991) has drawn attention to the high frequency of species with a very localised distribution in the huge and topographically diverse Southern Rocky Mountain system, the Great Basin, the Sierra Nevada, a large part of the Colorado Plateau and also the Pacific Coast Ranges. Many of these endemics might prove valuable additions to the rock garden although they remain largely unknown in this country

The climate varies greatly according to latitude. The western slopes of the Continental Divide receive about three quarters of the rain carried on the prevailing winds from the Pacific, but the actual amount depends greatly on how far the mountains are from the coast. Thus the Canadian Rockies, close to the ocean, experience much higher rain and snowfall than the mountains further south, especially those which are far inland with the Cascades and Sierra Nevada to protect them. In general, these are dry mountains which approach desert conditions at their southern end. In the southern Rockies summer thunderstorms are frequent, often almost daily, but much of the downpour quickly flows away and is lost to the plants. The drier climate is marked by greater fluctuation in temperature, both daily and seasonally, compared with the moderating effect of the ocean in Canada. At high altitudes day and night temperatures may differ by as much as 17°C. On the eastern slopes cold winter air from Canada may bring the temperature down to freezing only a few hours after warm winds have pushed it to 25°C. Insolation is also important. Ascent from sea-level to 3000m increases solar radiation by 30% but ultra-violet radiation by 90%. The mountain plants have responded to such rigorous conditions by developing adaptations such as dwarf or prostrate habit, to gain wind protection, a hairy coat to reduce evaporation and reduce heat loss, light colour of foliage to reflect the intense sunlight, tap roots to tap water at deeper levels and often succulent leaves to store water in especially arid sites.

The vegetation of the Rockies is commonly classified into four major Zones, according to altitude. The upper limits of the zones decrease northwards. Thus in Alberta the tree-line occurs between 2000 and 2300m whereas in Colorado it lies between 3300 and 3600m.

The Foothills Zone. This is the lowest zone which is more clearly defined in the US Rockies than in Canada where the species make-up of the forests changes rather gradually from one association to another. In the US Rockies the Foothills mark the transition from plain or prairie to the Montane Zone.

The Montane Zone. More relevant to our concerns is this zone which ranges from dense forest to open stands of trees. In Canada, Douglas fir and lodgepole pine, as well as trembling aspen are important constituents. In the northern US Rockies Douglas fir and in the southern Rockies ponderosa pine take precedence. This zone is very rich in trees, shrubs and flowering plants.

The Subalpine Zone. This extends from the upper margins of the Montane forest to the tree-less alpine zone. It is not greatly different along the length of the Rockies. Subalpine fir and/or Engelmann spruce, with a substantially ericaceous under storey, provide the main features. As the height increases the trees become more stunted and eventually peter out. Where the trees are dense enough they trap the snowfall and prevent it from melting quickly in the spring. The resulting moist conditions provide an ideal habitat for many choice species. A notable feature of this zone is the presence of species-rich alpine meadows.

The Alpine or Tundra Zone. This is essentially similar along the Rockies, extending from where the trees finally stop to the permanent snow fields. The alpine plants which occupy this zone often grow as mats or cushions so dear to the rock gardener.

No account, however brief, would be complete without reference to the important part played by fire, a natural event which may have a profound effect on the vegetation. Deciduous trees and many conifers require exposure to fire to set seed. The consequences of a fire depends on its nature and just where it occurs. In forests at high altitude, where there is plenty of moisture from melting snow, fire only occurs during drought periods when it may be widespread and disastrous, killing many trees. In the lower Montane Zone fires may occur frequently, especially in the southern Rockies, but they are generally not lethal and have a beneficial effect in keeping the forest open. The third type of fire often occurs in Douglas fir or lodgepole pine forests in dry situations. Such fires often spread widely but vary in intensity in the area covered. Where they have burned less fiercely the ground is soon covered with flowering plants and shrubs which profit from the warm, more nutritious and less acidic soil conditions. Fire, therefore, is one of the many factors which contribute to the distribution and composition of the Rocky Mountain flora.

Even a cursory acquaintance with the North American alpine and mountain flora reveals how greatly it is under- and unevenly represented in our rock gardens. Many have acquired a reputation for being difficult either because they are short lived, fail to flower or appear out of character compared with their native habitat. Panyoti Kelaidis of the Denver Botanical Garden is of the opinion that, apart from general differences in climatic conditions, an important factor may be the relative sterility of the dry, nutrient screes of the Rockies. Under usual rock garden conditions there is much greater scope for pathogenic soil organisms to kill or weaken the plants. To offset such hazards he advocates the need for particular cultural methods such as the use of slow release fertiliser, foliar feeding and the layering of the soil to provide both sharp drainage and the availability of essential mineral nutrients. In addition there is need for adaptation to our climatic and soil conditions. Most of the potentially desirable species are outbreeders, plentifully endowed with genetic variation in their physiological response to environmental conditions. For Himalayan species we have noted examples where initially discouraging experience gave way to later success. Although difficult to prove, it is likely that repeated introductions and the independent efforts of growers in different parts of the country led to the selection of hardier strains better adapted to the novel conditions. There is no reason why a similar experience should not be repeated with many American species. The practical requirements require the collection of seeds from a number of individual plants and from different populations growing in different areas, to maximise the genetic variation. Collaboration between a number of growers and field collectors could make a significant contribution to our rock garden flora by bringing many of the unfamiliar North American species into wider use.

A brief survey of the North American introductions can hardly avoid seeming rather arbitrary in the species which are chosen for comment. Some of the genera are immense and we cannot hope to do more than note some of the more notable representatives. We have particularly benefited from the observations of Mike and Polly Stone who have done so much to introduce North American species to the rock garden. Their comments are based on extensive field work as well as practical experience of growing many of the species in their garden at Askival. It appears from the SRGC Club seed lists that there is growing interest in North American species. This has encouraged us now and then to refer to species which, although not yet established in our gardens, are of sufficient promise to merit notice. As usual we shall deal first with the dicots.

Dicots
Asteraceae
Erigeron   This large genus of daisy-like flowers has a world-wide distribution, especially in temperate and mountainous regions. The centre of diversity is located in western North America. A small group has migrated into eastern Asia to develop a minor complex in the Himalayas while another group occurs in Europe and western Asia. The species are usually well defined, very often with a localised geographical range, as in more than a third of the approximately 130 North American species. The most important taxonomic criterion is the nature of the pubescence; every species has its characteristic combination of hair types. The species of horticultural interest are mostly small, erect plants with leaves which are often simple but may be finely divided, yellow disc florets and two or more whorls of ray florets which may be white, rose, purple, violet or yellow. Erigerons are often confused with asters from which they may be distinguished by the single or double row of involucral bracts of about equal length compared with three or more rows of overlapping bracts of unequal length of the asters. Also, the erigerons are flowers of the spring and early summer unlike the late-flowering asters. They are generally easily grown in scree conditions where they revel in sunshine. They are becoming more popular. Recent SRGC Club seed lists include nearly 50 species or varieties of which we can only note a few.

In *E. aureus* (Fig.126) the scape of about 10cm carries a solitary head with broad yellow rays. It is a native of alpine and subalpine zones in British Columbia and Alberta. The well known cultivar 'Canary Bird' was raised from seed by Jack Drake and may be a hybrid. *E. chrysopsidis* is a more tufted plant, growing to about 15 cm, with comparatively large daisy flowers in the best forms of this variable species. *E. compositus* (Fig.127) is a tufted, low growing species with rosettes of dissected leaves. It is a widespread, frequent mountain plant, found from Alaska and British Columbia to northern California; it even turns up in Greenland. There are several varieties among which var. *trifidus* is particularly attractive, with tiny, compact cushions and relatively large white rayed flowers. The Stones (1989) found a fine white, compact form in the Olympic Mountains, superior to what is generally offered, and also commend two other species: *E. peregrinus*, with violet flowers, and the truly alpine *E. pinnatisectus* (Fig.128) with rays of deep violet blue. *E. glabellus* is another tufted, larger species with large flowers on 12-20cm scapes and hairy grey-green foliage. The flowers are at first white, but change with age through pink to lavender. We cannot leave the erigerons without noting *E. karvinskianus* which spreads by rhizomes to form straggling little clumps smothered in flowers with white, pale lilac or reddish rays. Native to Mexico and Panama this cheerful little plant has colonised walls and rocky banks all over the warmer parts of Europe, including Britain. Once introduced into the rock garden it will often spread by both seed and runners. However, in New Zealand it is so unpopular as to be classed a rampant weed and its sale banned.

Hymenoxys This is an exclusively American genus, formerly known as *Tetraneuris*. *H. grandiflora* is one of the most conspicuous of mountain plants. The tap-rooted growth is tufted and extends to 10-30cm with leafy stems which carry one or more bright yellow flower heads which are usually about 5cm across but may reach 10cm, an attraction which outweighs its tendency to be monocarpic. It is widely distributed in the Middle Rockies on open, gravelly, limestone sites. It is known both as the alpine sunflower and the compass plant, because its flowers always face east. *H. acaulis* (Fig.129), a variable species, also has showy, yellow flowers growing out of a tuft of silvery basal leaves. It is a plant of the foothills, montane and alpine zones from Alberta to New Mexico. The compact variety *caespitosa* is the one most often seen.

Townsendia This genus of about 20 species includes perennial, annual or biennial herbs from western North America especially the Rocky Mountains. They are mostly found from 1000-1500m but a couple of them reach 4000m in Colorado. Such high level populations are generally apomictic i.e. reproducing asexually (Benman, 1957). Soil rather than climatic conditions often determines their localised distribution. They are generally small plants with clustered rosettes of short leafy branches. They often have very attractive, relatively large flowers with a yellow disk and rays which may be of various shades of pink, blue or white. Most are best suited to well drained composts in the alpine house, while some are worth trying outside in the raised bed in full sun although they may prove short lived. *T. condensata* (Fig.130), an uncommon species from high altitudes in Montana, Wyoming and Idaho, is particularly attractive. The relatively large, stalkless, daisy-like flowers, generally white but sometimes pink or palest purple, nestle in the compact rosettes of oblong, stalked leaves. *T. exscapa* (Fig.131) produces rosettes of linear leaves from which arise the almost sessile flowers with lavender-blue rays and a large yellow disk. Flowering early, it is popularly known as the Easter Lily, a name which is also used for *T. hookeri*, of similar appearance and regarded by some as belonging to the same species as *T. exscapa*. *T. parryi* produces robust stems of 10-20cm with striking blue to purple flowers which may be 5cm across. It occupies rocky slopes from the montane to alpine zone from southern British Columbia and Alberta to Colorado. In the low-growing *T. montana* (Fig.132) the sessile or stalked flower heads present a pleasing contrast between the yellow disc and the white to pink or purple ray florets. It is to be found in Utah, south west Montana and western Wyoming. *T. rothrockii*, a tap-rooted perennial from alpine levels in Colorado produces impressive, almost sessile, large flowers with bluish rays and the usual yellow disk .

Brassicaceae

Draba There are dozens of species of *Draba* with small, tufted habit and more often inconspicuous white or yellow flowers. Among those which have been offered in SRGC Club seed lists we can note three. *D. incerta* grows between 2 and 10cm with fine white hairs which give it a grayish appearance. The generally leafless stems carry clusters of small yellow flowers. It is a montane and alpine species of open slopes, found from Yukon to Wyoming. *D. oligosperma* is very similar except that there are dense hairs which are disposed on the lower surface of the leaves "like the teeth on a two-sided comb". It is like the previous species in both habitat and distribution. *D. ventosa* forms medium sized mats of very hairy leaves, with comparatively large, yellow flowers. It extends from British Columbia south and east to Wyoming and Utah.

Boraginaceae

Eritrichium There are several American species/sub-species of this genus. The most widespread is *E. nanum* which is circumboreal and also present at high altitudes in mountains of the North temperate zone. As might be expected there are a number of regional differences recognised as sub-species or varieties. In North America there are three sub-species: *E. n. elongatum*, like an attenuated *E. nanum*, from northern Wyoming, Montana and Idaho, *E. n. argenteum* from the southern Rockies and *E. n. aretioides* from Alaska and Yukon in which the newly opened flowers are violet, turning blue later. These all form mats or irregular cushions. *E. howardii*, which has larger, deep blue flowers about 1cm across, has abundant needle-like leaves. As it ages it produces rounded cushions, unlike the flatter *E. nanum*. It is found on limestone in Wyoming and Montana and is not confined to high altitudes. These are all plants for a sunny alpine house and are likely to prove difficult.

Mertensia This genus contains species from both Europe and Asia as well as North America, where they are commonly known as bluebells. In *M. alpina* the prostrate stems carry a terminal cluster of pale blue, tubular flowers. In the closely related *M. viridis*, the stems are upright and the flowers deep blue and scented. Unlike *M. alpina* the anthers extend beyond the end of the corolla. Both species are Rocky Mountain plants from 3000-4000m. *M. lanceolata* and *M. longiflora* are attractive small species which do not exceed 20cm, with the typical pendant flowers.

Campanulaceae

Campanula *C. lasiocarpa* is a small, upright hairbell generally less than 10cm in height, with dentate leaves and hairy, also dentate sepals. It occurs from Alaska to British Columbia and Alberta but also occurs in Japan and Kamchatka. It is really rather like a smaller version of *C. rotundifolia* which has a wide distribution in North America. There is a dwarf form of this species, var. *olympica*, found of course in the Olympic Mountains, which retains its dwarf stature in the garden. But the gem of the genus is *C. piperi* which has the remarkable ability to colonise hairline cracks on rock faces in the Olympics and cover large areas with its dark, evergreen foliage of small, toothed leaves and beautiful, blue bells which spread open to reveal handsome red anthers. It is often remarked that this species prefers to spread vertically rather than crossways. It is difficult to establish although cuttings take well and seed is readily set.

Cornaceae
Cornus   *C. canadensis* (Fig.133) covers the ground by means of vigorous rhizomes. The more or less oval leaves are in whorls at the stem tips. The numerous, tiny green to white flowers are densely packed in a head surrounded by four large and conspicuous white or pinkish bracts and succeeded by a cluster of bright red, shiny berries, hence the common American name of bunchberry. The wide distribution covers North America and into eastern Asia as far as Japan. This is typically a creeping plant of the open forest floor and damp, heathy situations. It is a close relative of the British *C. suecica*, which differs chiefly in the paired, opposite leaves and dark, reddish flowers. In the garden, *C. canadensis* will produce admirable ground cover, given moist, shady peat-bed conditions.

Ericaceae
Cassiope   This is a small genus which belongs to the boreal and tundra regions of the Northern Hemisphere. It includes small evergreen shrubs with tightly branching, wiry branches and tiny, appressed leaves. The flowers are bell shaped, white or tinged pink in some species. The North American species comprise *C. lycopodioides, mertensiana, tetragona* and *hypnoides*. Although C. *hypnoides* just about defies cultivation all the other species grow best under cool, moist peaty conditions. The prostrate *C. lycopodioides* occurs in northern British Columbia and Alaska but is better known from its locations in Japan. The variety 'Beatrice Lilley' is an attractive small version which produces plenty of flowers. *C. mertensiana* forms clumps which are 15-30cm across and about 30cm high. It can also be distinguished from the previous species by its four rows of leaves along a relatively wider stem, whereas in *C. lycopodioides* the leaves are irregularly arranged. There are several geographical races of *C. mertensiana* of which the most familiar is the floriferous variety *gracilis*. *C. tetragona* is sparingly branched and upright, growing to about 30cm. The lower leaves turn brown and are retained on the stem. This truly arctic species, adapted to cool, dry summers, is generally regarded as difficult to please, but there is a geographical race, *saximontana*, from the alpine meadows of the northern Rockies which is easier to grow. *C. hypnoides* is a wiry-stemmed, creeping, little plant from the tundra regions of both America and Europe. But only those willing to look for it in its native habitat are likely to enjoy the charming white bells, carried on short stalks,

and embellished with crimson sepals. *Cassiope* is prone to hybridisation. *C. lycopodioides* has been crossed to *C. wardii* to produce the popular and vigorous 'Muirhead'. Mike Stone (1998) has recently described distinct cultivars which are believed to be the result of crossing between the Sino-Himalayan *C. selaginoides* and respectively *C. lycopodioides* and *C. mertensiana*.

Kalmia *K. polifolia* var. *microphylla* (Fig.134) is a small evergreen, mat-forming shrub of 5-20cm, with stiff, dark, glossy green opposite leaves and quite large rose-pink, saucer- shaped flowers of great beauty. It is to be found on moist subalpine and alpine sites from Yukon south to Colorado, with similar requirements to those of *Phyllodoce*.

Phyllodoce This is another small genus with two species *P. empetriformis* (Fig.135) and *P. breweri* worth noting. The former is another native of boreal and north temperate regions which grows best on cool, moist, well drained peaty sites. It is to be found in the sub-alpine and alpine zones from Alaska to California, forming loose cushions which may grow up to 30cm and reach a metre across in the wild. The needle-like needles are light green. The bell-shaped erect or pendent flowers vary between pink and deep rose. *P. breweri* differs in its reclining or semi-prostrate branches which form mats and in the much larger, open, flowers which are carried in terminal rosy-purple clusters. It is confined to the Sierra Nevada of California at altitudes of 1800-3600m.

Fabaceae

Lupinus There is an immense number of lupins in America, including many hybrids, which together present a daunting taxonomic prospect, and also a reservoir of possible garden plants yet to be exploited. Two species must serve as token recognition of the genus. *L. breweri* forms mats, which can become quite large, on open slopes of mountains of California, Oregon and Nevada, where it grows on granite scree and volcanic sands. Silky hairs impart a silvery sheen to the leaflets. The white or yellowish flowers are borne in a dense raceme. There are varieties e.g. var. *bryoides* which is smaller and more alpine in its distribution and var. *grandiflorus* which is larger. This is a good alpine house plant which is also suited to the scree or raised bed outside. *L. lepidus* grows with a tufted habit to 30cm, although usually less. The underside of the leaflets is silvered with light hairs and the flowers are blue to violet. This is a prairie species from north west America. There are a number of varieties of which the best known is *L. lepidus* var. *lobbii*. Here the stout stems radiate to form a flat mat. Both stems and leaves are covered in fine hairs so that the whole plant presents a silvery appearance. The flowers are violet–blue with a white spot on the standard. This is a plant of the Cascades of British Columbia, Washington State and Oregon. *L. lepidus* is generally regarded as a rather difficult, short lived species but presents a challenge worth accepting.

Gentianaceae
Gentiana   *G. affinis* grows on moist, open sites from the foothills to the subalpine zone from British Columbia and Alberta to New Mexico. The leaves are lance-shaped and finely fringed and the blue, 2-3cm long tubular flowers are in clusters. *G. algida* (Fig.136), the Arctic Gentian, has an immense distribution. In America it occurs from Alaska to Colorado but it is also to be found in China, the Himalayas, Siberia and Japan, evoking interest on that score alone. But it is also a very beautiful gentian. The large trumpets are white or pale yellow, striped and variously marked with purple. The Stones (1989) found plants with 3.5–5cm long flowers of creamy-white with purple streaks and spots on the outside, borne on 20cm stems above rosettes of strap-shaped leaves.

Hydrophyllaceae
Phacelia   This large genus is predominantly North American. Most of the species are annual like *P. campanularia* which is appreciated for its broad bell-shaped blue flowers. But the plant which most of us would like to grow is *P. sericea* (Fig.138). One or more unbranched stems grow 10-20cm with alternate, pinnately lobed, silky leaves. The dense flower spike, 10-15cm long, is made up of open-faced, campanulate, violet to purple flowers from which the long, purple, yellow- tipped stamens elegantly protrude. Only the unpleasant smell, presumably to attract some pollinator, mars the effect. This attractive plant is found in open, montane to alpine sites from southern British Columbia and Alberta to Colorado. In the UK it is difficult and is best tried in the alpine house in well drained, lime-free soil.

Papaveraceae
Sanguinaria   *S. canadensis*, the bloodroot, has a wide distribution in eastern North America. It forms colonies by means of rhizomes which, in spring, send up shoots with rounded, broad lobed leaves and solitary flowers with 8–16 petals of gleaming white. At first the flower head is concealed in the folds of an adjacent leaf. The plant earns its name from the colour of the sap. There are several forms but the best one to grow is 'Plena', which is fully double and flowers longer. This striking species is best grown in light shade in moist, but well drained soil with plenty of organic matter.

Polemoniaceae.
Phlox   Apart from one Siberian representative, the tufted *P. Sibirica*, phloxes are entirely North American. They comprise a dominant element of the flora of the Great Basin. At the height of the flowering season they cover the landscape for hundreds of square kilometres with dazzling carpets of colour. In the rock garden their salver-shaped corollas of many hues are an indispensable component of the spring scene. They are notable for their variability in such characters as the presence of glandular hairs, shape of leaf,

glandular hairs, shape of leaf, length of pedicels and sepals, length of corolla tube, shape and colour of the petals, length of stamens and styles and even fragrance (Wherry 1955). Such variation may be due to intra-population genetic variation and/or introgressive hybridisation between otherwise distinct taxa.

Although predominantly of western distribution there are a few important eastern species such as *P. subulata*, the familiar, mat-forming, garden phlox with innumerable cultivars. This species is native to the north eastern United States and south eastern Canada where it grows on rather sterile, gravelly and sandy slopes. In the wild the petals may be entire or notched, most commonly purple to red but may vary to display all manner of shades between purple and white. Some of the cultivars attributed to *subulata* are derived from hybridisation with the mid-western to south eastern *P. bifida* or the south eastern *P. nivalis*. *P. bifida* has a tufted habit or forms creeping mats, from which arise 10-20cm shoots with a lax, 6-9 flowered inflorescence of more or less lavender coloured petals with a conspicuous notch. Typically it is a plant of sandy prairies. *P. divaricata* is decumbent and more or less evergreen, rooting at the nodes. The inflorescence becomes more lax with age. The flowers are light violet, ranging from lavender to pink or white, often with a darker eye and a honeysuckle-like fragrance. It occurs on wooded slopes in neutral to sub-acid soils from sea level to 1000m in the eastern half of North America. It is believed to have survived the Ice Age in the Appalachian area, spreading westward later. There are several horticultural cultivars including the familiar, but doubtfully hardy, 'Chattahoochee' with a crimson eye, a common plant on the show bench. *P. nivalis* is closely related to and often confused with *P. subulata*. It forms loose, spreading mats to 10cm with very leafy sterile shoots. The flowers are purple to pink, rarely white, with radiating stripes about the centre. It occurs in open pine woods on sandy soils from Virginia, northern Florida and Alabama. The hardiest and most intensely coloured form is *P. n. hertzii*. *P. stolonifera* forms a mat of decumbent leafy stolons, hence its common name of creeping phlox, with terminal rosettes. It makes excellent ground cover. The inflorescence is rather lax with flowers which span the range from lavender to purple it is adapted to humus-rich, open woodland from the Appalachians south to Atlanta. There are a number of 'Ridge' cultivars and a white one called 'Ariane'.

Among the western phloxes *P. adsurgens* (Fig.137) forms the rather usual mat of leafy stems, which root at the nodes only sparingly, with glabrous shiny leaves. The 6-12 fairly fragrant flowers are large, usually pale purple, lilac or pink and bear a deep-hued stripe toward the base of each petal. This beautiful species occurs on both humus-rich and rather sterile soils in deciduous or conifer woodland up to about 2000m on the western slopes of the Cascades. Several natural variants have been given names and introduced to gardens. 'Wagon Wheel' and the more garden-worthy 'Red Buttes' are examples. Several closely related species, formerly regarded as varieties of *P* and *hendersonii*. *P. caespitosa* forms a cushion-shaped mound with a 1-3 flowered inflorescence. The rather sweet scented flowers are lavender to white in colour. It ascends to 4000m in the Rockies. *P. diffusa* (Fig.139) is very variable. Within the range of a few metres the flowers range in colour from white to pink or various shades of purple, lavender or violet. In some of them the throat may be white, yellow or of a deeper hue. Also the petals may vary from narrow spokes to broad, overlapping blades which make up the salver-shaped corolla. Propagation is easy by rooted division or layering. *P. hendersonii* (Fig.140) is an endemic of the Northern Cascades where its compact mounds and almost white flowers occur at high altitudes. *P. hirsuta* (Fig.141) offers quite a challenge for it is not easy to keep going. It is a rare species, confined to two sites in Siskiyou County, California. It is a low growing shrubby plant with densely hairy, narrow leaves and clusters of purple to pink flowers. *P. hoodii* (Fig.142) is a densely tufted to cushion-forming species with linear to awl-shaped leaves, white to nearly lilac flowers and a wide distribution from British Columbia and Manitoba across the Prairies to Utah and Colorado, not really a mountain plant. *P. speciosa* (Fig.143) is usually a small shrub although it may reach a metre. The narrow pointed leaves are finely hairy on the upper side. The flowers are quite spectacular, about 2.5cm across, pale or white, often with a lighter eye and carried in clusters. It is a mountain species of open rocky ground in the States of Washington and Idaho. There are at least five sub-species which differ in shape and thickness of the leaves and the extent to which the petals are notched. *P. bryoides* is a low, cushion-forming species which can spread as it ages. The numerous, awl-shaped leaves closely overlap in a manner which has been likened to the leaves of a cassiope. The solitary flowers of about 1cm are white to lavender and of variable fragrance. The Stones have suggested that it might be more suited for a southern alpine house. *P. multiflora* is another mat-forming species with linear leaves and lilac-pink flowers which occurs widely in the Rockies among grass and low growing plants. There are several varieties which differ in plant and flower size, such as var. *depressa* which is smaller and more compact with comparatively large fragrant, solitary pink to white flowers. It is fitting to leave the phloxes with a quote from Kelaidis: "Once their cultural needs are mastered, the Western cushion phloxes provide an inexhaustible scope for horticultural study and enjoyment."

Polemonium *P. caeruleum* is rather large for the average rock garden, since it grows from 30 to 100cm, although it appears in the SRGC seed lists. The blue and white flowers are borne in cymes at the end of the stem or in the axil of the underlying bracts. It is widespread in North America from Alaska to California but is also native to Europe, including parts of northern England. *P. elegans*, from the northern Cascades, grows to about 15cm with hairy-edged, closely overlapping leaflets. The beauty of the deep blue, yellow throated flowers is marred only by the unpleasant scent which is characteristic of several species of *Polemonium*. *P. pulcherrimum* is a tufted plant which may be anything from 5 to 30cm tall. The alternate, pinnate leaves are divided into many leaflets. The more or less upright stems bear clusters of broadly bell-shaped flowers of blue to rose colour with a yellow eye. Comparatively indifferent to soil type and light exposure it is widespread from Alaska to Colorado.

In *P. viscosum* (Fig.144) the mostly basal, glandular, sticky foliage is in the form of whorled leaflets. The flowers are larger and more funnel-shaped than those of *P. pulcherrimum*. It occurs in stony places from the montane to alpine zone from southern British Columbia and Alberta to New Mexico. The leaves have the rather alarming property of exuding a skunk-like smell when bruised. To offset this the flowers are sweet scented and provided with nectar. The blue and part of the white areas of this and related species reflect ultra-violet light whereas other parts of the corolla absorb it. Thus visiting insects are presented with three colour zones which act as a guide to the nectar.

Polygonaceae
Eriogonum This is a large genus from the western and southern USA with a preference for arid sites. Although many of the species are annuals, shrubs or otherwise unsuited to the rock garden there are a number which are attractive and becoming increasingly popular. These are small plants with a basal rosette of often very hairy leaves and small flowers gathered into heads or umbels. All the species noted here do very well in the alpine house in gritty compost and most can be grown outside on a raised bed or scree, with the aid of a Dutch light to protect them from winter wet (Elliot 1993).

Many of the 50 or so Rocky Mountain species are difficult to identify. Taxonomic distinctions are based on differences in size, hairiness, the shape and abundance of leaves, flower colour and especially the structure and form of the involucre. It appears that such differences may be determined to variable and uncertain degree by the conditions of growth and development rather than by stable genetic differences (Kershaw, MacKinnon and Pojar, 1998). The seed, like tiny grape pips, germinates readily and cuttings are feasible, but division is likely to fail unless a peripheral rosette has already rooted.

Among the species and varieties most likely to interest the rock gardener are the following. *E. caespitosus* forms low mats which are made up of tiny rosettes of tomentose leaves packed tightly on the little branches. The almost globular, solitary flower heads are at first pale yellow but gradually become bright reddish orange as they age. It occurs from California to Idaho, Montana and Colorado. In *E. flavum*, a widespread species, the paddle-shaped leaves are heavily tomentose on the lower surface. The bright yellow flower heads are borne on 10-20cm scapes. The variety *piperi* (Fig.145) from Washington State grows a little larger to form mats, silvery below, with hairy yellow or greenish flowers, sometimes with red tips. There is also a high altitude variety, *xanthium*, from Colorado which is yellow at first but later becomes red. *E. jamesii* is another mat forming species with cob-webby paddle-shaped leaves. The flower heads are relatively large, white, cream or yellow and borne on short stalks. *E. kennedyii* forms a mat of compact rosettes of tomentose leaves. The flower stalks may be as tall as 15cm but are generally less. The flower heads are white but attractively decorated by the red mid-rib of the calyces. This is an easily grown species from California.

E. ovalifolium is a common plant which occurs from the sagebrush foothills to the alpine zone from California and British Columbia to Wyoming and Montana. Although named after its oval leaves, a distinguishing feature is the absence of leaves on the stem which lacks even the usual whorl of leaves below the involucre. The flowers are clustered in a dense head on a scape of variable height from a few centimetres in alpine sites to 20cm or more. The flowers are creamy white to yellow at first but later turn pink or purplish. This is a variable species with several subspecies and varieties, all of which are worth growing. *E. umbellatum* is usually prostrate, forming mats from which arise the flowering stems, which, like the previous species, may vary in length. Typically, the whorled basal leaves are spoon shaped and heavily tomentose on the underside, turning red in autumn, and the flower heads are pale yellow, often with a hint of pink. This is also a species with a wide distribution, from British Columbia and Alberta to New Mexico, with great variation of form such that there is little prospect of an amateur putting a meaningful subspecies or variety name to a wild specimen. But that should be no deterrent to growing any member of the species complex.

Portulacaceae
Lewisia   This genus of about 20 species is confined to western North America. It has been monographed by Brian Mathew (1989). The thick roots are starchy, surmounted by a caudex or thick basal stem. The leaves are mostly basal, often in a rosette and succulent to variable degree. An important taxonomic distinction between the species refers to whether the leaves are deciduous, shrivelling after flowering to reappear in the autumn, or whether they are evergreen.

For pot culture Mathew recommends for most but not all species a sharp compost of equal parts of John Innes Number 3, peat and grit or peat and grit in the ratio 4 to 3, but a number of the species can be grown outside in a manner which avoids crown rot Species are generally propagated by seed but the numerous interspecific and hence sterile hybrids must be reproduced vegetatively by naturally occurring or induced offsets. Among the deciduous species *L. brachycalyx* is nearly stemless, not exceeding 10cm in height with a tuft of basal leaves. The flowers are white, sometimes with pink veins or wholly pink. A native of California and Arizona it occurs in damp, upland meadows and among open stands of *Pinus ponderosa*. *L. nevadensis* occurs more widely from Washington to Colorado in sandy or gravelly sites, grass etc. where there is plenty of moisture. The flowers, nearly sessile or on almost prostrate stalks, are generally white or, less often, pink. *L.pygmaea* grows to under 10cm. There are several flower stalks, each with several flowers which vary from white to pink or shades of purple. It occurs in well drained, open sites at elevations up to 4000m, ranging widely from Alaska to California and eastwards to Colorado and neighbouring states. Mathew has noted that the species long known to gardeners as *L. pygmaea* is really *L. longipetala*. *L rediviva* (Fig.146) is the most showy of the lewisias, with large, cactus-like white or pink flowers. Success in the alpine house depends largely on providing plenty of water during the growing period and none after flowering. It ranges from British Columbia to California and east to Colorado on dry rocky sites or desert flats where it sometimes occurs in immense numbers. Among the evergreen species, *L. columbiana* has flat, fleshy basal leaves. There are several to many white or pink red-veined flowers in panicles on 15-30cm scapes. It is another widespread species from British Columbia south to central Oregon and across to Idaho. It is very variable, like so many of the lewisias, and has been split into several sub-species. Mike and Polly Stone have reported (1990) that *L. columbiana* and its sub species *L. c. rupicola* have proved the best species for their rock garden, establishing seedlings in any well drained soil. *L. cotyledon*, with its numerous, fleshy, basal leaves and many flowered panicles is familiar to all rock gardeners. It is also very variable. Although the flowers are typically pink-purple with light and dark stripes, they may also be white, apricot or yellow with orange stripes on a pale background. Various forms have been selected or are the products of hybridisation with several other species so the colours of the cultivars span the rainbow. Ashwood Nurseries in England have bred a new dwarf strain called 'Carousel Hybrids,' using *L. cotyledon* as a parent. These can stand any amount of winter wet, do not seed and so flower profusely for a long time. *L. tweedyi*, which many regard as the best of the genus, develops a loose tuft of basal leaves, a short caudex and a fleshy root. The generally 1-4 pink, peach, yellowish or more rarely white flowers are borne on scapes as long or a little longer than the leaves. It can be grown outside in a warm, dry spot. It is another species which likes dry conditions after flowering. There are several distinct, geographical races.

Primulaceae

Androsace Use of the name *Douglasia* rather than *Androsace* is rather a matter of personal preference or deference to custom since there are taxonomic grounds for including the species concerned in *Androsace*. *A. laevigata*, (Fig.147) which is a native of the Cascades and Olympic mountains of Washington and Oregon, and only rarely in British Columbia, forms dense mats of narrow, pointed, evergreen leaves with umbels of several bright rose-pink flowers with spreading petals. It makes an excellent trough plant. *A. montana* (Fig.148) from British Columbia to Idaho and Wyoming plant. *A. montana* (Fig.148) from British Columbia to Idaho and Wyoming produces solitary or occasionally paired flowers of pink to purple colour. It also is well suited to the trough. *A. chamaejasme* is another mat forming species which spreads by stolons. In Europe it is a familiar species of limestone mountains but it has an immense distribution across Asia, China and also North America where it occurs from Alaska to Utah. Naturally there are regional differences and, according to the Stones, at least some of the American forms are found on acidic soil. It is another good plant for scree or raised bed.

Dodecatheon This is an entirely North American genus of about 15 species. There are one or more rosettes of simple leaves which, in some species, are irregularly toothed or narrowed at the base into petioles. The inflorescence is in the form of a few to many-flowered umbel of nodding flowers. The generally five, but, in some species, four lobes of the corolla are reflexed cyclamen-like. The stamen filaments may or may not be united into a distinct tube. The protruding anthers come together to form a pointed cone, hence the name of shooting star. Adapted to cool, moist situations with plenty of humus, the dodecatheons are often regarded as the ecological equivalent of the primulas in the American scene. *D. alpinum* grows to about 30cm, with four purple petals in few-flowered umbels. Unlike some of the other species it keeps its leaves until the autumn. It grows in alpine meadows and by stream sides, generally about the tree-line, reaching 3500m. The range is from California and Oregon to Arizona and Utah. It is closely related to *D. jeffreyi*, which can grow to 60cm, with four- or five-petalled flowers of rose-purple with a yellow base and spreading stamens with deep purple anthers. *D. clevelandii* (Fig.149) grows to about 45 cm with irregularly toothed leaves and five-petalled flowers which are purple or less often white. The tube is maroon with a yellow band and the anther cone is almost black. There are several sub-species. This is a lowland plant from grassy places in open woodland in California and is better grown in the alpine house than outside. *D. conjugans* (Fig.150) is rather similar to *D. pulchellum*, with five petals, purple, pink or white flowers in umbels, with dark purple to black, occasionally yellow, anthers. It grows to about 25cm and occurs in the western coastal States and also inland to Wyoming and Montana. *D. dentatum* is a smaller species with distinctly petioled and toothed leaves. The flowers are white with a purple base to the petals and red-purple anthers. It occurs from British Columbia and Oregon and across to Utah. *D. hendersonii* is a robust species, growing to about 45cm and dying down after flowering. The flowers are of various shades of lavender or white with a yellow stamen tube and maroon anthers. Although rather similar to *D. clevelandii* in appearance, it differs by producing bulblets like rice grains on the roots. It ranges from Vancouver Island and southwards along the west of the Cascades. *D. meadia* can grow to 60cm with an often purple-spotted scape which bears an umbel of 10-20, and sometimes many more, flowers of

Fig. 142　*Phlox hoodii* (p.174)　　　　　Fig. 143　*Phlox speciosa* (p.174)

Fig. 144　*Polemonium viscosum* (p.175)　　Fig. 145　*Eriogonum flavum* var. *piperi* (p.175)

Fig. 146 *Lewisia rediviva minor* (p.177)

Fig. 147 *Androsace laevigata* (p.177)

Fig. 148 *Androsace montana* (p.178)

Fig. 149 *Dodecatheon clevelandii* (p.178)   Fig. 150 *Dodecatheon conjugans* (p.178)

Fig. 151 *Dodecatheon poeticum* (p.179)   Fig. 152 *Primula angustifolia* (p.179)

Fig. 153 *Primula parryi* (p.179)   Fig. 154 *Anemone multifida* (p.179)

Fig. 155 *Aquilegia jonesii* (p.180)

Fig. 156 *Caltha leptosepala* var. *sulphurea* (p.180)

Fig. 157 *Ranunculus adoneus* (p.180)

Fig. 158 *Pulstilla patens* (p.179)

Fig. 159 *Ranunculus eschscholtzii eximius* (p.180)

Fig. 160 *Elmera racemosa* (p.181)   Fig. 161 *Penstemon eriantherus* (p.184)

Fig. 162   *Penstemon newberryi* (p.183)

Fig. 163   *Penstemon procerus* var. *tolmiei* (p.183)

Fig. 164 *Iris douglasiana* (p.186)

Fig. 165 *Iris innominata* (p.186)

Fig. 166 *Iris tenax* (p.186)

Fig. 167 *Calochortus venustus* (p.188)

Fig. 168 *Erythronium grandiflorum* (p.189)

Fig. 169 *Erythronium hendersonii* (p.189)

Fig. 170 *Erythronium montanum* (p.190)

Fig. 171 *Fritillaria affinis* (p.190)

Fig. 172 *Fritillaria glauca* (p.190)   Fig. 173 *Fritillaria recurva* (p.191)

Fig. 174 *Trillium erectum* (p.191)

Fig. 175 *Trillium chloropetalum* (p.191)   Fig. 176 *Trillium luteum* (p.191)

Fig. 177 *Trillium grandiflorum roseum* (p.191)

Fig. 178 *Trillium rivale* 'Purple Heart' (p.191)

Fig. 179 *Trillium ovatum* (p.191)   Fig. 180 *Pernettya mucronata* (p.194)

Fig. 181 *Nassauvia revoluta* (p.193)

Fig. 182 *Oxalis adenophylla* (p.194)

Fig. 183 *Oxalis enneaphylla* (p.194)

Fig. 184 *Saxifraga magellanica* (p.197)

Fig. 185 *Calceolaria uniflora* (p.198)   Fig. 186 *Ourisia coccinea* (p.198)

Fig. 187 *Ourisia fragrans* (p.199)

Fig. 188 *Nierembergia patagonica* (p.199)   Fig. 189 *Tropaeolum incisum* (p.199)

Fig. 190 *Tropaeolum polyphyllum* (p.199)

Fig. 191 *Viola atropurpurea* (p.199)

Fig. 192 *Viola coronifera* (p.200)

Fig. 193 *Viola nivalis* (p.200)

Fig. 194 *Viola philippii* (p.200)

Fig. 195 *Viola sacculus* (p.200)

Fig. 196 *Alstroemeria pseudospathulata* (p.2

Fig. 197 *Epimedium grandiflorum* (p.203)

Fig. 198 *Adenophora triphylla* var. *japonica* (p.204)

Fig. 199 *Campanula chamissonis superba* (p.204)

Fig. 200 *Diapensia lapponica* var. *obovata* (p.205)

Fig. 201 *Shortia soldanelloides* forma *alpina* (p.205)

Fig. 202 *Shortia soldanelloides* 'Askival Icebell' (p.205)

Fig. 203 *Shortia soldanelloides* (p.205)

Fig. 204 *Andromeda polifolia* (p.205)

Fig. 205 *Cassiope lycopodioides* (p.206)   Fig. 206 *Gaultheria adenothrix* (p.206)

Fig. 207 *Phyllodoce aleutica* (p.206)

Fig. 208 *Rhododendron aureum* (p.207)

Fig. 209 *Rhododendron camtschaticum* (p.207)

Fig. 210 *Rhododendron dauricum* (p.207) Fig. 211 *Rhododendron keiskii* (p.207)

Fig. 212 *Gentiana triflora* (p.208) Fig. 213 *Glaucidium palmatum* (p.208)

Fig. 214 *Dicentra peregrina* (p.207)

Fig. 215 *Hylomecon japonicum* (p.208)   Fig. 216 *Primula japonica* (p.209)

Fig. 217 *Primula sieboldii* (p.209)

Fig. 218 *Primula takedana* (p.209)

Fig. 219 *Adonis amurensis* (p.209)

Fig. 220 *Aquilegia flabellata* var. *pumila* (p.209)

Fig. 221 *Astilbe simplicifolia* (p.210)

Fig. 222 *Arisaema japonicum* (p.211)

Fig. 223   *Celmisia angustifolia* (p.218)

Fig. 224   *Celmisia hookeri* (p.218)

Fig. 225   *Celmisia semicordata* (p.218)

Fig. 226   *Celmisia sessiliflora* (p.218)

Fig. 227 *Haastia pulvinaris* (p.219)   Fig. 228 *Leucogenes grandiceps* (p.220)

Fig. 229 *Leucogenes leontopodium* (p.220)   Fig. 230 *Raoulia eximia* (p.220)

Fig. 231 *Aciphylla aurea* (p.217)

Fig. 232 *Nothothlaspi australe* (p.221)

Fig. 233 *Nothothlaspi rosulatum* (p.221)

Fig. 234 *Gentiana serotina* (p.224)

Fig. 235 *Gentiana saxosa* (p.223)

Fig. 236 *Clematis marmoraria* (p.224)

Fig. 237 *Ranunculus buchananii* (p.225) Fig. 238 *Ranunculus lyallii* (p.225)

Fig. 239 *Bulbinella angustifolia* (p.229) Fig. 240 *Gazania krebsiana* (p.234)

Fig. 241 *Rhodohypoxis baurii* var. *baurii* (p.236)

Fig. 242 *Lapeirousia silenoides* (p.236) Fig. 243 *Romulea bulbocodium* (p.236)

different shades of rose, with white at the base and red-yellow anthers. Attractive varieties include a white and a crimson form. *D. poeticum* (Fig.151) grows to about 30cm. The leaves are more or less lanceolate and often toothed. The five-petalled flowers are rose-purple to lilac, with dark, rather purple stamens. This species is confined to southern Washington State and north Oregon where it occurs in moist, grassy and open woodland sites. *D. pulchellum* varies in height up to 45cm but generally less. The more or less lanceolate leaves are narrowed into a winged petiole and die down after flowering. The flowers are rose-purple, as usual varying in shade and sometimes white, with a yellow base, a purple wavy line in the throat and purple anthers. The range is immense, from Alaska to Mexico and from the plains to the alpine zone, with many forms and local variants. This is the most widely grown species with attractive cultivars such as the dark crimson 'Red Wings'.

Primula   *P. parryi* (Fig.153) is a strong growing, rather fleshy plant with stems of 10-40cm and erect, more or less lanceolate leaves and reddish purple flowers with a yellow eye. It occurs in moist, rocky banks of streams and the like in the subalpine and alpine zones from Idaho and Montana to New Mexico. It is reported to have a smell which some find pleasant and others regard as skunk-like, such is the variability of human olfactory response. There are a few other American species like *P. angustifolia* (Fig.152) and *P suffrutescens* which are not well known in the UK.

Ranunculaceae
Anemone and **Pulsatilla**   *A. drummondii* forms a tuft of finely hairy, petiolate leaves from which arises one or two 5-15cm scapes bearing a single white flower. It occurs from Alaska to Wyoming. The plant closely resembles the Balkan *A. baldensis*. *A. multifida* (Fig.154) is a larger plant, varying between 15 and 50cm in height, and also tufted with a thick rootstock. The chiefly basal, long stalked leaves are divided several times into small segments. The scapes carry 1-3 flowers which are essentially white although suffused with yellow or reddish pink to variable degree. It occurs in dry open places or woodland from Alaska to New Mexico. *A. narcissiflora* is more familiar as a European species, but there is an American version called *A. vilosissima* which is so similar that some would lump them into the same species. The inflorescence is in the form of panicles of white flowers tinged pink on the outside. *Anemone* or *Pulsatilla patens* (Fig.158) is a very beautiful species. It has the familiar pulsatilla habit with many, basal divided leaves and pale lavender or bluish flowers. The whole plant is protected by silky hairs. It is a plant of well drained slopes or prairies from the foothills to the alpine zone from Alaska to New Mexico. We have here another complex of species or sub-species since the typical American form is similar to the East Russian *P. p. flavescens*. To make a distinction, the American form has been classed as the sub-species *multifida* or even raised to specific rank.

place in the rock garden. *A. canadensis*, at about 30cm is more acceptable in its smaller forms, like var. *nana*. The flowers are generally bicoloured with red sepals and yellow petals. This hardy species has an immense distribution from Canada to the eastern United States, where it grows in woodland and stony places. *A. elegantula* is closely related but smaller than typical *A. canadensis*, with uniformly scarlet flowers in some forms. *A. jonesii* (Fig.155) is a dwarf, deep rooted, limestone species with striking blue flowers and "a gem of its race" to quote Heath. It is short lived but readily raised from seed. *A. saximontana* varies in height but the smaller forms of 5-12cm are very attractive scree plants with pale violet sepals and white or pale yellow petals. In *A. scopulorum* the flowers are typically of similar colour but larger. There are varieties of different colour, including red and also a dwarf blue form, *calcarea*, with blue flowers.

Ranunculus and **Caltha**   With the *R. eschscholtzii* group, found from the Yukon to New Mexico, we have yet another example of several sub-species/species, generally similar but distinguishable, in this case, by the degree and type of dissection of the leaves and often by distribution. The Stones have compared the different types for general charm and especially admired colonies of *R. e. suksdorfii* which formed clumps with many 15cm stems bearing impressive golden cups 3-4cm across. The variety *eximius* (Fig.159), from Montana, Idaho and Utah, has particularly large flowers. At the end of the range of leaf types, with the most dissected foliage, there is the truly alpine *R. adoneus* (Fig.157) which often occurs in immense colonies in the melting snow. It fills the same ecological niche in America as *R. glacialis* does in Europe and *R. nivicolus* does in New Zealand. *R. macaulayi*, closely related and another alpine species, forms small clumps with solitary or paired, bright, shining flowers. The basal leaves are oblong or spade shaped. It has a limited range in Colorado and New Mexico. *C. leptosepala*, found in moist, montane sites from British Columbia to Alberta and Colorado, with white flowers with blue or greenish tints is worth noting. There is also a yellow flowered variety *sulphurea* (Fig.156) and the rather larger alpine sub-species *howellii* from the western Cascades and Sierra ranges, with white flowers.

Rosaceae

Kelseya and **Petrophytum**   The species of these related genera, which are close to *Spiraea*, vie with one another for being the smallest shrub. *Kelseya uniflora*, a relict species and the only member of its genus, grows so slowly that at least 15 years are needed to produce a fist sized shrub. The solitary, pink, sometimes white, spiraea–like flowers have no particular distinction but the plant is grown for its diminutive form. The dense, leathery, grey-green leaves are in rosettes. It is a plant of limestone or volcanic rock faces in Wyoming, Montana and Idaho, where it has the capacity to form large colonies without any obvious means of subsistence. It may be grown either in the alpine house or outside in a well drained trough with winter protection.

Propagation is by seed or small rosettes may be detached and rooted in a frame. *Petrophytum* has but three species, all dwarf shrubs. *P. caespitosum* produces a very slow growing mat. The leaves are in rosettes, spade shaped with a sharp point and covered in fine silky hairs which give them a grey-green appearance. The many, small white flowers are tightly packed in 2-4cm racemes. The species occurs from Oregon and California across to South Dakota and Texas. *P. cinerascens* is very similar but the leaves have three instead of a single vein and the racemes are often branched. It is confined to Washington State where it grows on volcanic rock. *P. hendersonii* has a similar habit. The leaves are also three-veined, bluish-green above, pinkish on the underside and with longer racemes. It occurs in the alpine zone in the Olympic mountains. All these species require the same kind of sharply drained conditions as *Kelseya*, with plenty of water during the growing period and a dry but not desiccated regime during winter.

Saxifragaceae
Heuchera   Members of this genus are often considered border plants, especially the cultivars derived from *H. sanguinea*. However, among the approximately 50 species of perennial evergreens which are exclusively North American or Mexican, there are several species which are worth a place in the rock garden. These are generally small and more or less acaulescent in habit. The coarse root system is surmounted by a caudex or woody stem base which bears the leaves from the axils of which arise the branches, which carry the panicles of small but often colourful flowers. The species most often classed as a suitable plant for the peat bed or similar site is *H. racemosa*, although we must now call it *Elmera racemosa* (Fig.160) since it has been transferred to a different genus on account of its lobed petals and the apical slits of its seed capsule. The relatively large, light yellow calyces combine with the small, white flowers to make a modest but attractive show. In *Heuchera* proper, *H. cylindrica* from western America, produces scapes of 30-90cm bearing close panicles of white to greenish flowers. *H. micrantha*, in which the greenish flowers are suffused with red to varying extent, is very polymorphic and in some forms can attain 100cm in height and in others only about 10cm. *H. sanguinea*, from Mexico and Arizona, is the well known bright red 'Coral Bells', with many horticultural varieties which include hybrids with *H. micrantha*.

Scrophulariaceae
Penstemon   This large genus of about 270 species is, with one Siberian exception, now transferred to a different genus, entirely American. Those of rock garden interest are from the western United States, with the greatest concentration of often narrowly endemic species in the Great Basin region of Nevada and western Utah. They are either herbaceous or shrubby in habit, very often intermediate with a herbaceous top and woody base. The simple

very often intermediate with a herbaceous top and woody base. The simple leaves are opposite in pairs. The tubular flowers open with a two-lobed upper and a three-lobed lower lip. The fifth stamen develops as a sterile staminode, which may be hairy and conspicuous. The flowers are often very showy and come in endless shades of blue, violet, purple, lavender or pink with occasional albinos. Members of the genus span a wide range of habitats from sea level to high altitudes, from dry, rocky ridges and more or less desert conditions to wet meadows or open pinewoods. To bring conceptual order to this huge assembly botanists have classified the genus into six sub-genera according to the way the anthers open and other characters. Three of the sub-genera, Habroanthus, Penstemon and Saccanthera, have been further subdivided into respectively 2, 6 and 2 Sections with further subdivision of five of them into sub-sections with variable numbers of species. When describing species of this genus, it is better to do so according to section or sub-section, rather than alphabetical order, since related taxa are more likely to require similar treatment in the garden.

Until recently, apart from the shrubby sub-genus Dasanthera, most of the western American species were unfamiliar. To quote Panayoti Kelaidis (1991), who knows them well: "I have always suspected that rock gardeners are simply not aware of the wealth of dramatic, miniature, saxatile plants that exist in the genus. When gardeners finally learn to grow these plants, and a good selection of dwarf species is readily available, *Penstemon* will surely join ranks with *Saxifraga* and *Primula* as a giant treasure trove for rock gardens". But times are changing. Recent Club seed lists include some 50 species and a number of cultivars. David Way and Peter James (1998) have recently published an excellent sytematic account of the genus, while, nearer home, James Cobb, who has a distinguished reputation for growing choice alpines, already has experience of growing about 80 species, a number of which are not yet generally available (1999). He extols their virtues as being relatively easy to grow, with a huge choice of species, and valuable for providing colour in the rock garden into late summer. Although many may be short lived they are generally easy to propagate vegetatively by nodal cuttings, basal shoots or even flowering stems. Since many may have been deterred from growing the western penstemons by their reputation for being difficult it is worth noting that Cobb has had great success in his Fife garden with raised beds or troughs with a 15cm base of dung enriched soil, overlaid with 10cm of coarse sand with a top dressing of 15cm of rough stones of variable size. Some of the species are covered with lights from December to February. Plants are grown from seed which is often subject to dormancy and should not be discarded under three seasons. He makes the important observation that plants grown from seed often vary in performance and ability to flower well so, when a good one turns up, it should be propagated vegetatively. In deciding on which species to mention we have relied on the authors mentioned above as well as the comments of Mike and Polly Stone (1991), which are based on their

Not all the species mentioned here are readily available yet.

Sub-genus Dasanthera   This small sub-genus of nine species includes the majority of the shrubby penstemons which prefer acid soil and cool conditions. They are found especially in north western USA, a few stray into Canada or further south as far as Utah. They readily hybridise so that many of the plants in cultivation are of complex origin and do not correspond to natural species or varieties, while their names often compound the confusion. Although attractive they do have a tendency to die back irregularly. Perhaps *P. rupicola* is the most familiar species, forming low mats of scrubby stems with flowers of various shades of pink to rose-crimson. It is found in the coastal mountains from Washington to northern California. There are more than a dozen named cultivars, often of doubtful origin. The closely related *P. davidsonii*, of similar habit but with purple flowers, occupies rocky ledges and scree from British Columbia to California. Where their ranges overlap it hybridises with *P. rupicola* and *P. newberryi*. *P. fruticosus* is larger, 15-40cm and erect with flowers of various shades of blue to pale purple. It has a number of geographical races, such as the sub-species *scouleri* from about the Canadian border, generally with lavender-pink flowers and also a white form, 'Albus' and another variety *serratus*, called 'Holly', with toothed leaves and an ideal size for the rock garden. *P. newberryi* (Fig.162) grows erect to about 50cm, with a woody base. The flowers are red to pink with densely woolly, exerted stamens. It is one of the outstanding rock plants of northern California where it is known as 'Mountain Pride.'

Sub-genus Penstemon   Within the Section Penstemon, *P. procerus* has a wide distribution from Yukon to California and east to Colorado. There are a number of geographical races which have been ranked as sub-species. *P. p. formosus* forms a dense mat with intensely blue flowers and has often been sold as *P. pulchellus*. *P. p. tolmiei* (Fig.163) from the northern part of the range, has often a very dwarf habit, is hardy and produces spikes of flowers which may be yellow, white, pink or shades of blue or even bicolour. *P. p. brachyanthus* is larger, growing to about 15cm, with turquoise blue flowers. The Stones have reported (1991) that this sub-species and *tolmiei* have proved the best garden forms they have met with in the genus, free-flowering and even producing self-sown seedlings. *P. virens* forms large mats in woodland and rocky slopes up to 3500m in the eastern Rockies of Colorado and New Mexico. *P. humilis*, in the sub-section Humiles, grows to about 30cm and is very variable although Kelaidis claims that any variety can be relied on to produce vivid blue flowers above a mat of green rosettes. *P. virens* is like a larger version of *P. humilis*, forming large mats in woodland and on rocky slopes up to 3500m in the eastern Rockies of Colorado and New Mexico. Typically the flowers are a fine blue-violet to lavender although white and pink forms turn up. *P. whippleanus*, in the same sub-section and named after the man who first brought taxonomic order to the genus, has a broad range from Montana to New Mexico. It is generous with its deep purple flowers. *P.*

from Montana to New Mexico. It is generous with its deep purple flowers. *P. bracteatus* of the Anularius Section, an endemic from Utah where it grows in *Pinus ponderosa* woodland, with blue, rose to violet flowers, has proved an easy plant to grow without protection (Cobb loc.cit,). In yet another sub-section, *P. harbouri* is a true alpine endemic from Colorado with lilac blue flowers and a splash of gold contributed by the conspicuous, hairy staminodes.

In the Section Ericopsis within the same sub-genus Penstemon, the plants display small-leaved, branching stems which form more or less shrubby mats in the artemisia sage brush and in dry situations up to about 3000m. The centre of distribution is Colorado and adjacent States. The Stones singled out *P. crandallii*, especially the very local sub-species *procumbens*. It has small, dark green, cotoneaster-like leaves and bright blue flowers. The sub-species *suffruticosus* of *P. caespitosus* is recommended for its attractive pink-grey foliage. American authors extol the virtues of *P. acaulis*, a tiny 1-3cm plant of dry, sandstone rocks from parts of Wyoming and Utah, with turquoise bells and also *P. laricifolius*, from Wyoming, a larger plant with basal tufts of bright green leaves and light, rose-purple flowers, which make vivid splashes of colour on rocky hillsides. There is also a white sub-species *exilifolius*. Everyone is familiar with the accomodating *P. pinifolius* from Arizona to New Mexico, with its tubular, strongly two-lipped flowers which are typically scarlet but with a yellow cultivar 'Mersea Yellow'. *P. linarioides* is a robust species with a number of varieties of different habit, from loose mats to more upright growth to 20cm. The thin and spiky leaves recall those of *P. pinifolius* although the flowers differ in their blue violet colour. *P. teucrioides* is an attractive alpine from Colorado with bright blue flowers which is easily grown from cuttings (Cobb loc.cit.).

In the Section Auritor the species fall into two groups which are either lowland species or from the dry lands of the Great Basin and desert States. Among the former, the easily grown *P. eriantherus* (Fig.161) occurs in the north western Great Plains and Canada. Typically growing up to 50cm, it has a number of varieties. The foliage is grey-green. The medium sized flowers are typically lavender to blue-violet, with the throat filled by the golden-haired staminode, although pink to red-purple forms also occur. *P. gormanii*, from Alaska and Yukon, has smaller, rather lighter coloured flowers. Members of the second group appear to be strangers to our garden scene. Kelaidis has drawn attention to *P. grahami* from the oil shales of Colorado and eastern Utah. The 7cm stems produce 2/3 lilac-pink balls " that resemble a baby bird demanding to be fed". Although a native of a sterile, dry environment it responds to a well watered scree, so it sounds like a species worth a try.

The Sub-genus Habroanthus is the second largest after Penstemon. Many are too large for the rock garden although they are famous for splashing the western mountain slopes with dazzling blue. But Kelaidis asserts that 30-40 species are candidates for the rock garden with shiny, generally hairless leaves and generally large, prominently displayed flowers which span a range of blues and violets, set off by the white throat revealed by the down-turned lower lip. *P. alpinus*, which typically grows to 50cm, in common with other species, produces dwarfer forms at higher altitudes. The Stones (1991) commend *P. hallii* which forms clumps of rich green leaves, with flower stems of some 15cm or less bearing flowers of a deep purple hue which recalls that of *Gentiana veitchiorum*. *P. hallii* grows in immense numbers on the central mountains of Colorado. The other species they note is *P. compactus* which produces whorls of gentian blue flowers on 15-20cm stems.

Finally, in the highly variable Sub-genus Saccanthera we have, again according to Kelaidis, "the greatest untapped potential" in the genus. Many of the species, with a shrubby form and shiny leaves look rather like members of Dasanthera. *P. heterophyllus* is the mostly widely grown species in the US, in which one or other of its numerous cultivars are used for bedding. In spite of that fact, many would not be averse to seeing one or other of them in their rock garden here. Perhaps of more immediate interest might be *P. leonardii*, which has been fairly recently introduced to cultivation in America. Of common occurrence in Utah, and apparently rather indifferent to soil type, it produces clusters of violet blue flowers.

Monocots
Araceae
Arisaema   *A. triphyllum* (Fig.71) is a hardy plant of moist woods of eastern North America. It can grow to 60cm but is generally less with 1-3 pointed leaves. The spathe varies in colour from green to purple, with white or green stripes and a reflexed margin. The green or purple spadix stands boldly above the tube, hence the common name of jack-in-the–pulpit.

Iridaceae
Iris   The genus Iris is divided in to 6 sub-genera (Mathew1981) of which Limniris includes the North American species. There are two sections: Lophiris, the so-called evansia irises, with one or more crests on the petals, often dentate like a cockscomb, and the much larger Limniris, with as many as 16 series, from different parts of the world, distinguished by differences in their capsules and seeds. Five of these series, Californicae, Hexagonae, Longipetalae, Prismaticae and Vernae include species which are exclusively American while the sixth, Tripetalae, includes species from eastern Asia as well. The most important of these groups is Californicae. In the Section Lophiris, *I. cristata* is from the south eastern United States where it is found in montane woods and rocky places. It is a dwarf species, with slender rhizomes, growing to 15cm, in which the flowers are typically lilac-blue but vary between many shades of purple or violet. There is a white patch on the falls and three yellow or orange-brown crests. It is easily grown in humus-rich but well drained sites. *I. lacustris* is closely related and like *I. cristata* in

decorated with a golden crest. Its range is confined to the region of the Great Lakes. In the Section Limniris, the hardy *I. douglasiana* (Fig.164) is essentially a coastal species from California and Oregon. There is a stout rootstock and flattened stems which grow from 15 to 70cm, with broad leaves with a red coloured base. The branched stem carries several flowers which are extraordinarily variable in colour, ranging from pale yellow to deep purple, but most often some shade of deeply veined lavender- purple. *I. innominata* (Fig.165) is a well known species from the mountains of south west Oregon, discovered in the 1930s. It is typically brilliant yellow, but many colour forms occur in the wild, including shades of pink to violet, together with bicolours such as white/pink, white/violet, yellow/red etc. There are many named cultivars, both in the UK and USA, which are hybrids between *I. innominata* and *I. douglasiana* and these tend to be taller than the wild *innominata* and longer lived. *I. innominata* also hybridises with *I. tenax* in cultivation to produce very fine salmon, rose or reddish flowers. *I. macrosiphon* is another species from California where it can reach an altitude of 1000m. The one, or more usually, two flowers are variable in colour from cream to purple, generally with delicate veining. It is safer to grow it in the alpine house. *I. purdyi* grows to 15-30cm with a pair of white flowers with purplish pink veins and spots, although variable as usual. It is a coastal species of conifer woodland from California. *I. tenax* (Fig.166) forms clumps with light green leaves which pale to pink or straw colour. The 15-30cm stem carries 1-2 flowers of pearly grey, white apricot to deep purple, veined and often with a white base to the blade. The combinations of colours are so many and so subtle that any description must seem lame and inadequate when compared with the original. The range is from Washington to northern California.

The series Hexagonae and Laevigatae which includes *I. versicolor* and also our yellow flag, *I. pseudacorus*, are hardly plants for the rock garden. In the Longipetalae, *I. missouriensis* is found in hilly regions, montane meadows and by streams from the eastern side of the Great Divide. The rhizomes are stout and the roots fleshy. The scapes grow to about 50cm carrying 2-3 flowers on long pedicels. The colours vary about lilac-purple, veined and often with a yellow-white blotch at the base of the petals. The Tripetalae includes *I. setosa* which is really a complex of sub-species and varieties with an immense, northern distribution from eastern Asia, through Japan to Alaska as well as Labrador, Nova Scotia, down through Ontario to Maine. It is a lowland species of marshes and boggy places. It varies in height from 15 to 90cm with leaves which are often reddish at the base. The stem is usually branched with 2/3 flowers per branch. These are typically of a blue-purple colour, but there is great variation. This is an easy, hardy iris with some attractive geographical races like ssp. *canadensis*, a dwarf form from eastern Canada, with an unbranched stem and usually solitary flowers of a lighter shade.

Sisyrinchium   Although the approximately 100 species are mostly from

North or South America, with outliers in the Caribbean and the Falkland Islands, the smaller species suited to the rock garden are predominantly from western North America. They comprise small, tufted generally hardy plants with iris-like leaves, one or more leafy bracts which protect the buds and a succession of flowers which last but a day. Many species display great variability within populations and local varieties are commonly encountered. The taxonomy is difficult leading to much confusion about names. *S. bellum* is one of the taller species, growing up to 45cm in grassland along the coastal zone of California, with flowers of various shades of dark blue-purple, occasionally white, with a yellow eye. *S. californicum* grows as a rule to a similar height with bright yellow, black-veined flowers. A geographical race from the northern part of the distribution in California and Oregon, of distinctly shorter stature, has been widely grown under the name *S. brachypus*. *S. douglasii*, now known as *Olsynium douglasii*, because it is one of only two species which have rounded leaves and stems, grows to 15-30cm, has relatively large, nodding flowers in delightful shades of red-purple or white which appear fairly late in the season. It is another Pacific Coast species which extends northwards to British Columbia. The whole plant dies down after flowering. *S. angustifolium*, with several synonyms, from the eastern States, has become naturalised in Ireland, south west England and elsewhere. The 25 - 45cm stems carry violet blue flowers with a yellow throat.

Liliaceae
Allium   There are about two dozen North American species which are possible candidates for the rock garden or bulb frame or alpine house, although only a specialist would want to grow more than a few of them. The variable number of bell or cup-shaped or, less often, open, spreading flowers of various shades of pink or purple are carried in loose or more tightly packed umbels of roughly spherical or hemi-spherical shape. The best known species is *A. cernuum*, with 30-40cm stems rising from narrowly ovoid bulbs, typically with pink flowers but also with a white and a purple variety. This is a hardy species with a wide distribution from British Columbia to New York and south to Arizona and Colorado. It will often spread by seed to become a nuisance in the garden. *A. acuminatum* grows to 15-30cm with lilac, light or dark violet or pink flower of characteristic appearance since the outer tepals are recurved and the inner ones erect and pointed, hence the name. It occurs in western North America in pine forest and open ground to 1800m. The name *A. murrayanum*, which turns up in the seed lists, appears to be a selected form of *A. acuminatum* with broader tepals and deeper colours. *A. falcifolium* is a diminutive species of 5-12cm, with sword shaped leaves, from California and Oregon with attractive rosy purple bell shaped flowers. *A. siskiyuouense* is closely related, generally similar although even smaller and with a distribution which is restricted to the Siskiyou Mountains of Oregon.
Brodiaea   There are about three dozen species in this genus from western

Brodiaea There are about three dozen species in this genus from western North America. They are distinguished by their corms and their grass-like leaves which generally die off before the flowers which appear rather exposed on the naked stems. Propagation is easy by seed or offsets. *Brodiaea* is one of four closely related genera which include *Bloomeria*, *Dichlostemma* and *Tritelia* whose generic names have often been used interchangeably. Although the brodiaeas are mostly border plants a few are suited to the rock garden and merit notice. *B. elegans*, a forest and grassland species from California and Oregon, produces umbels of deep violet purple flowers and grows to about 40cm. *B. terrestris* hardly reaches 5cm with a few lilac to purple flowers. It is another open woodland species from California and Oregon which can easily be grown in scree or trough. There is a sub-species, *kernensis*, which is just a little larger.

Calochortus This is a substantial genus of about 60 species, with a range in western North America from British Columbia to Mexico and Guatemala, with their centre of diversity in California. It might seem self indulgence to devote space to them in a Scottish context, since they have a reputation for being difficult but this is not true of some species. The Stones flower about a dozen species outside while recent SRGC seed lists have included 15 species so it looks as if the difficulties are being overcome. Their charming flowers and rainbow hues make them desirable subjects for the bulb frame and alpine house, marred only by their tendency to flop on their slender stems. They require very well drained soil, a fair degree of water during the growing period and a great deal less after flowering until growth recommences about December. Propagation is by seed or by the bulbils which some species produce in the leaf axils. The bulbs have a membranous or fibrous outer coat. The perianth is made up of distinct sepals and petals which have a conspicuous gland at their base. The genus is divided into three Sections: Mariposa, the largest Section, with showy, erect flowers on more or less upright stems, with a very wide distribution and a preference for open, dry situations in sage brush; Eucalochortus with, mostly, nodding, often campanulate flowers, a single, broad, basal leaf and a more northern distribution in woodland and upland sites and Cyclobothra, also with a single, broad, basal leaf, flowers which may be upright or pendant and a distinctly southern distribution.

We can note just one or two of the easier species from each section. In Mariposa, *C. luteus* from the Coast Ranges of California and also inland, the broadly campanulate flowers are of a deep yellow colour, often marked with brown stripes and blotches. It grows to 20-40cm. *C. venustus* (Fig.167), from the Coast ranges and Sierra Nevada, grows to 60cm. There is great variation in flower colour which may be white, yellow, pink, purple or dark red, with a dark red patch on each petal. This can be grown outside in sheltered, well drained scree. Eucalochortus includes the Fairy Lanterns, which are usually regarded as a little easier to grow, especially if sharp drainage is combined with humus. *C. albus* varies greatly in height from 20 to 50 cm with several branches to the stems, each bearing several, white, bowl-shaped, pendant flowers. There is a delightful variety *rubellus* with rosy flowers. This species is native to northern California, preferring open woodland and scrub. In *C. uniflorus* the stem is quite short, 6-20cm, there are bulbils in the leaf axils and the generally erect flowers, carried on long pedicels, are lilac or pale pink, with a purple spot above the basal gland on each petal. This a lowland species of grassland in northern California and southern Oregon. Finally in Cyclobothra we can note *C. weedii* from dry, rocky sites of southern California and hence best suited to the alpine house. Here the broadly bell-shaped flowers are erect, yellow or orange, irregularly marked with brown and distinctly hairy within. It grows to about 40cm or more.

Erythronium This genus of some 20 species has a north temperate distribution with a few representatives in Asia and Europe, including the south European *E. dens-canis*, but the majority are North American, either from the east or, more importantly, from the west of the continent. The simple stem, with two or more unequal leaves, which appear almost basal, carries solitary or several large, more or less nodding flowers. In some species the leaves are mottled, earning them the popular name of fawn lilies. They are best grown in well drained, moist humus-rich soil, preferably in a lightly shaded site. *E. americanum* is the best known of the half dozen species from the eastern United States and Canada where it grows in damp woods and pastures. It grows to 15-20 cm with brown mottled leaves and solitary flowers in which the inner tepals are bright yellow and the outer ones reddish brown outside, spotted on the inside. In cultivation it often does not flower freely. Among the western species *E. californicum* is one of the best, growing to 30 cm or more, often branching, with a few to many creamy-white flowers with a yellow throat and reflexed tepals with a faint or more definite, brownish red ring. The leaves are mottled to varying degree. It is a native of the Coastal Ranges of California. It is probably best known for its vigorous cultivar 'White Beauty' which has often been wrongly attributed to *E. revolutum*. In *E. grandiflorum* (Fig.168) the leaves are unmottled and the flowers of a clear yellow with a white three-lobed style. Different forms are distinguished by red, yellow or white anthers. It is a widespread snow-melt species. *E. hendersonii* (Fig.169) from northern California and southern Oregon is of smaller size with mottled leaves and one to four nodding flowers with recurved tepals, pale to dark lavender in colour, with a dark purple base, surrounded by a lighter, white or yellow-tinged zone. *E. oregonum* ranges from Vancouver Island to Oregon, but is a lowland species and easy to grow. The flowers are white with a small, yellow throat, sometimes with an orange base and usually yellow anthers with flattened filaments which are not as wide as in *E. revolutum*. *E. revolutum*, with large, pink flowers and marbled leaves, grows to about 25cm. It occurs from British Columbia to northern California in damp woods, especially where the soil is sandy. There are several named varieties which differ in their shades of pink. *E. montanum* (Fig.170), the avalanche or glacier lily, has unmottled leaves and one to five large, white flowers with a yellow throat. It occurs at high elevations from British Columbia to Oregon, often in immense numbers, and is reported by the Stones to be shy to flower in cultivation.. *E. tuolumnense* is confined to only a few sites in California where it may be locally abundant. The plain leaves have long petioles. The approximately 25cm scapes carry golden yellow flowers with a pale, green-yellow base. A particularly large flowered form has been called 'Spindlestone' by Jim Jermyn, formerly of Edrom Nurseries. The popular, easily grown cultivar 'Pagoda', is the result of hybridisation between *E. tuolumnense* and 'White Beauty' of *E. californicum*.

Fritillaria In America the representatives of this widespread genus occur along a narrow coastal strip from the Aleutian Islands and Alaska to northern Mexico, extending eastwards to Nebraska and the Dakotas. Unlike most of the old world fritillaries which have a tunicate bulb, in the American species the flat, disk-shaped bulb is provided with small scales and, usually, tiny bulblets like rice grains, although in a few species there are a few, broad scales instead. With the exception of *F. camschatcensis*, which occurs also in Asia, these species are exclusively American. They span a wide range of habitats including grassy sites, sometimes at sea level, open conifer or deciduous woodland or rocky slopes and screes extending into the subalpine or even alpine zone in a few instances. They have a reputation for difficulty and are on the whole subjects for the bulb frame or alpine house. Most of the species noted here have appeared in the SRGC seedlists. *F. affinis* (Fig.171) is very variable in height and may reach 120cm although it is generally much less. It occurs from British Columbia to central California and inland to Idaho in grassy sites and is easily grown outside. The several, bell-shaped flowers are green marked with brown. *F. biflora* grows to about 30cm with variable coloured flowers which are very dark, blackish or brown-purple, sometimes with a dash of green. Like several of the species it produces a scent which some find unpleasant. *F. camschatcensis* varies from 20 to 65cm in height. The 1-8, sometimes more, flowers are dark, green-bronze to purple-brown, rarely spotted yellow, with an unpleasant smell which is reported to attract blowflies. This is the species which occurs from Alaska to Washington and westwards to Kamchatka and Japan, often on lowland or coastal sites in America but up to 2000m in Honshu. *F. glauca* (Fig.172), from northern California and southern Oregon, occupies screes and rocky places to moderate elevation. The bulb is provided with only a few scales. The 4-10cm stems carry one to several yellow bells, sometimes with brown markings of variable extent. *F. grayana* differs chiefly from typical *F. biflora* in the white ground colour of the tepals, marked with rusty brown. *F. pudica* is a small species of 7-20cm, typically with one, or less often, two open bell-shaped flowers which open bright yellow and develop an orange shade as they age. This attractive species has been split into several varieties on the basis of size, flower colour and leaf type. It ranges from British Columbia to California and eastwards to Montana and New Mexico on dry sites up to 4000m. *F. recurva* (Fig.173) is an outstandingly beautiful fritillary with a slender, habit up to 60cm and one to several or even many, open bells with recurved tips to the petals and of scarlet colour, spotted with orange and yellow.

Trillium The distribution of this north temperate genus of about 50 species comprises three regions: Asia, eastern and western North America. The Asian species have affinities with those of western America. The erect, unbranched stems arise from short rootstocks. The whorl of three leaves near the top of the stem subtends the tripartite flower which may be sessile or stalked. The sepals are usually green while the petals may be white, pink, purplish, yellow or reddish brown. They are in most cases attractive, hardy plants with a preference for moist humus-rich conditions. The seed is slow to germinate and it may take five years for the flowers to appear. R. J. Mitchell has monographed the genus (1989). Considering first the western species, *T. chloropetalum* (Fig.175), from the redwood forests of California, grows to 30-60cm, with round-ovate, sessile, usually mottled leaves and sessile flowers. The erect petals vary from yellow to green or dark purple or reddish brown, according to variety. This species may be considered too big for the rock garden, but makes a brave show if it can be accomodated. *T. ovatum* (Fig.179) grows to about 40cm with leaves which are sessile or nearly so. The white petals of the stalked, erect flowers, set off by yellow anthers, sometimes change to rose as they age. This is the 'Coast Trillium', which is the most widespread of the western species, ranging from British Columbia to California and east to Montana and Colorado. There is a dwarf subspecies *T. o. oettingeri* and an even smaller variety *hibbersonii*. *T rivale* is a small, rhizomatous plant of 10-15cm. The flowers are borne on slender pedicels and are at first erect, later nodding. The petals are white or pale rose with purple spots at the base of the petals with the cultivar 'Purple Heart' (Fig.178) having attractive flowers which are deep purple at the base. Among the eastern species *T. cernuum*, with a wide distribution in the eastern States and Canada, has wavy edged, white or pink recurved petals; the flowers tend to hang below the leaves. It is a strong grower, perhaps more suited to the border. In the sessile leaved *T. erectum* (Fig174), which grows from 20 to 60cm, the stalked flowers are typically maroon but may also be white, yellow or green. It occurs from eastern Canada to Georgia. *T. grandiflorum* (Fig.177), with sessile leaves grows to about 40cm. The white petals, which often turn pink with age, are erect at the base but then spread outwards. The range is from Quebec to North Carolina and Missouri. *T. luteum* (Fig.176), with sessile, mottled leaves and sessile, lemon scented, bright yellow flowers is native to Tennessee and North Carolina. *T. sessile* is closely related, with similarly sessile leaves and flowers, but the erect petals are purple to green while the range is from Pennsylvania to Florida. *T. undulatum*, with a similar distribution, is an acid loving species from boggy sites in coniferous and mixed woodland. The petals, with wavy margins, are white with a basal arc of purple or crimson stripes. It is a more difficult species which requires greater effort to reproduce its natural substrate.

Tritelia This is a small genus, only debatably distinct from *Brodiaea*, which is native to western North America and Mexico. It is distinguished by the possession of corms and grass-like leaves. *T. hyacintha* reaches 20-50cm in height, with compact umbels of many white or pale blue star-shaped flowers. Its range is from British Columbia to California and Idaho, usually in moist habitats. *T. laxa* grows to about 30cm but varies greatly in height. The scape carries loose umbels of blue or sometimes white flowers. It occurs in California and Oregon in open, often wooded sites up to 1400m. *T. uniflorum*, now correctly called *Iphieon uniflorum*, is the familiar, spring flowering bulbous plant which grows to about 15cm. with white, mauve or pale blue, star shaped petals which emerge from a tubular base. The whole plant has a slight aroma of onion when bruised. In spite of its origin in Uruguay and Argentina it is perfectly hardy, floriferous and multiplies rapidly to form clumps which should be periodically divided to maximise the display.

South America

South America poses a problem as to where to draw the line in an account of introduced species. There is an immense Andean alpine flora which includes so many plants of dazzling beauty, so well illustrated in the Encyclopaedia of Alpines, and yet for most rock gardeners they will be just a name and perhaps a memory of an illustration. The Andean flora is still in the early days of introduction and testing for use in the garden and alpine house. This new flora will present a challenge for many years to come. There has not yet been time for selection of genotypes suited to our conditions. The situation is reminiscent of early introductions from the Sino-Himalayan region when so many fell by the wayside, although there is the impression that the Andean species are generally more exacting in their requirements. Many gardeners are deterred from trying them by the reports of difficulties in seed germination, reluctance to flower or atypical growth in our climate, problems which seem best left for the specialists to grapple with. Given this situation we have restricted our comments to the better known species from especially the southern Andes, Patagonia and the floristically related Falklands, especially those which have appeared in Club seed lists.

Dicots
Apiaceae
Bolax There are only two species in this genus which is close to and sometimes combined with *Azorella*, which also has a much greater

distribution along the Andes. *B. gummifera* produces compact cushions made up of rosettes of small, leathery leaves supported by deep roots. In the wild the cushions, which may grow up to a metre or more in height and as much across, are reminiscent of the New Zealand vegetable sheep. The insignificant flowers in simple umbels are greenish-white. It occurs in peaty soil among quartzite rocks where it makes a major contribution to its ecological association in the south of Chile, Argentina and the Falklands. It is quite hardy and can be grown in a well drained scree or raised bed although it is unlikely to grow very big.

Asteraceae
Nassauvia This is a genus of about three dozen species which are distributed among the mountains of South America and the Falklands. They are low-growing shrubs, many of which form cushions like the best know *N. gaudichaudii* which is a Falkland endemic. Here the tight cushions are constructed from branching stems which bear rosettes of deep green narrow, glabrous, spine-tipped leaves. The old leaves remain attached to the lower branches. The strongly scented flowers, about 6 cm in diameter, are cream coloured and sometimes in such profusion as to cover the bush. This is a reliable scree or raised bed species. *N. pygmaea* is altogether smaller, as befits its name. The woody, branching, procumbent stems are provided with small, overlapping spine-tipped leaves. It occurs in screes and rock crevices in Chile and Argentina and is a likely candidate for a well drained trough.

N. revoluta (Fig.181) is a true alpine since it is to be found as high as plants go in the Andes of Chile and Argentina, growing in loose volcanic sand. It forms cushions of abundant, rigid pointed leaves which are downy white on the underside. The globular infloresences are white.

Perezia This genus of some three dozen species of herbaceous or shrubby habit is distributed along the Andes from Columbia southwards to Patagonia. *P. recurvata* from Patagonia and the Falklands is another low-growing shrub which forms mats or cushions with branching, woody stems. The tough, often spiny leaves occur in terminal rosettes. The solitary white or blue flowers, about 2.5cm across, are carried clear of the foliage and strongly scented. There are several forms which differ in leaf size or inflorescence, e.g. var *patagonica* which has small, non-spiny leaves and bright blue flowers.

Gutierrezia The best known of this small genus is *G. baccharoides* which ranges from high alpine communities in Chile and Argentina to sea-level in Patagonia. It forms small, squat cushions of a few cm with masses of sessile yellow flower-heads which smother the plant. It is reported that cuttings take readily and that it is best grown in a sandy compost on a south-facing raised bed.

Ericaceae
Pernettya   *P. mucronata* (Fig.180) is a stout, bushy shrub, spreading by suckers, with prickly, leathery leaves. The small, white, urn-shaped flowers are borne in the upper leaf axils. However, it is not the flowers but the large, globular fruits which make it a garden favourite, especially for winter decoration. They range in colour from white through all shades to deepest purple, with many named forms. Since the plants are dioecious, male and female plants should be grown together. Although not too demanding, damp, peaty conditions suit it best. It is a native of central Chile and western Argentina.

Loasaceae
Loasa   This is a comparatively large genus of mainly Andean plants although some species extend as far north as Mexico. Many of them are notorious for their stinging hairs but in some of the smaller species these are sufficiently reduced to be acceptable as alpine house plants. The annual *L. triphylla* var. *vulcanica* has appeared in the Club seed lists. It grows to about 40cm with a tendency to climb. The serrated leaves are simple or trilobed. The flowers, about 2cm in diameter, are white and enlivened by the yellow nectar scales which are barred red and white.

Myrtaceae
Myrteola   This is a small genus, often included under *Myrtus*, which includes the familiar *M. nummularia* from southern Chile and Argentina as well as the Falklands. It forms a creeping mat of paired, opposite, leathery, deep green leaves. The solitary white flowers arise from the leaf axils and are followed by pink or red, edible berries. In the wild it occurs in the drier parts of peaty bogs and, in cultivation, should be treated like an acid loving erica. It may be propagated by cuttings, rooted stems or seed and may be grown outside or in the alpine house.

Oxalidaceae
Oxalis   This huge genus has a world wide distribution but has two centres of diversity, in South Africa and South America from where the best known rock plants have come. *O. adenophylla* (Fig.182) is a stemless, herbaceous species which develops from brown, scaly tubers. The stalked leaves are carried erect or spreading, with numerous folded leaflets and of a shining, silvery grey appearance. The peduncles carry 1-3 attractive, funnel-shaped flowers, embedded in the foliage. They vary in colour from pink to violet with darker veins and a lighter throat. This is a hardy plant for a well drained site, flowering in late spring to early summer. It occurs in the mountains of Chile and Argentina at lower levels in southern beech woodland and scrub. At higher elevations, up to 2600m, it forms more compact hummocks and the colours are deeper and more intense. *O. enneaphylla* (Fig.183), closely related

but extends also to the Falklands. It has a similar habit, spreading by rhizomes which are covered in white scales which bear bulbils in their axils. The many, obcordate, rather fleshy leaflets are often partly folded. The flowers are white to rose-purple, elegantly veined and sweet scented. According to Watson (1994) there is regional variation in the frequency of flower colour. On the mainland a variety of pink shades predominate and white is uncommon, but in the Falklands white prevails and pinks turn up only occasionally in the west of the islands.

O. laciniata is another rhizomatous plant of similar habit to the foregoing, although the rhizomes make a chain of small, scaly bulbils. The narrow leaflets are folded, glaucous green with an often purplish wavy margin. The solitary, salver-shaped, fragrant flowers are very variable in colour, ranging from violet and crimson to pale blue. It occurs in Patagonia in stony, well drained sites at lower elevations. It can be grown outside in a trough but is superb in the alpine house. It is closely related to *O. squamosa-radiacata*, which may be a form of *O. laciniata*. They differ in leaf shape. In *O. laciniata* the narrow leaflets are pointed but rounded with a notch in *O. squamosa-radicata*. Both often grow together in the wild. This was first collected by Ruth Tweedie at Estancia Stag River and received a Preliminary Commendation when shown in 1958. *O. loricata* is another species of the same group, also collected at Stag River by Ruth Tweedie and also given a Preliminary Commendation when shown in 1963. Apparently it was grown about that time at Edrom Nursery but now appears to have been lost although Erskine (1994) has suggested that it may be lurking in Scotland under the invalid name of *O. patagonica*. *O. loricata* occurs in the southern Andes in scree near summits and in the wet sand of upland river sides. According to Erskine (loc.cit), although spreading by rhizomes, *O. loricata* sends up separate shoots which appear to be separate plants. The rounded leaflets are folded, notched, with a red margin and of a distinctive green when young. The solitary cup-shaped flowers are white, pink on the underside, and with purple veins in the throat.

Portulacaceae
Calandrinia This is a large genus from especially tropical and sub-tropical regions, especially South America. It is allied to *Lewisia*. The flower has two sepals which are often conspicuous and used in classification, 5-9 petals and up to 40 stamens. The flowers may be solitary or multiple in cymes or racemes. The genus is split into Four Sections:
<u>Acaules</u> Small, clump-forming species with a fleshy tap root from which the solitary flowers arise directly. These include the species most like *Lewisia* from which they are distinguished by the way the seed capsules split longitudinally instead of by an apical cap.
<u>Dianthoideae</u> These are stout perennials with leafy stems and the flowers most often but not always in clusters.

Andinae Succulents with leafy stems, clustered flowers and sepals with purple to black wavy stripes.
Hirsutae Tufted, mat or cushion habit with leafy stems, narrow leaves and covered with hairs which may be fine and velvety to very coarse.

The calandrinias are increasing in popularity. Nine species and several, recently introduced varieties appear in the Club seed lists. Taking the Sections in turn, in Acaules, the specific name of *C acutisepala* refers to the distinctive oval-triangular sepals. The tufted rosettes grow to a height of about 10cm, with narrow, grass-like leaves which do not exceed the flower stem in length. The bright and attractive flowers vary between white and pink. This is a true alpine which is at home in loose, volcanic scree between 1200 and 2700m in the southern central Cordillera of Argentina. In *C. caespitosa* the leaves are rather narrow and pointed, gradually reduced in width toward the base and hairless, like the rest of the plant. The flower stalk is noticeably longer than the leaves. But the rest of the plant presents great variation in growth form, ranging from loose rosettes and pale blue flowers which fail to open to a compact cushion of small leaved rosettes with striking, gleaming red, star-like flowers with a green-gold centre and there is still another form in which the larger petals are golden orange. These different forms differ in their distribution. Thus the orange golden one occurs in the Argentine Lake District in unstable scree at 2000m. The red form occurs near the upper limit of vegetation at 2500–4000m while pink forms appear at lower altitudes from further south. Clearly taxonomic revision is overdue. This species is not too difficult in cultivation and so both the red and the orange forms merit wider interest.

In the Dianthoideae, *C. cistiflora* occurs in the Central Cordilleras of Chile and Argentina in stony soils at 1700-3200m. Spreading by rhizomes it forms a slender erect bush with narrow, linear leaves and 5-6 narrow, pointed petals which are white or pink.

Of the species in the Hirsutae. *C. gilliesii* produces a thick tap root and small cushions of grassy, silvery leaves. The flowers are in terminal clusters. This species appears to be polymorphic since members of the same population may be either white or pink flowered. It is another high alpine since it occurs in exposed sites in the central and northern Andes at 2000-4000m. *C. sericea* also forms cushions which may be rather lax. The narrow leaves have a silky appearance, are blue-grey and mostly but not entirely basal. The inflorescence consists of cymes of several magenta, 2cm wide flowers with a central boss of many golden stamens. To add to the shiny effect the narrow, pointed red-brown sepals are coated with silky hairs which may be silver or warm brown in colour. It occurs in the Chilean central plain and Cordillera. It looks as if this species is making a successful transition into cultivation.

C. umbellata has a rather similar growth form, with mainly basal, tufted, grassy leaves. It produces a few to many 2cm wide flowers which vary between rich violet to deep magenta. The short-lasting flowers open in the afternoon sun. The range is from sea level to 2700m, as usual according to latitude, in poor, exposed, gravelly soils. It occurs in the Andes from the central valley to northern Patagonia. It is widely grown commercially and usually treated as an annual.

Primulaceae
Primula *P. magellanica* forms loose rosettes of spoon shaped leaves which narrow basally into a stalk, with a mealy underside. The scape is usually between 5 and 15cm, occasionally much more, standing well above the leaves. It carries a terminal umbel of a few white flowers with a yellow eye, rarely tinted lavender. It occurs in wet places in Patagonia, Tierra del Fuego and the Falklands.

Ranunculaceae
Anemone *A. multifida* is a bit of a mystery since it is recorded from both North America and the southern part of South America. The basal leaves have three lobes which are further indented. The 20-30cm scape carries 1-3 flowers which are very variable in colour and may be white, cream, yellow or almost red. It occurs in open ground in stony places among scrub or woodland. It makes a good scree plant and is quite hardy. According to the Encyclopaedia of Alpines the typical white flowered form is sold under the name *A. magellanica*.

Ranunculus *R. guzmannii* is to be found in damp grassland from southern Columbia to Ecuador at high altitudes (3300–4800m) and often on limestone. It grows from a stout rhizome to 10-15cm with trilobed leaves which are hairy, especially on the underside. The 1-3 flowers make a splash of colour. The large sepals are shining red and the smaller petals orange.

Saxifragaceae
Saxifraga There are only a few saxifrages in South America so it is worth noting *S. magellanica* (Fig.184) which extends from the extreme south of the Andes to Peru. It forms low cushions of three-lobed leaves with a broad petiole. The flowers are white. It is described as similar in general form to the rare Scottish native *S. cespitosa*.

Scrophulariaceae
Calceolaria This is an essentially South American genus, although it does extend as far north as Mexico. *C. biflora* spreads by rhizomes to form clumps 10-30cm high with basal rosettes of leaves which vary in shape from oblong to more lanceolate with dentate margins. The inflorescence consists of two or occasionally more yellow flowers with the characteristic inflated lower lip of the corolla. The specific name embraces a complex of forms which differ in habit, leaf shape and other respects but which apparently agree in favouring

peaty, moist sites from sea level to 2800m in south Chile and Argentina and also rarely in the Falklands. *C. fothergillii* is closely related to the *C. biflora* complex. Rather woody at the base, the rosette of oval or spade-shaped leaves taper uniformly toward the base. The solitary flowers are borne on 10cm scapes The upper lip of the corolla is bright yellow while the enlarged, sack-like lower lip varies from yellow with small red spots to red streaks or is entirely dark red. It occurs in Patagonia and the Falklands in conditions similar to those of *C. biflora*. *C. polyrhiza* spreads by woody stems to form mats of tufted, oblong leaves with wavy margins. The flowers are usually solitary and yellow. It occurs in open, sunny spots in Chile and Patagonia. According to the Encyclopaedia of Alpines, the plant commonly known by this name may really be one of the forms of the variable *C. lanceolata* which has a wide distribution in Chile and Argentina. The familiar *C. tenella* is a small, delicate mat-forming species with short stalked more or less oval leaves which have a few teeth. The inflorescence, on peduncles less than 10cm, consists of a single yellow flower or a simple two-branched cyme, each with 1-3 flowers. This is another species which is found on moist, well drained rocky sites, in southern Chile and Argentina. *C. uniflora* (Fig.185) is everyone's favourite. It is found in the same kind of places as the preceding species and grows between 4 and 10cm, with more or less upright leaves which are roughly oblong, of variable shape and tapering basally. The ground colour of the flower is orange-yellow but there is variation in the degree of red or chestnut spotting in the throat and on the outside of the lower lip. At the junction of the throat and lower lip there is a conspicuous white band. There are several varieties of which the best known is the larger and generally admired var. *darwinii* with a very large lower lip. Ruth Tweedie introduced a form of this, with silvery leaves, from Estancia Stag River. The species occurs in Chile and Argentina including southern Patagonia. It is generally treated as an alpine house subject which needs an acid, humus-rich compost, plenty of ventilation and avoidance of winter wet.

Ourisia This is one of the genera which perhaps bears the imprint of former land connections since it has representatives in New Zealand, South America and Tasmania. They are all rhizomatous low-growing species with a decided preference for moist situations. The petiolate leaves are usually basal. About 18 species have been found in the Andes. In the New Zealand species the flowers are white and this is true of the South American species which are insect pollinated but where humming birds are the pollinators the flowers are red. Only a few Andean species have been established in cultivation. Probably the best known is *O. coccinea* (Fig.186) from southern Chile. It forms mats of oval, clearly veined, dentate leaves from which arise the 20cm stalks carrying a terminal panicle of drooping, 4cm long, tubular flowers, with protruding cream coloured stamens. In the wild it prefers, moist, peaty sites and some shade. Given similar conditions it grows happily, often vigorously, in the garden. To maximise flowering it is advisable to divide and replant the rhizomes when they become too congested. As noted earlier, *O. coccinea* is one parent in the cross to the New Zealand *O. macrophylla* which gave rise to that excellent cultivar 'Loch Ewe'. *O. elegans* is very similar in habit, distribution and ecological preference, differing chiefly in having more triangular and lobed leaves. In *O. fragrans* (Fig.187) the groups of several, rather tubular scented white to pink flowers are borne on approximately 8cm stalks which spring from the leaf axils. It occurs in shady rocky places up to 2000m in Argentina and Chile. *O. microphylla* is quite different since it is a dwarf shrub with fine, branched roots and branching stems with small pointed leaves arranged in four rows, rather reminiscent of a cassiope. The solitary flowers, carried on short stipes, are pink or occasionally white and often produced in great profusion. It occurs in Chile and Argentina from the southern central Cordillera to the Lake District, in lava cliffs from 1500 to 1800m i.e. at tree-line level. Given its habitat it is no surprise that it is a subject for the alpine house.

Solanaceae
Nierembergia *N. patagonica* (Fig.188) forms broad cushions of rigid linear leaves. The shallow, cup-shaped flowers are dusky yellow or pale violet with darker, netted veining. It is an endemic of southern Patagonia and is not easy but worth trying in a sheltered raised bed with winter protection.

Tropaeolaceae
Tropaeolum This is another South American genus which stretches north to Mexico. Apart from the climbing *T. speciosum*, the other two hardy species are *T. incisum* and *T. polyphyllum*. *T. incisum* (Fig.189) resembles *T. polyphyllum* in its procumbent habit. The leaves are lobed and the long-spurred flowers typically yellow, although in some forms they may be orange with purple veins. It occurs in volcanic detritus up to 3000m in Argentina. It appears to be fairly hardy given sharp drainage. It is not a climber but will straggle in a prostrate and pleasing fashion. In *T. polyphyllum* (Fig.190) the grey-green leaves are divided into 5-7 or more lobes. The clustered flowers, with the typical, sepaloid spur, are usually yellow, although lemon and dark orange forms occur in the wild. (Watson, 1994). There is a compact, orange flowered form known as 'High Alpine Form' which can be recommended. In Chile and Argentina this species occurs in alpine screes which are snow covered in winter.

Violaceae
Viola When we come to this immense, world wide genus we are brought up short by the South American species. Illustrations of wild plants reveal many with amazing saxatile form and charming, idiosyncratic flowers which fascinate. But, with few exceptions, their cultivation poses great difficulties. According to the AGS Bulletin (1994), some species like *VV. atropurpurea*

(Fig.191), *coronifera* (Fig.192), *dasyphylla* and *fluehmannii* germinate easily and a few, such as *VV columnaris, coronifera, cotyledon, dasyphylla* and *philippii* (Fig.194), have been grown to flowering size. Other attractive species include *V. nivalis* (Fig.193) and *V. sacculus* (Fig.195). In the former, from Ecuador, where it grows to high elevations in damp grassland, the flowers are white, often with bluish veins and a yellow throat. In the latter, from Argentina, Chile and Patagonia, the overlapping leaves are arranged spirally and the white, yellow throated flowers form a ring round the tips of the outer leaves. V. *reichii*, a yellow flowered species introduced recently from southern Chile by Gardiner and Knees of the Edinburgh Botanic Garden, grows well enough outside in a moist, sheltered spot. But, in the present context, we shall have to leave the South American violas to the few specialists with skills and patience enough to unravel their special needs and look briefly at some attractive monocots.

Monocots
Alstroemeriaceae
Alstroemeria There are over 60 herbaceous species in this genus which is well represented in Chile and southern Brazil. A number of the alpine species are receiving increasing interest, evident in the Club seed lists. It appears that the high altitude species, from over 1500m, will often do best outside in sparse compost in as sunny a place as possible. Which of them can get by without a protective glass pane during winter can only be determined by experiment. In general, since so much has yet to be learnt of the needs of different species, it would be wise to split batches of their seedlings into samples which are given different treatments. *A. angustifolia* is a dwarf which grows to about 10cm, with rather grassy leaves which are twisted and pointed. The inflorescence consists of umbels of 20 or more funnel shaped flowers with green pointed outer tepals and unequal sized inner tepals of which the upper two are yellow banded with red stippling. It occurs in the Santiago region of Chile. There is a sub-species *velutina*, in which, as the name suggests, the leaves are provided with a covering of fine hairs. *A. hookeri* is also a small species, although it can grow tall and out of character under glass. The outer tepals are broadly ovate, the inner ones narrower and more lanceolate, all with a pointed tip. There are four sub-species with more or less funnel shaped flowers which differ in their bright colour patterns and subtle shades which can only be conveyed by a photograph. *A. pelegrina* is taller, growing to about 25cm, often less. The stems are covered with succulent, twisted leaves. The single or, usually several, striking, large, widely open flowers per umbel are pink with crimson and yellow markings. There is also a white variety 'Alba'. This species occurs on Chilean sea shores and cliffs. *A. pseudospathulata* (Fig.196) grows between 5 and 20cm. The funnel-shaped flowers are bright yellow. It occurs in central and southern Chile on granite ridges. *A. pulchella* is taller still, growing between 25 and 45cm with twisted,

petiolate, oblong to lanceolate leaves which are located near the end of sterile shoots. The inflorescence is a simple umbel of 4-6 flowers which are dark red, brown spotted, with green tipped tepals. This is a hardy species which will grow outside in a sunny, sheltered spot. *A. pygmaea* is a very small, almost stemless species with a rosette of narrow leaves. The flowers are yellow with red spots. This is an alpine from altitudes of 3500-4500m and open stony places in Argentina, Bolivia and Peru. Apparently *A. patagonica* has sometimes been called *A. pygmaea*. *A umbellata* varies in height between 10 and 25cm with succulent, spade-shaped leaves with a marginal fringe of hairs. Typically the flowers are warm pink, occasionally white, and in umbels of 2-10. It occurs in Chile and Argentina in scree at 2000 – 3000m.

Tecophilaeaceae

Tecophilaea There are two species in this Chilean genus from north of Santiago, *T. cyanocrocus* and *T. violiflora*, both with corms, the former with several leaves and the latter only one. *T. cyanocrocus* is one of those species which cause a gasp when first seen. The crocus-like, fragrant flowers are a brilliant gentian blue. It is not an alpine. It has not been seen in its native habitat for some time and is commonly presumed extinct although Watson (loc.cit.) has speculated that might be a premature conclusion. Fortunately it is not too difficult to grow in the alpine house and there is plenty of material in cultivation. *T. violiflora* is very variable in colour, not exclusively violet, and may be white, purple or even blue and of a shade which rivals that of *T. cyanocrocus*.

§ CHAPTER 10 §

Japan

Japan is a mountainous country with peaks exceeding 3000m and therefore home to many desirable alpine plants. The chain of islands stretches so far north and south that the climate ranges between semi-arctic to semi-tropical. Honshu is the largest island, Hokkaido to the north is next in size with the much smaller Sakhalin and the Kurile Islands further north still. The proximity to the sea has a general ameliorating effect on the climate. There are annually two monsoons, a cold one in winter from Siberia and a warm, moist one from the Pacific in summer. The vegetation can be classified in four categories according to altitude. The lowland zone which extends up to about 500m is dominated by bamboo forest. The montane zone, which extends from 500 to 1550m, is characterised by a cold temperate flora in which the dominant trees include species of oak, beech, birch, cherry and many conifers such as *Cryptomeria*, *Pinus* and *Abies*. From 1550 to 2500m we have the subalpine zone in which conifers predominate, accompanied by maples and birches. Above 2500m to the snow-line we have the true alpine zone, where snowfall is heavy, the growth of trees and shrubs is stunted and the commonest 'tree' is the creeping pine, *Pinus pontica*. Above the tree-line great areas of moorland, broken by cliffs, rocky outcrops and peaty patches, form a characteristic feature of the Japanese landscape. Here ericaceous species of such genera as *Phyllodoce*, *Gaultheria*, *Vaccinium*, *Empetrum*, *Rhododendron*, *Ledum* and *Loiseleuria* dominate the vegetation. In many of these plants the foliage in autumn turns to various shades of crimson, yellow and orange to paint the hillsides in dramatic colour. In the references to plant localities below, Japan includes Hokkaido and Honshu. Sakhalin and the Kurile isles are distinguished separately since they have a rather distinct flora.

The Japanese flora has close affinities with that of Asia and America, traceable to former physical connection to both continents. Many species recorded from Japan also occur in places like Korea, Kamchatka, eastern China or Siberia. There is also a strong circumpolar element. The contribution of species from different floristic regions is evident in the origins of the alpine flora. Out of the 574 species of the alpine zone just over 32% are endemic, 28% are Asiatic, 22% are circumpolar, 11% are North American while the rest have affinities with more distant floras in Europe and western Asia and the Pacific region (Kuyama, 1989). Among the dicots from Japan and often neighbouring regions of eastern Asia we can note the following.

Apiaceae
Bupleurum   This has a wide distribution through Eurasia. The species are easily recognised by their tightly packed, often compound umbels which

frequently arise from a whorl of leafy bracts. The flowers are tiny and often yellow. The leaves are generally simple and alternate. *B. longeradiatum* grows between 30 and 90cm, with clustered umbels of small yellow flowers. The typical form occurs in Japan, Korea and China. The variety *shikotanense* is much smaller, 20-30cm, with thicker leaves and less dense umbels. It is confined to the alpine regions of Hokkaido and the Kuriles.

Asteraceae
Artemisia   The members of this genus small enough to be admitted to the rock garden are grown primarily for their attractive foliage. *A. schmidtiana*, from Japan, Sakhalin and the Kuriles, ranges from the sea-shore to mountain slopes. The branching stems produce a dense mat. The preferred variety is 'Nana' with silvery-leaved hummocks. *A. stelleriana*, with a distribution which also includes Korea and Kamchatka, spreads by stolons to produce large mats. The leaves, which are densely covered in fine, white hairs, provide an effective background for the narrow panicles of small, yellow flowers.

Leontopodium   Species of edelweiss, wherever they come from, are sure to persuade some rock gardeners to find a place for them. *L. discolor* has long-stalked woolly leaves, grows from 15 to 30cm and is found only in the alpine zone of Hokkaido and the Kuriles. *L. kurilense* is another edelweiss of similar size, from the Kuriles and eastern Siberia. *L. fauriae* is much smaller, 6-15cm and endemic to the alpine zone of Honshu.

Berberidaceae
Epimedium   This is a genus of woodland plans adapted to shady conditions where they can spread by means of rhizomes. *E. grandiflorum* (Fig.197) grows to about 30cm. The leaves are divided into at least nine leaflets. The flowers vary from white or yellow to pink or purple. It is a native of south and central Japan. The specific name embraces an aggregate of sub-species, geographical races and varieties which have given rise to a number of excellent garden cultivars which differ in flower colour, time of flowering and growth habit. *E. setosum*, from south west Honshu is semi-evergreen, turning crimson in winter. The leaves are divided into several prickly leaflets and the flowers white. Its taxonomic status is uncertain since it may be a hybrid between the Japanese *E. diphyllum* and a sub-species of *E. grandiflorum*.

Campanulaceae
Adenophora   This genus is closely related to *Campanula* but differs in the presence of a tubular or glandular disc at the base of the style. Most of the species are late flowering and worth attention on that account. Most of the cultivated species, often from west China, are too big for the average rock garden but there are a few acceptable, smaller ones like *A. takedae* from Japan with a willowy stem which grows to 60cm with racemes of violet blue

flowers. Better still there is an alpine variety, *howozana*, which only reaches 15cm. *A. triphylla* (Fig.198), from Japan, Taiwan and China, with pale violet flowers, can grow to about a metre but it includes several much smaller varieties like *puellaris*, a local Japanese, alpine endemic.

Campanula *C. chamissonis*, better known by its synonym *C. pilosa* (Fig.199), spreads by rhizomes to form clumps with rather floppy stems up to 15cm. The oblong leaves are in loose rosettes. The solitary blue flowers are provided on the interior of the corolla with white hairs. This is to be found on sandy or gravelly soil at alpine levels in Japan, including the Kuriles, Sakhalin and across to Alaska and the Aleutians, illustrating the American affinities noted above. *C. lasiocarpa* has a similar distribution but occurs in Kamchatka as well. It forms loose mats from which arise the single flowers, which may be oriented horizontally or vertically, and are of an attractive, medium blue colour. *C. punctata* is a robust species which spreads by rhizomes to form colonies with erect stems which grow to about 30cm. The large bell-shaped, pendulous flowers, in a terminal raceme, are typically rose-purple often with dark flecks within the corolla, but they may also be cream or pink. It is found in grassy lowland sites and foothills in Japan. This handsome plant has given rise to a number of cultivars which differ in size and colour, including the familiar variety 'Alba' which is white splashed with purple, and also the smaller version 'Alba Nana'. This species is closely related to the Korean border plant *C. takesimana*.

Crassulaceae

Sedum *S. cauticolum*, a herbaceous species of 10-15cm has round, paired, stalked and rather fleshy grey leaves with rounded teeth and purple flecks. The flowers are deep purple in terminal cymes. This is a hardy, cliff-dwelling species from Japan which has given rise to a number of cultivated forms which differ in colour. *S. ishidae*, as its synonym *Rhodiola* suggests, is very similar to the circumpolar roseroot, except that the leaves are green, narrowed at each end and strongly toothed with clear margins. It occurs in the mountains of Hokkaido and Honshu. *S. pluricaule* forms mats of pink-grey, succulent, almost circular leaves. The inflorescence, borne on 3-6cm scapes, consists of branched, dense cymes of light purple colour. It occurs on mountain slopes from eastern Siberia to Sakhalin. It is reported to have been confused with the rather similar *S. ewersii* var. *homophyllum* in which, however, the leaves are less succulent and not glaucous. *S. polytrichoides* is a Japanese endemic from Honshu with a densely tufted, erect habit and comparatively few flowers.

Diapensiaceae

Diapensia *D. lapponica* forms low hummocks of bright, evergreen foliage which sets off the upright, cup-shaped cream coloured flowers of 1-2cm. The distribution is circumpolar with sporadic appearance of the species in alpine situations further south as in Scotland, for example, where it is restricted to a single site. With such a wide distribution several geographical races are recognised;. The Japanese one is var. *obovata* (Fig.200), which has relatively larger, more ovate leaves and slightly larger flowers. It is notoriously difficult to establish *D. lapponica* in cultivation but it is reported that the Japanese form may be a little more responsive.

Shortia   This is a small genus from north east Asia and eastern North America. They are primarily woodland plants which require cool, moist, humus rich soil and a site where they will be sheltered from drying winds and bright sunshine. They spread by rhizomes to form small clumps or mats. In *S. soldanelloides* (Fig.203) the round leaves produce mats of foliage from which arise the 15cm stems bearing clusters of pink or white bell-shaped corollas with very evident fringed, soldanella-like margins. It is found in mountain woods in Japan. There are several cultivars which differ in habit, such as the elegant 'Askival Icebell' (Fig.202) and the high alpine and tiny var. m*inima* and *alpina* (Fig.201), with only one or two barely fringed flowers per stem. *S. uniflora* forms clumps of bronzy, round leaves from which arise the 12cm stems carrying a single pink flower. It occurs in eastern Honshu. The variety *grandiflora* has larger flowers which are likely to be more abundant than in other forms. Shortias require careful attention to detail in culture, even in the cool conditions of Scotland.

Ericaceae

Andromeda   *A. polifolia* (Fig.204) is a northern circumpolar species adapted to tundra and moist acidic conditions. Like so many of such species it also turns up on mountains further south, as in Japan, and also occurs locally in Britain on upland, peaty moors. It is a small evergreen with tough, linear or oblong pointed leaves. The flowers are in terminal umbels of 2-8. The five petals are fused to form a short lobed corolla which is typically pale pink, with a reddish calyx. There are a number of cultivars which differ in size, growth form and corolla colour.

Arcterica   There is only one species in this genus, *A. nana* which is a very small, creeping, evergreen shrub which forms mats or cushions. The leaves occur in whorls of three near the stem tips. The flowering stems of a few cm carry terminal clusters of several, pendant, scented white flowers. It is to be found on rocky, alpine sites in north and central Japan, the Kuriles and also Kamchatka. This is an excellent but slow growing species for the peat bed or its politically correct equivalent, provided it is not overgrown by moss. It offers the bonus of crimson autumn foliage.

Arctostaphylos   *A. alpina* is another mat-forming shrub, which, however, is deciduous. The oblong to lanceolate leaves are bright green in summer and finely toothed at the margin. The small clusters of pendulous white or pink tinted urn-shaped flowers arise in the leaf axils. In autumn the leaves turn a brilliant crimson and add their quota to the transformation of the Japanese moorlands at that season.

Cassiope   *C. lycopodioides* (Fig.205) is also a prostrate shrub which constructs a mat of inter-locking branchlets clothed in tiny appressed leaves. The charming, bell-shaped flowers are white to cream with green, red-tipped sepals. It is a plant of peaty sites from northern Japan and Alaska. Among the several geographical races var. *globularis* has more rounded flowers and var. *gracilis* is an attractive dwarf form, both Japanese.

Gaultheria   *G. adenothrix* (Fig.206) is an evergreen shrub which forms a low-growing bush some 15cm high with rather ovoid leaves. The solitary, urn shaped pendant flowers are white, but set off by the bright red calyx. They are succeeded by even brighter red berries. In the garden they need the usual treatment for ericas.

Ledum   *L. palustre* is a fairly large, evergreen, aromatic shrub which can grow to about one metre. The more or less linear leaves with recurved margins are dark green on the upper side but rust coloured below. The white flowers are produced in terminal clusters. The typical form has a wide circumpolar distribution including Japan, Sakhalin, the Kuriles, Korea, Siberia and beyond. There are a number of regional varieties one of which occurs at one or two sites in Scotland. The plants concerned belong to the sub-species *groenlandicum* and there is little doubt that they are introduced.

Menziesia   This is a small genus of dwarf shrubs from Japan, eastern Asia and North America. The best known species is *M. ciliicalyx* which grows as an erect shrub to 60cm or more in the wild. The hairy leaves are ovate to oblong. The several bell-shaped flowers, borne in terminal umbels, are yellow or greenish-yellow, tipped with purple. This is a montane endemic from Honshu. The variety *purpurea* has light purple flowers. There are several dwarf forms including 'Buchanan's Dwarf'. *M. pentandra* can grow to one metre or more. The narrowly elliptic leaves are green above and hairy, paler below. The nodding, small, urn-shaped flowers are whitish. It occurs above the tree line in Japan and is another of the autumn glories since its leaves turn to gold and flame before they fall. Both these species thrive in peaty conditions.

Phyllodoce   This is another small genus of low-growing evergreen shrubs of northern or circumpolar distribution. They are distinguished by hard, narrow, needle-like leaves and terminal umbels of pendulous flowers. *P. aleutica* (Fig.207), from Japan, Sakhalin, the Kuriles, Kamchatka and the Aleutian Islands has the typical low-growing habit of 10-30 cm, with urn-shaped groups of flowers which are greenish, yellow or white. *P. caerulea* is a circumpolar species which extends into north temperate mountains. It occurs at one site in Scotland and is a member of the moorland flora of Japan. We have met it before in the account of North American species. In spite of its name the flowers are not blue but purple or pink and only turn blue when dried. *P. nipponica* is smaller in stature, 10-20cm with white or pinkish flowers. It is confined to the Japanese alpine zone.

Rhododendron There are about 40 species of this genus in Japan of which only a few of the smaller ones can be noted here. *R. aureum* (Fig.208) grows to about one metre with comparatively small, more or less ovate leaves. The three centimetre flowers are broadly bell-shaped and yellow with interior spotting. At the highest elevations the shrub may be quite prostrate. The distribution is wide – Japan, Korea, northern China and eastern Russia. *R. camtschaticum* (Fig.209) is a low-growing, often prostrate, deciduous species with upright flower stems of 15cm or less. The hairy, bell shaped flowers are rosy-purple or occasionally white. This is an upland species from Japan, Alaska and the neighbouring region of Russia. The foliage contributes to the autumn colour by turning to shades of yellow, orange and red. *R. dauricum* (Fig.210) is a rather straggling shrub which can grow to 1.5m but includes smaller forms of value. Typically it is semi-deciduous with pink or violet-pink flowers and occurs in Japan, China, Mongolia and eastern Siberia. It is notable for flowering in winter or early spring. It is a complex rather than a single species and has been split into three taxa, largely according to the colour and scaliness of the leaves, and these have given rise to a series of cultivars like 'Arctic Pearl' and 'Hokkaido', the winter flowering semi-evergreen 'Midwinter' and the dwarf 'Nanum'. *R. keiskei* (Fig.211), another native of Japan, can become far too big for the rock garden but there are dwarf forms which are quite acceptable. They have dark green, scaly leaves and pale yellow funnel-shaped flowers. 'Yaku Fairy' is a desirable mat forming variety with groups of several bright yellow flowers. *R. kiusianum* grows nearly to a metre with semi-deciduous, rusty coloured leaves. The flowers are rose pink or, less often, purple. This Japanese species is quite famous in the history of cultivated rhododendrons since both the Kurume Azaleas and the Obtusum cultivars owe their origin to hybridisation between this species and *R. kaempferi*. *R. degronianum* ssp. *yakushimanum*, often called *R. yakushimanum*, has been among the most widely grown dwarf rhododendrons since its introduction from Yakushima Island, southern Japan in the 1930s. It has been the most popular plant for breeding in recent years and there are now hundreds of 'Yak' hybrids. It is a hardy free flowering species.

Fumariaceae
Dicentra This is a small genus of herbaceous perennials with representatives in North America, the Himalayas, Siberia and Japan. The most desirable Japanese species is the frustratingly difficult but small and beautiful *D. peregrina* (Fig.214) which grows to about 10cm. The outline of the basal, stalked leaves is triangular but the blade is finely divided into narrow segments. The four-petalled flowers are heart-shaped; the outer two petals have spurs at their base and are pouched. Their colour is purplish-rose or pink, occasionally white as in the form 'Alba', and they are carried in pendant racemes of 2-3 flowers. It has the wide distribution characteristic of

the genus but is not recorded from the Himalayas. In Japan it favours volcanic scree where it encounters little competition from other species. Although it is difficult to grow successfully in Scotland it is an easy plant in Japan where it is kept in window boxes or grown even in garage forecourts in a soil mixture which contains 50% ground pumice.

Gentianaceae
Gentiana   G. *algida* is the alpine gentian we have met before with the immense distribution from Alaska, China, the Himalayas, Korea, Hokkaido, Sakhalin and the Kuriles. G. *triflora* (Fig.212) is a slender, branched leafy plant which grows erect to 60cm but is usually less. The lanceolate leaves have three veins. The flowers, carried in spikes from the axils of the upper leaves, are narrowly bell-shaped, deep or purple blue, usually with white bands on the outside of the corolla. It occurs in both lowland and upland sites in Japan, Sakhalin, Korea and eastern Siberia. There is a subspecies *montana* which is smaller overall.

Glaucidiaceae
Glaucidium   This is a genus with only a single species, G. *palmatum* (Fig.213), from the mountain forests of Japan. Spreading by rhizomes it sends up erect stems of about 20cm topped by a pair of maple-like leaves. The solitary, terminal flower of some 8cm across consists of four, broad pale to darker lilac or even white sepals surrounding a mass of stamens. As a woodland species it delights in well drained, humus-rich soil. It may be readily grown outside in a sheltered site. Seed should be sown as soon as ripe.

Papaveraceae
Corydalis   This genus is growing in popularity although some of them need special care. *C. fumariifolia*, a variable species, has a wide distribution which includes China, Japan, Kamchatka, Sakhalin and the Kuriles. The flowers, in racemes, are described as softly blue to muddy pink in the Encyclopaedia of Alpines but when they are of the soft blue form they are wholly delightful.

Hylomecon   There is only one species *H. japonicum* (Fig.215), from Japan, Korea and east China. It forms herbaceous clumps to about 30cm. The mostly basal leaves are pinnate with several pairs of broadly lanceolate toothed leaflets. The stalked and erect solitary flowers have four yellow or orange tinted petals and many yellow stamens. This is an easily grown woodland species which requires well drained, humus-rich soil and some degree of shade. Seed should be sown as soon as ripe.

Primulaceae
Primula   The obovate to cuneate leaves of *P. cuneifolia* (Section Cuneifolia) are rather fleshy, dentate and narrow basally into a stalk. The relatively large flowers are rose-purple with a yellow eye, rarely white, and carried in umbels

on 10-15cm stems. This species occurs in wet meadows, often by the coast, in Japan, Siberia and thence into Alaska and British Columbia. It is not too difficult in cultivation, given a rich soil, which is never allowed to dry out, and plenty light although it does tend to be short lived. *P. japonica* (Fig.216) is too familiar to require comment. In *P. modesta* (Section Cuneifolia) the more or less elliptic leaves taper into long winged petioles and are provided with yellow meal on the lower surface. The peduncles of varying height, 3-13cm, bear umbels of several pink flowers. This is a native of Japanese mountains and sea cliffs. The variety *fauriae* is smaller. *P. sieboldii* (Section Cortusoides) (Fig.217) is to be found in wet meadows in Japan and north east China. It spreads by rhizomes and dies down completely at the end of summer. The flowering stems rise to 15-40cm and carry up to 10 white, pink or purple flowers with a white eye. As might be expected it grows best in well drained, moist, humus-rich soil. It has been grown in Japan since the latter part of the 17th century and reached a peak of popularity between 1780 and about 1850. A great many forms were selected from wild populations and, though it is hard to credit, up to 3000 varieties were in cultivation (Kuyama, 1989). Of course most of these have vanished but shows and competitions devoted to this species have continued since 1804. *P. takedana* (Section Reinii) (Fig.218) is a Japanese endemic of mountain meadows. The rounded leaves are basally cordate, lobed, toothed and hairy. The few flowered umbels grow to 15cm, but generally less, with white bell to funnel-shaped flowers with oblong lobes. *P. yuparensis* (Section Farinosae) has lanceolate to elliptic leaves which narrow basally into a winged petiole and are provided when young with white meal on the lower surface. The two or three purple flowers are carried on a 5cm stipe. It occurs in Japan in upland meadows.

Lysimachia *L. japonica* is a mat forming 'Creeping Jenny' with broad ovate leaves with long petioles. From the leaf axils arise the 1cm peduncles carrying the solitary yellow flowers. The distribution includes Japan, Taiwan, China and Malaysia. There is a very dwarf form, *minutissima*.

Ranunculaceae
Adonis *A. amurensis* (Fig.219) is a perennial herb which grows to a height of 15-25cm with divided stem leaves with long petioles. The flowers are 3-4cm in diameter with lilac sepals and numerous yellow petals which are bronze coloured on the exterior. It flowers very early in late winter or early spring. It occurs in Japan, Korea, China and eastern Siberia. Although the petal colour is normally yellow there are several alternatives such as orange, green and white, as well as doubles. This was also a Japanese florist's plant. In the middle of the nineteenth century more than 160 varieties were grown.

Aquilegia *A. flabellata* is an interesting species. It is a native of the mountains of Japan, Sakhalin, the Kuriles and Korea. According to the Encyclopaedia of Alpines the plants in cultivation are probably descended from the dwarf variety *A. f.* var. *pumila* (Fig.220), while the status of the tall, typical form is obscure. The cultivated plant with blue-purple sepals and yellow to white petals is a first class rock garden plant. There is also a white form, 'Alba'.

Thalictrum *T. kiusianum* spreads by rhizomes to form small colonies which grow to about 15cm in height. The leaves are generally biternate with lobed or toothed leaflets. The flowers are in small racemes with purple or white sepals and protruding lilac stamens. It is a mountain species confined to Japan.

Rosaceae
Geum *G. pentapetalum* is a high moorland plant, generally from above 1500m in Japan. It occurs also in Sakhalin, the Kuriles, Kamchatka and the Aleutians. It is of sub-shrubby habit, forming mats of deep green, shiny, divided leaves which turn a brilliant crimson in autumn. The solitary, cup-shaped flowers on short stalks are succeeded by feathery seed-heads. Although considered not too easy to establish it makes an excellent plant for peaty conditions or the like.

Saxifragaceae
Astilbe A few of the smaller species of this genus, which has representatives in eastern North America and eastern Asia, are suited to the rock garden, where their rhizomes are most at home in moist, well-drained, humus-rich conditions like so many of the Japanese upland plants. The tiny 4-5 petalled flowers are arranged in upright, branching panicles which have a feathery appearance in the smaller species. *A. microphylla*, from mountain meadows in Japan, grows to about 30cm with a mass of divided leaves. The inflorescence of pink or white flowers stands clear of the foliage. *A. simplicifolia* (Fig.221), an endemic from Honshu, can grow to as tall as 40cm but is generally less. The narrow inflorescence bears many small white flowers. It has long been prized for a cool, moist spot in the rock garden and has been used in hybridisation to produce a great many cultivars.

Saxifraga *S. fortunei* has large, basal, approximately round, rather fleshy, petiolate leaves with marginal waves, coloured attractively red-brown on the under side. The inflorescence, which appears in autumn, may reach 50cm in exceptionally well grown specimens. It comprises a panicle of narrow-petalled white flowers, hanging from reddish pedicels. This species is to be found in sheltered, upland sites in Japan, China and Korea where it has given rise to several geographical races. Some cultivars like 'Rubrifolia' and 'Wada' have attractive red foliage.

Scrophulariaceae
Penellianthus This genus has been recently defined to include what was formerly called *Penstemon frutescens* – the specific name has been retained - which was always a subject of curiosity since it was the only non-North American representative of *Penstemon*. A native of Japan and eastern Russia,

it is found in exposed, rocky sites where it spreads by rhizomes to form mats from which arise the short scapes bearing the 2.5cm long, pale mauve flowers, flushed purple with darker lines and markings. The whole flower is covered with hairs.

Valerianaceae
Patrinia This is a small genus with representatives across temperate Asia, including Japan. The mostly basal leaves are pinnate or lobed. The inflorescence is made up of many small flowers gathered into heads which may be compact or looser. In the commonly grown *P. gibbosa* the stems grow about 20cm tall and the flower heads are flattened and yellow. *P. triloba* is larger, growing to about 60cm, with more golden tinted, fragrant flowers. The cultivated var. *palmata* is barely distinguishable from the type.

Violaceae
Viola *V. dissecta* forms small colonies of 5-12cm. The leaves are palmately divided into five deeply toothed lobes. The flowers are white with purple veins. It occurs in the mountain forests of Japan. *V. grypoceras* is like a larger version of our own *V. canina*. *V. keiskei*, a mountain species from Japan and Korea, has white flowers with purple veins on the lower petals. *V. mandschurica* is to be found in fields in Japan, the Kuriles, China and Korea. Here the leaves vary from triangular to ovate with bluntly toothed margins. The flowers are usually deep purple, but forms occur in which they are white with purple veins. *V. verecunda* grows to 10-20cm. The leaves are more or less kidney-shaped and the flowers are white with purple veins on the lower petals. It has a wide distribution which includes Japan, Sakhalin, the Kuriles, Taiwan, China and Korea. There are several geographical races including dwarf forms like var. *fibrillosa* and the even smaller var. *yakusimana*, from high altitudes in Yakushima. It must be in the running for the smallest violet since the leaves are only about 5mm long and the flowers barely 1cm across. *V. yedoensis* is a lowland species with purple flowers from Japan, China and Korea.

Monocots
Araceae
Arisaema Not so long ago it would have seemed a little odd to include arisaemas among rock garden plants. But fashions change. About 16 species now appear in the Club seed list so we can hardly ignore them. *A. amurense* ssp. *robustum*, as its name suggests, is a hardy plant from Japan, Sakhalin, Korea, northern China and eastern Siberia. It grows to some 45cm. The 10cm spathe is pale green with a purple margin and may also be decorated with white stripes or be entirely purple in var. *atropurpurea*. In the woodland species *A. japonicum* (Fig.222), the spathe, carried well above the usual pair of divided leaves, is purple with white stripes. It is from montane forests in

Japan. *A. ringens* grows to about 30cm, with a short spathe of 3-4cm, which varies in colour and may be green or purple with white stripes or just pale green, topped by a helmet of similar shade. The rather dramatic *A. sikokianum* grows to 50cm with a 15cm spathe which is purple or brown, set off by the stout, white spadix sticking out of the spathe opening and by the terminal blade, which is suffused with greenish tints. This is a hardy species from Japan.

Iridaceae
Iris *I. gracilipes* is an Evansia Iris of the Section Lophiris. It forms clumps, 10-25cm high, with narrow grass-like leaves. The notched flowers are lilac-blue with a white central patch and a yellow and white crest. A native of Japan and China, it is an attractive, hardy species for a moist, humus-rich site and can be readily increased by division. *I. japonica*, from Japan and northern China, belongs to the same Section. The branched stems grow to 30-45cm or more and carry loose racemes of many delicate, short lived flowers which are lilac to pale lavender, with an orange, white-headed crest ringed by purple spots, although there is the usual variation. The standards are about equal in length to the falls. *I. tectorum* is very similar to *I. japonica* except that the leaves produced in spring do not persist through the winter and the flowers are bright lilac with finely serrated white and blue crests and more rounded falls. Although a native of south west China it wins inclusion here because it is widely grown in Japan on straw thatched roofs. There is a pure white form, 'Alba'. *I. setosa* is one of those species with an immense distribution from Japan to North America. It has already been noted in the section on North America.

Liliaceae
Polygonatum *P. humile* generally grows to about 15cm or over with one or two flowers on long stalks, of a pale yellow to green colour. It has a wide distribution from Siberia, northern China, Korea to Japan. It is a useful peat bed species. The much taller *P. falcatum* often appears under the invalid horticultural name of *P. pumilium*. *P. odoratum*, from China, Korea and Japan, grows about twice as high as *P. humile*, with an angled stem and alternate leaves. The scented, white, green-tipped flowers occur alone or in pairs. There are several varieties which differ in size from the type and with minor differences between the leaves.

Tricyrtis This is a small genus with an eastern distribution in which most of the species are too big for the rock garden. They spread by rhizomes. The leaves are usually attached to the stem and ovate or lanceolate in shape. The inflorescence is terminal or arises from the upper leaf axils with six tepals to the corolla. *T. hirta* is hairy and grows to about 80cm with heart-shaped leaves which clasp the stem. The flowers are white with purple spots. It a native of Japan. It is sometimes confused in the trade with the Chinese *T.*

macropoda which is less often hairy while the flowers are between white and purple with smaller purple spots. *T. hirta* has given rise to a number of attractive cultivars. In *T. latifolia* the stem is erect and hairy and varies between 40 and 90cm in height although in cultivation it is likely to be at the lower end of the range. The leaves clasp the stem and the flowers are yellow or with a greenish tinge with purple spots. It occurs in both Japan and China. *T. macrantha* can grow to 90cm, with amplexicaul, clasping leaves and pendulous, yellow flowers with brown spots inside the corolla

§ CHAPTER 11 §

New Zealand and Australia

New Zealand
The New Zealand flora is remarkable on several counts. About half of the nearly 1000 species which can be broadly classed as alpine or sub-alpine occur between 1000 and 2150m with a handful ascending above 2500m. Since only about 10% are found in North Island it is the larger South Island which excites the interest of rock gardeners. To quote from a perceptive article in the Club Journal by Jack Drake (1972): "To appreciate the New Zealand alpines one must free oneself entirely from the mental picture of the alpine plants of Europe, for they are entirely different." The most obvious difference lies in the predominantly white flower colour, which means that attention is more focused on the endless diversity of habit, foliage and fruit. Many species develop mounds or cushions which may be spiky or hard enough to stand on, velvety or woolly, while the colour ranges from silver or white through grey, gold, copper and all shades of green with all manner of subtle combinations. The larger herbs and dwarf shrubs, some with needle-like spines, similarly vary in foliage colour. Many of the low growing species produce brilliant berry-like fruits which may be white, various shades of blue, pink, bright orange or crimson, making the point that the whiteness of their flowers does not lie in any lack of capacity to produce pigments. About 97% of this alpine flora is endemic and quite often the distribution of species and /or sub-species is quite local. A number of genera, which are predominantly from New Zealand, also have representatives in Australia, especially Tasmania, as well as South Africa and South America. As we have already noted, such a disjunct distribution of species of the same genus has been related to an ancestral home in the old land mass of Gondwanaland before tectonic plate action led to its break-up. But we must also remember that winds are a likely vehicle of airborne seeds, from Australia on westerlies and from elsewhere, resulting in sporadic colonisation followed by adaptive radiation, as in other oceanic islands like Hawaii. Other, endemic genera may have evolved in New Zealand and be of great age.

The mountain ranges of New Zealand are of recent origin. It is believed that the present topography began to take shape about 20 million years ago and that the alpine landscape was formed within the last two million years, so these are some of the youngest mountains to be found anywhere. The endemic species which extend into the alpine zone probably evolved during this period of mountain formation from a pre-existing lowland flora. Glaciation, followed by on-going erosion by water, ice, frost and wind, have been the major, recent factors in sculpting the forms and shapes of the Southern Alps and determining the distribution of the alpine flora. The rocks which make up the

New Zealand mountains fall into several major categories. Metamorphosed sedimentary rock known as greywacke accounts for the non-volcanic mountains in North Island which are continued in South Island along the Southern Alps to north Otago where the greywacke merges with more highly metamorphosed schist which stretches eastward. The mountains of Fiordland and Stewart Island in the south are mostly ancient, durable gneiss and granite. Greywacke is very susceptible to frost shattering and erosion which result in the formation of the unstable scree slopes which are home to a specialised flora. In North Island the highest mountains are volcanic, some still active and here, of course, the topography is very recent and the flora depauperate. It is interesting that botanists have concluded that the chemical nature of the rocks has little effect on the the distribution of particular species of plant, except for north west and south west South Island where the marble and limestone formations are associated with a more distinct flora.

The most important environmental feature of South Island is the difference in rainfall between the west and the east sides of the Main Divide. The west coast, facing the prevailing winds, is very wet with a luxuriant vegetation. In the rain shadow, east of the Divide the rainfall may be only a tenth of that on the western side. Most of the rock garden plants in cultivation have come from the eastern side. A number of more or less well defined plant associations have been recognised. As might be expected their precise altitudinal limits vary with latitude and local conditions. According to Mark (1995), in the approximately 1000m of elevation between the tree and the permanent snow line, New Zealand displays a greater range of types of vegetation than in most other alpine regions. Tall snow tussock grass, mostly of the genus *Chionochloa*, extends about 500m above the tree line. This grass forms clumps and does not fuse to form an alpine sward, leaving space and shelter between plants for a wide variety of species. Above the tussock zone four categories have been recognised. Fellfield occurs where the rocks are fairly stable and the density of plants is low but they are very diverse, with many cushion and mat-forming species, especially on non-volcanic rocks. Scree refers to loose talus, often very extensive on the eastern slopes and known locally as 'shingle slips'. This habitat supports some two dozen species, belonging to different families, which are highly adapted to this rigorous environment, where the stones may be too hot to handle when the sun shines and yet, a few centimetres below, the roots are in contact with ice-cold water trickling down from the melted snow. Most observers comment on how closely the colour of these shingle slip plants resembles that of the grey-green stones among which they grow. Screes vary from mobile to comparatively stable, and often species show a preference in such respects. Cushionfield refers to the association of plants which occupy windswept plateaux on mountains, especially in central South Island. Finally we have the Snowbank habitat where the snow persists well into the growing season.

There is good evidence that a number of the major New Zealand genera as *Celmisia*, *Hebe* and *Aciphylla* are in a state of on-going evolution. Hybridisation is frequent. Where several species of the same genus grow in the same area this can lead to taxonomic confusion since there may be many intermediate forms linking the 'species'. Even groups distinct enough to merit generic distinction may hybridise. Such a situation is most likely a consequence of the rapid erosion and climatic changes encountered by colonists of mountainous regions in which glacial action had exterminated vascular plants over a large area, as in central South Island, and where post-glacial habitats are inherently unstable. The perennial query about the prevalent white colour of New Zealand flowers has been answered in recent years. To put the issue in perspective, Godley (1979) has noted that 61% of the New Zealand flora is white, compared with 48% for Tierra del Fuego and 25% for the British flora. But, more significantly, 78% of the New Zealand mountain flowers are white compared with only 37% for the coastal lowlands, whereas in South America there is no such difference in frequency between mountain and lowland species. The white colour is a special feature of the alpine habitat in New Zealand. Richards (1995) has reviewed the evidence and concluded that the explanation lies in the nature of the pollinating insects. Typically the New Zealand alpine flowers have a bowl-shaped form which, by reflectance of the sun's rays especially from a white surface, creates at the centre of the corolla a warm spot — the so-called solar furnace which is attractive to insects, especially flies. As in other oceanic islands, New Zealand has an unrepresentative insect fauna which, in this case, lacks the presence of indigenous social bees, which gather both pollen and nectar and which are major pollinators elsewhere. There are social bees, but these have biting-mouthparts suited for collecting pollen only. Thus the alpine flora has to rely for pollination on visits from a wide variety of insects with unspecialised mouth parts. When insect visitors are scarce, as on a cold and windy mountain, it is an advantage for different species of plants to share a common advertisement of where insects can find both food and a warm place to rest. White colour appears to meet that need particularly well.

Before noting the more important rock garden species it is worth inserting a tip from an expert grower (Booker, 1995), to the effect that seedlings of New Zealand species do not relish a British winter and that everything other than composites should be sown during December and January, to allow temperature changes to break dormancy and initiate germination the following spring. Hence it may be necessary to store seed in the refrigerator until the right time has arrived. Seed of Composites like *Celmisia*, *Craspedia* and *Leucogenes* will only germinate well if sown fresh, so they should be sown as soon as possible. The seed trays should be exposed to light and air, with careful watering, while young seedlings should be protected in a frame or glasshouse from November to spring.

We consider now some of the more important alpine plants.

Dicots
Apiaceae
Aciphylla This genus comprises some three dozen species of which all but two from Australia commonly occur in the New Zealand sub-alpine and grassland zones up to 1900m. They display a range of form from the primitive, with typical umbels of flowers and non-spiny habit, to the specialised with tough, rosettes of hard leaves which are divided into fiercely spiny segments which must be approached with caution. They are commonly given the name of 'Spaniard' or, far more appropriately, 'Speargrass'. The plants are unisexual and, in larger species, the flowers are arranged in imposing golden-yellow, orange, brown or even darker coloured spikes. Most of them, like *A. colensoi, ferox, horrida* and *scott-thomsonii*, which produce formidable tussocks and imposing spikes, are too big for other than the large rock garden where they can make dramatic specimen plants. People tend to be either attracted to or repelled by aciphyllas. It has been suggested that even those who do not like them may find a use for the smaller species as an insurance against cat damage when planted among choicer alpines. But for those who like to grow the smaller species in the scree or on raised beds several are worth noting. *A. aurea* (Fig.231), the Golden Spaniard, from the tussock grassland of South Island can grow to a metre. The sharp leaf segments are edged with gold and the male inflorescence is also golden. *A. monroi*, from the northern mountains of South Island, is of more acceptable size. It is a small tufted plant with the usual, sharp pointed leaves and 30cm scapes which carry the golden-yellow inflorescence. *A. pinnatifida* is rather a curiosity. It is a creeping, stoloniferous species with prostrate leaves which are divided into many pairs of parallel linear segments, which have been likened to a fish skeleton. *A. spedenii* is suitable for the scree or raised bed. It produces rosettes of stiff, pointed leaves with a fan-like arrangement of the leaf segments. It is an alpine species from South Island. *A. squarrosa*, the Common Speargrass, has black, rigid leaves. The flower stalk, from 60–200cm, carries sweetly scented, yellow flowers in racemes of small umbels. *A. subflabellata*, from south east South Island, is rather similar but the leaves are more brown or grey in colour.

Asteraceae
Celmisia There are some 70 species in this genus, a few in Australia and the rest in New Zealand where they comprise a major feature of the alpine communities. Indeed, they are to be encountered in every ecological situation other than standing water. They are easily recognised by their white, daisy-like flowers. Although they conform to a common structure their habit, stature and leaf shape display great variety. The leaves are entire, sometimes dentate and often appear white on either the lower or both sides due to a coating of closely packed hairs which often create a brilliant, silvery effect. They are self-sterile and hybridise readily. In the wild as many as ten different species

may grow side by side to produce a swarm of hybrids and a taxonomic headache. They are generally easily grown in well drained soil, provided it does not dry out, is not too rich or of high pH. The genus includes a number of excellent rock-garden species. So many have been introduced that we can notice only a few which illustrate different types of growth. *C. alpina* is a small, tufted species from the boggy sites in the mountains of South Island, found between 600 and 1600m, with very narrow, sharp pointed leaves and solitary white flowers. It is not easily grown. *C. angustifolia* (Fig.223) is a small, graceful, woody shrub in which the lower branches are clothed with dead leaves and produce the new leaves at their tips. The aromatic leaves are leathery and strap-like with white hairs on the underside. The 2-4cm flowers are carried on 15cm, sticky scapes. It occurs in grasslands and rocky places from Arthur's Pass to the Humboldt Mountains in South Island. *C. argentea* forms dense, silvery cushions with almost stemless flowers. When grown in a trough it is most attractive when young since it tends to die back when older. *C. bellidioides* creeps and branches forming roots as it grows, to form a wide, green mat from which the short stalked flower heads arise. It makes a fine trough or pan plant which needs to be kept moist, as might be expected from its preference for water inundated gravel and wet rocks in South Island. *C. coriacea*, the large mountain daisy, more correctly known as *C. semicordata* (Fig.225), is a robust, tufted plant with more or less silvery leaves when young, turning dark green when older and growing up to 60cm. The large flowers are borne on, fluffy, woolly scapes up to 40cm or more. This is the largest of the celmisias, found in alpine and sub-alpine fellfields and grasslands throughout South Island. *C. gracilenta* belongs to a group of species with narrow, linear leaves. In this species they taper from the base and the margins are rolled back almost to the midrib. The flowers are on slender stalks which may grow to 40 cm but are usually less. It occurs widely in different habitats from Coromandel in North Island southwards to Stewart Island. *C. hectori* ascends to 2000m. It is a many-branched, low shrub which can reach one metre across. The branches produce rosettes of leathery leaves the upper surface of which is covered with scale-like, brilliant white hairs while the lower surface is covered with satiny-white hairs. A single 2-2.5cm flower grows from each rosette. It is found from Arthur's Pass southward in South Island. In *C. hookeri* (Fig.224), a plant of lower elevations in South Island, the undersides of the tough leaves are densely woolly but its chief distinction lies in the vary large flowers which may be up to 10cm in diameter. *C. sessiliflora* (Fig.226) is a branched sub-shrub with overlapping, thick leaves which forms irregular cushions of loose rosettes which may spread across a metre in the wild. The almost sessile flowers arise from the tips of the rosettes. It is found in the mountains of South Island up to 1800m in damp sites among short snow-tussock or herbfield. *C. spectabilis* is a short tufted herb with the usual leathery leaves which are shiny on the upper surface and felted with buff or whitish hairs on the lower side The flowers are carried singly on white, woolly stalks of 8-25cm. This is a variable and easily grown species. It is the most widespread of the celmisias, occurring commonly in the mountains of both Islands in a great variety of habitats. *C. traversii* is a large and handsome species with large flowers. The underside of the leaves and the leaf margins are densely clothed with rich brown velvety hairs, except for the purple midrib, hence the common name of Brown Mountain Daisy. It has an odd distribution since it occurs in high rainfall areas both in the north west and the south west of South Island and not in-between. The plant sold under this name is a hybrid of uncertain origin.

Cotula The cotulas are known for their button-like heads made up of many tiny tubular flowers. The smaller ones make attractive subjects for the rock garden although some like the aromatic *C. pectinata* and *C. pyrethrifolia* as well as *C. squalida* may be invasive. *C. potentillina* forms mats of creeping stems with one cm yellow heads. It is found in moist sites on the Chatham Islands. Undoubtedly the most striking and desirable species is *C. atrata*, commonly called the black daisy. This is a true member of the eastern screes of South Island, found between 1250 and 2000m. The branching stems creep among the stones and turn up at the ends to support a cluster of thick, fleshy, pinnatifid leaves which are often coloured with a bronzy pink tint like the colour of the stones among which they grow. The florets of the two centimetre flower heads, on short stalks, may be either black-purple or brown in colour, contrasting with the bright yellow stamens. There is also a variety called *dendyi* in which the flower heads are much lighter, more yellowish in colour.

Craspedia This is a small genus from New Zealand and Australia. The species form basal rosettes from which rise solitary flower heads made up of many small tubular florets. *C. incana* grows to a maximum of about 30cm with white, densely woolly leaves and white or yellow flower heads. Height, leaf shape, hairiness and also size of flower head vary in the wild. It is a plant of the greywacke screes of South Island. *C. uniflora* has soft leaves with white hairs on their margins. The flower stalk of 15-35cm carries a single white to yellow globose head which may be up to three cm across. This species is widespread in both Islands in moist grassland and snow tussock or herbfield.

Haastia There are three species in this genus, all alpines confined to the mountains of New Zealand. They include *H. pulvinaris* (Fig.227), which rivals and sometimes exceeds *Raoulia* in the production of 'vegetable sheep'. From a central stem a large number of closely packed branches grow out to form the body of the cushion. Covered with hairy leaves, they form a hard surface. This species is to be found on stable screes on the eastern side of South Island, ascending to 2750m. Growth is extremely slow so large specimens are very old. Although they have a reputation for being impossible to grow, some growers have kept them going in the alpine house by paying scrupulous attention to watering and avoiding winter wet. The other two species of the genus, *H. recurva* and *H. sinclairii* are more normal, shrubby plants also found in the screes and rocky places of South Island.

Helichrysum   This large genus includes small plants of the 'everlasting' habit. *H. bellidioides* is prostrate, creeping and rooting as it goes to produce woolly branches to 60cm. The leaves are similarly woolly on their undersides. The yellow flower heads, one per stalk, are surrounded by a stiff collar of white bracts and are produced in profusion. It occurs throughout New Zealand from lowland to montane exposed, rocky sites and grassland. *H. microphyllum* produces small bushes, up to 20cm in cultivation, with closely, overlapping tiny, scale-like leaves, as the name suggests, and small yellow or brownish sessile flowers. It is recommended for the alpine house. *H. selago* is very similar, except that it has smaller, creamy white flowers. Both species are from South Island and both grow in crevices in rocky outcrops up to 1600m although *H. selago* is more widespread..

Leucogenes   This genus includes two alpine species in which the leaves are covered in silvery white wool, *L. leontopodium* (Fig.229) and *L. grandiceps* (Fig.228). The clustered yellow flowers are surrounded by a ring of many woolly, white leaves. Their general appearance recalls the European Edelweiss and so in New Zealand they are known as respectively the North and South Island Edelweiss although the former extends into the northern end of South Island. Both form mats. *L. leontopodium* has bigger leaves and flower heads than *L. grandiceps*. Both these mountain plants of rocky outcrops make excellent subjects for the trough or raised bed.

Raoulia   The species of this genus occur predominantly in New Zealand, although there are a few in New Guinea. They form mats or cushions packed with tiny simple leaves and generally small flower heads made up of tiny tubular florets. In some species the cushions can become immense (vegetable sheep) but there are a number of smaller species admirably suited to the raised bed or alpine house. *R. australis* is a densely compacted creeping herb which can form bronzy-green mats up to two metres wide in the wild. The tiny yellow flower heads are produced in profusion. It occurs in dry, gravelly sites in both Islands. *R. glabra* forms green prostrate patches of creeping and rooting growth. The creamy white flower heads are produced in abundance. It occurs in both lowland and sub-alpine, damp rocky places from Lake Taupo southwards. It is not reliably hardy outside. *R. haastii* spreads across stones and shingle to form hummocks and cushions which are bronze-green in winter and bright green in summer. This species is fully hardy and well suited to the scree. *R. hookeri* is the commonest species, found throughout New Zealand. It has a similar habit to *R. australis*, but is more grey-green in colour and the flowers occur at the tips of the little branches. There are two varieties, var. *albo-sericea* from North Island with white haired leaves and dark tips to the scales which surround the flower heads, and var. *apice-nigra*, from South Island in which the bracts are black tipped. *R. tenuicaulis* forms bright green mats which become silvery if the site is open and sunny. The fragrant, comparatively large flower heads are white. This hardy species, found in both Islands, deserves to be more widely grown. *R. eximia* (Fig.230), the common vegetable sheep, is a rather different proposition. It occurs in dry, greywacke scree in the mountains of Nelson, Marlborough and Canterbury, South Island. It grows extremely slowly to form tight cushions which may be 20-60cm high and up to 2m across. The smooth surface is made up of innumerable, tiny, densely packed, woolly leaves. Successful culture wins unqualified respect. *R. mammilaris* is very similar but does not generally become so big although it grows a good deal faster. The two species can often be found growing on the same terrain. Its culture poses similar problems to those of its relative.

Boraginaceae
Myosotis There are several New Zealand Forget-Me-Nots which can be easily grown. *M. australis* is an erect herb, growing to 15-40cm in tussock grassland and rocky places throughout the islands. The narrow leaves are hairy on both sides and the flowers are white or yellow. *M. colensoi* has a prostrate, creeping habit with lax branches up to 6cm and white flowers which may occur singly but more usually in short clusters. It is a rare species which occurs on limestone rocks in the vicinity of Canterbury. *M. explanata* is a neat, tufted herb up to 30cm in height with leaves covered in soft white hairs. The funnel-shaped white, or occasionally blue, fragrant flowers are grouped in short, terminal cymes. It is confined to rocks and stream sides in the vicinity of Arthur's Pass in South Island and is best grown in the alpine house.

Brassicaeae
Notothlaspi There are just two or perhaps three, species in this endemic genus and both belong to the specialised fraternity which inhabits the shingle slips of eastern South Island, although they prefer sites which are partially stabilised. *N. rosulatum* (Fig.233) is a fleshy herb with many overlapping olive-green to purplish, dentate leaves which form a compact rosette which may be 12cm across The central flower stalk, which may reach 25 cm, carries a head of fragrant white flowers. It is monocarpic, taking two years to develop the flowers after which it dies. This is popularly known as the penwiper plant, but since most people these days would not recognise a penwiper if they saw one the name has lost its descriptive value. *N. australe* (Fig.232), the mountain cress, produces fleshy rosettes which are entirely covered with fragrant white flowers borne on the usually branched stem. The deeply subterranean rootstock produces new rosettes of leaves over several years. This species often occurs in large colonies, often along with *N. rosulatum*. Both are suitable for the scree although the alpine house may be a safer place.

Campanulaceae
Lobelia *L. angulata* forms, spreading mats, with small orbicular leaves and small white flowers on short stalks, succeeded by purple-red berries. It prefers moist, humus rich conditions. There are several geographical races which

have been introduced e.g. var. *treadwellii* which is generally larger and can be invasive. *L. linnaeoides*, from the mountains of South Island, also forms mats, with orbicular leaves which are green above, tinted purple below and toothed toward their ends. The erect, solitary flowers are pale blue to white. It has a reputation for impermanence derived from its aversion to drought rather than lack of winter hardiness. *L. roughii* is quite different in its requirements since it is a member of the shingle slip flora. Growing to about 5-10cm, the stems and branches twist about between the stones to produce thick, leathery leaves with large, red-tipped teeth. The white or reddish flowers are borne on stout 5cm stalks. Although rare in cultivation, this bizarre little plant merits more attention.

Wahlenbergia This is a southern hemisphere genus with many species in South Africa, and Australia as well as New Zealand. They are related to *Edraianthus* but differ in having usually solitary flowers on long stalks. They are classified into three groups according to habit. In the group of long lived perennials with slender rhizomes *W. albomarginata*, known as the New Zealand bluebell, is a small, tufted herb with elliptic leaves usually with nearly smooth white margins. The 1-3cm nodding, white to lavender bells are borne singly on slender pedicels. It occurs especially on river terraces and in tussock grassland in South Island between 600 and 1550m. *W. congesta* is a lowland species which grows among sand dunes and along the west coast of South Island. It has a creeping habit, forming mats, with short flower stalks which carry a single, pale blue or white bell. It makes an excellent trough plant. *W. pygmaea*, unlike the other species noted, is a native of North Island from Lake Taupo southwards as well as South Island. It is rather like *W. albomarginata* but much smaller, growing only 1-3cm high, with wide open bell-shaped flowers, at least as wide as long. It displays a great deal of local variation which offers scope for selection of different forms. *W. matthewsii* belongs to a different group, with a sub-shrubby habit. It produces many leafy branches and often branched flower stalks which carry single, large, pale blue bells It occurs only on limestone on the Kaikoura coast and in Golden Bay, South Island. Given a lime enriched compost it is easily grown and will survive outside if the winter is mild; otherwise it can be grown in the frame or alpine house.

Epacridaceae

Cyathodes The members of this Australasian family resemble the South African heaths both in appearance and ecology. The New Zealand *C. colensoi*, well known in the UK, is a prostrate or weakly upright, branching shrub which may form open or dense hummocks up to 1m high and twice as much across. The leaves and branches are usually reddish, making it easy to spot at a distance, but they may also be bluish-green. The inflorescence is in the form of 2-5 flowered, terminal racemes. The small fruits may be white, pink or crimson. It occurs in fellfields, grasslands and rocky places.

Dracophyllum Of this Australasian genus 35 species occur in New Zealand, including about 18 mainly from the sub-alpine zone. They are commonly known as grass trees from the presence of numerous, narrow leaves which overlap at the base and make them easily mistaken for a monocot at first sight. They are not often seen in this country although a few growers, such as the Stones, have successfully grown a number of species. The small, cylindrical bell-shaped flowers are either solitary or in terminal spikes, racemes or panicles. They are plants with a rather exotic charm, very redolent of the New Zealand scene. They merit more attention since they appear be quite amenable to culture outside. *D. muscoides*, the smallest species, forms small moss-like mats with overlapping, stiff leaves and solitary, white flowers. It grows on exposed plateaux and well drained sites up to 2000m. *D. pronum* grows more loosely to form a trailing shrub up to 50cm in height and prefers fellfield and exposed ridges at high elevation..

Ericaceae
Gaultheria *G. antipoda* is a plant of the sub-alpine zone throughout New Zealand. It grows erect from 30 to 200cm, with branches which are clothed with black or yellowish bristles mixed with fine down. The thick, leathery leaves have bluntly toothed margins. The small red or white flowers are succeeded by bright capsular fruits which may be white, pink or deep red. *G. crassa* is a branched, rather untidy shrub which grows up to one metre in height but less at higher elevations, with lily-of-the-valley white flowers, set off with red-tipped sepals, followed by brown fruits. *G. depressa*, is a mat-forming species, with a preference for alpine herbfield, which produces a crop of large white, or rarely, red berries. It is like *G. antipoda* in bearing solitary flowers but differs in habit and distribution.

Gentianaceae
Gentiana There are several very attractive alpine gentians in New Zealand in which the flowers are solitary or in clusters. Several of them are easily grown although not long lived so, for a succession, one must rely on seed which is generally freely set. *G. bellidifolia* produces small tufts which grow to about 10cm, with many, mostly basal, rather fleshy leaves. The terminal cymes of 2-6 large, white, uptilted flowers are often decorated with fine purple veins. It prefers damp places in sub-alpine grassland where it is not uncommon in both North and South Island. There is a larger flowered, high alpine, attractive variety, *australis*, which is confined to South Island. *G. patula*, the alpine gentian, sometimes covers acres with a dazzling white display. It grows, rather laxly, to 20-50cm. The basal leaves are in a rosette from which arises the handsome spray of delicately veined, white or occasionally pink flowers It occurs in montane grassland. *G. saxosa* (Fig.235) forms 5cm high clumps of crowded, brownish-green leaves with shallow, white, upturned cups borne on wiry stems. This is not an alpine since it is

found along the coast in sand dunes and the like. It is easily grown. There are several other fine gentians which offer more of a challenge to the grower such as *G. serotina* (Fig.234) which is a good trough plant, or *G. corymbifera* which grows from 10 to 50cm tall with erect stems which are branched above to produce many large, white flowers. It is a plant of the drier tussock areas of South Island up to 1500m. It takes two or three years to flower after which it may die.

Geraniaceae
Geranium   There are not many geraniums in New Zealand but *G. sessiliflorum* wins a mention not only because it has become quite a popular rock garden plant but also on account of the interesting distribution of its sub-species which occur also in Australia, including Tasmania and South America from Peru to Tierra del Fuego. The New Zealand sub-species, *novaezelandii* has 5-7 lobed, orbicular, incised leaves which may be either green, or dark bronze coloured in the variety *nigricans*. Both sorts occur in the same natural populations, suggesting a simple polymorphism. The flowers are white or pink-purple. It occurs in lowland to sub-alpine grassland in both North and South Island.

Onagraceae
Epilobium   *E. crassum* is a small mat-forming species which occurs on screes to 1800m. The leaves are often red or purple on the lower side; the small pink or white flowers arise singly in leaf axils, followed by long erect capsules. *E. glabellum* is an alpine species, found in fellfields, in grassland and stony riverbeds where it forms wide patches. It has a tufted, shrubby habit and grows to about 30cm, with terminal spikes of several white or pink flowers which emerge from long buds. It occurs from East Cape southwards and is quite widely grown in the UK. One or two of the New Zealand epilobiums are now widespread weeds in the Northern Hemisphere. *E. pedunculare* commonly occurs at the edge of mountain streams in the UK and has spread to become a rock garden weed, albeit of quiet charm and no terrible propensities.

Ranunculaceae
Clematis   *C. marmoraria* (Fig.236) is a newcomer since it was discovered in the early 1970s growing in crevices in marble rock at 1450m in the Mt. Arthur Range of northern South Island. It is a small, non-climbing, evergreen shrub with a suckering habit, which grows to 10cm or less in height but spreads to form a low bush. The sexes are on separate plants. The clustered, cup-shaped, white flowers have a greenish tint and are larger and hence more showy in the males. It can be grown outside on the scree or raised bed or treated as a pan plant in the alpine house. It has been hybridised with *C. paniculata* and *C. petriei* to produce a variety of forms which tend to be more

vigorous and lack the restrained growth of *C. marmoraria*. As noted earlier, in 1983 the Taylors raised from a batch of *C. marmoraria* seed a splendid cultivar 'Joe' which consistently won prizes at the Shows from then onwards. The Youngs went a step further and crossed 'Joe' to what is commonly called *C. cartmannii* (*C. marmoria* x *C. paniculata*) to produce a compact, low-growing shrub which they named 'Craigton Comet'.

Ranunculus There are a number of fine alpine buttercups in New Zealand but not many of them have appeared in cultivation. Best known is *R. lyallii* (Fig.238), known as the 'Mount Cook Lily' but not confined to that region. The largest of its genus, it can reach a metre or more tall in the wild, with panicles of as many as 70 shining white flowers, although it is hardly likely to grow as big in cultivation. It needs moist, well drained, organically rich soil and patience since it may take several years to flower but is worth waiting for. The closely related white flowered *R. buchananii* (Fig.237), with which *R. lyallii* hybridises, has a more refined appearance but is more difficult to flower. But a real challenge is offered by *R. haastii*, which is a member of the shingle slip flora. It grows to about 15cm, with broad, fleshy, deeply divided, grey-green leaves, yellow flowers and long fine roots which reach down into the moist sandy soil below the scree. It is found between 1400 and 1850m in the mountains of Nelson and Canterbury. Although these species are notoriously difficult to keep some have succeeded. Thus *R. lyallii* is successfully grown in gardens such as Cluny while *R. haastii* was grown for many years at Inshriach. *R. crithmifolius*, a scree species, was successfully grown for years by Harold Esslemont who also grew *R. paucifolius* which was rescued from extinction in New Zealand only by careful 'gardening' in the wild and which survives in cultivation in a few nurseries such as Jim Sutherland's Ardfearn.

Rosaceae
Acaena Although this genus is best represented in New Zealand and Tasmania it has outliers as far away as California, Mexico, Central America and Hawaii. The cultivated species are creeping plants which make good ground cover where their invasive habits can be tolerated. The foliage of toothed leaflets is quite pleasing, especially when of a grey or bronzy tint, but their distinction lies in their globular flower heads and burr-like fruits which may be 2-3cm or more in diameter in some species and may range in colour from bright green or yellow to rusty or bright red or purple, according to species. Their hooked fruits make them very unpopular among New Zealand sheep farmers. There are many species but only a few can be noted. *A. buchananii* is a strong grower with yellow brown burrs. It includes a variety *picta* with crimson to purple burrs and another, *inermis*, which earns a mention since it lacks spines. *A. microphylla*, from the volcanic soils of North Island, produces bright red burrs which make vivid splashes of colour when the plant is in flower. *A. novae-zelandiae*, widespread in both Islands, the

flowering heads are large and globular with purple spines. Those looking for a more aristocratic and refined acaena might consider *A. glabra* which favours the margins of scree slopes from 600 to 1400m in South Island. The flower heads are purple green and the spines are without hooks.

Rubiaceae

Coprosoma There are 45 species of this genus in New Zealand, many of them inhabitants of sub-alpine and alpine scrub. They are very variable in habit. The sexes are generally separate and differ in appearance. They are chiefly noted for their brightly coloured fruits (drupes). Not all are hardy in the UK. 'Beatson's Gold', a hardy hybrid of uncertain origin, grows as a shrub to one metre or more, with bright red fruits. *C. cheesemanii* forms a sprawling, more or less prostrate shrub with globose fruits which are generally orange, but may also be white, yellow or red, according to locality. Several wild forms of different habit and fruit colour have been brought into cultivation. *C. petriei* is prostrate, rooting as it grows, to form large, dense mats. It occurs throughout New Zealand and has given rise to a number of local varieties with different coloured, shining fruits which may be greenish-white, green, pale blue, orange or red to purple in colour.

Scrophulariaceae

Hebe There are about 100 species of *Hebe* in New Zealand, generally inhabiting rocky outcrops, sometimes at high altitudes. The woody habit chiefly distinguishes this genus from *Veronica*. The species fall into two groups distinguished by whether they have normal leaves or belong to the whipcord type in which the small, scale-like leaves overlap, often very closely, in a manner reminiscent of *Lycopodium*. The inflorescence is generally that of a spike-like raceme, but in the whipcord group the flowers are solitary and borne in the axils of the leaves. Most often the flowers are white but there are also species in which they are magenta or pale blue. Many species have been introduced, hybridisation is widespread and hence the taxonomic status of many forms is in doubt. Many of the species are easily grown, given good drainage, although montane species used to winter snow cover may suffer from frost. They are generally easily propagated by cuttings although these do not strike so easily in the whipcord species. *H. albicans*, the Mount Arthur Hebe, is a densely branched, low-growing shrub, which can attain a metre but is generally much less, with sessile, blunt-ended leaves and dense spikes of little white flowers which arise in the leaf axils and bear purple anthers. There are several varieties and hybrids which differ in habit, the colour of the leaves and/or the flowers, such as 'Red Edge', with mauve flowers and red leaf margins, and 'Cranleigh Gem' with a dense, rounded habit. *H. amplexicaulis* is very similar but with more rounded leaf tips. *H. buchananii* is a shrub, growing to 20cm with thick, leathery, concave leaves and tight groups of sessile white flowers at the tips of the branches. It is a native of

South Island, from Mt. Cook southwards. *H.* x *'Carl Teschner'* is an attractive, violet flowered, mat-forming hybrid between *H. pimeleoides* and *H. elliptica* which arose in the Christchurch Botanic Garden. In *H. epacridea* the leathery, rigid leaves are arranged in four overlapping rows. They have thickened, reddish, partly hairy leaf margins. The closely related *H. haastii* is rather similar. Both are from South Island and both are suitable for a raised bed. *H. hectorii* is one of the whipcord types, growing to about 70cm, with closely appressed, scale-like leaves, each with a small, keeled tip and terminal spikes of few to a dozen or so white flowers. The variety *demissa* is smaller. Both occur in damp montane scrub and grassland in the vicinity of Canterbury and Otago. *H. hulkeana*, from rocky places, up to 900m, in the northern part of South island, forms a loosely branched shrub to 60cm. The numerous flowers are crowded in terminal spikes and of a white to lavender colour, earning it the title of 'New Zealand Lilac'. *H. lycopodioides* is a sub-alpine, whipcord species from South Island. It is a fine, erect, branching shrub growing up to one metre, in which the four-angled stem is closely covered in thick concave-convex leaves. The 3–12 white flowers occur in short, terminal spikes. As its name suggests it looks at first rather like a clubmoss. *H. pinguifolia*, from dry, rocky sites on the eastern side of South island, grows only to about 15cm. It has thick, shining broadly based leaves and crowded, sessile white flowers at the tips of the branches. It is variable, with a number of forms of which the best known is the hardy, mat-forming variety 'Pagei', with slightly concave, glaucous leaves. *H. rakaiensis*, from South Island, produces a rounded bush, with crowded, shiny green leaves. The white flowers are in dense racemes. Plants with this name are generally represented by the cultivar 'Golden Dome', which usually does not exceed 60cm in height but can spread laterally to form a wide dome, with rather yellowish leaves and short racemes. *H. raoulii* is a neat little shrub from the limestone Marlborough area of South Island. It and its variety *pentasepala* make easy and hardy trough plants. *H. vernicosa*, from the northern part of South Island, especially under Southern Beech trees, is semi-erect or prostrate. The small, deep green leaves, with twisted petioles, have a lustrous appearance. The heads of white flowers arise laterally towards the tips of the branches.

Ourisia This is another genus with the characteristically disjunct distribution often encountered in Antipodean genera since it has representatives in New Zealand, South America and one in Tasmania. *O. caespitosa* has a prostrate, branching habit, rooting at the nodes, to form thyme-like mats of bright green leaves.. The broadly lobed white flowers, with a yellow eye, are carried, generally in pairs, on hairless stalks up to 10cm. It occurs throughout New Zealand in damp, rocky places. The variety *gracilis* has slightly smaller flowers, one or two per scape. It is confined to South Island. This is easily grown provided it is provided with plenty of moisture. *O. macrophylla*, from North Island, also has a prostrate, rooting stem. The stout flower stalk, up to 60cm, carries at least one whorl of leaves below the first cluster of white flowers. There are regional varieties which differ in leaf size and shape. They all occupy damp sub-alpine sites. The pink cultivated form known as 'Loch Ewe' is a hybrid between *O. macrophylla* and the Chilean *O. coccinea* with scarlet flowers and is of intermediate flower colour. One is led to wonder how long ago they diverged from a common ancestor. The widely grown cultivar 'Snowflake' is a hybrid between *O. macrocarpa* and *O. caespitosa* which arose at the Inshriach Nursery. It closely resembles a naturally occurring form of probably similar parentage.

Parahebe This genus of some 30 species, spread between New Zealand, Australia and New Guinea, is closely related to *Hebe*. Many of the species are admirably suited to raised beds and walls and are easily grown. Consequently they are well represented in trade lists which include many hybrids. *P.* x *bidwillii* (*P. decora* x *P. lyallii*) is a naturally occurring hybrid with white flowers with radiating pink veins. *P. catarractae* is a variable, low, open-branched shrub with both prostrate and ascending stems. The numerous, attractive flowers, carried in racemes on long stalks, are white with a red basal ring and red veins. There are a number of forms and regional varieties. *P. c. diffusa* is more compact, with often red-edged leaves and pale pink flowers. *P.c.* ssp. *catarractae* is a robust form reaching 60cm, from Fiordland. *P. hookeriana* has a similar growth form to *P. catarractae* but with leathery leaves. The flowers, with a crimson base, are white or pale lavender. *P. linifolia* branches profusely from a woody base to form a sprawling mat or sometimes is more erect. The relatively large flowers, generally 2-4 per raceme, are white, pink or blue. It favours wet, rocky places in South Island. It is well known in cultivation. The vigorous variety 'Blue Skies' has violet-blue flowers with a yellow eye. *P. lyallii* is a prostrate, rooting shrub which forms small mats on wet rocks in South Island. The flowers, arranged in racemes, have the usual red eye and are faintly veined pink. There are several charming varieties in cultivation e.g. 'Clarence' and 'Mervyn'. It is an interesting observation that, although *P. lyallii* and *P. catarractae* thrive in wet places, if picked and put in water the corollas drop off almost immediately. But if kept in a plastic bag or left in the open the flowers will remain intact for several days (Salmon 1968).

Pygmaea This is a genus of only six species, all confined to New Zealand and all alpine. With one exception, *P. tetragona*, which resembles a dwarf *Hebe*, they form small, compact, evergreen cushions decorated by small white flowers with black, purple or orange anthers. *P. pulvinaris* makes a dense cushion only 2-4cm high and about 10cm across, giving the impression it is composed of some deep green moss. The tiny more or less linear leaves are moderately provided with long, stiff hairs which impart a characteristic sheen to the cushion. This species occurs above 1500m in rocky and stony places from Nelson to Canterbury, South Island. It appears to be quite hardy, except for severe winters, and is well suited to the scree and raised bed.

Monocots
Although grasses, especially species of snowtussock or *Chionochloa*, form the most important constituent of the low-alpine flora above the tree line, New Zealand monocots make only a marginal contribution to the rock garden. One of the snowtussocks, *C. rubra* has appeared in Club seed lists. It has a wide distribution throughout New Zealand, from low levels to 1500m. The leaves are often reddish with shining brown sheaths. It is probably best grown as a specimen plant since the flowering shoots grow to a height of one metre.

Liliaceae
Arthropodium Only one species of this small genus, scattered across the southern Hemisphere, is worth noting for growing outside i.e. *A. candidum* which is found in damp, upland sites in both North and South Island. It has a tufted habit and grows to 10-25cm, with grass-like leaves and a conical tuber. The white flowers are carried in dainty panicles. There are cultivated forms with bronze or purple leaves and another with spotted leaves. *A. cirrhatum* is much larger, more tender and best suited to pot culture.
Astelia This genus has a wide distribution in the Pacific region with 13 New Zealand species, about half of which can be classed as alpine. *A. nervosa* produces leafy tufts with handsome, long, arching leaves which are coated with silky hairs, felt-like, on the lower and variably hairy on the upper surface. The orange red berries, sitting in yellow cups, are more conspicuous than the small, sweet smelling flowers which are rather hidden in the foliage. These are evergreen plants which make clumps which occur in damp places up to 1100m on both Islands. *A. nivicola*, only from South Island, is similar to *A. nervosa*, although substantially smaller while the under side of the leaves is covered with a warm brown felt.
Bulbinella This is a small genus of clump-forming species from New Zealand and South Africa, another disjunct distribution. The only species which have been widely grown in the UK are *B. angustifolia*, known in New Zealand as Maori Onion, and *B. hookeri*. Both are hardy plants which produce bright yellow-flowered spikes which are clearly longer in *B. angustifolia* (Fig.239) which is also distinguished by its narrower leaves, in which the edges are rolled inwards towards the tips. They are widespread throughout both Islands, often present in great numbers, especially in tussock grassland.

Australia

Australia has contributed few species to the rock garden for rather obvious reasons. On the mainland the alpine flora is chiefly confined to the Australian Alps in the south east of New South Wales and the north east of Victoria. The subalpine and alpine zones occur between 1700 and 2200m on an uplifted plateau, with Mt. Kosciusko as its highest point. The rocks are made up of the remains of ancient, eroded and metamorphosed sediments in the form of schists, slates and quartzites, with massive granite intrusions which dominate the highest regions about Kosciusko. During the Pleistocene, although the area was not heavily glaciated, glacial action was sufficient to determine the present appearance of the landscape. Snow lies for 6–7 months of the year and, although there is no persistent ice, isolated snow patches may remain throughout the year. Tasmania is very different. It is quite mountainous and a large area in the centre and west of the island is above the tree-line. It is believed that Tasmania was originally separated from the mainland some 65 million years ago but, during the Pleistocene, the intervening sea retreated at least twice to allow migration of animals and plants to and from the mainland. Of the approximately 2000 species of flowering plants recorded from Tasmania about 10% are endemic. But there is still another part of Australia which may have untapped potential for the rock garden. The Stirling Ranges in the south west of Western Australia, with the highest peaks around 1100m, with some snowfall during the winter, are home to a substantial number of small, attractive, saxatile and often endemic species which are worth investigating since nothing much seems to be known about their behaviour in cultivation (Dempster 1985).

Asteraceae
Brachycome *B. nivalis*, commonly called the snow daisy, is a conspicuous feature of the alpine scene. It produces neat rosettes of variable divided foliage with white rayed flowers on six inch scapes. There is a stoloniferous variety, *alpina*, which has a similar distribution but occurs also in Tasmania. *B. rigidula* from eastern Australia and Tasmania is not classed as an alpine species. It forms small clumps with 10-30cm stems with a few narrow lobed leaves and approximately two centimetre diameter flower heads with purple blue rays. Both species are suited to the alpine house.
Celmisia The Australian celmisias are not as diverse as their New Zealand relatives. The best known is *C. longifolia* which comprises several closely related forms which make spectacular displays in the Snowy Mountain uplands. The flowering stem grows to about 15cm. It is not difficult to grow and reproduce by cuttings.
Cotula *C. coronopifolia* occurs in Australia, Tasmania and also South Africa. It is one of those species which has spread throughout the world and may be too much of a common weed to be given a place in the rock garden.

Nonetheless it produces cheerful, yellow button heads about one centimetre across and varies in height between 15 and 40cm.

Craspedia   There are a number of forms of what has been called *C. glauca* growing in the Australian alpine areas. Solitary flower stalks arise from tufts of basal leaves to variable height and carry globular flower heads which may be white, cream, bright yellow or orange. They are commonly known as billy buttons. Smaller forms from higher elevations are to be preferred. If grown in scree or gravelly soil they are fairly hardy outside but should be given a glass cover to protect from winter wet. They rarely set seed in the UK.

Helichrysum   *H. hookeri* is an aromatic, woolly shrub which can grow to one metre but is usually less, with small, sessile, sticky leaves. The small, everlasting type flower heads are straw coloured. It occurs in the subalpine and alpine zones of the Australian Alps and on the mountains of Tasmania. It goes by the common name of kerosene bush since it burns so easily but, being fire-adapted, it generally recovers.

Olearia   *O. frostii* forms a spreading bush with dark green, very hairy leaves. The flower heads are in shades of lilac. It is native to upland sites in north east Victoria. *O. phlogopappa* is a mountain species from both Tasmania and the Australian Alps. It is a small, 30-75cm shrub with woolly branches and small, crowded, sessile leaves which are felted on the underside and hairy above. The ray florets of the terminal flower heads are white. Both these species are fairly hardy.

Campanulaceae
Lobelia   *L. pedunculata* is a vigorous, creeping, mat-forming species which can be invasive, especially in its preferred moist sites. It is found in south east New South Wales, north east Victoria and Tasmania. Typically, the two-lipped flowers with their much larger three-lobed lower lip, are blue or purplish. but forms have been introduced from Tasmania which are of various shades of blue including pale and deep violet.

Wahlenbergia   *W. ceracea* is a native of the Australian Alps and Tasmania, growing to about 15-30cm with slender stems carrying pale blue to pale violet nodding flowers. It is a good alpine house plant. *W. gloriosa* is very closely related to *ceracea*, differing chiefly by the mainly opposite, more crowded leaves, compared with the mostly alternate leaves of *W. ceracea,* and the deep, purple-violet flower colour. It is also rather less alpine and is uncommon above the treeline. It is easily grown both in alpine house and outside, where however it will only survive mild winters.

Epacridaceae
Epacris   These are evergreen shrubs with many small leaves and tubular flowers, which arise singly in the leaf axils The corolla has five spreading lobes. Some are worth trying outside in a sheltered spot but they would all be safer in the alpine house. *E. impressa* has narrow, spreading or recurved

leaves and handsome large flowers of 1-2cm which vary in colour between red, pink and white. It occurs in southern Australia, Victoria, New South Wales and Tasmania and is solely for the alpine house. *E. petrophila* is a common species of alpine and subalpine grassland of the Australian Alps and the mountains of Tasmania. It is an erect shrub which can grow to about 40cm or the stems may be prostrate and rooting. The leaves are thick, sessile, tightly packed and shiny. The solitary more or less sessile, white flowers occur in small clusters at the ends of the stems.

Myrtaceae
Leptospermum The only species worth noting is *L. humifusum*, a hardy species from Tasmanian mountain slopes to 1600m. It forms a wide mat with typically leptospermum white flowers

Stylidiaceae
Stylidium This genus is entirely Australian except for one species from New Zealand. The only species likely to be encountered is *S. graminifolium* which grows from sea level to the alpine zone, where the plants are shorter, 30-45cm, and much preferred to lowland forms which can grow to 120cm. The basal leaves are closely tufted, stiff and grass-like. The scape bears a spike of handsome deep pink or purplish flowers with four large paired lobes and a small reflexed one. This species bears the name of 'Trigger Plant' from the remarkable pollination mechanism in which the style forms an irritable column which is held to one side of the flower and, when touched, sweeps across to allow the stigma to pick up pollen from the visiting insect Best in the alpine house but a sheltered site outside is possible although the plants have a reputation for being short lived.

Monocots
Hypoxidaceae
Hypoxis *H. hygrometrica* is an alpine house species from Tasmania and eastern Australia. It grows to about 15cm with grassy, basal leaves and bright yellow star-like flowers. It is generally found in damp sites. This genus is closely related to the South African *Rhodohypoxis*.

Iridaceae
Diplarrhena *D. moraea* is very common in Tasmania where it ascends to 1200m. It also occurs less frequently in New South Wales and Victoria, preferring coastal heathland and damp sandy sites. It is very variable in size; upland forms are only half as big as those from the lowlands which may grow to 45cm. It produces large clumps of iris-like evergreen leaves. The outer perianth parts of the lovely, scented flowers are white and the inner ones suffused with yellow or purple. Hardier cultivars from Tasmania can be grown outside in a sheltered position and in peaty soil. *D. latifolia* is endemic

to the mountains of Tasmania. The flowers are larger than in *D. moraea* and the inner segments are conspicuously veined purple. It is also a hardier species which flowers freely, can easily be grown from seed and should be divided in winter.

Libertia   *L. pulchella* has a very disjunct distribution since it occurs in eastern Australia, Tasmania, New Zealand and the mountain forests of New Guinea. Growing to about 10cm it forms small clumps of narrow, floppy, pointed leaves. The white flowers are carried just clear of the leaves. It is best given some shade, since in the wild it occurs in rain forest country under southern beech forest, near mountain streams or, above the tree line, in the shelter of boulders or scrub. It may be propagated by division or from seeds.

Liliaceae

Arthropodium   This is a small Australasian genus with more or less narrow basal leaves and racemes or panicles of starry flowers. The New Zealand *A. candidum* is the most widely grown species, but there is also the attractive *A. milleflorum* which is widespread in southern New South Wales and Tasmania where its scented flowers have earned it the name of vanilla lily. They may be white, mauve or lilac coloured and are carried in panicles above the leaves to a height of about 45cm. In cultivation light shade is preferred and the plants can get by without too much water.

§ CHAPTER 12 §

South Africa

The flora of South Africa is immensely rich, comprising just under 20,000 species. Within this vast assembly the Cape Flora of some 8000 species is recognised as a Floral Kingdom by virtue of the number of families, genera and species represented. However, only a tiny fraction of this wealth of species can tolerate our climate. Of course, were we to extend the limits of our survey by including plants suited to the frost-free greenhouse the number of beautiful South African species would be legion, but that route is barred so we have to be content with a very short chapter and confine our attention to a few more or less hardy species although there is little doubt there is potential for augmenting their number by new introductions from the Drakensberg mountains and other comparable sites.

Asteraceae
Euryops This is a widespread Africa genus of both herbs and shrubs with stalked, composite flowerheads, usually with a yellow disc. The hardiest species is *E. acraeus*, commonly referred to as *E. evansii*. It forms a shrubby bush a little over 30cm high with narrow silver hairs and plenty of yellow flowerheads two to three centimetres across. A native of the Drakensberg in Basutoland, it is quite hardy except for the occasional severe winter. The somewhat larger *E. tysonii* is not quite so tolerant.
Felicia This is another wholly African genus which includes many annuals which contribute to the brilliant colour displays of the spring veldt. *F. amoena* forms a shrubby bush of about 30cm or more in height with narrow leaves and solitary, quite large, bright blue flowerheads. In the wild pink and purple colour forms occur. This colourful species does quite well outside in sunny, sheltered sites but like *Euryops* will perish in a hard winter. *F. petiolata* has a prostrate habit with lanceolate leaves and solitary white to violet or pink to rosy flowerheads, borne on short stalks. It is also fairly hardy given a sunny spot. *F. rosulata* is another blue flowered South African species, which spreads by rhizomes to form small clumps. *F. uliginosa* forms mats of spreading, rather woody branches. The comparatively large flowerheads are blue to lilac. Although found in marshy places at 2800m and over in Natal and Lesotho it struggles to keep going in our climate.
Gazania Among these showy daisy-headed species which contribute so much to the veldt spring display *G. krebsiana* (Fig.240) is a fairly low-growing, mat-forming species with orange red florets shaded with brown towards their base. It is best treated as an alpine house subject but there is a sub-species *serratula* from the Drakensberg with brilliant yellow daisy-heads and a hardier constitution which may tolerate a sheltered spot outside.

Helichrysum This immense genus is particularly well represented in Africa. *H. milfordiae* spreads by stolons to form small, shrubby cushions about 15cm high, with densely hairy silvery leaves. The quite large flowerheads are subtended by silvery white bracts which are crimson or brown on the underside. Native to Natal and Basutoland at high elevations this is quite hardy on raised bed or scree. *H. sessiloides* is rather similar and is often confused with *H. milfordiae*. Deep green leaves with silvery hairs form cushions in which nestle the sessile white flowerheads which may be faintly flushed yellow or pink. It also has bright bracts or phyllaries below the involucre. This is also a mountain species which is tolerably hardy outside although both these species do very well in the alpine house. There are further species worth noting like *HH. pagophilum* and *splendidum* which have the same general habit of growth, are excellent in the alpine house and worth trying outside for those who like experimenting.

Campanulaceae
Wahlenbergia We have met this genus before in New Zealand and Australia. Its appearance in South Africa provides yet another example of the kind of disjunct distribution already discussed. The best known and most attractive species is *W. undulata*, a slender but robust species with quite large, solitary pale lavender flowers. Although a perennial in its native habitat it is best treated as an annual.

Hilliard and Burtt (1987) believe there are likely to be potential additions to both alpine house and sheltered garden among other species from high elevations in the Drakensberg.

Scrophulariaceae
Diascia This genus is confined to South Africa. The species are generally too big for the rock garden but one or two are worth noting. *D. barberae* and *cordata* are very similar in forming dense mats with oval, toothed leaves and pink flowers with two lateral spurs. The garden form 'Ruby Field' appears to be derived from *D. barberae*. Both species can be grown outside but will require periodical renewal.

Monocots
There are innumerable monocots of dazzling beauty but we can only consider a few.
Iridaceae
Gladiolus This genus includes many African species of which none of the smaller southern ones can be classed as hardy, so they are alpine house subjects. Half a dozen or so appear in the SRGC seed lists and a few of them are mentioned here. *G. carinatus* grows up to 60cm with small, scented, mauve and yellow flowers which, as in most of these species, vary in colour, often in subtle ways which often make descriptions rather inadequate. Of

roughly similar size, *G. cardinalis* produces large, crimson flowers while in *G. gracilis*, with narrow leaves and slender stems, the flowers are blue. *G. tristis*, which has been long in cultivation and is regarded as the hardiest of this group of Cape bulbs, since it can be grown outside in southern England, has very fragrant, large, pale yellow flowers, splashed red on the outside. There is an attractive sulphur-yellow variety *concolor* without the red tints.

Hesperantha This is a purely African genus. Two species appear in the SRGC seed lists: *HH. baurii* and *falcata*, both confined to the alpine house. In the former the basal leaves are grass-like and the spike of pink flowers grows to about 20cm. The corolla spreads widely above a basal tube. *H. falcata* is rather similar in size with a spike of white or deep yellow flowers. Apparently populations are polymorphic for the presence of scent. White flowered individuals are fragrant, not so the yellows.

Ixia In this South African genus, propagated by corms, the leaves are narrow and the flowers rather crocus-like and carried on terminal spikes. They are notable for their wide range of colours. Some of the species, like *I. monodelpha*, include a number of varieties which encompass a remarkable diversity of colour combinations.

Lapeirousia This genus includes a number of particularly beautiful, low growing, perennial herbs with a corm. One of the most charming is *L. silenoides* (Fig.242), with many close packed flowers of magenta to cerise colour with pale yellow markings at the base of the petals. This is definitely a plant for greenhouse culture.

Romulea This is a large, wide ranging genus with species in Europe, the Middle east as well as Africa. They are closely related to *Crocus* which they resemble in the presence of a corm and the structure of the flower but differ in their very short stem which makes the flowers appear to be sitting on the ground. There are many Cape species which differ greatly in colour. One of the commonest is *R. bulbocodium* (Fig.243) with small (2-3cm) star-shaped yellow flowers. Another is *R. macowanii*, also yellow but flushed with orange. *R. rosea* is a deep pink. They produce coloured forms in the wild, none more arresting than var. *speciosa* of *R. rosea* with large flowers of dazzling carmine.

Hypoxidaceae
Rhodohypoxis A small genus of some six species from East Africa on damp grassland. The leaves are basal, gray-green and hairy, the rhizomes rather squat, the flowers solitary with spreading lobes. All are good alpine house subjects but *R. baurii* grows well outside in a sheltered place, although the occasional hard winter will kill it. In var. *baurii* (Fig.241), the leaves are narrower and the flowers are of a deep, rich pink colour. In var. *confecta* the flowers are white to red. In var. *platypetala* the leaves are broader and the flowers pale pink. These plants have become very popular in recent years and many nurseries list several forms.

§ CHAPTER 13 §

The Future

Here we must end our survey of introduced species suited for either rock garden or alpine house. There are plenty of attractive species we have not mentioned due to the limitations of space and time but, at least, we have tried to represent the more important genera and demonstrate how the major regions differ in which families and genera have contributed most to our rock garden flora. At this point perhaps we may be forgiven for opting to peer speculatively into the uncertain mists of the future.

Whatever our attitude to a Millennium celebration, awareness of the passage of time acquires an added significance. Reflection on past events leads naturally to speculation as to what the future might hold for us. Within the modest confines of our rock garden theme we have considered how we have arrived thus far on our journey and are compelled now to look to the way forward. But to what end? To make confident predictions for any domain of human activity is to indulge a vacuous fancy. Extrapolation from former experience is the only prudent choice. At least it will give our successors a laugh to see how wrong we were but we shall not be present to be discomfited or share in the joke, so why worry?

What are the prospects of a substantial increase in the rock gardener's repertoire of species? The unexplored regions of the world are shrinking so fast that a massive injection of new species comparable with the influx from the Sino-Himalayan region or North America seems improbable. Given the way in which people get to the most unlikely places with unprecedented ease it is increasingly unlikely that an undiscovered El Dorado of alpine plants is secretly blooming in some remote, sequestered valleys. That said, there is no shortage of potential additions to the scree and raised bed from many different parts of the world. For example there is evidence that the Rocky Mountain flora is ripe for detailed attention. Merely to exploit fully the potential of the genera *Phlox* and *Penstemon* would add a great deal to the colour and flowering period of Scottish rock gardens.

We have only to read in the SRGC Journal and the AGS Bulletin travellers' accounts of botanical forays in places like southern Russia, eastern Turkey or central Asia to find descriptions of many species, presently known only to botanists, which sound as if they should be introduced as garden plants. The nearest approach to an El Dorado appears to occur in the flora of the Andes. Any rock gardener must gaze with wonder at the photographs of so many dazzling species from so many different genera — species which, for the most part, are beyond reach since they are so difficult to grow and, when they do flower, often appear as a disappointing reflection of their wild glory. If anyone can discover how to fool these plants into believing they are growing in a metre or so of volcanic scree, bathed in ultraviolet rich sunlight at 4000m, then the influx of South American plants could be the event of the 21st century.

So a prime limiting factor in expanding the diversity of rock plants is adequate understanding of the physiological needs and special adaptations of many difficult species, leading to new techniques of cultivation. But to be maximally effective such techniques must be accessible to the gardener of limited resources. Related to this consideration is the capacity of the trade to sustain an ever-expanding diversity of species. On average, the greater the number of species on offer the fewer the number sold per species. The only practical solution to the effects of such an inverse relationship depends on the viability of a sufficient number of small specialist nurseries.

A further consideration turns on the fact that already the gardener has access to an immense number of alpine and rock plants, far in excess of the needs or capacity of the average, small suburban garden. So, in practice, there is a limit to the increase in diversity of species on offer. What is more likely is that fashions will change in unpredictable ways so that the popularity of given species wax and wane over time. Just now the genus *Corydalis* is in the ascendant while *Arisaema* is coming on fast. But who would care to predict what will succeed them?

There are other entirely different considerations which could affect the future rock garden flora. Until recently it has been traditional to grow only wild species or naturally occurring forms of the kind which turn up in polymorphic populations. Even hybrids were eyed with suspicion not so long ago. But times are changing. Forms which arise in cultivation are favoured while hybrids between related taxa are now respectable. This change in attitude may spring from the realisation that hybrids often occur in the wild while, in many taxa, there is such an inter-grading of forms which are actively exchanging genes that the notion of a 'pure' species is hardly relevant. We have only to mention the situation in some of the North American irises, the ornata gentians from the Himalayas or the campanulas of south west Asia to make the point. Hybridisation and selection is such instances have already been put to practical use.

It is a short step from there to pose the question, quite blasphemous to some, as to whether rock and alpine plants will become objects of genetic manipulation by the arts and science of the plant breeder. Compared with so many of our familiar border species alpine and rock plants are 'unimproved'. Some would hold that many of them are beyond improvement and that is a tenable view. But the longer any species is in cultivation and seeds and/or propagules are derived preferentially from one individual rather than another, some degree of selection is entailed. Indeed more or less unconscious selection for ability to grow under garden conditions has most likely been one of the reasons why many species which were once impossibly difficult are no longer so. By comparison with what plant breeders have achieved in both annual and perennial border plants, not to mention agricultural crops, there is no doubt that great changes could be effected in the size, growth form, flowering time, colour etc. of rock plants. Of course, with so many species in cultivation, there would be a practical, economic limit to the number which could be subjected to a systematic breeding programme. Most likely a few of the more popular species would be chosen for this purpose. If such a route were followed there is no obvious limit to the variety of form and behaviour which could be realised by use of contemporary methods of gene transfer and manipulation. If, at some future date, the supply of new species of rock plants dried up, for one reason or another, it is a reasonable guess that such methods would be invoked to expand the development of novelty and diversity of form.

And there we had better stop trying to imagine what might happen in the future. What is certain, unless some catastrophe befalls our western society, there will be enthusiastic rock gardeners scanning the catalogues for new species a hundred years from now but what they might be doing come the next Millennium, we dare not even guess.

BIBLIOGRAPHY

Abdalla, S. T. & McKelvie, A.D. (1980) The Interaction of Chilling and Giberellic Acid on the Germination of Seeds of Ornamental Plants. Seed Sci. and Technol. 8, 139-144.
Archibald, J. (1963) Among Moroccan Mountains. Quart. Bull AGS, 31 (4), 314-340.
---------------- (1991) Survivors – Some specialised Endemics of the American West, 197-206. A Century of Alpines, AGS & SRGC Publication.
Beckett, K. (Ed) (1993) *Encyclopedia of Alpines*. Vol 1, Vol 2. AGS Publication, Pershore, Worcs.
Benman, J.A. (1957) The Systematics and Evolution of Townsendia (Compositae). Contrib. Gray Herb. CLXXXIII, 69-71.
Bird, R. Ed. (1991) *A Century of Alpines*. AGS & SRGC Publication.
Booker, C. (1995) Down under in the Pennines. Quart. Bull. AGS, 63 (3), 237-241.
Christie, I. (1995) Plant Portraits: Gentiana coelestis (CLD 1087). Jour. SRGC XXIV (2), 172-173.
Clay, S. (1937) *The Present Day Rock Garden*. T.C & E.C. Jack, Ltd. London.
Cobb, J. L.S. (1989), *Meconopsis*, Helm, London; Timber Press, Oregon.
---------------- (1994) Good-bye Meconopsis. Jour. SRGC, XXIV (1), 38-48.
---------------- (1999) Penstemons. Jour. SRGC, XXVI (2), 120-132.
Cooper, R. E., Curle, A. O. & Fair, W. S. (1935) *George Forrest VMH*. Scottish Rock Garden Club
Conquist, A. (1948) Revision of the North American Species of Erigeron. Brittonia, 6, 121-302.
Costin, A.B., Gray, M., Totterdell, C.J. & Wimnbush, D.J. (1979) *Kosciusko Alpine Flora*. CSIRO and W. Collins, Ltd. Australia.
Cowan, J.M. (1952) *The Journeys and Plant Introductions of George Forrest V.M.H*. Oxford University Press, London.
Cox, E.H.M. (1953) Some Dwarf Rhododendron Species. Jour. SRGC, No.12, 171-174.
----------------(1945) *Plant Hunting in China*. Collins, London.
Cox, P.A. (1973) *Dwarf Rhododendrons*. B.T. Batsford, London.
-------------(1985) *The Smaller Rhododendrons*. B.T. Batsford, London.
Cox, P. A. & Cox, K. E., (1997) *Encyclopedia of Rhododendron Species*, Glendoick Publishing.
Cullen, J. (1978) Asiatic Gentians of Series Ornatae. Jour. SRGC, XVI (2), 85-96.
Darlington, P.J. Jr. (1965) *Biogeography of the Southern End of the World*. Harvard Univ. Press.
Davidian, H. H. (1963) Rhododendrons for the Rock Garden. Jour. SRGC, VIII (4), 252-261.

Dempster, H. (1985) Mini Plants in Western Australia. Quart. Bull. AGS, 53 (2), 146-159.
Drake, J. (1972) Plant Hunting in New Zealand. Jour. SRGC, XIV (3), 214-227.
Elliott, J. (1993) Eriogonums. Quart. Bull. AGS, 61 (2), 200-214.
Erskine. P. (1994) *Oxalis enneaphylla* and its Cousins. Quart. Bull. AGS, 66 (3), 345-352.
Farrer, R. (1922) The English Rock Garden. T. C. & E. C. Jack.
Fletcher, H.R. (1975) *A Quest of Flowers. The Plant Explorations of Frank Ludlow and George Sherriff.* Edin. Univ. Press.
Fletcher, H.R. & Brown, W.H. (1970) *The Royal Botanic Garden Edinburgh 1670-1970* HMSO.
Forrest, G. (1973) George Forrest, 'The Man', Jour. SRGC, XIII (3), 169-175.
Godley, E.J (1979) Research in the vegetation of New Zealand. New. Zeal. J. Bot. (17), 441-446.
Grey-Wilson, C. (1984) A survey of Incarvillea in cultivation. The New Plantsman, 1 (1), 36-52.
Grierson, A. J.C. (1991) More on Saussureas. Jour. SRGC, XX11 (3), 278-279.
Grierson, A. J. C. & Long, D. G. (1983) *The Flora of Bhutan.* Edinburgh Royal Botanic Garden.
Griffiths, M. (1992) *Index of Garden Plants.* The New RHS Dictionary. Macmillan.
Halley, P.C. (1986) Glacial History of the Rockies. *Rocky Mountain Alpines* 22-30. Timber Press.
Handel-Mazetti, H. (1996) *A Botanical Pioneer in South West China.* David Winstanley, Brentford, England.
Harley, P.V. Geologic History of the Rockies. *Rocky Mountain Alpines.* Timber Press.
Heath, R. (1981) *Collectors' Alpines.* Collingridge Books.
Hedge, I.C. (1986) Labiatae of South West Asia: diversity, distribution and endemism. Proc. Roy. Soc. B Edin. 89, 23-36.
Hilliard, O. M. & Burtt, B.L. (1987) *The Botany of the South Natal Drakensberg.* Annals of the Kirstenbosch Botanic Garden (15).
Hulme, J. (1982) Heritage in Trust Quart. Bull. AGS, 50 (3), 183-185.
Kelaidis P. (1991) Dwarf Phlox and Penstemon. *Rocky Mountain Alpines*, 88-194. Timber Press.
-----------. (1991) Dwarf Phlox and Penstemon. *A Century of Alpines*, 88-104. AGS and SRGC Publication.
Kershaw, L. , Mackinnon, A. & Pojar, J. (1998) *Plants of the Rocky Mountains.* Lone Pine Publishing. Edmonton, Vancouver, Renton.
Kinsman, D.J.J. (1998) Rhododendrons in Yunnan, China: – pH of associated soils. The New Plantsman, 5 (1), 32-38.
--------------------(1999) Rhododendrons and associated plants growing in soils overlying limestone. The New Plantsman, 6 (1), 21-22.
Kurschner, H. (1986) The subalpine thorn-cushion formation of western South

West Asia: ecology, structure and zonation. Proc. Roy. Soc B. Edin. 89, 169-180.
Kuyama, A. (1989) Alpines in home gardens. Quart. Bull, AGS, 57 (2), 235-241.
Lawrence, W. J. C. & Newall, J. (1962) *Seed and Potting Composts*. Allen & Unwin.
Lawson, J. C. (1996) Inshriach Nursery. Jour. SRGC. XXV (1), 20-28.
Livingstone, D. (1983) Post-War Memories. Jour. SRGC. XVIII (2), 102-104.
Lowe, D. (1991) Growing Alpines in Raised Beds. B. T. Batsford.
MacKenzie, W. G. (1983) The SRGC – Pre-War Days. Jour. SRGC, XVIII (2) ,93-101.
Mark, A. F. (1955) The New Zealand Flora and Vegetation. Quart. Bull. AGS. 63 (3), 245-259.
Masterton, R. S. (1979) Notholirion. Jour. SRGC, XVI (4), 270-271.
--------------------(1976) Asiatic Primulas Growing in Scotland in 1975. Jour. SRGC, XV (1), 11-29.
Mathew,B. (1981) *The Iris*. B.T. Batsford Ltd.
Mathew,B. (1989) *The genus* Lewisia. Christopher Helm.
Matthews, J. R. (1966) Personal and Otherwise. Jour. SRGC. X (1), 36-40.
McAleese, A.J., Rankin, D. W.H. & Hang Sun (1999) Rhododendrons do grow on limestone. The New Plantsman 6 (1), 23-29.
McGough, N. (1993) Alpine Plants and Conservation Legislation. Quart. Bull. AGS, 61 (3), 238-253.
McNaughton, I.H. (1996 a) Autumn Gentians Part 1: Their introduction and improvement through breeding and selection. Jour. SRGC, XXIV (4), 341-356.
---------------------- (1966b) Autumn Gentians Part 2: Their propagation, cultivation and place in the garden. Jour. SRGC, XXV (1), 84-98.
Mitchell, R..J (1983) The Sino-British Expedition to Cangshan 1981. Jour. SRGC, XVIII (2), 127 - 134.
-----------------(1989) Trillium – Part 1. The Asiatic Species. The Plantsman. 10 (4), 216-231.
-----------------(1989) Trillium – Part 2. The West North American Species. The Plantsman, 11 (2), 67-79.
-----------------(1989) Trillium – Part 3. The Eastern Species. The Plantsman. 11 (3), 132-151.
----------------(1990) Trillium – Part 4. The Pedicellate Species of Eastern North America. The Plantsman. 12 (4), 44-60.
Neese, E. (1986) Plants of the Great Basin and the Western Slopes. *Rocky Mountain Alpines*, Timber Press, 92-104.
North, C. (1978) New Lilies by Embryo Culture. Jour. SRGC. XV1 (1), 97-99.
------------(1979) *Plant Breeding and Genetics in Horticulture*. Macmillan.
------------(1997) *A Botanical Tour Round the Mediterranean*. New Millennium.
Pattison, G. (1993) Garden Plant Conservation. Quart. Bull. AGS. 61 (3), 310-313.
Philipson, W.R. (1960) Scree Plants of the Southern Alps. Jour. SRGC, VII (2), 115-120.

Polunin, O. (1980) *Flowers of Greece and the Balkans.* A Field Guide. Oxford University Press.
Radebaugh, R. (1986) Geography and Climate of the Rocky Mountains. *Rocky Mountain Alpines,* 14-22. Timber Press.
Read, D.J. (1996) The Structure and Functions of the Ericoid Mycorrhizal Root. Ann. Bot. 77, 365-374.
Reid, A.D. (1969) Miniature Rhododendrons. Jour SRGC, XI (3), 202-206.
Richards, A.J. (1993) *Primula.* B. T. Batsford Ltd.
------------------(1995) White Flowers and the New Zealand Flora. Quart. Bull. AGS, 63 (3), 275- 278.
Rix, M. & Phillips, R. (1981) *The Bulb Book.* Pan Books Ltd. London.
Salmon, J.T. (1968) *Field Guide to the Alpine Plants of New Zealand.* A. H. & A. W. Reed.
Stone, M. (1989) 'The Stone Column'. Jour. SRGC, XXI (2), 125-141.
-------------(1990a) Some Western American Alpines: A Personal Commentary Part Two. Jour. SRGC, XXI (4), 389-406.
-------------(1990b) Some Western American Alpines: A Personal Commentary Part Three. Jour. SRGC, XXII (1), 90-103.
-------------(1991) Some Western American Alpines: A Personal Commentary Part Four. Jour. SRGC, XXII (2), 195-214.
Stone, M. (1998) The Askival Hybrid Cassiopes. Quart. Bull. AGS, 66 (4), 484-492
Stone, P. & M. (1983) Primulas, Quart. Bull. AGS, 51 (3), 241 – 244.
Sutherland, J. (1978) The Garden Walls. Jour. SRGC. XVI (2), 110-114.
Symons-Jeune, B.H.B. (1936) Natural Rock Gardening. Country Life Ltd, London.
Synge, P.M. (1971) *Collins' Guide to Bulbs.* Collins, London.
Taylor, G. (1934) *Meconopsis.* Waterstone, London.
Watson, J. (1994) South American Alpines. Quart. Bull. AGS, 62 (3), 293-352.
Way, D. & James, P. (1998) *The Gardener's Guide to Growing Penstemons.* David & Charles, Newton Abbot.
Wherry, E.T. (1955) The genus Phlox. Morris Arboretum Monographs III, 1-174.
Wilkie, D. (1950) *Gentians.* Country Life Ltd. London.
Young, I. & M. (1996) Bulb Growing. Jour. SRGC. XXV (1), 30-44.

INDEX OF PEOPLE PLACES AND TOPICS

Aberchalder Nursery, 6
Aberconway, Lord, 7
Aitken, David, 79
Aitken, James (Jimmy), 50
Aitken, J. A., 57, 62
Aitken, John, 43, 79
Alden, B., 15
Alexander, J. C. M., 15
Almond, Michael J.B., 28, 46
Almond, Lynn. A., 28, 46
An Cala Garden, 70
Anderson, Brenda, 46
Anderson, John, 46
Archibald, James, 25, 26, 62, 163
Archibald, Jenny, 27
Ardfearn Nursery, 28, 62
Arduaine Garden, 76, 77
Ascreavie Garden, 11, 45
Askival, 25
Bainbridge, Dr. Carole, 32
Bainbridge, Dr. Ian, 32
Balbithan Nursery, 62
Bannatyne & Jackson Nursery, 61
Balfour, Sir Isaac Bayley, 3, 4, 64
Balfour, Andrew, 63
Balfour, John Hutton, 3, 64
Barr, Peter, 20
Bees Ltd. 4
Benmore Specialist Garden, 68
Bezzant, Lyn, 52
Blackmore, Stephen, 64
Boyd-Harvey, John, 50
Boyd-Harvey, Christina, 50
Branklyn Garden, 74, 75
Brickell, Chris. D., 51
Brodick Castle Garden, 76
Brooker, Dr. Ian M., ix
Buchanan, William, 50, 51
Bulley, Arthur, R., 3, 4, 7
Burnett, Peter, 56
Burnett, Sybil, 76
Bute, The Marquesses of, 72
Campbell, Archie, 32
Carrie, Fred, 22, 43, 62
Carrie, Monika, 62
Castlefield Nurseries, 62
Chadwell, Chris, 22, 23
Chamberlain, David, J., 14, 15, 16
Chambers, Anne, 27, 52
Cherrybank Garden, 70
Christie, Ian, 22
Christie's Nursery, 62
Chudziak, Bill, 28
Clark, Miss Jenny, 62
Clark, Miss Helen, 62
Clarke, E. S., 16
Cluny Garden, 56
Cobb, James, 47
Cooper, Roland, E., 9, 10, 31, 34
Correvon, H., 65
Corsar, Kenneth, 32, 49
Cowan, J. MacQueen, 4, 8, 73
Cowley, E. J., 15
Cox, E. H. M., 7, 20
Cox, Kenneth, 22
Cox, Peter A., 14, 15, 16, 21
Crarae Garden, 70
Crathes Castle Garden, 75, 76
Crawford, S., 16
Crosland, Jack, 32, 42
Cruickshank Botanic Garden, 72
Cunnington, Peter, 15
David, Père, 4
Davis, Cath, 44
Davis, Peter, H., 18
Dawyck Specialist Garden, 68
Delavay, Abbé, 4
Dickie, Prof. G., 87
Dobbie & Co., 61
Drake, Jack, 27, 52, 53
Duff, John, 57
Duguid, Alec, 26, 44
Dunkley, A., 16
Edrom Nursery, 28, 44, 61

Elliot, Roy, 80
Erskine, P., 195
Esslemont, Harold, 28, 32, 41, 82
Evans, Alf, 32, 34, 65
Farrer, Reginald, 7, 65
Finnis, Valerie, 36
Fletcher, Harold. R., 5, 10, 34, 64
Forrest, George, 4, 5, 6, 7, 8
Gardner, M.F., 16
Glass, F., 30
Glassel House, 30
Glendoick Nursery, 62
Graham, Robert, 64
Grants of West Calder, 62
Grey-Wilson, Christopher, 15, 16
Grierson, A. J. C., 17
Halley, Joyce, 48
Handel-Mazzetti, H., 6, 7
Hans, G., 15
Hardy Plant Society, 90
Harley, Andrew, 30
Harrow, R. L., 5
Hedge, Ian, 18
Henderson, Douglas, 64, 73
Henry, Augustine, 4
Hicks, J. H., 12
History of the SRGC:
 Foundation and development, 30–34
 Plants at the Shows, 34-35
 Early Shows, 36
 Cushion Plants, 36
 Bulbs, 37
 To feed or not to feed, 37
 Fashions, 38
 Common Plants, 38
 Forrest Medals, 38
 New Introductions, 39
 Trade Stands, 39
Holmes, Wilfred, 43
Hooker, Sir W. J., 13
Hunt, Fred, 27, 48
Hunt, Terry, 44
Hutcheson, Sir Peter, 15, 16

Hulme, Joy, 90
Hyam, R.D., 15
Ingram, David, 64
Inshriach Nursery, 53, 61
Inverewe Garden, 73, 74
Ivey, Bette, 52
Izat Miss, Grovemount Nursery, 62
Jermyn, Jim, 27, 44
Keillour Castle, 55
Kessels, Mervyn, 86
Kildrummy Castle Garden, 68
Kilmory Castle Garden, 71
Kilpatrick, Peter, 32
Kingdon Ward, Frank, 87
King & Paton of Dalbeattie, 62
Kirkpatrick, George, 16
Kittock Mill, 71
Knott, D. G. F., 16
Knox Finlay, Major George, 28, 55
Knox Finlay, Mary, 28, 55
Lafong, Dr Cyril., 45, 46
Laing, Mrs. J., Nursery, 62
Laird, Eric P., 30
Lancaster, R., 14
Lawrence, Sir William, 30
Lawson, John, 52, 53
Leith Hall Garden, 75
Leslie, A.C., 15
Leven, Sandy, 58
Lilley, Richard, 27
Livingstone, David, 32, 51, 52
Litton, Mr., 8
Logan Specialist Garden, 68
Logan Home, The Misses Edith and Mollie, 44
Long, D.G., 15, 16, 17
Lowe, Duncan, 79
Ludlow, Frank, 5, 10, 11
Lumsden, K. 11
Lyles of Maryfield Nursery, Fife, 62
Main, John, D., 16
Mann, D.G., 16
Martin, Ian, 62
Masterton, Bobby, 27, 28, 56

Masterton, Betty, 28, 56
Mathew, Brian, 27
Matthews, Prof. J.R., 44
Mattingley, John, 56
Mattingley, Wendy, 56
Maule, Sheila, 28, 49
Mawson, Thomas, 72
Maxwell, Bob, 43
Maxwell-Macdonald, D., 16
McBeath, Ron J. D., 15, 16, 17, 27
McClaren, D.M., 7
McDouall Brothers, 67
McKean, D.R., 16
McKelvie, Alastair, 22, 23, 32, 34
MacKenzie, Bill, 30
Mackenzie, Osgood, 73, 74
McMurtie, Mary, formerly of Balbithan, 43, 62
McNab, James, 64
McNab, William, 64, 67
McNaughton, Ian, 108, 110, 111
McNeil, John, 64
McWatt, John, 45
Millais, E.G., 15
Milne, Harley, 50
Mitchell, J.M., 15, 17, 18, 191
Mitchell, Robert. J., 1, 4, 32, 70
Mount Stuart Gardens, 72
Mowat, John, 32
Murray-Lyon, Major General, D. M., 57
National Trust for Scotland; Gardens, 77
Noltie, Henry J., 15, 16, 17
North, Dr. Chris, 57
Paterson, D.S., 15, 16
Paton, Bill, 66
Pattison, Graham, 90
Pontecorvo, Prof. G., 51
Ponton, J.R., Kirknewton, Earlston Nurseries, 62
Potterton, R., 15
Rae, D. A. H., 16
Ramsay, Magnus, 27

Renton, Dorothy, 28, 54, 55
Renton, John, 28, 30, 54, 55
Richards, Dr John A., 119, 216
Robb, James, 72
Robertson, Prof. Forbes W., x
Rutherford, Bob 72
Salzen, Dr. Heather, 27, 43
Sawyer, Mairi, 73
Schilling, A. D., 15
Sherriff, George, 5, 10, 11, 45
Sherriff, Elizabeth, 12, 45
Sibbald, Robert, 63
Simson-Hall, Ian, 50
Simson-Hall, Kathleen, 50
Simpson, David, 50
Simpson, Isobel, 50
Sinclair, W. J., 15
Sinnott, M., 16
Smarzty, S., 16
Smith, Eric, 26
Smith, Ian, 54
Smith, Joel, vi
Smith, Mrs Mary Guthrie, 62
Smith, Sir William, W., 4, 5, 64
Sprunt, Glassford, 58, 59
St. Andrews Botanic Garden, 70
Stead, Dr. Don, 52
Stead, Joan, 52
Stewart, L.B., 4
Stevens, Dr Evelyn, 59
Stitt, Col., of Blairgowrie Nursery, 62
Stone, Mike, 24, 53, 82
Stone, Polly, 24, 53, 82
Stonefield Castle Garden, 71
Strangman, Elizabeth, 15
Sutherland, Alasdair, 62
Sutherland, Fred, 72
Sutherland, James, 63
Sutherland, Jim, 28, 62
Symons–Jeune, E. H. B., 78
Swift, Mike, 71
Taylor, Sir George, 10, 12, 13
Taylor, Henry, 23, 46, 117

Taylor, Margaret, 23, 46, 117
Technical Topics
Rocks, 78
Raised Beds, 79,
Tufa, 80
Soils, 80, 81
Pots, 81
Watering, 82
Alpine Houses and Frames, 82, 83
Horticultural Chemicals, 84,
Propagation, 85
Genetic Advances, 86
Conservation, 87–89
NCCPG, 90-91
Threave Garden, 77
Tod, Dr Henry, 28, 49, 81
Torosay Castle Garden, 71
Tough Alpine Nursery, 63
Trotter, D. G., 54
Tweedie, Ruth, 26
Walmsley, Major Alan, 32, 49
Watson, Eric, 82
Watson, M. F., 15, 17
Wester Balruddery, 24
Willtshire, T., 15
Williams, J. C., 7
Wilson, Brian, 43
Wilson, Maureen, 43
Wintergill, D. of Thornliebank Nursery, 62
Worth, Dr Henry, 28
Wylie, Jean, 59
Young, Ian, 42, 43, 79
Young, Margaret, 42, 43

INDEX OF PLANTS
Synonyms in italics

ACAENA
buchananii Hook. f., 225
var. picta, 225,
var. inermis, 225
glabra J. Buch., 226
microphylla Hook. f, 225
var. robusta, 225
novae-zelandiae T. Kirk, 225
glabra J. Buch., 226

ACANTHOLIMON
armenum Boiss. & Huet., 140
glumaceum Boiss., 140
sp. ?, Fig. 91
ulcinum Boiss., 140
A. androsaceum
A. echinus
venustum Boiss., 140

ACHILLEA
ageratifolia (Sibth. & Sm.)
Boiss., 151, Fig. 80
clavennae L., 151
holosericea Sibth. & Sm., 151
tomentosa L., 151
umbellata Sibth. & Sm.

ACIPHYLLA
aurea W. Oliv., 217, Fig. 231
colensoi Hook. f., 217
ferox W. Oliv., 217
horrida W. Oliv., 217
monroi J.R. & G. Forst., 217
pinnatifida Petrie, 217
scott-thomsonii Ckn. & Allan, 217
spedenii Cheesem. 217
squarrosa J.R. & G. Forst., 217
subflabellata W. Oliv., 217

ACONITUM
fletcherianum, 126
hookeri Stapf., 126
pulchellum Hand.-Mazz., 126
violaceum Jacq. ex Stapf., 126

ADENOPHORA
takedae Mak., 203
var. howozana, 204
triphylla (Thunb.) A. D C., 204
var. japonica, Fig. 198
var. puellaris, 204
verticillata Syn.

ADONIS
amurensis Regel & Radde, 209, Fig. 219
brevistyla Franch., 95
chrysocyathus Hook. f. & Th., 126

AETHIONEMA
armenum Boiss., 134
cordifolium Hort. ex Boiss., 134
Iberis jucundum
grandiflorum Boiss. & Hohen., 134
A. pulchellum
iberideum Boiss., 135
oppositifolium Boiss., 135
A. bourgaei
A. rubescens
Eunomia oppositifolia
saxatile R. Br., 135
A creticum
A. graecum
A. ovalifolium
A . pyrenaicum
x warleyense, 135
'Warley Rose', 135
'Warley Purple', 135

ALLIUM
acuminatum Hook., 187
cernuum Roth., 187
A. recurvatum
A. alleghaniense
falcifolium Hook. & Arn., 187
narcissiflorum Vill., 24
A. grandiflorum
siskiyouense Munz & Keck ex Ownbey, 187

ALSTROMERIA
   angustifolia Herb., 200
   ssp. velutina, 200
   hookeri C. Gay, 200
   A. hookeriana
   patagonica R. Phil., 201
   pelegrina Vell., 200
   'Alba', 200
   pseudospathulata, 200, Fig. 196
   pulchella L. f., 200
   pygmaea Herb., 201
   Shickendantzia pygmaea
   umbellata Peyen., 201
ALYSSUM
   cyclocarpum Rupr., 151
   Ptilotrichum cyclocarpum
   corymbosum Boiss., 151
   markgrafii O.E. Schulz., 151
   montanum L., 151
   ssp. brynii, 152
   murale Wald st. & Kit., 152
   saxatile L., 152
   Aurinia saxatile
   Aurinia arduinii
ANARTHOPHYLLUM
   desideratum Benth. 27
ANCHUSA
   cespitosa Lam., 41
   A. caespitosa
   leptophylla Roem. & Schultz, 134
   ssp. incana, 134
ANDROCYMBIUM
   A. striatum, 24
ANDROMEDA
   polifolia L., 24, Fig. 204
ANDROSACE
   albana Steven., 157
   armeniaca Duby., 158
   var. macrantha, 158
   cantabrica (Losa & Montseriat) Kress, 24
   chamaejasme Wulf. in Jacq., 96, 178
   delavayi Franch., 117, Fig. 58
   geraniifolia Watt., 121
   hedraeantha Griesb., 158, Fig. 92
   himalaica Hand.-Mazz., 117
   A. sempervivoides var. *tibetica*
   laevigata (A. Gray) Wendelbo, 177, Fig. 147
   Douglasia laevigata, 49
   lanuginosa Wall., 117
   montana (A. Gray) Wendelbo, 178, Fig. 148
   Douglasia montana
   muscoidea Duby., 117
   var. longiscapa, 117
   obtusifolia All., 158
   sarmentosa Wall., 117
   sempervivoides Jacq. ex Duby., 117
   spinulifera (Franch) Knuth, 57
   strigillosa Franch., 117
   studiosorum Kress 'Doksai', 24
   villosa L., 158, Fig. 93
ANEMONE
   appenina L., 141
   baldensis L., 179
   blanda Schott & Kotschy., 141
   drummondii S. Wats., 179
   multifida Poir, 179, 197, Fig. 154
   narcissiflora L., 180
   obtusiloba D.Don., 127, Fig. 61
   patens L., 180
   Pulsatilla patens
   rivularis Buch.-Ham. ex DC., 127
   rupicola Cambess., 57, 95, 127, Fig. 60
   rupestris Wallich ex Hook. f. & Thoms., 127
   trullifolia Hook. & Thomps., 127
   villosissima (DC.) Juz., 180

AQUILEGIA
    canadensis L., 179
    var. nana, 179
    elegantula Greene, 179
    flabellata Sieb. & Zucc., 209
    var. pumila, 209, Fig. 220
    'Alba', 209
    fragrans Benth., 209
    jonesii Parry, 179, Fig. 155
    saximontana Rydb, 179
    scopulorum Tiedstr., 179
    var. calcarea, 179
    viridiflora Pall., 127
    var. atrorubens, 127
ARABIS
    androsacea Fenzl., 135
    bryoides Boiss., 152
    caucasica Willd. ex Schdl., 135, Fig. 81
    A. albida
    ferdinandi-coburgi Kellerer & Sunderm, 152.
    'Variegata', 152
    procurrens Waldst. & Kit., 152
ARCTERICA
    nana (Maxim.) Mak., 205
ARCTOSTAPHYLOS
    alpina (L.) Spreng., 205
    Arctous alpina
ARISAEMA
    amurense Maxim., 211
    ssp. robustum, 211
    var. atropurpurea, 211
    candidissimum W.W. Sm., 129, Fig. 68
    flavum (Forsk.) Schott., 129, Fig. 70
    japonicum BL., 211, Fig. 222
    A. serratum
    nepenthoides (Wall.) Mart. ex Schott, 129, Fig. 69
    ringens (Thumb.) Schott., 212
    sikokianum Franch ex Savat., 212

triphyllum (L.) Torr., 185, Fig. 71
    A. atrorubens
ARTEMISIA
    schmidtiana Maxim., 203
    stelleriana Besser., 203
ARTHROPODIUM
    candidum Raoul., 233
    cirrhatum (Forst. f.) R. Br. 229
    milleflorum L., 233
ASPERULA
    daphneola O. Schwarz., 142
    lilaciflora Boiss. 142
    ssp. lilaciflora, 142
    nitida Sibth. & Sm., 142
    ssp. hirtella, 142
ASTELIA
    nervosa Ckn. ex Cheesem., 229
    nivicola Banks & Soland. ex Hook. f., 229
ASTILBE
    x 'William Buchanan', 51
    microphylla Knoll, 210
    A. chinensis var. *japonica*
    simplicifolia Mak., 210, Fig. 221
ASYNEUMA
    limonifolium (Boiss. & Heldr.) Bornm, 152.
AUBRIETA
    canescens (Boiss.) Bornm., 135
    A. deltoidea var. *canescens*
    columnae Guss., 152
    deltoidea (L.) DC., 152
    gracilis Sprun. ex Boiss., 152
    libanotica Boiss. & Hohen., 135
    parviflora Boiss., 135
    A. kotschyi
    pinardii Boiss., 135
BOLAX
    gummifera (Lam.) Spreng., 193
    B. glebaria
BRACHYCOME
    nivalis F. Muell., 230

var. alpina , 230
B. cardiocarpa var. *alpina*
rigidula (DC.) G. L. Davis,
230
A. squalida
BRODIAEA
   elegans Hoover, 188
   terrestris Kellogg, 188
   B. coronaria var. *macrocarpa*
   ssp. kernensis, 188
BRUCKENTHALIA
   spiculifolia (Salisb.) Rchb., 156
BULBINELLA
   angustifolia (Cockayne &
   Laing), 229, Fig. 239
   hookeri (Hook. f.) Cheesem.,
   229
BUPLEURUM
   longiradiatum Turcz., 203
   B. aureum
   var. shikotanense, 203
CALANDRINIA
   acutisepala Suarez , 196
   caespitosa Gill., 196
   cistiflora Gill., 196
   gilliesii Hook. & Arn., 196
   sericea Poepp. & Walp., 196
   umbellata (Ruiz. & Pav.) DC,
   196
CALCEOLARIA
   biflora Lam., 197
   fothergillii Soland.
   lanceolata Cav., 198,
   polyrhiza Cav., 198
   tenella Poepp. & Endl., 198
   uniflora Ruiz. & Pav., 198, Fig.
   185
   var. darwinii, 44, 198
CALLUNA
   vulgaris L.
   'Kinlochruel', 48
CALOCHORTUS
   albus Dougl. ex Benth., 189
   luteus Nutt., 188

uniflorus Hook. & Arn, 189
C. lilacinus
venustus Benth., 188, Fig.167
weedii Alph. Wood, 189
CALTHA
   leptosepala DC., 180
   var. sulphurea, 180, Fig. 156
   ssp. howellii
   C. biflora
CAMPANULA
   abietina Griesb. & Schrenk.,
   152
   C. patula ssp. *abietina*
   alpina Jacq., 152
   aucheri A. DC., 136, Fig. 83
   betulifolia C. Koch , 136, Fig.
   84
   C. betulaefolia
   calaminthifolia Lam., 153
   cashmeriana Royle, 136
   C. evolvulacea
   chamissonis Fed., 204
   C. dasyantha,
   C. pilosa var. *dasyantha*
   'superba', Fig. 199
   collina Bieb. Non Sims., 136
   coriacea Davis, 136
   fenestrellata Feer, 153
   ssp. fenestrellata, 153
   ssp. istriaca, 153
   C. garganica ssp. *fenestrellata*
   garganica Ten., 153
   glomerata L., 153
   hagelia Boiss., 136
   hawkinsiana Hausskn. & Heldr.,
   153
   lasiocarpa Cham., 169, 204
   C. algida
   moesiaca Velen., 153
   morettiana Rchb., 41
   oreadum Boiss. & Heldr., 153
   petrophila Rupr., 136
   piperi T. J. Howell , 170
   portenschlagiana Schult., 153

C. *muralis*
punctata Lam., 204
C. *takesimana*,
'Alba', 204
' Alba Nana', 204
raddeana Trautv., 136
rotundifolia L. , 169
var. olympica, 169
rupicola Boiss. & Sprun., 153
sartorii Boiss. & Sprun., 153
thessala Maire., 153
thyrsoides L., 153
tridentata Schreb., 136, Fig. 83
C. *biebersteiniana*
C. *bithynica*
versicolor Andrews., 153, Fig. 85
waldsteiniana Roem. & Schult., 153
CARDIOCRINUM
giganteum (Wallich) Mak., 130
CASSIOPE
fastigiata (Wall) D.Don, 99, Fig. 24
hypnoides (L.) D. Don, 170
Harrimanella hypnoides
lycopodioides (Pall.) D. Don, 170, 206, Fig. 205
var. globularis, 206
var. gracilis, 206
'Beatrice Lilley', 170
mertensiana (Bong.) D. Don, 170
var. gracilis, 170
selaginoides Hook. f. & Th., 42, 95, 100, Fig. 25
var. nana, 100
tetragona (L.) D. Don, 170
var. saximontana, 170
wardii Marq., 170, Fig. 26
'Bearsden', 100
'Muirhead', 100, 170
CELMISIA

alpina (Kirk) Cheesem., 218
angustifolia Ckn., 218, Fig. 223
argentea T. Kirk, 218
bellidioides Hook. f., 218
semicordata Petri3, 218, Fig. 225
coriacea Hort.
gracilenta Hook. f., 218
hectori Hook. f., 218
hookeri Ckn., 218, Fig. 224
longifolia Cass., 230
sessiliflora Hook. f, 218, Fig. 226
spectabilis Hook. F., 218
traversii Hook. f., 219
CENTAUREA
triumfettii All., 151
ssp. stricta, 151
CHINOCHLOA
rubra Zotov. 229
CLEMATIS
marmoraria Sneddon, 35, 37, 48, 224, Fig. 236
'Joe', 35, 37, 45
paniculata Gmel., 224
petriei Allan., 224
x cartmanii, 225
'Craigton Comet', 225
CODONOPSIS
clematidea C.B. Cl., 98
convolvulacea Kurz., 99
meleagris Diels., 99
ovata Benth., 99
thalictrifolia Wallich., 99
vinciflora Kom., 99
COLCHICUM
pusillum Sieb., 161
turcicum Janka., 161
ssp. variegatum, 162
C. *parkinsonii*
COPROSMA
cheesemanii W. Oliv., 226
petriei Cheesem., 226

CORNUS
- canadensis L., 170, Fig. 133
- *Chamaepericlymenum canadense*
- suecica L., 170
- *Chamaepericlymenum suecicum*

CORYDALIS
- bulbosa (L.) D C., 157, Fig. 89
- cashmeriana Royle., 55, 112, Fig. 36
- flexuosa Franch., 112
- 'Blue Panda', 112
- 'China Blue', 112
- ' Père David' , 112
- fumariifolia Maxim, 208
- *C. ambigua*
- lutea (L.) DC., 157.
- ochroleuca Koch, 157, Fig. 90
- solida (L.) Sw., 24
- *C. decipiens*
- 'Highland Mist', 24

COTULA
LEPTINELLA
- atrata Hook. f., 219
- var. dendyi , 219
- coronopifolia L., 230
- pectinata Hook. f., 219
- potentillina (F. Muell.) Druce, 219
- *C. muelleri*
- pyrethrifolia Hook. f., 219
- squalida (Hook. f.) Hook. f., 219

CRASPEDIA
- glauca (Labill.) Spreng., 231
- 'Billy Buttons'

CREMANTHODIUM
- delavayi (Franch.) Diels. ex A. Lev., 97
- ellisii (Hook. f.) Kitamura, 97, Fig. 23
- *C. plantagineum*
- nepalense Kitamura, 97
- *C. oblongatum*
- rhodocephalum Diels, 97

CROCUS
- abantensis T. Baytop & B. Mathew, Fig. 102
- ancyrensis (Herb.) Maw., 144
- biflorus Miller, 144, Fig. 103
- ssp. alexandri, 144
- ssp. weldenii, 144
- cancellatus Herb., 143, Fig. 105
- ssp. cilicicus, 143
- chrysanthus (Herb.) Herb., 144, Fig. 104
- 'Blue Pearl', 144
- 'Cream Beauty', 144
- 'Snow Bunting', 144
- 'Zwanenberg Bronze', 144
- cvijicii Kosanin, 160
- dalmaticus Vis.,160
- flavus Weston, 144
- fleischeri Gay., 144, Fig. 106
- *C. aureus*
- *C. luteus*
- gargaricus Herb., 144
- ssp. herbertii, 144
- hadriaticus Herb., 160
- karduchorum Kotschy ex Maw.
- korolkowii Regel ex Maw., 144
- kosaninii Pulevic., 160
- kotschyanus E.Koch., 143
- var. leucopharynx, 143
- *C. zonatus*
- malyi Vis., 160
- niveus Bowles., 160
- olivieri Gay., 144
- ssp. balansae, 144
- ssp. olivieri, 144
- oreocreticus B.L. Burtt, 144
- pallasii Goldb., 160
- *C. albanus*
- *C. elwesii*
- ssp. *pallasii*, Fig. 107
- pestalozzae Boiss., 144
- pulchellus Herb., 143
- reticulatus Stev. ex Adams., 144
- robertianus C. Brickell, 160

scardicus Kosanin, 161
scharojanii Rupr., 143
sieberi Gay., 161
　ssp. sublimis, Fig. 108
　ssp. atticus, 161, Fig. 109
speciosus M. Bieb., 143
thomasii Ten., 161
tommasianus Herb., 161
veluchensis Herb., 161
CRUCKSHANKIA
gracilis, 26
hymenodon Hook. & Arn., 26
CYANANTHUS
delavayi Franch., 99
lobatus Wall. ex Benth. 95, 99
'Sherriff's Variety', 99
microphyllus Edgew., 99
C. integer
CYATHODES
colensoi Hook. f., 222
CYCLAMEN
cilicium Boiss. & Heldr., 140, Fig. 94
coum Miller, 140
hederifolium Aiton, 140
C. neapolitanum
intaminatum (Meikle) Grey-Wilson, 140
C. cilicum var. *alpinum*
mirabile Hildebr., 140
parviflorum Pobed., 140, Fig. 95
trochopteranthum Schwarz., 140
DABOECIA
x 'William Buchanan', 51
x 'William Buchanan Gold', 51
x 'Jack Drake', 53
DAISWA
polyphylla (Sm.) Raf., 130, Fig. 79
Paris polyphylla
var. alba, 130

violacea (Lev) Takht., 130
Paris violacea
yunnanensis (Franch.) Takht., 130
Paris yunnanensis
DAPHNE
x hendersonii, Hodgkin ex. C.D. Brickell, 24
'Rose Bud', 24
oleoides Schreb., 159, Fig. 100
petraea Leyb., 41
retusa Hemsl., 129
tangutica Maxim., 129
DELPHINIUM
brunonianum Royle, 95, 127
cashmerianum Royle, 127
muscosum Exell & Hill, 127
pylzowii Maxim. ex Reg., 127
tatsienense Franch., 127, Fig. 65
DIANTHUS
anatolicus Boiss., 136
brevicaulis Fenzl., 136
freynii Vandas., 154
fruticosus L., 154
D. arboreus
haematocalyx Boiss. & Heldr., 154
　ssp. pindicola, 154
　var. alpinus, 154
microlepis Boiss., 154.
myrtinervius Griesb., 154
D. myrtinervis
nardiformis Janka, 154
pavonius Tausch, 53
D. neglectus
'Inshriach Dazzler', 53
petraeus Waldst. & Kit., 154
pinifolius Sibth. & Sm., 136
D. androsaceus
scardicus Wettst., 24, 154, Fig. 87
simulans Stoj. & Stef., 154
squarrosus Bieb., 136

'Nanus', 137
zederbaueri, 137
DIAPENSIA
  lapponica L., 204
  var. obovata , 205, Fig. 200
DIASCIA
  barberae Hook., 235
  cordata N.E. Br., 235
  'Ruby Field', 235
DICENTRA
  peregrina Makino, 207, Fig. 214
  'Alba', 207
  D. pusilla
DIGITALIS
  lanata Ehrh., 159
DIONYSIA
  afghanica Grey-Wilson, 141
  archibaldii Wendebo, 26
  aretioides (Lehm.) Boiss., 38, 41
  D. demawendica
  bryoides Boiss. & Buhse., 141
  curviflora Bunge. , 36, 141
  diapensifolia Boiss., 141
  freitagii Wendelbo, 141
  involucrata Zapr., 141
  lamingtonii Stapf., 141
  michauxii (Duby) Boiss, 141.
  tapetodes Bunge., 141
  viscidula Wendelbo, 141
DIPLARRHENA
  moraea Labill., 232
  latifolia Benth., 232
  moraea var. *latifolia*
  D. moraea var. *alpina*
DODECATHEON
  alpinum (A. Gray) E. Greene, 178
  clevelandii E. Greene, 178, Fig. 149
  conjugans E. Greene, 178, Fig. 150
  D. glastifolium
  dentatum Hook., 178
  hendersonii A. Gray, 178
  D. atratum
  D. cruciatum
  D. latifolium
  jeffreyi van Houtte, 178
  D. lancifolium
  D. tetandrum
  D. viviparum
  meadia L., 178
  D. hugeri
  D. pauciflorum
  poeticum L. F. Henderson, 179, Fig. 151
  pulchellum (Raf.) Merr., 179.
  D. amethystinum
  D. puberulum
  D. radicatum
  'Red Wings', 179
DRABA
  cappadocica Boiss. & Bal, 135
  D. calycosa
  incerta Pays. 169
  longisiliqua Schmalh., 135
  mollissima Steven, 36, 41, 68, 135
  oligosperma Hook., 169,
  oreades Schrenk, 98, Fig. 21
  polytricha Ledeb., 135, Fig. 82
  D. reuteri
  rigida Willd., 135
  rosularis Boiss., 135
  ventosa A. Gray, 169
DRACOCEPHALUM
  calophyllum Hand.-Mazz., 112
  forrestii W.W. Sm., 12
  isabellae Forr., 112
  nutans L., 112
  wallichii Sealey, 112
  D. speciosum
DRACOPHYLLUM
  muscoides Hook. f., 223
  pronum W. Oliv., 223
EDRAIANTHUS
  dalmaticus (A.DC.) A. DC., 153

graminifolius (L.) A. DC., 153, Fig. 86
pumilio (Portenschlag) A. DC., 154
Wahlenbergia pumilio
serbicus Petrovic., 154
serpyllifolius (Vis.) A. DC., 154
'Major', 48
tenuifolius (Waldst. & Kit.) A.DC., 154
E. bosniacus

ELMERA
racemosa (S. Wats.) Rydb., 181, Fig. 160
Heuchera racemosa
Tellima racemosa

EMBOTHRIUM
E. coccineum Forst. & Forst. f., 56, 69

EPACRIS
impressa Labill., 231
petrophila Hook. f., 232

EPILOBIUM
crassum Hook. f., 224
glabellum Forst. f., 224
pedunculare A. Cunn., 224

EPIMEDIUM
diphyllum Lodd., 203
grandiflorum Morr., 203, Fig. 197
setosum Koidz., 203

ERIGERON
aureus Greene, 167, Fig. 126
'Canary Bird', 167
Haplopappus brandegeei
chrysopsidis A. Gray, 167
compositus Pursh., 167, Fig. 127
glabellus Nutt., 167
karvinskianus DC., 167
peregrinus (Pursh.) Greeene., 167
pinnatisectus (A. Gray) Nels., 167, Fig. 128

ERIOGONUM
caespitosus Nutt., 175
flavum Nutt. 175
var. piperi, 175, Fig. 145
var. xanthium, 176
jamesii Benth., 176
kennedyi Porter in S. Wats., 176
ovalifolium Torr., 176
umbellatum Torr., 176

ERIOPHYTON
wallichii Benth., 43

ERITRICHIUM
howardii (A. Gray) Rydb., 169
nanum (L.) Schrad. ex Gandin., 41, 169
ssp. aretioides, 169
ssp. argenteum, 169
ssp. elongatum, 169

ERYNGIUM
amethystinum L., 150

ERYTHRONIUM
americanum Ker-Gawl. 189
californicum Purdy., 189
'White Beauty', 189
grandiflorum Pursh. 189, Fig. 168
hendersonii S.Wats., 189, Fig. 169
montanum A. Wats, 190, Fig. 170
oregonum Appleg., 189
revolutum Sm., 189
tuolumnense Appleg, 190
'Pagoda', 190

EUPHRASIA
officinalis agg. L., 96

EURYOPS
acraeus M. D. Henderson, 234
E. evansii Hort.
tysonii Phillips, 234

FELICIA
amoena (Sch. Bip.) Levyns, 234
petiolata (Harv.) N.E. Br., 234

Aster petiolatus
rosulata Yeo, 234
Aster natalensis
uliginosa (Wood & M. Evans) Grau., 234
FRITILLARIA
acmopetala Boiss. 146, Fig. 114
affinis (Schultz) Sealy, 190, Fig. 171
F. eximea
F. lanceolata
F. lunellii
F. mutica
armena Boiss., 146
assyriaca Bak., 147
aurea Schott, 146
F. cilico-taurica
biflora Lindl., 190
bithynica Bak., 146, Fig. 115
F. citrina
F. dasyphylla
F. pineticola
F. schliemannii
F. subalpina
bucharica Reg., 146
camschatcensis (L.) Ker-Gawl., 190
caucasica Adams., 146
conica Boiss., 48, 162
crassifolia Boiss. & Reut., 48, 147, Fig. 116
ssp. crassifolia, 147
davisii Turrill., 162, Fig. 117
ehrhartii Boiss. & Orph., 162
elwesii Boiss., 147
gibbosa Boiss., 38, 41
glauca Greene, 190, Fig. 172
graeca Boiss. & Sprun., 162
ssp. graeca, 162
F. guicciardii
ssp. thessala, 162
grayana Rchb. F. & Baker, 190
F. biflora var. *ineziana*
F. roderickii

latifolia Willd., 147
var. *nobilis*, Fig. 118
meleagris L., 147
messanensis Raf., 162
ssp. gracilis, 162
michailovskyi Fomin.
olivieri Bak., 147
persica L., 147
F. eggeri
F. libanotica
pinardii Boiss., 147
F. alpina
F. fleischeri
F. syriaca
pontica Wahlenb., 147
pudica (Pursh) Spreng., 190
F. olympica
recurva Benth., 191, Fig. 173
F. adamantina
F. coccinea
sibthorpiana (Sm.) Bak., 147
tubiformis Gren. & Godron., 48
uva-vulpis Rix., 147
GAULTHERIA
adenothrix (Miq.) Maxim., 206, Fig. 206
antipoda Forst. f., 223
crassa Allen
G. rupestris var. *parvifolia*
cuneata (Rehd. & Wils.) Bean, 100
depressa Hook. f., 223
G. antipoda var. *depressa*
nana C.Y.Wu & T.Z. Hsu
nummularioides D. Don, 100
var. minuta, 100
thymifolia Stapf., 100
G. thibetica
trichophylla Royle, 100
GAZANIA
krebsiana Less., 234, Fig. 240
ssp. serratula, 234
GENTIANA
affinis Griesb. ex Hook., 172

algida Ball., 171, 208, Fig. 136
G. nubigena
G. romanzovii
bellidifolia Hook. f., 223
var. australis, 223
cachemirica Desne., 112, Fig. 36
coelestis H. Smith, 110
corymbifera T. Kirk, 224
depressa D. Don, 22, 109
farreri Balf. f., 24, 44, 108, 109, 110
frigida Haenk., 156
G. algida ssp. *frigida*
georgei Diels., 111, Fig. 32
gracilipes Turrill, 111
G. purdomii
hexaphylla Maxim. ex Kuzn., 111, Fig. 33
Inshriach Hybrids
'Blue Heaven', 53
'Darkness', 53
'Drake's Strain', 53
kuroo Royle, 111
loderi Hook. f., 111
oreodoxa H. Smith
ornata Wall., 22, 107, 109
patula Cheesem., 223
prolata Balf. f., 109
pyrenaica L., 156
G. dshimilensis
saxosa Forst. f., 224, Fig. 235
serotina Ckn., 224, Fig. 234
sikkimensis C.B. Cl., 111
sino-ornata Balf. f., 24, 107, 108, 109,110,Fig. 34
'Brin Form', 54
x 'Margaret', 24
stragulata Balf. f. & Forr., 111
tenuifolia Petrie, 24
trichotoma Kuzn., 111
G. hopei
triflora Pall., 228, Fig. 212

veitchiorum Hemsl., 107, 108, 109, Fig. 35
x bernardii, 110
x caroli, 110
x 'Devonhall', 110
x 'Farorna', 110
x 'Inverleith', 110
x macaulayi, 110
x stevenagensis, 10
GERANIUM
dalmaticum (Beck) Rechb., 156
libani P.H. Davis, 138
G. libanoticum
peloponnesiacum Boiss., 156
renardii Trautv., 138
sessiliflorum Cav., 224
ssp. novaezelandii, 224
var. nigricans, 224
tuberosum L., 138
versicolor L., 156
G. striatum
wallichianum D. Don, 138
GEUM
pentapetalum (L.) Mak, 210
GLADIOLUS
cardinalis Curtis, 235
carinatus C. H. Wright, 235
tristis L., 235
var. concolor, 235
GLAUCIDIUM
palmatum Sieb. & Zucc., 208, Fig. 213
G. paradoxum
GUTIERREZIA
baccharoides Sch. Bip., 193
GYPSOPHILA
aretioides Boiss., 137
briquetiana Schischk., 137
nana Bory & Chaob., 155
tenuifolia Bieb., 137
HAASTIA
pulvinaris Hook. f., 38, 219, Fig. 227
recurva Hook. f., 219

sinclairii Hook. f., 219
HEBE
   albicans (Petrie) Ckn. 226
   'Red Edge', 226
   'Cranleigh Gem', 226
   amplexicaulis (J.B. Armstrong) Ckn. & Allan, 226
   x 'Carl Teschner', 227
   buchananii (Hook. f.) Ckn. & Allan, 226
   elliptica (Forst. f.) Pennell, 227
   epacridea (Hook. f.) Ckn. & Allan, 227
   haastii (Hook. f.) Ckn. & Allan, 227
   hectorii (Hook. f.) Ckn. & Allan, 227
   var. demissa, 227
   hulkeana (F. Muell.) Ckn. & Allan, 227
   'New Zealand Lilac', 227
   lycopodioides (Hook. f.) Ckn. & Allan, 227
   pimelioides (Hook. f.) Ckn. & Allan, 227
   pinguifolia (Hook. f.) Cockayne & Allan, 227
   'Pagei', 227
   rakaiensis (J.B. Armstr.) Ckn., 227
   'Golden Dome', 227
   raoulii (Hook. f.) Ckn. & Allan, 227
   var. pentasepala, 227
   vernicosa (Hook. f.) Ckn. & Allan, 227
HELICHRYSUM
   bellidioides (Forst. f.) Willd. 220
   heldreichii Boiss., 151
   hookeri (Sonder) Druce, 231
   Ozothamnus hookeri
   microphyllum (Hook. f.) Benth. & Hook., 220
   milfordiae Killick., 235
   orientale (L.) Gaertn., 151
   pagophilum M.D. Henderson, 235
   praecurrens Hilliard,
   selagao (Hook. f.) T. Kirk, 220
   sessiloides Hilliard, 235
   H. sessile
   splendidum (Thumb.) Less., 235
   H. trilineatum
   H. alveolatum
HELLEBORUS
   cyclophyllus (A. Br.) Boiss., 58, Fig. 100
   foetidus L., 54
   'Wester Flisk', 54
   niger L., 54, 158
   'Trotter's Wheel', 54
   odorus Waldst. & Kit., 158
   orientalis Lam., 54
   'Trotter's Spotted', 54
HESPERANTHA
   baurii Bak., 235
   H. mossii
   falcata (L. f.) Ker-Gawl., 235
HEUCHERA
   cylindrica Douglas ex Hook., 185
   micrantha Douglas ex Lindl., 185
   racemosa S. Wats., 185
   Elmera racemosa
   sanguinea Engelm., 185
   x ' Coral Bells', 185
HORMATHOPHYLLA
   reverchonii (Degen & Hervier) Greuter & Burdet, 42
HYL0MECON
   japonicum (Thunb.) Prantl & Kundig, 208, Fig. 215
HYMENOXYS
   acaulis (Pursh) K.F. Parker, 168, Fig. 129
   Actinella acaulis
   Actinella simplex

Tetraneuris acaulis
  grandiflora (Torr. & A. Gray)
  K.F. Parker, 168
  Actinella grandiflora
  Rydbergia grandiflora
HYPERICUM
  athoum Boiss. & Orph., 155
  cerastoides (Spach) N. Robson, 137
  H. rhodoppeum
  delphicum Boiss. & Heldr., 155
  fragile Heldr. & Sart., 155
  linarioides Boisse., 137
  H. repens Hort.
  olympicum L., 137, 155
  'Grandiflorum', 137
  ' Sulphureum', 137
  H. polyphyllum Hort.
  pallens Soland. in Russell, 137
  H. cuneatum
  polyphyllum Boiss. & Bal., 137
  H. olympicum var. *minus*
  richeri Vill., 155
HYPOXIS
  hygrometrica Labill., 232
INCARVILLEA
  arguta (Royle) Royle
  compacta Maxim., 98, Fig. 22
  delavayi Bur. & Franch., 98
  mairei (Lev) Grierson, 98
  var. grandiflora, 98
  I. brevipes
  I. grandiflora var. *brevipes*
IPHEION
  uniflorum (Graham) Raf., 192
  Tritelia unifloum
IRIS
  afghanica Wendelbo, 145, Fig. 110
  attica Boiss. & Heldr., 145, Fig. 111
  bakeriana Foster, 145, 146
  I. reticulata var. *bakeriana*
  cretensis Janka, 161

I. cretica
  cristata Solander, 185
  danfordiae (Baker) Boiss., 145
  douglasiana Herbert., 186, Fig. 164
  forrestii Dykes, 52
  gracilipes A. Gray, 212
  histrio Reichb. f., 145
  var. aintabensis, 146
  histrioides (G.F. Wilson) S. Arnott, 146
  innominata Henderson, 186, Fig. 165
  japonica Thumb., 212
  lacustris Nutall, 185
  macrosiphon Torrey, 186
  I. amabilis
  missouriensis Nuttall, 186
  pseudacorus L., 186
  pumila L., 145
  purdyi Eastw., 186
  reticulata M. Bieb., 145, 146
  sari Schott. ex Baker, 146
  setosa Pall ex. Link, 186
  ssp. canadensis, 186
  suaveolens Boiss. & Reut., 145
  I. mellita
  tectorum Maxim., 212
  'Alba', 212
  tenax Douglas ex Lindl., 186, Fig. 166
  unguicularis Poir., 161, Fig. 112
  I. stylosa
  versicolor L., 186
  winowgradowii Fomin., 37, 145, Fig. 113
IXIA
  monodelpha Delaroche, 237
JANKAEA
  heldreichii Boiss., 41
KALMIA
  polifolia Wangenh., 171, Fig. 134
  var. microphylla, 171

K. glauca
KALMIOPSIS
  K. leachiana (Henderson) Rehd., 41
  Rhododendron leachiana
  Rhodothamnus leachiana
  'M. le Piniec', 41
KELSEYA
  uniflora (S. Wats.) Rydb., 41, 49, 180
LAPEIROUSIA
  silenoides (Jacq.) Ker-Gawl., 236, Fig. 242
LEDUM
  palustre (L.), 206
  ssp. groenlandicum, 206
LEONTOPODIUM
  discolor Beauv., 203
  L. japonicum ssp. *sachalinense*
  fauriei (Beauv.) Hand-Mazz., 203
  L. alpinum ssp. *fauriei*
  kurilense Tak., 203
  L. kamtschaticum
LEPTOSPERMUM
  humifusum A. Cunn. ex Schau, 232
  L. rupestre
  L. scoparium prostratum
LEUCOGENES
  grandiceps (Hook. f.) Beauv., 36, 220, Fig. 228
  leontopodium (Hook. f.) Beauv., 36, 220, Fig. 229
LEWISIA
  brachycalyx Engl. ex A. Gray, 37, 59, 176
  columbiana (Howell ex A. Gray) Robinson, 177
    ssp. rupicola, 177
  cotyledon (S.Wats.) Robinson, 177
    'Carousel Hybrids', 177
    'Sunset Strain', 53, 177

longipetala (Piper) S. Clay, 177
nevadensis (A. Gray) Robinson, 59, 176
L. bernardina
pygmaea (A. Gray) Robinson, 177
rediviva Pursh, 177, Fig. 146
tweedyi (A. Gray) Robinson, 177
LIBERTIA
  pulchella Spreng., 233
LILIUM
  lophophorum Franch., 130, Fig. 74
  L. lophophora
  Fritillaria lophophora
  nanum Klotzsch, 16, 130, Fig. 73
    var. flavidum, 130, Fig. 72
  Nomocharis nana
  sherriffiae Stearn, 96, 130, Fig. 75
  souliei (Franch.) Sealy, 130, Fig. 76
LINUM
  capitatum Kit. & Schult., 157
LOASA
  triphylla Juss., 194
    var. vulcanica, 194
LOBELIA
  angulata Forst. f., 221
  Pratia angulata
    var. treadwellii, 222
  linnaeoides (Hook. f.) Petrie, 222
  pedunculata R. Br., 231
  Pratia pedunculata
  roughii Hook. f., 222
LUPINUS
  breweri A. Gray, 171
    var. bryoides, 171
    var. grandiflorum 171
  lepidus Douglas ex Lindl., 171
    var. lobbii, 171

LYCHNIS
　viscaria L., 66
LYSIMACHIA
　japonica Thunb. 209
　minutissima, 209
MAIHUENIA
　poeppigii (Otto & Pfeiff.) A. Weber, 47
MECONOPSIS
　aculeata Royle, 75
　betonicifolia Franch., 115
　M. baileyi
　cambrica (L.) Vig., 113
　chelidonifolia Bur. & Franch.,113
　dhwojii G. Tayl. ex Hay, 75, 114
　gracilipes G. Taylor , 22
　grandis Prain, 45, 75, 116, 117, Fig. 38
　'GS 600', 117
　' Sherriff 6oo', 117
　x sheldonii, 116
　horridula Hook. f. & Thoms, 75, 113, 116, Fig. 37
　M. prattii
　integrifolia (Maxim.) Franch., 75 , 115, Fig. 39
　M. soulei
　x 'finlayorum', 56
　'Ivory Poppy', 115
　M. harleyana
　latifolia (Maxim.) Franch, 116.
　napaulensis DC., 22, 75, 115, 116
　M. wallichii
　paniculata (D. Don) Prain, 114, 115, Fig. 40
　pseudointegrifolia (Maxim.) Franch..., 115, Fig. 41
　punicea Maxim., 59
　quintuplinervia Reg., 75, 115, Fig. 42
　regia G. Tayl., 75, 114
　x sheldonii G. Tayl., 75
　'Branklyn', 55
　'Jimmy Bayne', 59
　sherriffii G. Tayl., 45
　simplicifolia (D.Don) Walp., 115
　superba King ex Prain, 96, 114
　villosa (Hook. f.) G. Tayl., 113, Fig. 43
　Cathcartia villosa
MEGACARPAEA
　polyandra Benth., 55
MENZIESIA
　ciliicalyx (Miq.) Maxim., 206
　'Buchanan's Dwarf'
　pentandra Maxim., 206
MERTENSIA
　alpina (Torr.) G. Don., 169
　lanceolata (Pursh.) A.DC. , 169
　longiflora Greene., 169
　viridis (A. Nels.) A. Nels. , 169
MINUARTIA
　juniperina (L.) Maire & Petitm., 155
　Arenaria juniperina
MUSCARI
　armeniacum Bak., 147
　M. cyaneo-violaceum
　M. polyanthum
　M. sosnovskyi
　M. steupii
　M. szovitsianum
　M. woronowii
　'Blue Spike', 147
　'Heavenly Blue', 147
　aucheri (Boiss.) Bak., 147
　M. lingulatum
　comosum (L.) Mill. , 147
　Leopoldia comosa
　latifolium T. Kirk, 147
　macrocarpum Greene, 148, Fig. 119
　M. moschatum var. *flavum*
　moschatum Willd., 148

M. muscarimia
M. ambrosiacum
MYOSOTIS
  australis R. Br., 221
  colensoi (T. Kirk) Macbr., 221
  M. decora
  explanata Cheesem., 221
MYRTEOLA
  nummularia Berg, 194
  Myrtus nummularia
NARCISSUS
  cantabricus DC., 24
  x christopheri, 24
  'Camaro', 24
  romieuxii Br.-Bl. & Maire, 24
  rupicola Dufour
    ssp. watieri, 28
NARDOPHYLLUM
  bryoides (Lam.) Cabrera, 27
NASSAUVIA
  gaudichaudii (Cass.) Cass. ex Gaud., 193
  pygmaea (Cass.) Hook. f., 193
  revoluta D. Don, 193, Fig. 181
NIEREMBERGIA
  patagonica Speg., 199, Fig. 188
  Petunia patagonica
NOMOCHARIS
  aperta (Franch.) Wils., 131, Fig. 77
  farreri (W. E. Evans) R. Harrow, 131
  N. pardanthina var. *farreri*
  pardanthina Franch., 131, Fig. 78
  mairei Lev., 131
  saluenensis Balf. f., 131
NOTHOLIRION
  bulbiferum (Lingl.) Stearn, 131
  N. hyacinthinum
  campanulatum Cotton & Stearn, 131
  macrophyllum (D. Don) Boiss., 132

thompsonianum (Royle) Stapf., 132
NOTOTHLASPI
  australe Hook. f., 221, Fig. 232
  rosulatum Hook. f., 22, Fig. 233
OLEARIA
  frostii (F. Muell.), 231
  O. stellata var. *frostii*
  Aster frostii
  phlogopappa (Labill) DC., 231
OMPHALOGRAMMA
  delavayi Franch., 118
  elegans Forr., 118
  elwesiana (King ex G. Watt) Franch., 118
  vinciflorum (Franch.) Franch., 57
  O. engleri
  O. rockii
  O. vincaeflorum
  O. viola-grandis
ORNITHOGALUM
  lanceolatum Labill., 148
  oliogophyllum Clarke, 148, Fig. 120
  O. aucheri
  O. balansae
  O. brevipedicillatum
  sibthorpii W. Greuter, 148
  O. nanum
  sigmoideum Freyn. & Sint., 148
  umbellatum L., 148
OURISIA
  caespitosa Hook. f., 227
    var. gracilis, 227
  coccinea Comm. ex Jus., 198, Fig. 186
  O. elegans
  fragrans Phil., 199, Fig. 187
  O. suaveolens
  macrophylla Hook. f., 227
  x 'Loch Ewe', 198, 227
  macrocarpa Hook. f., 228
  'Snowflake', 228

microphylla Poepp. & Endl., 199
OXALIS
  adenophylla Gillies ex Hook., 194, Fig. 182
  'Brenda Anderson', 24
  enneaphylla Cav., 194, Fig. 183
  laciniata Cav., 26, 195
  loricata Dusen, 195
  patagonica Speg., 195
  squamosa-radicata Steud., 195
PARAHEBE
  catarractae (Forst. f.) W. Oliv., 228
  Veronica catarractae
  ssp. diffusa, 228
  ssp. catarractae, 228
  x bidwillii (Hook. f.) W. Oliv., 228
  decora Ashwin, 228
  Veronica bidwillii
  hookeriana (Walp.) W. Oliv., 228
  linifolia (Hook. f.) W. Oliv.
  Veronica linifolia
  'Blue Skies', 228
  lyallii (Hook f.) W. Oliv., 228
  Veronica lyallii
  'Clarence', 228
  'Mervyn', 228
PARAQUILEGIA
  anemonoides (Willd) Ubr., 43, 55, 57, Fig. 62
  P. microphylla
PATRINIA
  gibbosa Maxim., 211
  triloba Miq., 211
  var. palmata, 211
PELARGONIUM
  endlicherianum Fenzl., 138
  quercetorum Agnew., 139
PENNELLIANTHUS
  frutescens, 210

Penstemon frutescens
A.B. Lambert
PENSTEMON
  acaulis L.O. Williams, 183
  alpinus Torr., 184
  bracteatus D.D. Keck, 182
  caespitosus Nutt. ex A. Gray, 183
  ssp. suffruticosus, 183
  compactus (Keck) Crosswhite, 184
  crandallii A. Nels., 183
  ssp. procumbens, 183
  davidsonii Greene, 182
  eriantherus Pursh., 184, Fig. 161
  fruticosus (Pursh) Greene, 182
  ssp. scouleri, 182
  'Albus', 182
  'Holly', 182
  gormanii Greene, 184
  hallii A. Gray, 184
  harbourii A. Gray, 183
  heterophyllus Lindl., 184
  humilis Nutt. ex A. Gray, 183
  laricifolius Hook. & Arn., 183
  ssp. exilifolius, 183
  leonardii Rydb., 184
  linarioides A. Gray, 183
  newberryi A. Gray, 182, Fig. 162
  'Mountain Pride', 182
  pinifolius Greene, 183
  'Mersea Yellow', 183
  procerus Douglas, 183
  ssp. brachyanthus, 183
  ssp. formosus, 183
  ssp. tolmiei, 183, Fig. 163
  rupicola (Piper) Howell, 182
  teucrioides Greene, 184
  virens Pennell, 183
  whippleanus A. Gray, 183
PEREZIA
  recurvata (Vahl.) Less., 193

ssp. patagonica, 193
PERNETTYA
   mucronata (L. f.) Gaudich & Spreng., 27, 194, Fig.180
   Gaultheria mucronata
PETROPHYTON
   caespitosum (Nutt.) Rydb., 181
   Luetkea caespitosum
   Spiraea caespitosum
   cinerascens (Piper) Rydb., 181
   hendersonii (Canby) Rydb., 181
PHACELIA
   sericea (Graham) A.Gray, 172, Fig. 138
   campanularia A. Gray, 172
PHLOX
   adsurgens Torr. ex A. Gray, 173, Fig. 137
   'Red Buttes, 174
   'Wagon Wheel', 174
   bifida (L.) C. Beck, 173
   bryoides Nutt., 174
   P. muscoides bryoides
   caespitosa Nutt., 174
   P. douglasii var. *caespitosa*
   diffusa Benth., 174, Fig. 139
   P. douglasii var. *diffusa*
   divaricata L., 173
   ' Chattahoochee', 173
   P. canadensis
   douglasii Hook., 174
   P. piperi
   P. caespitosa var. *rigida*
   hendersonii (Canby) Rydb., 174, Fig. 140
   hirsuta E. Nelson, 174, Fig. 141
   P. stanburyi var. *hirsuta*
   hoodii Richards, 174, Fig. 142
   P. canescens
   Inshriach Hybrids
   'Crackerjack', 53
   'Red Admiral', 53
   multiflora Nels., 174
   var. depressa, 174

   nivalis Lodd. ex Sweet, 173
   var. hertzii, 173
   sibirica L.
   speciosa Pursh., 174, Fig. 143
   stolonifera Sims., 173
   'Ariane', 173
   'Ridge Hybrids', 173
   subulata L., 173
   triovulata Thurb. Ex Torr., 41
   mesoleuca Hort.
   nana glabella
PHYLLODOCE
   aleutica (Spreng.) A. Heller, 206, Fig. 207
   breweri (A. Gray) A. A. Heller, 171
   caerulea (L.) Bab., 206
   empetriformis (Sm.) D.Don, 171, Fig. 135
   nipponica Mak., 49, 206
PIERIS
   formosa (Wallich) D. Don, 51
   var. forrestii, 57, 69
   japonica (Thunb.) D. Don ex. G. Don,
   'William Buchanan',
PLEIONE
   albiflora Cribb & C. Z. Tang, 132
   bulbocodioides (Franch.) Rolfe, 132
   P. pogonioides
   P. henryi
   P. delavayi
   forrestii Schltr., 42, 132
   x confusa, 132
   formosana Hay, 132
   P. hui
   P. pricei
   humilis (Sm.) D. Don, 132
   'Frank Kingdon Ward', 42, 132
   limprichtii Schltr., 132
   P. bulbocodioides ' Limprichtii'
   'Shantung Hybrids', 132

'Ducat', 48
praecox (Smith) D. Don, 132
speciosa Ames & Schltr., 132
POLEMONIUM
caeruleum L., 174
elegans E. Greene, 175
pulcherrimum Hook.,175
viscosum Nutt., 175, Fig. 144
POLYGONATUM
falcatum Gray., 212
humile (Maxim.), 212
graminifolium Hook., 212
P. pumilum
odoratum (Mill.) Druce, 212
POTENTILLA
anserina L., 96
arbuscula D. Don, 128
P. fruticosa var. *rigida*
atrosanguinea Lodd. ex D. Don, 95
P. argyrophylla
cuneata (Wall.) Lehm., 128, Fig. 64
eriocarpa Wall ex Lehm., 128, Fig. 66
multifida L., 96
PRIMULA
algida Adams., 141
angustifolia Torr., Fig. 152
alpicola Stapf., 125
var. alba, 125
var. luna, 125
var. violacea, 125
amoena Bieb., 141, Fig. 96
P. elatior
ssp. *meyeri*
angustifolia Torr., 179, Fig. 152
anisodora Balf. f. & Forrest, 120
atrodentata W.W. Sm.,
aurantiaca W.W. Sm. & Forrest 120
aureata Fletcher, 23, 35, 36, 41, 85, 124, Fig. 44
ssp. fimbriata, 124

beesiana Forrest, 120
bellidifolia King ex Hook., 122
P. menziesiana
bhutanica Fletcher, 56, 125
'Tantallon, 56
bracteosa Craib, 9, 124
bulleyana Forrest, 120
burmanica Balf. f. & Kingdon-Ward, 120
buryana Balf. f., 22, 126
calderiana Balf. f. & Cooper, 123, Fig. 47
ssp. strumosa, 123
capitata Hook., 121
var. capitata, 121
var. mooreana, 121
var. sphaerocephala, 121
chasmophila Balf. f., 9
chionantha Balf. f. & Forrest, 123, Fig. 53
clarkei G. Watt., 121
cockburniana Hemsl., 120.
cusickiana A. Gray, 49
cuneifolia Ledeb, 208
denticulata Sm., 121
deuteronana Craib., 22
dryadifolia Franch, 44.
eburnea Balf. f. & Cooper, 9
falcifolia Kingdon-Ward, 22
flaccida Balakr., 45, 126
P. nutans
floribunda Wall, 122
forrestii Balf. f., 37, 55, 119, Fig. 48
geraniifolia Hook. f., 121
glomerata Pax., 121
gracilipes Craib, 124, Fig. 56
griffithii (Watt) Pax., 123
heucherifolia Franch., 121
Inshriach Hybrids
'Bonfire', 53
'Christine', 53
'Dianne Hybrids', 53
'Drake's Form', 53

'Inshriach Hybrid', 53
'Inverewe', 53
involucrata Wall, 121
ioessa W.W. Sm., 125, Fig. 46
japonica A. Gray, 209, Fig. 216
kingii Watt, 44, 45, 119
macrophylla D. Don., 121, 123, Fig. 52
P. moorcroftiana
magellanica Lehm., 197
P. decipiens
Mc Watt Hybrids,
'Mc Watt's Blue', 45
'McWatt's Cream', 45
'McWatt's Crimson', 45
melanops W.W. Sm. & Kingdon-Ward, 123
minutissima Jacq., 122, Fig. 54
modesta Bisset & S. Moore, 209
var. fauriae, 209
muscarioides Hemsl., 122
nana (Hook. f.) Pax., 22, 124
var. alba, 124
'Ghose Strain'
P. edgeworthii, 61
P. winteri
nepalensis Smith, 124
parryi A. Gray, 179, Fig. 153
petiolaris Wall, 124
poissonii Franch., 120
prolifera Wall, 120
P. helodoxa
pulverulenta Duthie, 120
reidii Duthie, 55, 126, Fig. 55
var. williamsii, 45, 126
reptans Hook. f. ex Watt, 122
rosea Royle, 122, Fig. 57
rotundifolia Wall, 125
serratifolia Franch., 120
sherriffae Smith, 44, 45, 126
sieboldii E.Mori., 209, Fig. 217
sikkimensis Hook. f., 95, Fig. 49
var. hopeana, 9, 22, 125
sinoplantaginea Balf. f., 123
sinopurpurea Balf. f., 120
sonchifolia Franch., 21, 54, 124
strumosa Balf. f. & Cooper, 9, Fig. 45
ssp. calderiana
suffrutescens A. Gray, 179
takedana Tatew., 209, Fig. 218
tanneri King, 124, Fig. 50
tsariensis Smith, 124
umbratilis Balf. & Cooper, 9
vialii Delavay ex Franch, 126.
P. littoniana
waltonii G. Watt. ex Balf. f., 125
wattii King, 126
whitei W. E. Smith, 125, Fig.51
xanthopa Balf. & Cooper, 9
yargongensis Petitm., 122
yuparensis Tak., 209
PTEROCEPHALUS
perennis Coult., 156
P. parnassi
PULSATILLA
halleri (All.) Wild., 158
montana (Hoppe) Rchb., 158
patens (L.) Mill., 180, Fig. 158
P. nuttalliana
ssp. flavescens, 180
vernalis (L.) Mill., 158
PYGMAEA
CHIONOHEBE
pulvinaris Hook. f., 228
tetragona (Hook. f.) Ashwin, 228
RAMONDA
myconi L.) Rchb., 157
nathaliae Pancic & Petrovic, 157
serbica Pancic., 157, Fig. 88
RANUNCULUS
adoneus A. Gray, 180, Fig. 157
buchananii Hook. f., 225, Fig. 237
crithmifolius Hook. f., 225
ssp. paucifolius, 225
eschscholtzii Schdl., 180
var. exiimus, 180, Fig. 159

ssp. suksdorfi I, 180
  glacialis L., 180
  guzmannii H.B. & K, 197
  Krapfia gusmannii
  haastii Hook. f., 225
  lyallii Hook. f., 225, Fig. 238
  macaulayi A. Gray, 180
  nivicolus Hook., 180
  parnassifolius L.,
  'Gowrie', 24
  'Nuria, 24
  paucifolius T. Kirk, 225
RAOULIA
  australis Hook. f, 220
  eximia Hook. f., 41, 220, Fig. 230
  glabra Hook. f., 220
  haastii Hook. f., 220
  hookeri Allan., 220
  var. albo-sericea, 220
  var. apice-nigra, 220
  x loganii Cheeseman, 27
  mammilaris Hook. f., 221
  tenuicaulis Hook. f., 220
RHODODENDRON
  anthopogon D. Don, 23, 95, 103
  var. hypenanthum, 103
  'Betty Graham', 103
  aureum Georgi, 207, Fig. 208
  calostrotum Balf. & Kingdon-Ward, 105
  ssp. keleticum, 105
  R. radicans
  campylogynum Franch., 104
  var. myrtilloides, 104
  camtschaticum Pall., 207, Fig. 209
  charitopes Balf. & Farrer, 104
  ciliatum Hook., 105, Fig. 29
  cowanianum Davidian, 106
  dauricum L., 207, Fig. 210
  'Arctic Pearl', 207
  'Hokkaido', 207
  'Midwinter', 207
  'Nanum', 207
  degronianum Carr, 207
  ssp. yakushimanum, 35, 42, 207
  falconeri Hook., 76
  fastigiatum Franch., 105
  flavidum Franch., 105
  forrestii Diels, 107
  var. repens, 107
  var. tumescens, 107
  glaucophyllum Rehd., 96, 104
  var. tubiforme, 104
  hanceanum Hemsl., 42, 106
  'Nanum', 106
  hippophaeoides Balf. f. & W.W.Sm., 104
  impeditum Franch., 104
  kaempferi Planch., 207
  keiskei Miq., 207, Fig. 211
  'Yaku Fairy', 207
  kiusianum Mak, 207
  lapponicum (L.) Wahlenb., 164
  laudandum Cowan, 103, Fig .27
  var. temuense, 103
  lepidostylum Balf. & Forrest, 106
  lepidotum G. Don, 16, 23, 106, Fig. 30
  leucaspis Tagg, 103
  lowndesii Davidian, 105
  ludlowii Cowan, 106
  x 'Chikor', 106
  x 'Curlew', 106
  megeratum Balf. & Forrest, 103
  orthocladum Balf. f. & Forrest, 104
  var. microleucum, 104
  pemakoense Kingdon-Ward, 104
  polycladum Franch., 105
  R. scintillans
  R. compactum
  primuliflorum Bur. & Franch, 101, Fig. 28
  pumilum Hook., 16, 106
  racemosum Franch, 106, Fig. 31
  rupicola W.W. Sm., 105

var. chryseum, 105
sargentianum Rehd. & Wils. 103
sherriffii Cowan, 45
sinogrande Balf. f. & W. W.
Sm., 76
trichostomum Franch., 103
R. sphaeranthum
wardii W.W. Sm., 21
williamsianum Rehd. &
Wils., 107
RHODOHYPOXIS
baurii (Bak.) Nel., 236
var. baurii, 236, Fig. 241
var. confecta, 236
var. platypetala, 236
RODGERSIA
nepalensis Cope & Cullen, 17
ROMULEA
bulbocodium (L.) Sebast. &
Mauri, 236, Fig. 243
R. grandiflora
Trichonema bulbocodium
macowanii Bak., 236
R. longituba
rosea (L.) Ecklon, 236
var. speciosa, 236
R. sicula
Trichonema purpurascens
thodei Schlechter, 24
ROSCOEA
alpina Royle., 132
auriculata Schum., 132
R. sikkimensis
cautleoides Gagnep. 132
humeana Balf. & Smith, 132
purpurea, 132
var. procera, 132
ROSULARIA
aizoon (Fenzl.) A. Berger, 138
alpestris (Kar. & Kir.) A.
Boriss., 138
chrysantha (Boiss.) Takht., 138
Umbilicus chrysanthus
rechingeri Jansson, 138

sempervivum (Bieb.) A. Berger,
138
serpentinica (Werderm.)
Muirhead, 138
SANGUINARIA
canadensis L., 172
'Plena', 171
SAUSSUREA
gossypiphora Wall, 97
laniceps Hand-Mazz., 97, Fig. 20
longibracteata Decne., 97
obvallata Wall., 97
SAXIFRAGA
andersonii Engl, 16, 128
brunonis Wallich ex Ser., 128
S. brunoniana
cespitosa Scop., 197
cinerea, H. Smith, 16
diversifolia Wall, 128
federici-augusti Biasol, 159.
ssp. *federici-augusti, 159*
ssp. *grisebachii*, 159
flavum H. Sm., 96
fortunei Hook. f., 210
'Rubrifolia', 210
'Wada', 210
hypostoma H. Sm., 129, Fig. 67
lowndesii H. Sm., 16
magellanica Poir., 197, Fig. 184
marginata Sternb., 159, Fig. 99
matta-florida H. Sm, 129.
sempervivum K. Koch, 195,
Fig. 98
S. porophylla var. *sibthorpiana*
sherriffii H. Sm., 51
stolitzkae Duthie ex Engl. &
Irmsch, 129.
stribryni (Velen.) Podp., 159
SCUTELLARIA
diffusa Benth., 139
orientalis L., 139
ssp. alpina, 139
ssp. pectinata, 139
pontica C. Koch, 139

salvifolia Benth., 139
SCILLA
   bithynica Boiss., 148
   mischtschenkoana Gross, 148
   S. tubergeniana
   sibirica Haw., 148,
   S. cernua
   ssp. *armena,* Fig. 121
   'Alba', 148
   'Atropurpurea', 148
   'Spring Beauty', 148
SEDUM
   cauticolum Praeger, 204
   fastigiatum Hook.f. & Th., 99
   Rhodiola fastigiata
   ewersii Ledeb., 204
   Hylotelephium ewersii,
   ishidae Miyabe & Kudo, 204
   Rhodiola ishidae
   kirlowii Reg., 99
   Rhodiola kirowii
   pachyclados Aitch ex Hemsl.,137
   pluricaule Kudo, 204
   Hylotelephium pluricaule
   pilosum Bieb., 137
   Hylotelephium pilosum
   polytrichodes Hemsl. ex. Hemsl. & Forb., 204
   primuloides Franch., 99
   Rhodiola primuloides
   spurium Bieb., 138
   stoloniferum S.G. Gmel., 137
SHORTIA
   soldanelloides (Sieb. & Zucc.) Mak., 205, Fig. 203
   Schizocodon soldanelloides
   var. *alpina,* Fig. 201
   'Askival Icebell', 204, Fig. 202
   var. *minima,* 204
   uniflora (Maxim.) Mak, 205
   var. grandiflora, 205
SILENE
   alpestris Jacq., 155
   S. quadrifida
   Heliosperma alpestre
   asterias Griesb., 155
   lerchenfeldiana Baumg., 155
   parnassica Boiss. & Sprun., 155
   pusilla Waldst. & Kit., 155
   S. quadrifida
   saxifraga L., 155
   vallesia L, 155
   ssp. graminea, 155
SISYRINCHIUM
   angustifolium Mill., 187
   S. graaminoides
   ssp. humile, 24
   bellum S. Wats., 187
   S. maritimum
   californicum Ait., 187
   S. boreale
   S bradypus
   douglasii A. Dietr., 187
   S. grandiflorum
   S. inflatum
   Olsynium douglasii
SPIRAEA
   hemicryptophyta J. C. Grierson
STELLERA
   chamaejasme L., 129
STERNBERGIA
   candida B. Mathew & Baytop, 149, Fig. 122
   clusiana (Ker-Gawl) Spreng., 149
   S. grandiflora
   S. latifolia
   S. macrantha
   S. spaffordiana
   S. stipitata
   colchiflora Waldst. & Kit., 149
   S. alexandrae
   S. aetenensis
   S. dalmatica
   fischeriana (Herb.) Rupr, 149.
   lutea (L.) Spreng., 148, Fig. 123
   sicula Tineo ex. Guss., 149, Fig. 124

S. lutea var. *graeca*
SYMPHOSTEMON
    lyckholmii, 27
STYLIDIUM
    graminifolium Sw., 232
TECOPHILAEA
    cyanocrocus Leyb., 38, 48, 201
    violiflora Leyb., 201
TELSONIX
    jamesii (Torr.) Raf., 34
    Boykinia jamesii
THALICTRUM
    alpinum L., 96
    kiusianum Nak., 210
THYMUS
    cilicicus Boiss. & Bak., 139
    leucotrichus Hal., 139
    T. hirsutus ssp. leucotrichus
    polytrichus A. Kern ex. Borbas, 139
    T. praecox
TIARELLA
    polyphylla D. Don, 95
TOWNSENDIA
    condensata Parry, 168, Fig. 130
    exscapa Porter, 168, Fig. 131
    hookeri Beaman., 168
    montana M. E. Jones, 168, Fig. 132
    parryi Eaton, 168
    rothrockii A. Gray, 168
TRICYRTIS
    hirta (Thunb.) Hook., 212
    latifolia Maxim., 213
    macrantha Maxim., 213
    macropoda Miq., 213
TRILLIUM
    cernuum L., 191
    chloropetalum (Torr.) Howell, 191, Fig.175
    erectum L., 191, Fig. 174
    grandiflorum (Michx.) Salisb., 191, Fig. 177
    luteum (Muhlenb.) Harb., 191, Fig. 176
    ovatum Pursh., 191, Fig. 179
    ssp. oettingeri, 191
    var. hibbersonii, 191
    rivale Wats., 191
    'Purple Heart', 191, Fig. 178
    sessile L., 191
    undulatum Willd, 191.
TRITELEIA
    hyacinthina (Lindl.) Greene, 192
    laxa Benth., 192
TROLLIUS
    pumilus D. Don., 128, Fig. 63
    ranunculinus (Sm.) Stearn, 142, Fig. 97
    yunnanensis (Franch.) Ulbr., 128
    T. pumilus var. *yunnanensis*
TROPAEOLUM
    incisum (Spreng.) Sparre., 199, Fig. 189
    polyphyllum Cav., 199, Fig. 190
    'High Alpine Form', 199
    speciosum Poepp. & Endl., 199
TULIPA
    biflora Pall., 149, Fig. 125
    T. polychroma
    clusiana DC., 149
    T. aitchisonii
    var. chrysantha, 149
    var. stellata, 149
    hageri Heldr., 149
    kolpakowskiana Reg., 149
    linifolia Reg, 149
    ssp. batalinii, 149
    ssp. maximowiczii, 149
    orphanidea Heldr., 149
    T. thracia
    T. whitallii
    sylvestris L., 149
    T. australis
    T. celsiana
    tarda Stapf., 149
    T. dasystemon Hort.
    urumiensis Stapf., 149

VACCINIUM
   delavayi Franch., 107
   nummularia Hook. f. & Th., 107
VERONICA
   armena Boiss. & Huet., 142
   austriaca L., 142
   ssp. teucrium, 142
   V. jacquinii
   bombycina Boiss. & Kotschy., 142
   caespitosa Boiss., 142
   gentianoides Vahl., 142
   pectinata L., 142
   peduncularis Bieb., 143
   V. penunculata
   telephiifolia Vahl, 143
   V. glareosa
   V. minuta
VIOLA
   aetolica Boiss. & Heldr, 159.
   V. saxatilis ssp. *aetolica*
   atropurpurea Leyd., 199, Fig. 191
   bhutanica Hara, 96
   biflora L., 96
   cenisia L., 159
   columnaris, Skotsb., 200
   coronifera Becker, 200, Fig. 192
   cotyledon Ging., 200
   V. columnaris
   dasyphylla Becker, 200
   V. cotyledon ssp. *lologensis*
   dissecta Ledeb., 211
   elegantula Schott., 159
   V. bosniaca
   fluehmannii Phil., 200
   graeca (W. Beck.) Halacsy, 159, Fig. 101
   grypoceras A. Gray, 211
   V. canina var. *japonica*
   V. sylvestris var. *japonica*
   V. sylvestris var. *grypoceras*
   keiskei Miq., 211

   mandschurica W. Becker, 211
   V. patrinii
   nivalis Benth., 200, Fig. 193
   orphanidis Boiss., 160
   philippii Leyb., 200, Fig. 194
   reichii Skottsb., 200
   sacculus Skottsb., 200, Fig. 195
   stojanowii W. Becker., 160
   verecunda A. Gray, 211
   var. fibrillosa, 211
   var. yakusimana, 211
   yedoensis Makino, 211
   zoysii Walfen, 160
   V. calcarata var. *zoysii*
WAHLENBERGIA
   albomarginata Hook. f., 222
   ceracea Lothian, 231
   congesta (Cheesem.) N.E. Br., 222
   W. saxicola
   gloriosa Lothian., 231
   matthewsii Ckn., 222
   pygmaea Colenso, 222
   undulata (Thumb.) A. DC., 235

Note. In two cases no authority is quoted since it does not appear in the Kew Index.